Bye Bye I Love You

Bye Bye I Love You: The Story of Our First and Last Words

Michael Erard

The MIT Press
Cambridge, Massachusetts
London, England

The MIT Press would like to thank the anonymous peer reviewers who provided comments on drafts of this book. The generous work of academic experts is essential for establishing the authority and quality of our publications. We acknowledge with gratitude the contributions of these otherwise uncredited readers.

This book was set in ITC Stone Serif Std and ITC Stone Sans Std by New Best-set Typesetters Ltd. Printed and bound in the United States of America.

Library of Congress Cataloging-in-Publication Data is available.

ISBN: 978-0-262-04942-9

10 9 8 7 6 5 4 3 2 1

For Iver and Orri, with love

It seems, in the end, that an obsession with words . . . is nothing less than a search for proof that time existed.

—Ange Mlinko

We must always keep in mind that the ancestor sleeps within the child, and the child within the ancestor.

—Sabina Spielrein

It takes two to know one.

—Gregory Bateson

Contents

Prelude: Into the Puckerbrush

Who knows how she got into the puckerbrush. Perhaps she wandered into the brushy overgrowth in a druggy haze, or maybe someone deposited her body. Her name was Toina Hanson, pronounced "ton-ya," and she lived on the streets of Portland, Maine, until she died somehow in the weedy hinterlands of the city, unseen and unheard, so physically slight that the goldenrod and blackberry canes were barely inconvenienced by her collapse.

One afternoon about a year later, I was blithely foraging for wild blackberries in that hinterland, and as I picked my way through the puckerbrush, I saw. Tumbled yellowing bones. Some organic matter slathered in the mat of grass. Shredded clothing. I couldn't recognize what it was—and this confusion immediately suggested, to my horror, what I was looking at. Several weeks later, the newspaper divulged her identity. For a year no one had noted her absence, until I encountered her.

This unexpected shock led, in a meandering fashion, to this book.

For years I felt haunted, trapped in a role with no name with a person I'd never met. Crucial to my recovery was reading about the cultural diversity of practices surrounding death and burial, in particular a seminal essay by an early twentieth-century French sociologist named Robert Hertz. His emphasis on the care of the dead struck me, as I'd never taken such responsibilities seriously, let alone understood their role in maintaining the well-being of the living. Hertz argued for the critical importance of maintaining good relations between the communities of the living and the dead, particularly by performing the right rituals and observances. These questions were put before me: In what way was Toina "my dead," and how should I care for her?

The eventual answer, when it came, made me increasingly sympathetic to the notion that the dead don't really leave us, because they need us, and us them. The secret about living isn't loving life; it's knowing how to be with the dead. A younger version of myself would be eager to point out that this position is at odds with my committed materialism. *But you don't believe that consciousness persists after death*, he'd say. I'd reply that I reconcile the contradictions through the Jungian notion that some deep remnant of an ancestral self within us hungers, and that if we honor those hungers, we might survive, even thrive, in the material world. Finding a balance between these positions is the closest thing I have to a religion.

I began thinking about interactions at the deathbed, where it seemed that modern people first confront their responsibilities to the dead. Given that I write about language, I became curious about how this care might be enacted through paying attention to a dying person as they transition from linguistically capable to whatever they become. *Attention as a form of care.* From there it was easy to think about Toina, what she might have spoken to the summertime stars, how only the puckerbrush heard her. And from there it's easy for my heart to leap out to all the unheard, unseen moments from people who have ceased to exist, except in the memories of the living.

Like the narrator of Dante's *Inferno*, I was halfway through the journey of life when I became lost in that dark wood of reckoning. When I finally emerged, I was armed with this wisdom: we age, we sicken, and we die, and in some circumstances, we die in ways that preclude the proper observances, leaving the living with the task of rewriting the balance, if they can. The stakes could be very high indeed. Here was the theme of my elderhood, the lesson of the puckerbrush.

Then, three years later, my wife and I had another baby. Beginnings. Endings. So it goes.

A home birth is extraordinary for many reasons. One is the way it binds you to the moment, stripping you of your plans and protocols, as you watch your partner summon a strength that's so animal in its pure vitality that she sheds, in that space, her human guise. On that breezy summer night, the baby, a boy, came so quickly that I almost earned my midwifery badge. He and his older brother (who had come more leisurely, also at home, six years earlier) have grown into jouncy, flouncy specimens of young humans whose joyous right-nows often make an Eeyore like me hold his head in his hands. Yet I have to acknowledge that my escort in the dark woods brought me not to the threshold of elderhood but spiraling back to beginnings. There a new version of myself was born, too, somehow attuned to appreciating the span of a life in the same way that a simple geometric shape can be apprehended in a glance. First and last words, just another way to say from cradle to grave, seemed of a piece.

Working on this book, I've shuttled between the beginnings of language in development and evolution and its endings in aging, sickness, and death. It has been something like walking back and forth between two ends of a long beach. In this movement, I couldn't help but hear familiar melodies echoing in the other. You might try reading it in that fashion, too, and see how, when you read in one area, you find the other topic singing out from under the rocks, then go to the other part, where the rocks are singing about the first. I'm not suggesting that first and last words amount to the same song. Rather, they harmonize. Someone asked me if I had a theory to connect first and last words. No, I said, just an intuition. Of a resonance. A rhyme. Of a metaphor to be made. This book is an attempt to get my hands around that metaphor, and with it some of the story of life itself.

Introduction

Mama. I love you. Thank you. Oh wow.

With our earliest utterances and gestures, we announce ourselves—and are recognized—as persons ready to participate in social life. With our final ones, we mark where others must release us to death's embrace. Language scientists have thoroughly explored the former, called "first words," but they've paid surprisingly little attention to the latter, called "last words," and certainly not treated them as part of the same continuum.

Until now, that is. In this book, I open a window into our cultural, biological, and personal entanglements with first words and last words, trying to capture their beauty as intimate, emotionally profound language moments. Why do this? Because there's so much more to wonder about them. Toni Morrison famously said in her Nobel Prize acceptance speech that how we do language may be the measure of our lives. This book takes up the question of where that measuring begins and ends.

It's easy to assume that people, across cultures and eras, have found first and last words interesting for the same reasons, mainly that we all learn language and we all die. Despite these universal experiences, it turns out that people don't possess the same expectations about the linguistic behaviors that mark the beginning and end of the signifying self. Across cultures and historical eras, those behaviors are framed in many different ways. This book is, in part, an attempt to capture and explain that range, so that you might situate yourself, where you come from, what you desire.

Such a starting point seems to commit me to aggregating cute stories about the toddler's first words, mixing them with emblematic stories of wise words from the lips of the dying. But I see quite a few more possibilities.

In fact, our first and last words are culturally significant beyond the anecdotal. They shed light on practices and beliefs about babies, the dying, language itself, and the very nature of existence. As personal, anthropological, and historical accounts show, first words and last words have been connected to a cornucopia of ideas and beliefs, from the sweet to the serious. They tell us that a baby learns to talk when a god helps it or after it eats corn, or that parents eagerly anticipate their baby's first words, or that a first word should only be the first utterance that has the form of an adult's, or that it's always "shit!," or that it makes for a good tale. They tell a story about dying as well: that a dying person must have a prayer or a god's name on their lips when they expire, or that they always tell the truth, or that a person need only say "yes," or that they should abstain from pain relief so that they can speak lucidly, or that some last words are inevitable—one should not, under any circumstances, greet that dark night in silence—or even that babbling by infants and by the elderly amount to the same language of the spirit world. Or that neither matters at all.

When I surveyed these beliefs, I found a tremendous variety in how the firstness and lastness of these moments get treated. Even their "wordness" is up for debate. I began to see that only certain behaviors undergo cultural transformation. Moreover, only certain transformations occur. All of this variety is bound up in family behavior, parenting, education, medical care, grief, and even the structure of daily life. Here the groups for whom I've written this book—families, caregivers, medical professionals, chaplains and social workers, linguistic scholars, and memoirists, among others—will find their needs and experiences reflected. Yet my goal isn't to pull down anyone's myths and rituals. Rather, I aim to lay out the full panoply of what it might be possible to believe alongside a description of all that occurs, so that we might understand better our experiences of the beginning and end of language and perhaps revise our ways of doing things to be better suited to our needs and hew closer to what's enduring and true. Doing so requires something of a reset, one that's drawn from historical understandings and, above all, the language sciences. Only then can we find real opportunities to make different decisions about what the right thing is to do.

§

When you take first and last words together, it immediately becomes obvious that they can both be freighted with more than words usually bear. As the Austrian writer Karl Kraus once wrote, "The closer one looks at a word, the farther away the distance from which the word looks back." Here this adage seems particularly true.

What is the first word of a baby? It's an inheritance of the species, bestowed by the community. It's not the seed of language but its sprout, which has already sought the warm light of interaction. What is the last word of a dying person? It amounts to some final articulation of consciousness (and not just a word, by the way) that passes through a closing window of interaction. What I mean here will unfold in the coming pages. Language at the end of life is so much more than a diminishment. Yes, it's a debris of language, a rubble of interactive abilities and expressive behaviors. But it also puts on display what has sustained an individual's language powers from the beginning—even before their first word. And so the circle is complete.

I'll discuss many of the shared linguistic facets of first and last words, along with their differences. As I explored these topics, many other themes and symmetries became apparent. In cultures where first and last words are associated with existential significance, they activate rituals and other recipes that people bring to bear on encounters with mysterious boundaries. This need coexists with—and sometimes crashes against—that demand of modernity that people apprehend things as they really are, even if courage is required for facing naked truths. When you read this cultural history of first and last words, you'll see a glimpse of how these two forces have been threaded together over many centuries—and what we have inherited.

Another theme is that people don't live their own first or last words in a manner that they can reflect on—the self that's bookended by these moments is unable to directly access them and will not be judged by them. The dead can't feel embarrassment for what they did or didn't utter; a baby can, but not in the moment. No matter what linguistic talents you might develop in your lifetime, they'll begin and end without the *you* who claims them. This makes first and last words utterly personal but also strangely alien, as much for the person who produces them as for whomever is lucky enough to be entrusted with such weighty existential cargo.

There are also persistent frictions between the private and public dimensions of first and last words: what they mean, and to whom, in which intimate or public spheres, and how the traffic between them runs. One such friction is that the public versions of first and last words, as cultural ideals, can serve as models for behaving in private that may be frustratingly unattainable. There's an ethic of privacy that surrounds the moments in which first and last words appear, one that's accompanied by a desire (and sometimes a need) to transform them into memorials, slogans, inputs for artistic and scientific projects, and other public purposes. (It occurs to me to playfully offer that one reason linguistics doesn't tackle last words is because the scientific discipline must repay a cosmic debt accrued by exposing so many first ones to public view. But it's probably due to the simple fact that linguists are people, too, wanting to process the loss of loved ones like everyone else. Even linguistic curiosity has its limits.)

Then there's the way that this public-private tension contrasts with the simple but far more predominant reality that the vast majority of humanity's first and final articulations of consciousness have been uttered to a void and lost to time—washed away, as the cyborg Roy Batty says at the end of *Blade Runner*, like tears in rain. Part of me wants to imagine a god of the puckerbrush, whose divinely capacious perception can't let a single articulation of consciousness slip by, whether they happen in the royal bedroom or the slum. Yet even the notion that these are sacred moments is itself a belief about them—which demonstrates a bit of what's difficult about holding first and last words at the proper distance to understand better how one might hold them close.

§

A few years ago, a friend of mine helped her brother care for his infant son. For many months, she signed in American Sign Language to her nephew, so it wasn't surprising when he began signing back. "Are you comfortable?" she signed to him one day. "Comfortable," he replied. A first sign! His mother was chagrined that he didn't speak his first word, but my friend (who is Deaf) was *delighted*.

§

A couple from Tbilisi, Georgia, had a baby whose first word was *mama*—a quite unremarkable first word. Yet complications stemmed from what "mama" means in Georgian, which is "father," while in Russian (a language brought to the mix by the nanny) it's "mother." In this way, an innocent first word touched bilingualism, language politics (the two languages are often at loggerheads in Georgia), and even gender politics. Which meaning would the adults agree upon?

§

One day, my wife forgot to give our son a book to look at while she changed his diaper. So he asked for one. This was his first English word, at about twelve months old. He quickly added "bike" and "bock" (for "box") to his repertoire. At the time, we were moving to Europe, and I was describing to someone that we were bringing bicycles. They asked how. "In a bike box," I said. My son's eyes widened at the opportunity to say 66 percent of his expressive vocabulary in one swoop. "Bike bock?!" he said.

§

A woman was at home, dying of cancer, in tremendous pain. Her struggle to breathe was eased with an oxygen mask, which she hated because it blocked her speech.

"Help me take off this mask, it's unbearable," she whispered to her daughter, who complied. A few seconds later, the woman passed away.

For years after, the daughter drank heavily, guilty that she had killed her mother, and she told this story as she herself struggled to stay alive.

§

A British man was dying of AIDS. His parents persuaded him to return to their house. He was deaf and signed, which they'd never bothered to learn. Lying in bed at the end of his life, he moved his hands. After he passed, his mother called a Deaf friend of his, who came to sit with the body with her.

"He tried to sign to me," she told the friend, chuckling nervously. "I don't know why he tried to do that, I can't sign." *You missed his last words,* was all the friend could think.

§

Along with these moving personal experiences—a tiny sample of the ones I've encountered—is a broader story that I seek to tell about first and last words. (For more on how I encountered them, see "A Note on Sources.")

My first clue to this story arose when I noticed a profound asymmetry in first and last words' visibility on the modern cultural landscape. I wanted to put them on the same footing. What might the nature of last word-iness reveal about first word-iness, and vice versa?

"Last words" has long been a distinct literary genre—a directly quoted utterance that is a "final, self-validating articulation of consciousness in extremis," according to Karl Guthke, a scholar who wrote the authoritative work on the genre. Realistic and dramatized portrayals of such expressions abound in the media, films, music, literature, and pop culture of modern North America, Europe, and elsewhere. They've been collected and published in multiple languages, often as distillations of longer deathbed scenes. (From Guthke's book I learned that "last words" is a category in the US Library of Congress classification scheme.) Such anthologies reflect prevailing ideas about gender; in European anthologies, the only women are either royalty or religious figures.

Nowadays, it's easy to find websites with the last words of doomed pilots or last text messages of car crash victims. Unlike Guthke's meditations on mortality, these highlight death as spectacle. A famous person's last words are a familiar trope in their obituaries and biographies, and at points in the past the average citizen's cultural literacy could be measured by their knowledge of Harriet Tubman's last words, or Marie Antoinette's, or Johann Wolfgang von Goethe's. Let's have a quiz: Who said, "Thanks, Ollie"? Who said, "Into your hands, I commend my spirit"? Who said, "Oh wow. Oh wow. Oh wow"? (For answers, check the notes.) Encounters with finality are so desperately desired that last words have been attributed to animals (Alex, a famous research parrot, said, "You be good. See you tomorrow. I love you") and machines ("my battery is low and it's getting dark" was popularly attributed to the Mars rover *Opportunity*).

They're often a key ingredient of morbid jokes. A linguistics professor was guest lecturing at a prison. "Is it true that your last words are the first ones you say?" a prisoner asked him afterward. "That's not true," another prisoner said. "I shot a guy, and his last words were, 'Don't shoot.'" The last words of the condemned have long been objects of fascination, and there's legitimate forensic and psychiatric interest in, and a morbid fan culture of, suicide notes. Nevertheless, I'm exclusively concerned here with dying from disease as well as death from old age, what is called "illness dying," but not dying in non-illness contexts, such as homicides, suicides, wars and disasters, death rows, or death camps. I emphasize that I'm mapping language behavior during ordinary dying to say something about language in *this* world, and as a mirror of beliefs about death, dying, or what comes next, not as evidence for or against those beliefs.

"Nana, it's fine if those are your final words, but it's also O.K. if you want to take another stab at them."

Figure 0.1
As of this writing, the *New Yorker*'s cartoon archive contains twelve cartoons about last words—but only four about first ones. Reproduced with permission from the *New Yorker*.

Often the real meaning of last words is most available when you appreciate how they're embedded in private lives. Poignant stories are often treasured by family members, where they are elements of a tool kit for grieving. A woman told me that her Dutch-speaking grandmother inexplicably said, in English, "I go," before collapsing. Not getting to share last words with someone can be a lasting regret. A man's dying grandmother wanted to tell him something but her mouth was too dry. "Four times she tried to say it," he told me, then paused, a bit wistful. "I wish I knew what she wanted to say." And sometimes people find meaning in a mere semblance of a last word. As a man held his dying wife's hand, he told her he'd be okay, that he'd meet her again someday, and when she moved her lips soundlessly, as if in response, it seemed to comfort him when he remembered it. She'd heard him; she knew.

§

By contrast, first words have the scantest of public lives, real or imagined. Beyond the realm of science and scientists, they appear mainly in narrow cultural niches, like celebrity memoirs (we learn from singer Julie Andrews that her first word was "home"), parenting blogs, and a few sitcoms—Bart Simpson's first words, upon discovering his parents in bed, became his catchphrase, "*Ay caramba!*"

Cute sayings by older kids have long entertained family get-togethers and social media lurkers. But first word-iness is little discussed, nor is the first word as a cultural symptom, even though, as linguists assure us, everyone has first words. Yet they're not attributed to animals and machines; there's no library classification that pairs them with last ones. A quiz about famous first words would be futile. Even Guthke, in his encyclopedia of famous last words, discounts the first ones. He wrote that they "belong with anecdotes of childhood, whose biographical value is inversely proportionate to their charm." His ire was provoked by 1988 US Democratic presidential candidate Michael Dukakis's reported first words, in Greek, *monos mou*, or "all by myself," which foreshadowed Dukakis's reputation as a technocrat.

What's going on here? Do we indeed care about entrances, beginnings, the new? The reason, as Guthke saw, isn't complicated: Most first words lack glamor and drama. There's nothing to chew on. You can't really use them to distinguish one kid from another—they're not monumental. They don't make history.

But leave it to the language sciences, with their extensive studies of infants acquiring vocabulary and grammar, to produce fascinating insights about *groups* of first words, such as when they emerge and what they tend to be about. In so doing, they divulge secrets about the lives of young human selves, most reliably if those selves come from wealthy, Anglophone societies. For instance, if the emergence of the signifying self is interesting to you, then you should know that the baby's *first point* may be more unambiguous fruit than a signed or uttered first word. There's also the theory that language evolved in many places, the so-called "polygenetic theory." One implication is that there's no single *first* first word for the human species to hang its humanity on, but plausibly millions of them. Think about it: our language lives don't trace back to a single Adam-and-Eve-like word (apple? snake? darn!) but to a bounteous, and probably sloppy, squall. No matter the words themselves, in each of those millions of instances they likely arose through the interactions of caregivers and offspring.

To me, this is only the beginning of a story about why humans notice, remember, record, and memorialize first words. The story isn't simple, for there's a surprising diversity to what adults make of early language, even though—this is important—virtually all children end up skilled users of their community's languages. All of this is covered in the first half of this book, which connects every baby's first word to an expansive evolutionary and cultural legacy, whether that word is signed or spoken, on time or late, noticed or overlooked. First words may not make history, but they're bound up with it. They also make a human place in it. I propose that over the longer term of language history, people have developed an anxiety about time's passage and where they fit, an anxiety whose revelatory symptom is a fascination with children's first words.

§

I also propose that the life of first words can help us recognize compelling insights about groups of last words.

The great irony of last words' oversized cultural salience is that no information about actual language at the end of life has been collected in one place. Perhaps you're curious because you're engaging in a dark existential tourism, or you're quelling some anxiety about your own mortality, or you're interested for scientific or medical reasons. Maybe it's a unsettled mix of all three.

In any case, your curiosity will be difficult to satisfy, your intuitions hard to confirm. What "famous last words" and such give us are akin to rainbows, a beautiful sight, rare and evanescent, caused by a narrow set of specific conditions. Yet we live in and with the rain, not rainbows. So we might wish to know where the rain falls, and when, and how it tapers or rages. The simple fact is that there's no catalog of possible linguistic behaviors, one that's unframed by expectations of any sort, whether spiritual or cultural, and no account of what will stand in the way of a dying person's linguistic powers. More than a few people told me that they wished for a road map for communication at the end of life, so one of my aims is to get as close to that as possible. I have in mind what a nurse in an online forum once wrote in a thread about moaning. "If you mention everything that could happen before it does, it takes the panic away. Because instead of [family members] going 'Oh, no what is that?' they say, 'Oh, that is what she was talking about.'" As readily as mental shorthands for baby talk come to mind, it might help us to have them for language, interaction, and communication at the end of life too.

Until now, linguists haven't examined any of this. Their field's theoretical preoccupations with children preclude any interest in the patterned linguistic phenomena that occur during ordinary, illness dying. Some information is spread throughout the medical literature, but language is described there in the broadest strokes, if at all, because facts about the state of the body overshadow all else. Meanwhile, health communication research focuses on what people say, less so how they say it—which is a puzzling gap, given that the *how* often shapes the *what*. Some popular works aim to provide psychological and emotional support to family and friends of the dying, making last words a function of the living. Others explore hypotheses about the afterlife: in fact, until recently, the overwhelming thrust of the story of last words has cast them in the broader story of death and the afterlife. But in today's world, while religion plays a strong role for many, it no longer covers the topic adequately. So what then are we to make of last words?

The second part of this book provides a much-needed basic decrypting, and it disentangles language facts from beliefs about dying. I focus on the period closer to actual expiration, within the last week to the last few days and hours. There the myths originate, the existential gravity presses down, and unmeetable expectations rise.

My approach is anchored to an obscure but historically significant study on the process of dying, conducted in the early twentieth century by renowned physician Sir William Osler (1849–1919). This is embedded in a broad-ranging discussion of why dying people would be expected to produce language in the first place. To illuminate things further, I draw from published research as well as my own interviews with speech-language pathologists, medical interpreters, palliative care physicians and nurses, end-of-life doulas, chaplains, linguists, other language scientists, and communications experts. "We have no cultural history to guide us when health and well-being fade and dying becomes a branch of bioengineering," wrote historian Thomas Laqueur. This book is a start in that direction.

Framing my explanation is the fact that, in wealthy industrialized countries, the bulk of the population will die—if they live the long lives of their hopes and dreams—of multiple chronic conditions after long declines. At their deathbeds, they won't invent fancy speeches or heartfelt quotables. They'll use whatever language remains available, if any at all, and they'll likely do so in a hospital, nursing home, or hospice. Silence will prevail. The chance of rainbows will be low, that of drizzle very high. The people at those bedsides, hungry for connection, will look for expressive purpose in the dying person's vocalizations, facial expressions, hand squeezes, pointing, eye gazes—and someday perhaps brainwaves on a monitor. They may even resort to finding closure not through the dying person's words to them but their words to their loved one.

Even so, they may not fully appreciate the importance of the last time someone plays their part in the back-and-forth of an interaction. Maybe it helps to know that this coordination of communication, called turn-taking, is attested across the animal kingdom and is something that human babies learn to do within weeks of being born. This may be our most salient final expression of consciousness as an individual, as a human, as a being. It's the beauty of the rain.

§

My eagerness to tackle first and last words together stems partly from the fact that during the time that I conceived and wrote this, my family moved to Europe, then to America, then back to Europe, each period of residency an intense mini-lifetime that imprinted me not only with the finiteness of things but with their boundedness. It was soothing to gather up the sprawls of living within a single sweep of memory, marked by firsts and lasts.

Also relevant is that I began having children at an age when my mortal limits had come into view as concrete prospects. There's the way that young children threaten a writer's productivity—the sun's not up yet, they're downstairs burbling and chirping like birds, I haven't slept a full night in weeks, much less written anything. Is this how it's going to be, that their wildly raucous first words are deeply implicated in my last?

Under these circumstances, it occurred to me that first and last words had to be connected. It seemed impossible that no one had explored the way they mimicked the shape of the world. Irresistible to the linguist in me is that they're often fuzzy. If you're the one on the scene with intact, mature language abilities, you find yourself asking, Is that a grimace of pain or a smile? Is that a babble or my name? *Is this an utterance from the organism or the expressive self?* Here the stakes seem immense—if someone isn't producing language, who are they? To themselves, their family, their community, and even their god or gods?

I wanted to call on the science to get first and last words to divulge some linguistic secrets. They remind us how language is embodied, as much about what we do with our eyes, hands, and faces as with our brains and mouths. First and last words are often taken to be singular expressions of the individual person. However, in linguistic terms, responsibility for them is shared. We negotiate them; we make them *together*. In that sense, your first and last words are never yours and yours alone.

At the same time, the historian in me is fascinated by what these linguistic moments mean to caregivers and observers of different eras and to what end. To paraphrase the question posed by the anthropologist Gregory Bateson, How did people do their knowing about these phenomena? With what kinds of attention, which tools, which beliefs? How do contemporary people, as opposed to denizens of the past, do their knowing?

The poet in me recognizes that beginnings entail endings, and endings beginnings. I want to hold life from beginning to end in my hands, to stand outside human existence (even my own) and see it as a piece. First words and last words translate the massive geological and cosmological scales against which human civilization is a mere speck into something you might, if you really try, get your hands around.

In that larger sense, first and last words are tied up with our human moment, threatened now with anthropogenic disasters from global climate change and human incursions on animal habitats, thereby creating vectors for pandemics. Where do preoccupations with last words intersect with fantasies—and realities—about the end of the world? Why are we so fascinated with ruins? Karl Guthke published his book in the early 1990s, when the apocalypse seemed a comfortable distance away and, with the fall of the Berlin Wall, the fear of nuclear war seeming to dissipate. I'm at a less comfortable distance and think about collapsing ice sheets, weird weather, and rampant viruses all the time. Every baby's first word isn't the beginning; it's also an homage to the first words in the human past, themselves a first step toward our current moment. And a last word isn't the end. Embedded in any final utterance is the rumor of someone who receives it, which offers memorials and the possibility of cycles of renewal. In this book I'm going to attempt to capture these Möbius-strip stylings of beginnings and endings, where parallels emerge and then fade while asymmetries persist.

Mama. I love you. Thank you. Oh wow.

A List of Questions

If you have specific questions about first or last words, here's a guide to the exact place in the book with the answers.

- What is the oldest first recorded actual word? Page 46.
- What is a likely first word that caregivers miss? Page 35.
- What was the first human word ever spoken by an ape? Page 80.
- Do babies who sign produce a first word before babies who speak? Page 23.
- The last things that Jesus spoke are well-known, but what were his first words? Page 65.
- What are the most frequent first words of English-speaking American babies? Page 110.
- Do girls have different first words than boys? Pages 111–112.
- What is the first word that humans ever produced? Pages 68, 73.
- Does teaching signs to babies make them smarter? Page 95.
- What do people most often say as their last words? Pages 233–237.
- What do multilingual people say at the end of life? Pages 231–233.
- Do people's last words have anything to do with their first words? Pages 248–249.
- Can we predict what someone's last words will be? Pages 239–242.
- Does a person's language become different as they approach death? Pages 224–227.
- Can people who use sign language stay in communication longer than people who only speak? Pages 175, 230–231.

- What happens in the brain of a dying person that affects their language? Pages 142–145, 146–147.
- Is it true that hearing is the last sense to go? Pages 213–217.
- What are some ritual last words in religious traditions? Pages 180–186.
- What is the difference between "mama" from babies and "mama" from the dying? Page 249.

A Note on Sources

This book contains many last utterances and final moments, nearly all of which came from people I didn't know personally. I've been careful to try to earn the privilege of handling their last-word stories, which I never ask for outright. If they were offered, I always asked, when possible, for permission to use them. Whether the example is recent or from the past, I have never let myself forget that it's attached to someone's grief.

Often that grief was so palpable, I cried. It was the most natural response.

Because language at the end of life hasn't been researched systematically, many of the examples I use had a life as anecdotes. I've tried to tease out their kernel of truth while preserving how the anecdote itself humanizes; these are stories about intimate personal moments shared with me not only because someone thought I'd be interested but because someone trusted that I'd do the right thing with them. I'm honored by their trust, and I hope to show I deserved it.

I also want to acknowledge stories that I didn't hear because people didn't get to experience the last words of a loved one. This point is central to the aim of my book: all too often, circumstances frustrate achieving a cultural ideal, which actually was never typical in the first place. People may know better, yet they still feel guilty for missing out, for grieving improperly, for letting someone down. In fact, once you know what's ordinary, you know that the absence of last words, at least in their stereotypical form, is the normal condition, and perhaps there's some solace in that.

1 The Four Expectations

What follows is a journey to visit four types of expectations that adults across space and time have about young children's first words. Before we set off, an illustrative anecdote:

One Friday in 1977, a one-year-old named Nathaniel living in Leiden, Netherlands, said "mowuh." His English-speaking parents enthusiastically greeted this innocent "mowuh" (or /mɔwə/, in the notation of the International Phonetic Alphabet) as his first word. That weekend he pointed to things when he said it, so his parents responded by giving him more of that thing. It was obvious to them that "mowuh" meant "more."

Fast-forward to Monday evening. The Dutch-speaking babysitter had been excitedly waiting all day to give Nathaniel's parents this news: their son said his first word! It's *mooi*, the Dutch word for "pretty" (pronounced /moːi̯/ by adults). The babysitter reported—proudly, since she was present for it—that whenever he had pointed at something and said "mowuh," she agreed. "*Ja, ja, dat is mooi!*" "Yes, yes, that's pretty!"

As far as first words go, a word expressing a desire (such as wanting to have more) was as likely as one describing a thing. Which did Nathaniel intend? His subsequent silence, after the babysitter went home and then for weeks after, made clear that he hadn't been remarking on the beauty of his surroundings. As his mother later wrote, a full day of not getting "more" for "mowuh" had "either confused or discouraged Nathaniel sufficiently that he stopped using the word completely and didn't pick up any replacements for several months." By normal standards, he became a late talker, though "he's made up for it since," she said when I spoke with her about her essay. (The last time I checked, Nathaniel is a professor in Canada.)

This particular mother was Catherine Snow, later a Harvard linguist and prominent in child language studies. She began her research career in the late 1960s, suspicious of claims that children didn't use inputs from their social environments, particularly their mother's language, in their language development. "Though I had no personal knowledge about young children or their language environments," she remembered of her first encounters with the linguistics of the day, "it struck me as unlikely that the language they heard was as garbled, ungrammatical and impenetrable as presupposed by the linguists." Her dissertation was one of the first studies about the simplified language directed at children, now known as "motherese" or "parentese." One implication is that a baby's first word isn't a ribbon-cutting of their language project but the tip of an iceberg's worth of linguistic knowledge that they've already acquired.

Yet that iceberg tip can be tricky to spot. The truth is that there's no bright line between baby babbling and crystalline enunciations of adultlike language. Despite the first word's potential theoretical cachet, scientists of Snow's era also had difficulty putting a finger on it, something that parents and caregivers have presumably also dealt with. You'd think it would be easy, but the first word never announces itself as such. Rather, word-like forms wriggle one by one from the phonological mush like proto–land animals crawling from Protozoic seas. *More* sounds like "mowuh," *light* sounds like "dai," and *all done* sounds like "a-da," while a fully open hand with all fingers spread while the palm smacks the middle of the chin could be the American Sign Language (ASL) sign for "mother," "water," or "eat."

Inconveniently, the first word doesn't come with a tag—but that's also what makes identifying it fun.

§

All babies are noisy. They grunt, squeal, and coo from the moment they arrive, four to five times per minute, three thousand times per day when they're awake. Mostly vowels at first, then consonant-ish sounds, all of which becomes a semi-coordinated mess of babbling around two months.

This noisiness is important. It's some of the linguistic raw material that will be culturally transformed, and it might have played an important evolutionary role in how humans got words in the first place. Babies also move their hands, wave their arms. Out of the babbling mess emerges a more ordered, repetitive babbling at around seven months. Linguists call this "canonical" babbling, because the syllables come out like Platonic ideals of syllables: a single consonant, then a vowel. These syllables are repeated in long strings. Interestingly, hearing babies babble with their hands (as well as with their mouths), while signing babies babble with their mouths (but mainly with their hands). Around this time, babies begin pointing and making other gestures, sometimes to indicate things they're interested in but also for purposes like waving goodbye. This appears to be the real turning point, where they understand how to use their bodies to manipulate others' attention.

Then babbling typically changes again, as hearing babies gain control over their tongues. Varied consonants and vowels appear in the babbled string. This sets them up to produce more words that match what they hear adults say, via feedback from others and through the loop of hearing themselves vocalizing.

What emerges at this point are words—though not everyone calls what emerges "words." For babies who speak, this moment comes at about twelve months, while signing babies arrive here months earlier. (Perhaps it's because they can see the articulators clearly, whereas tongues and vocal cords are hidden and breath is invisible.) By about fifteen months, most babies can produce about ten words. The earliest events to be labeled words are the ones that attentive Anglophone parents extract from canonical spoken babbling, like "mama" or "dada." The most frequent first handshape of deaf children in ASL environments is all fingers extended and spread, the so-called 5-hand ✋. Conveniently, opening and closing those fingers is taken to be the ASL sign for "milk," a frequent first word, though the ✋ is an element in many other signs.

In the next stage come strings of sounds or handshapes that occur only in certain situations, such as "hello" or "thanks." These aren't just social niceties but also reflect how the semantics of early utterances can be as swampy as their phonetics. Linguist John Dore tells how "shoe" was an early word of his son, but only when he was getting dressed. Eventually the utterances free themselves of the context, and they have a broader meaning so that you can say, "Can you get a shoe?" and the child will fetch a shoe. As linguist Michael Halliday put it, the child "learns how to mean." The semantics firms up; the words map onto things and actions in the world that adults recognize.

Fully describing the learning of words, both making and understanding them, deserves more than these neatly trimmed paragraphs, which clean up what's really a messy, now-frontward, now-backward process, with

strange alleys, roundabouts, and dead ends. "A lot of kids have this discon-
certing all-over-the-placeness with their early vocalizations, and there's no
magic definition for how much stability of reference they have to have,"
cognitive scientist Michael Tomasello told me. Early words are fuzzy, which
makes them fascinating, especially when parents confidently claim to have
identified them clearly.

This interests me a lot, because in reality, first words can manifest as such
a mash of sounds or handshapes that their *wordness* isn't the most obvious
thing about them. To grant this moment a status as a word, you have to
account for how well the baby can control their tongue, lips, and jaw or
hands and fingers. You have to pay attention to what they think (or what
you think they think) words can do. Every child seems to have their own
idea about what they are doing. They might say something consistently in
a certain context but not outside it. They use "papa" for their father but
also for the mailman, their uncle, the pastor—is that a word? And if, like
/mɔwə/, it doesn't sound like an adult word, does it count? What if the word
doesn't behave according to certain rules about how words are formed—
does it count? What about something they imitate? Can a name be a first
word? What about a onomatopoetic sound like "vroom"? My oldest son
used to pant in an apparent attempt—I suspect—to refer to "dogs." (Not
a word, we decided.) Animal sounds, like "meow" and "moo," often label
animals. Are these words? Would they be counted as *first* words? And does
the pragmatic generosity of a grown-up—that willingness to interpret an
utterance as something intentional and meaningful—make an incomplete
utterance first-word-like in ways it could never otherwise count as a word
(say, in a game of Scrabble)? Especially because it comes from the baby, with
all the connotations of that word: compellingly helpless, aggressively new,
the apple of your eye, a mystery unfolding. A stranger.

The *firstness* of first words can be even harder to pin down. They emerge
gradually, Catherine Snow said. "There's a slow transition from something
that's definitely not a word to something that definitely is a word, with the
point in the middle where the shift is very hard to establish. It definitely
happens, we know the shift happens, but the point at which it happens is
somewhat indeterminate."

It's like a small town—if you blink while you're driving through, you
miss it. But it's still close to miraculous. Back in the early twentieth century,
a professor named W. G. Bateman became so enamored of his children's

language that he ventured outside his usual chemical researches, publishing about a small collection of first words from various sources. He noted that "the most frequently named object is the paternal parent," named "papa," "dada," "ata," or "daddy"—though he identified his daughter Jane's first utterance as "hello hello hello hello." He compared the "sudden advent of the first word" to other natural processes that change in the blink of an eye. "At one moment something *is not* and at the next moment it *is* and we do not know what miracle fills the infinitesimal gap."

It's easy to agree with Bateman—a whole world of possibilities comes into being in that moment, which until then had existed only as a rumor or a promise. And even though we find many ways to communicate with our children before their words appear, the first word marks a state change. And a desperately needed one, too—maybe with words we can coordinate this creature's care *with the creature itself.* We need a miracle to enable less crying, less stress, and some desperately needed quiet.

Which makes the first word's fuzziness, for those of us as obsessed as Bateman, something of a letdown. Snow touched on this in her essay "The Last Word." There she declared that "the first word is a theoretical rather than an empirical problem." This means that the harder you push on this linguistic state change, the fuzzier it becomes. You can't observe away its indeterminacy. Moreover, how you resolve it may depend on your take on deeper linguistic matters. In any case, in the end, it's you, the receiver (the parent or the scientist), who decides what to crown as a first word, and thus the advent of this miracle. You bring to bear your definition of a word, your interpretation of what the kid is doing. Those can vary wildly from parent to parent, even from child to child. For instance, in nuclear families that notice such things, first children tend to have more linguistic stories about them than subsequent children.

You didn't *perceive* the word as much as *negotiate* it. The mom says "ball," the baby says "baba," the mom says, "Yeah, bubble, a ball is like a bubble." This makes the first word an interpersonal artifact as much as a cultural one.

As Snow aptly observed in her essay, "The first word is a reflection of the culture's decisions about many matters—the status of child versus parent, the attribution of intentionality, language socialization beliefs and prac-tices, and beliefs about the social and communicative capacities of prelin-guistic members, as well as theories of language and of meaning."

I love this sentence, which draws me back constantly. It's a remarkably good tool for unpacking what we know about this linguistic milestone, how we know what we know, and why beliefs and practices about first words vary so much. It's true that children utter things based on how they see the shapes of the world and judge adults to be under their control, but adults recognize those utterances based on how they see the shape of children as beings that naturally do linguistic things. And that's only a bit of what Snow is getting at.

At another level, when you declare what your child's first word is, when you recognize and remember it, you're plucking it from the web of social relations in which it arose and cleaning off the dangly contextual bits of the moment to better allow it to serve its role: an attractive trophy, a part of the story about a miracle, an augury, a memento mori. I'm not diminishing the feelings that motivate the jobs that first words get. I just want us to recognize that one thing we're doing here is wiping off the vestiges of the private for a broader public consumption. What were people on the scene doing? Who identified it, who decided what it meant? Do they believe a mystical force to be involved? Why did someone have the time to be noticing the utterance in the first place?

One reason that I love Snow's quote is that it ushers those dynamics back to the scene. It opens the world of first words as an intimate story about how children are socialized in families and how parents are trained to engage with children's language, as well as the broader environment those families live in. The moral of Snow's work is: a first word is less something a baby produces and more something that babies and adults do *together*.

Her quote also closes the door to merely demolishing myths about first words, as if the decision to observe baby behavior wasn't itself a cultural decision. Let parents have their myths—in fact, let's have more myths, and better ones.

Another reason is that it also applies as well to last words, but that's a matter I'll take up in a bit.

§

As fuzzy as a baby's first words are, you also have to be careful with evidence from other times and places for parents' interest in first words.

One day I came upon this sentence in a 2008 scholarly history of daily life among the Aztecs, before the Spanish conquest: "The first words of a child were greeted with joy, and it is easy to imagine the delight of parents as they made offerings to thank the gods for bringing their children fully into their expressive and articulate world." My attention ensnared, I scrambled to find *Primeros Memoriales*, the book compiled by a fascinating Franciscan friar named Bernardino de Sahagún that the historian had cited. Sahagún arrived in Tenochtitlan in 1529, eight years after the Spanish conquest, and immediately began collecting information from the Aztecs, in the Nahuatl language, about their culture. The historian's quotation suggested that Sahagún had also collected what we would now consider ethnographic information about family life, including attitudes about child language.

Magnus Pharao, a linguist who studies Nahuatl, texted me a photo of the passage in his copy of an English translation of *Primeros Memoriales*. There it was:

> The priest of Ixtlilco was responsible for, saw to, called for the offerings when the children—boys and girls—spoke their first words. They went carrying their offerings of flowers or *copal*. All the different kinds of offerings were prepared, which they carried.

"Seems to be correct," Pharao texted.

"I'll be damned," I replied. Amazing! Valuable textual evidence of premodern interest in first words in Mesoamerica. Of course, I already presumed that Aztec parents paid attention to this linguistic arrival, having read that Nahuatl songs and poems described children as "flowers" and "precious jewels," and that Aztec society prized spoken eloquence. How easily this is overlooked, I thought. From the modern perspective, Aztecs look sophisticated, sumptuously violent (all that human sacrifice), and ultimately tragic. Yet here they were, listening for their children's first words, celebrating them just like us! Perhaps my first-word obsession (and the interest of middle-class parents) wasn't so idiosyncratic. After all, it had been shared by others, far away, long ago.

Except that it was too good to be true.

To his credit, Pharao's instinct was to check the Nahuatl text. It had no mention of "first words," in the modern sense of a baby's early utterance. In context, the passage did seem to describe children doing something for the first time. But what? The clue lay in the Nahuatl word *motenmanalia*, which means "to give lip" or "to offer lip"—or to make an offering by saying something. A prayer, perhaps.

It seemed as if Sahagún had described how Aztec children brought offerings of flowers and copal (an aromatic tree resin, burned as incense) to the temple at Ixtlilco, where they said prayers, maybe for the first time. Perhaps Sahagún was struck by a parallel with Catholic children, who must go through a First Communion ceremony. Indeed, the temple, dedicated to a deity called Ixtlilton, or "the Little Black Faced One," was a place of healing for children. But there are no mentions of children speaking or their first words in other existing texts about Ixtlilton, who was an avatar of Tlaltecuhtli, "Earth Stamper." In Nahuatl, the word for "word" (literally "mouth") is *cama-tl*, and there's a family of nouns and verbs built on the root *cama-*. However, none of them appear in descriptions of Ixtlilco. Sahagún's texts also doesn't use any Nahuatl words for babies who aren't yet talking: *ocatl, xochtic, octototl, conechichilli*. Who knows why the translator, an esteemed Classical Nahuatl scholar and Sahagún expert named Thelma D. Sullivan (who died in 1981), chose "first words" instead of something like "first prayers."

Thus, the evidence for Aztec parents' interest in first words foundered on a mistranslation. As far as information about babies, the chronicles of pre-Hispanic life in Mexico contain very little.

Yet my quest for evidence about beliefs about early language wasn't in vain. At the base of the mighty Mexican volcano Popocatépetl is a thriving Nahuatl-speaking community that lies near the border between the states of Morelos and Puebla. In that town, babies of seven or eight months who haven't babbled "na" or "ta" syllables yet (for "mother" and "father" in Nahuatl baby talk) raise the concern of their parents. To coax them to speak, the *abuelas* thread small, oblong corn tortillas called *memelitas* (or in Nahuatl *mehmelahtzitzinti*) on a string, which is hung around the necks of babies, who then eat the *memelitas* off the necklace. (This resonates with the beliefs in other communities in Mexico that animals represent "imperfect humans" because they cannot speak, an ability they gain when they taste corn.) Such recalcitrant babies are also fed fruit that parrots eat, so that if the baby cannot speak they might still be able to sing like a bird. I learned this from Claudia Zavala Amaro, Pharao's wife, who grew up in the town of Hueyapan. The *memelita* necklace wasn't common there, she remembered, and was offered mainly to babies who are exposed to both Spanish and Nahuatl at home, not just Spanish, and she wasn't sure if this is now a thing of the past.

These details, I love them. When we stop impressing our beliefs on others, when we get out of our own way, a broader range of emotional attachments—ones that we could have, too—comes into view.

§

One lesson of Catherine Snow's observation that first words reflect culturally specific decisions is that *all* ideas and beliefs about first (and last) words reflect such decisions—including scientific facts. Note these are *decisions*. There's not a straight causal line between noticing first words and parental love, literacy rates, class, or a love for the verbal arts. They're not expressions of a cultural essence either. We can't catalog all of the decisions—there are too many villages, too many *abuelas*—but we can look for patterns in what we do know.

Based on my investigations, the world's cultures of child-rearing and person-making fall into four styles or modes of engaging with first words. You might also think of them as four types of expectations about how the signifying self appears. In any case, mapping them can help us appreciate the diversity of cultural decisions about first words (and eventually about last words, too). Stories about them are woven through the following chapters.

The unscripted first word. In this style, adults notice a change, subtle or grand, in how a baby does language-like things. However, there's no given or expected word, type of word, utterance, gesture, or tone of voice that marks the change. This makes it rather *laissez parler*, or "say what you will," meaning that a variety of behaviors can serve as a plausible threshold to personhood and belonging in the community.

In the contemporary bourgeois household, this manifests as an expectation that linguistic behaviors that emerge from the child are particular to that child. This allows the parent to foretell whether they have a future animal lover, a stargazer, a daredevil, or whatnot. By contrast, in other communities or eras, this linguistic threshold amounts to a reassurance that the child isn't a demon, ghost, or animal but a *human*. In the 1930s, American anthropologists Leslie Spier and Edward Sapir noted that among the Wishram Chinook, an Indigenous community in the Pacific Northwest, babyhood lasts "until they could talk clearly." Until then, only guardian spirits, dogs, and coyotes can understand the babblings of babies, who can in turn understand dogs and coyotes, until they "grow old enough to speak and understand the tongue of [their] parents." The point is, whatever counts as "clear" speaking is more situational and subjective than some established threshold.

The reassurance that early speech or a first word marks humanness takes an inverse form among the Beng people, a small ethnic group in Côte d'Ivoire, who believe that babies come from the soul realm or afterlife, the *wrugbe*, where mingling souls can speak each other's languages with ease. Only after living in this world do these souls, now babies, forget all of those other languages, focusing only on Beng. But if they utter an identifiable Beng word before the appropriate time, it's a bad omen. Apparently any word of Beng will serve—though it puzzles me how someone might deliberately try *not* to hear an adult word in baby babbling, particularly if they speak a language like Beng that's made up of open syllables. Anyway, this premature first word is undesirable because it bends toward last words. It means a baby has left the *wrugbe* too early, requiring a cosmic rebalancing that involves the death of a grandparent.

In multilingual families, and also families where there's sign and speech, the first word is *laissez parler* by necessity, given that cultural mixing makes for inconsistent expectations about the first word, while diverse linguistic inputs make the child's outputs a toss-up. Cognitive neuroscientist Narly Golestani, who was born in Iran and lived in Switzerland with a German-speaking partner, told me that her daughter's first word was "hubaba," for helicopter (or *hubschrauber* in German). But another early word, "dada," stumped the family. In Persian, it's a baby talk form to describe leaving or going out, like "bye bye" (because *dar* means "door," "dada" might literally be "door-door"), though it could also have been a variant of "baba," which means "father" in Persian and Bavarian German. (Not all multilingual families have this issue—a Mandarin-speaking mother living in Britain told me her bilingual child's first word was an unambiguous English "book.")

A surprisingly old example of this *laissez parler* mode belonged to the ancient Roman religion, as described by the classical writer Marcus Terentius Varro (116–27 BCE). When a certain linguistic capacity emerged in a child, their parents (most certainly members of the elite) brought an offering to a temple of Farinus, who was the god of first words. I became excited when I read about Farinus, mentally booking my pilgrimage to the marbled temple of this forgotten god. Unfortunately, no buildings have survived and no images of the god exist, but we know Farinus wasn't alone, as other spirits were in charge of walking and babbling.

These Roman parents would be celebrating the arrival of *fari*, their word for this newly hatched language quality, which amounts to a sort of authoritative speaking, the same attributed to oracles and prophets. (*Fari* is an archaic form of *fans*, a word that refers to speaking, from which we derive the word "infant," or someone without speech, *infans*—without *fari*.) A linguist, unaccustomed to prophecies and oracles, would want to know the properties of *fari*—an adultlike pronunciation, perhaps? A spontaneous, willful word? This isn't clear. Suffice it to say that Farinus was believed to have joined his power and ability as a speaker to the child, not simply teaching them but carrying them over the threshold, before which the child was *infans*—without speech, and therefore not truly human. On the other side, they were raw material for socializing in the ways of the community.

This concept of *fari*, which you could recast as linguistic agency, recurs throughout the discussion of first words. Often this agency is shared, not located in one person. Rather, it can be spread across humans and gods, humans and other humans, and even humans and technological devices. It also takes many linguistic shapes—sometimes it's vocal, sometimes it's indubitably intentional too. Is it possible to accelerate the arrival of *fari*, say by teaching a baby to sign? And once you're considering its arrival, its departure comes quickly to mind. Who doesn't produce language, who loses *fari*? Can such a human be considered a person? In reality, babies aren't the only *infantes*, and people who are dying might be wholly or teetering at the edge of it as well, where we who will bear their passing find ourselves in relation to them and their *fari*.

If this concept of *fari* is still too vague, another way to unpack what Farinus offered to little Augustus or Flavia came from sociologist Erving Goffman. In the 1970s, he wrote about the subtleties in the idea of the "speaker" of an utterance. For instance, it's assumed that the source of someone's intention to produce an utterance is the same source as the utterance's content. In lots of cases, this plainly isn't true. When a prime minister reads a speech written by an assistant, who is the "speaker"? What about when a baby imitates something her mother has just done? In both cases, as well as many others, the "speaker" actually combines several roles into one. Goffman very helpfully proposed that the one who produces the message, or is its "sounding box" (its animator), is distinct from the one who devises the message or "scripts the lines" (its author). In turn, both are distinct from the one who gets social credit for the message or "the party to whose position the words attest" (its principal). The prime minister is that principal; it's "her" speech. And the imitating baby may or may not be the principal.

In the Roman case, little Augustus or Flavia was the animator, and Farinus's authorship made it possible for the baby to be credited as principal. Throughout the rest of this book, there will be many opportunities to see the language producer's myriad roles emerge, shift, and reverse themselves—in first words as well as last ones.

The cultural first word. This *laissez parler* style contrasts with another in which the form of the first word is prescribed and widely culturally shared—and therefore timeless. Sometimes parents pull something like an adult word from the baby's babbling, using a fairly rigid matrix of phonological expectation. Sometimes they repeat a word, which the child eventually imitates. Sometimes the child may produce a good number of recognizable words, but only when a specific utterance occurs do the adults acknowledge what the child has achieved. (There's more about cultural first words in chapter 4.)

Examples of this struck me as profoundly exotic when I first read about them. For instance, the Samoans, as the linguistic anthropologist Elinor Ochs described in the 1970s, believe a child's first words are composed of a curse, *tae*, which means "shit," as in "eat shit!" (or *ai tae*).

What does it say about a culture that a baby knows the word for shit? The answer is the same as how the baby knows that "mama" means "mother" or the 5-handshape 🤚 means "milk": the babies *don't* know what those sounds or hand movements mean, but adults are happy to author a meaning for the motor movements. Meanwhile, the babies animate the utterance, yet as soon as they're aided by the adults, they can win credit for "saying" a word.

Ai tae, "mama," and other conventionalized first words can be called "cultural" or "ideological" first words, in the sense that language is expected to reflect the ordering of selves and society. The ideological form is the default, in the absence of an actual observation, which it sometimes even withstands.

We can be oblivious to the fact that "mama" as mother isn't really universal, nor preordained. Better to think of the mama-first meme as culturally required. It's one way that a parent projects their desire to be recognized by their offspring. I argue that the mama-first meme has its own history, embedded in shifting family configurations and a glorification of the mother as keeper of the private domestic sphere, perhaps as a back-lash to new opportunities in public for women. It was fully convention-alized in Europe and North America until the twentieth century, when parents became socialized to look and listen instead at what babies actually produced.

Before I go further, I should say that I'm not claiming that any one of these styles is more advanced. They don't represent levels of evolutionary superiority or any better way to bring children into language. Neither are they static—in fact, they're quite vulnerable to the conditions of people's everyday lives and their beliefs about language. These styles blend with each other and even clash, as I will show, and new ones also pop up.

The observed first word. That's what happened with the third style. Its roots are in nineteenth-century positivism, which turned infants into subjects of scientific curiosity from educational reformers, psychologists, linguists, and social scientists. Here, adults engage closely with all of the things that babies do, including language. This involves cultural decisions to turn babies into science projects, to process private family matters for analysis and consumption outside the family, and even to enlist parents as quasi-scientists. This approach dovetails quite nicely with the *laissez parler* style, which it amplifies and informs.

You can track this observational style through the ideas from contem-porary experts in child language that are threaded through these chapters. One consequence of its rise is that parents and other adults, in many social strata around the world, now pay close attention to how their children develop language. The adults' long-term goal is to prepare the child for the rest of the child's life. However, many parents might agree that when you uncork children's verbal expressiveness, you also shift the center of family action to what and how they use language. This often works to the detri-ment of adult priorities; you spend more time dealing with immature view-points than instilling mature ones. Yet it's supposed to be worth it, because there's an economic—and even moral—value attached to precocious lin-guistic achievements. The observational style is thus deeply entwined with a capitalist ethos that judges the human being as a producer. It's also wrapped in middle-class routines of childcare that attempt to coordinate the chaos and hope for fewer tears. Yes, people may want their babies to express themselves, but actually in service of the needs of their nuclear fam-ily and the aspirations of the institution.

Occasionally these experts, including linguistics, psychologists, and cognitive scientists, display a shocking cultural arrogance by assuming that others share their views. To take one example, two linguists asserted in a 1999 textbook that "parents impatiently await their infant's first words and regard this as one of the most exciting milestones in development." Experts are needed for describing how first (and last) words begin biologically and socially. But this unreflective casting of the world in the shape of their own practices reflects cultural decisions too.

And yet language scientists have given us a fascinatingly comprehensive picture of first words, predominantly in Anglophone settings and developed societies. This has elevated what's known from the anecdotal to a developed subfield, with its own journals, researchers, and dedicated databases. For example, first words often rank high in a trait called "babiness." Simply put, this means they're words that have to do with babies, their immediate surroundings, and concrete objects that are relevant to them. One implication of this sort of insight is to reduce the first word's value as a window into the child's future; the choice of first word tells you more about the state of being a baby than a trait of the individual baby.

First words reflect vocabulary items that babies see or hear frequently, and which are emotionally relevant to them. At first glance, this seems obvious, but there's some fascinating nuance. For example, among their first fifty words, English-speaking babies don't say "diaper," but they have been known to say "socks" and "shoes." They learn to produce the names of things they can use or change, but not all the things they often see. Tellingly, they don't produce words for couches, beds, desks, or even cribs. They also learn words for things that themselves change. If a thing sits there and has no moving parts, its name isn't learned early. Early speech privileges objects small enough for babies to handle, which include toys. "Helicopter" and "airplane" might be outliers, but then you remember they're often high in the sky, thus small, and also loud. (Linguist Julie Hochsegang's oldest son's first sign was "airplane," which he signed when he saw or heard a plane—they lived near an airport.) One more important tidbit: early words emerge for things and actions that happen together in a frequent cluster, called an "action scheme." In one study, "Mommy," "Daddy," "dog," "hi," and "ball" were the most frequent words in the first ten that English-speaking children said. This is because first words emerge not randomly but in specific contexts, along with gestures and other bodily actions. (More about this appears in chapter 5.)

Attention by science has also uncovered what might be called a "shadow" first word. Linguists call them "demonstratives," words familiar in their adult forms as "here" and "that," but which can also be expanded into phrases like "here it is" or "look at that." Every language in the world has demonstratives, generally two or three terms, and babies everywhere have them among their earliest words. (One of the most famous first words is a demonstrative, in fact, as I'll describe in chapter 3.) However, parents tend to overlook demonstratives, for two main reasons. First, they sound like babbled noises—take the English "da," for "that," which is apt to be ignored if adults don't expect it. Second, adults are more clued in to words than gestures and may have a linguistic bias toward noticing children's nouns and verbs over grammatical function words. Though they fly under the radar, demonstratives are important pivots in the child's communicative life because they are key—along with pointing—to manipulating others' attention, particularly to a third entity. That manipulation begins with saying "here it is."

Any single first word in isolation might be worth little more than a nod, until you take a large enough sample to spot patterns—and even predict when they will occur. This was the work of an American cognitive scientist named Elizabeth Bates, who headed a team in the 1980s and 1990s that collected first words at a massive scale. Their most visible product became known as the MacArthur-Bates Communicative Development Inventory, or more conveniently as the CDI, and it established a baseline for early vocabulary growth in children learning dozens of languages. By aggregating samples from thousands of children, scientists could effectively resolve the fuzziness of the first word and tie it to other aspects of how language develops.

To achieve this, they had to enlist parents and recruit the private family sphere for what were essentially public ends. Such practices reflect cultural decisions about parents as citizen scientists, the need for detailed information about huge samples of children in the first place, and what such an approach might obscure along the way.

The ignored first word. The high level of expectations that my culture has about early utterances is probably an anomaly in the history of our species. The most likely fate of first words? Like most last words, they're more likely memorialized in the records of the gods, not the record of humans.

To some readers, this indifference to first words may be the most shocking revelation of this book. But it's not that people don't notice their kids—it's that other milestones matter more. In some societies, the more important milestone is when a child is no longer carried by their mother, when they begin to go unswaddled, or when a second set of molar teeth grows in. In hunter-gatherer societies, a child's achievements in prosocial, cooperative behavior, such as controlling one's anger, sharing, and understanding kinship structures, are considered to be milestones. In other societies, the milestones are about social but nonlinguistic behavior. For example, in Navajo (or Diné) families, the baby's first laugh is eagerly awaited—and often prompted—reflecting the importance of laughter as a "healing aspect of the human spirit." After the laugh arrives, there's a party, hosted by the person who made the child laugh. Elsewhere, family structures or economic pursuits constrain whether or not anyone notices early language milestones. For instance, in some communities, a child is cared for by a group of adults, not only one or two biological parents. This raises the suspicion that people in nuclear families focus on first words merely as a function of being cooped up with a baby.

Observers of various cultures have given us ample evidence about how language acquisition in preindustrial societies goes uncelebrated. In Europe prior to the seventeenth century, children's cognitive development would have been a questionable thing for grown-ups to monitor and track. This was its own form of care, in the sense that it freed adults to celebrate other things, such as baptisms and the wearing of pants by boys. For a contemporary example, consider the Tseltal, an Indigenous community that numbers about half a million and lives mainly in the Mexican state of Chiapas. According to the work of linguistic anthropologists, the Tseltal don't organize community or family life around babies, who have opportunities to see what's going on around them but have very little speech directed at them, particularly by parents. Somali society reportedly has similar practices. A composite character of a Somali-born woman who lived in the United States said, "I used to laugh when I would see these woman talking to babies who cannot respond: Why are these women wasting their time?" Many groups are like this. Why? If the first words reflect the cultures in which they arise, so does their absence, probably due to the demands of daily life.

From the scientific viewpoint, it's notable that children, whether they're medieval or contemporary European, develop language on the same basic trajectory and timeline as children from Indigenous rural communities. Across diverse situations, the inevitability of this achievement is why the ignored first word evolved in the first place, in societies that experience more infant mortality and lack the expectation of universal literacy. Yet this style, and its generally positive outcomes, has been almost wholly overlooked by middle-class Westerners who take their own interest in child language as normative. As younger children in those same families can attest: if your first words get ignored, it's not the worst thing that can happen to you.

§

Across these four expectations, one thing appears to be true: as far as I have been able to find, in no place or time have a child's first words prompted a collective celebration, not even in cultures where verbal fluency is prized. I've wrestled with this apparent fact—why is the Roman god Farinus the only such deity? Posting to social media, as contemporary parents do, doesn't count as a celebration—I mean stopping the day's activities to mark a special time because a child uttered /mɔwə/, in the same way that first teeth, first laughs, first menses or nocturnal emissions, literacy, recitations of family lineages, and other achievements are communally recognized in various parts of the world. I asked Catherine Snow about this invisibility. "Perhaps it's because first words are too ambiguous, too subjective," she mused.

Maybe it's just that they're celebrated privately. In that case, let me add more reasons to celebrate with the next two chapters. Even the most banal first word, spoken or signed, late or on time, has extraordinarily rich, deep cultural, historical, and evolutionary dimensions. Sure, the first word may not necessarily offer insight into the life of the individual who produces it or their personality. However, it does tell us why early utterances became so treasured and, just as significantly, why they happen at all.

2 The Story of a First Word (or Why We Pay Attention to First Words at All)

Round-round.

If someone were writing the story of an ordinary infant's first word, the utterance itself, no matter what it might be, whether "knuffle bunny" or "piz" (supposedly Picasso's first word, from the Spanish for "pencil," *lapiz*), would take up a speck of territory on the first page.

Hello. Bye bye. Da. Didda.

But we won't stop there. The setting, perhaps mundane, would have to be described. A baby in a high chair, a stroller. What was directed to whom might be drawn out, the perceptions of parents probed, the reactions of friends and family related. The career of the story of the first word might hint at the child's future—does it tell something fruitful about the person the child will become?

Round-round.

My eldest son's first discernible adult-sounding and semantically endowed spoken word occurred when he was thirteen and a half months old, at a bed-and-breakfast in a snow-blanketed village in Quebec. These facts are relevant because over the bed was a ceiling fan, switched on to circulate the room's heat. We didn't have such an apparatus at home. He and I were on the bed. I was changing his diaper, he was babbling away and looking up past my head, and suddenly I realized that he wasn't just babbling. "Woun-woun," he was saying, "woun-woun."

"Did you just say . . . 'round-round'?" I asked. "Are you calling the fan a 'round-round'?"

He smiled, gurgled, wiggled his limbs. I was so happy, proud of us both.

A nouny first word is fairly common, if he'd been labeling the fan. This one was deliciously ambiguous—it could also have been his admiration of its movement (such descriptions are more rare) or expressing a desire to do something with it. As it turns out, "round-round" foretold a highly kinetic boy's great love of wheeled things, especially trains and bikes, and anything with forward motion (arrows, runners, airplanes). My story is this, and I'm sticking to it: his love has lasted fourteen years and counting. Many first words survive as stories exactly because in retrospect, they line up with the character who spoke them.

All this would take up a few pages of the word's story. In the case of "round-round," there's a twist: this utterance won the "firstness" crown because his parents' narrow sense of what counted as a word distracted them from other things, word-like in their own ways, yet alien and hence easy to brush off. But undeniably a threshold, even if we saw it only in retrospect.

One example was his syllable "ka."

Linguists used to not dare call something like "ka" a word. They labeled them "nonsense words," "protowords," "prewords," "call-sounds," "quasi-words," or "vocal conventions." To them a "true" word embraced the arbitrary nature that's traditionally taken as the hallmark of the linguistic symbol. The "true" word sounded or looked like the adult form. It was pronounced consistently, referred to something consistently, and wasn't chained to a specific activity or contexts. In that sense, "hello" or "thank you" couldn't be a "true" word. The baby throws the stuffed animal out of the crib and says, "Kitty!" Not a word. The baby points and says, "Dat." Not a word. (Many linguists now disagree.) Nor, for that matter, most utterances that parents would call "first."

"Ka" was more than a mere protoword, I want to testify. It was deliberately and repeatedly uttered, with some significant purpose and stubborn intention. It was a big dose of *fari*. The problem was, its meaning was indiscernible to us.

"Ka, ka," he'd say, over and over, pointing. (Often, "ka" came with an emphatic straight arm, index finger outstretched, but by then he'd been pointing for a while.) The first time, at a car. That's easy, my wife thought. "Car" was indeed pronounced "kah" by some people in Maine, in that stereotyped New England fashion.

Then he pointed at a small statue of the Hindu god Ganesha. "Ka," he said.

"I don't think he's saying 'car,'" I remember saying. Something else is going on. Who says "ka" must refer to an object? Maybe it's just a word about communication that means "Look at that with me, isn't that interesting?"

Looking back, that's probably what it meant. "Look at that." One of the mysterious demonstratives, in fact. And like so many other parents, we'd overlooked it!

He didn't say "ka" every time he pointed at something interesting (or that he'd been interested in before). We went to a coffee shop, where a painting with large circles garnered a point and a "ka," as did a ceiling fan. (The boy liked his spinning things!) These instances suggested that my wife (who thought "ka" was a specific noun) and me (who thought "ka" was not only managing our attention but had embedded in it a sentence's worth of meaning, what linguists refer to as a *holophrase*) were both wrong. It seemed equally as likely that "ka" labeled an abstract category, visible only to young minds, of *circly things*.

This all happened long enough ago that I was still on Facebook, where I posted my question about the meaning of "ka," hoping for responses from my friends there. Gary mentioned that "ka" is a Vedic term for "god." That might explain the pointing at Ganesha and at wheels, a Vedic symbol of divinity. I was puzzled. My son, plugged into mythological archetypes?

The best suggestion came from Susan, who quoted American writer Shirley Jackson (1916–1965) on the holophrastic meaning of her son's first word, "dewey," as "Observe my latest achievement, far surpassing all my previous works in this line, a great and personal triumph representing perhaps the most intelligent progress ever accomplished by a child of my years." As for "ka," by the time we realized that personal triumph, weeks had passed; we were already celebrating another triumph, in the slightly obsessive, self-centered way that only first-time, middle-class American parents can.

More recently, linguists have relaxed their standards. They've recognized that vocabularies are built from iconicity, meaning that many words contain a resemblance between their sound or shape and what they represent. In fact, children learn more iconic words earlier, while adults use iconic words more frequently when they're talking to children. Others, who hold that language is built for interaction and social coordination, argue that learning to be polite ("hi!") or disagreeable ("no!") are eminently plausible words too. The consequence is that what counts as a first word is now broadened, while the protoword category is obsolete.

If "ka" were something akin to "dat," here was the miraculous threshold-crossing, ushering him to the place where he could manipulate his parents' point of view relative to his. A cognitively and socially significant milestone—and we'd missed it.

§

The next part of any first word's story covers broader cultural territory: Why do parents like me spend any energy puzzling about "ka" and "round-round"?

Partly, my wife and I wanted to understand this mysterious creature. What was going on in that little bald head? What did he make of what he could see? And what could he show us about our own experiences as babies, decades ago? Could he give us a glimpse into the inaccessible portions of our own lives?

More practically, it was about our sanity as parents. Maybe if he had words, it would make things easier—maybe we could finally figure out what he wanted. Anything to stop the crying. We were on our own, my wife and I, with family far away, dealing with our first crying, puking, shitting, screaming infant, as obsessed with not messing him up as we were with coming across as competent to the rest of the world. To be honest, it was stressful, as it is for many other parents. Maybe like them we thought that if we taught him some baby sign, it would ease things. Only one sign stuck: "more." (If you're wondering, this happened after the first spoken words.) Like many people in our predicament, we waited for the lexical dam to break, for the chance to be able to hear the answer to the perpetual question "What do you *really* want?"

But we also maintained a nobler rationale. It's partly about family tradition. I wanted to catch my son's first words because I was raised with stories of my own—allegedly "money" and "dubbaday," by my mother's recollection. I was the oldest child, so she has more stories about me. Such habits of noticing and storytelling seemed natural for a family of word-lovers. Yet they're rooted in circumstances too: my mother sent regular letters, filled with details about me, to my father, who was serving in the military in a faraway war for my toddlerhood. Daily life drives how you pay attention, I can't forget, as much as your stated values do. Yet in the Catholic tradition into which I was born, the word becomes flesh at every Mass, from which I derived the notion that a first word has a holy aura. *In the beginning was the Word.* Your first word, a gift to the world, like a radiant baby Jesus in the manger. Yet another part of me acknowledged that my family's love of language is tied to beliefs about, and indeed a deep faith in, the power of literacy, cultural and intellectual capital, and ultimately class achievement. The first word is the first step in the cognitive project that destines a child for success.

Where did that view originate? It's inconceivable that anyone comes to this naturally. So how did the middle class get socialized into the idea that these utterances mattered in the first place?

For parents who live in the West (and in places where Western ideas about parenting have been imported), such attitudes have been around since the early modern period in the seventeenth century. That's when Europeans, or at least the European elite, began to show more interest in how children developed. As a matter of parenting practice, this first took root among the Dutch. In its so-called Golden Age, the Netherlands enjoyed economic surpluses at a societal level before other European countries, thereby escaping the Malthusian trap in which the secular world was doomed to a cycle of surfeit and famine. The idea of a society of steady growth accompanied a new view of society's responsibility to children. As a result, they were to be nurtured and taught; most of them, including girls, went to school. This reorientation of the Dutch family toward the production of literate individuals was noticed by English philosopher John Locke (1632–1704). Exiled in the Netherlands for three years, he was so impressed by Dutch parenting that he imported these ideas back to England. From there, they spread.

Prior to this, European children had been treated more as either chattel or miniature adults. They were loved, of course, but no one conceived of childhood as a developmental period with its own needs and logic. Children weren't taught as much as disciplined, to counter their natural tendency to sin. And the family wasn't a venue for sentiment but a machine intently focused on survival, with parents (especially fathers) ruling over the children. Only under the Dutch model did parents take on roles as teacher and guide. It's hard to say how much this applied to children of the non-elite; probably their fortunes improved much later.

Slowly, a concept of childhood recognizable to us moderns emerged. Among its effects was more attention to how children talked. "It is a rare thing for literature, even of the most popular kind, to preserve traces of children's jargon," wrote French historian Philippe Ariès (1914–1984), adding that "references to children's jargon are unusual before the seventeenth century." (In French, *jargonner* means to speak unintelligibly.) Engravings from 1657 of children playing are captioned with "the jargon of infancy" and "school boy slang." Sometime after 1671, French aristocrat Françoise-Marguerite de Sévigné (1646–1705) wrote to her mother about her young daughter's amusing speech, transcribing it as "titota, tetita, y totata."

Ariès's ideas about childhood in *Centuries of Childhood: A Social History of Family Life* caused an uproar when they first appeared in English in 1962, because he was taken to suggest that parents of yore might not have loved their children. Many other histories of childhood have been written since then, but one of the immediate responses to Ariès came from Linda Pollock, now a history professor at Tulane University, whose PhD project analyzed 416 English-language diaries from the sixteenth to nineteenth centuries. She concluded that Ariès was wrong: even if parents' dotings didn't resemble modern ones, they held their children dear, worried about their futures, mourned their deaths.

I was interested in Pollock's work because she had tracked mentions of various child development phenomena, including infant speech, in these diaries, and I could make incidental use of her data. Only nineteen of the diaries, across four centuries, mentioned infant and child speech at all, and only nine of those mentioned first words or early utterances. These writers were all Anglophones, of course. But the fact is that most people live successful, happy lives without giving everyday language a single passing thought. You have to be taught to treat linguistic things as interesting in their own right.

In Pollock's survey, the earliest attention to child speech occurred in the early sixteenth century, in England, when Anne Clifford had a child "brought to speak with me" and Nehemiah Wallington described his three-year-old daughter as "prattling prettily." The earliest instance of a *specific* first word in Pollock's diaries came from a Puritan judge in Massachusetts named Samuel Sewall. In early 1686, he recorded that his eighteen-month-old son, Hull, "speaks Apple plainly . . . this the first word." Other historical sources explain how Sewall (who served as a judge in the Salem witch trials of 1692) was a devoted father, increasingly distraught by the stillborn babies and infant deaths that he and his wife, Hannah, endured—four in the span of five years. Of their fourteen children, only six survived to adulthood; only three survived him. It's easy to imagine that this interest was sparked by Hull's health—for the sickly boy to say anything at all was remarkable. The boy died five months later, just three weeks shy of his second birthday.

Diary mentions of child language increased over time, at least in Pollock's account: two per century in the sixteenth and seventeenth centuries, seven in the eighteenth century, and eight in the nineteenth—"da-da" (from a ten-month-old), "bow-wow" (from another ten-month-old), and "papa" (from a seventeen-month-old).

What factors explain this increase? One influence undoubtedly came from philosophers such as Jean-Jacques Rousseau (1712–1778), whose 1763 book about the proper education of the young mind, *Emile*, conditioned European parents to attend to babies' language development—not in order to improve or boost it but so as not to rush it, because they come to language on their own. "Whatever we do," Rousseau wrote, "they all learn to talk in the same way, and all philosophical speculations are utterly useless." Thus, parents didn't need to intervene. One mistake—"a much greater evil," he said—is the push to make children speak too early, which teaches them to misvalue words. "That fatal facility in the use of words we [meaning adults] do not understand begins earlier than we think." If children were introduced to language properly, even their first words would infuse the republic with virtue.

Elsewhere it also became important for children to testify to their Christian faith. For radical Protestants of Germany, the Netherlands, and England, the early words of children were of key importance—that ability was key to their confession of faith, which had to proceed their baptism. Meanwhile, Catholics and other Protestants baptized babies, who did not have the onus of speaking placed on them. On this basis, it seems reasonable to predict that radical Protestant communities favored a *laissez parler* approach.

Undoubtedly the material conditions of people's lives also improved, including public health innovations that allowed more children to survive infancy. For most of human history, the great majority of deaths had occurred in the first years of life. Historian Hugh Cunningham has estimated that in Europe as a whole up until the middle of the nineteenth century, between one in four and one in five of all children died before their first birthday. It seems reasonable to conclude that people have paid less attention to babies' language because keeping them alive took priority (and paid correspondingly more attention to their crying, which has been a consistent plaint of parenting literature as far back as the Akkadian civilization in 2500 BCE). That attention amounted to an investment in a child; the more likely they were to die, the riskier that investment. Thanks to efforts in public health and child development, infant mortality rates eventually declined around the world in the early twentieth century. In the United States, the largest decreases occurred in babies between one month and twelve months old. This increased survival, along with the involvement of professionals in childcare, mutually reinforced each other, boosting the attention paid to child language and first words—however, as we will see, only in some communities.

§

The first extensive noticings of baby's first words occur in the early modern period, with its crosscurrent of a new print culture, a dawning sense of economic growth, and the new importance given to the child as a child. The Puritan Sewall's record of "Apple" isn't, in fact, the earliest. We have more extensive records thanks to Jean Héroard, a physician who was assigned to keep a diary about the growth and development of the dauphin who would become Louis XIII. His father, French king Henry IV, was steeped in the humanistic culture whose brightest light was Michel de Montaigne (1533–1592), who had described in his *Essays* what languages he spoke (Latin, Greek) and the immersion to which his father subjected him. (Montaigne's outlook on death would prove pivotal in the treatment of last words, as we will see.) Thus, in 1602, at eight o'clock in the morning on September 15, the royal infant shouts "*hé*" to an arriving servant. In English it could be translated as "hey."

The fuzziness intrinsic to many first words raises its head here. Does "*hé*" count? Some people might say that such an attention-managing protoword wouldn't. In fact, Héroard himself identified a different utterance as a first word, one that occurred in a humorous interaction between the saucy prince and his wet nurse.

Nurse: Well, sir, when I am very old and go with a stick, will you love me more?

Baby: No.

I can't let the prince's august "no" be considered a first word—he was only four months old, after all, when linguistic communication is developmentally impossible. Assuming that the whole exchange isn't an invention by the nurse, this was likely simple phonation, no matter the impression that the cheeky back-and-forth imparts.

These and other linguistic anecdotes take a different cast once you learn that Héroard's six-thousand-page project obsessively describes twenty-six years of the prince's every spoonful of food and bowel movement (as a child) and sexual act (as an adult). Not surprisingly, the entire six thousand pages have never been published in full, likely because its grinding obsession is "more than enough to discourage the most ardent curiosity," as literary historian Elizabeth Wirth Marvick wrote. She also noted that Héroard was less a benign, disinterested observer than a keenly political operator. The twenty-first-century mommy blog has little in common with Héroard's diary, a record of his fealties that also served to hide his manipulations of the prince from a very early age. It seems worth noting that the saucy talking baby grew up to have a violent stutter, whose first occurrence Héroard faithfully noted on January 12, 1604.

Several decades later, the Dutch composer and diplomat Constantijn Huygens Sr. (1596–1687), another astute observer of his children, noted in his ninety-page diary how their speech developed, including their pronunciations and what words they understood. Huygens had an affinity for languages, and perhaps for the essays of Montaigne as well, both of which may explain his detailed notes on the topic, such as Lodewijk's half-words at a year old or Philip's ability at six months to answer in gestures. Though we might place Huygens in the avant-garde of noticing child language, he still didn't write down any of their first words in any language, and in general didn't mark milestones, including their birthdays. The point here is that material surplus, fascination with languages, and parental attention might have created the conditions for noticing first words. Only the idiosyncratic few actually did so.

§

After the dauphin's "*hé*" and Sewall's "Apple," the next first word that I found came from an 1828 book on progressive education by a Swiss intellectual, Albertine-Adrienne Necker de Saussure (1766–1841), who had four children. Apart from her intellectual achievements, she was also the great-aunt of prominent linguistic pioneer Ferdinand de Saussure, who knew her writing. In those days, a mother's perspective on such topics wasn't commonly found in books, and she foreshadows the modern study of infant language, for instance by relating gesture to words and by proposing that rote scenarios are the contexts in which the earliest words arise. (Linguists would later call these "action schemes.") Some of the first words she noted were "no," "yes," "warm," "papa," "mama," and "pretty." It's impossible for me to know whether she'd written these down at the time or was remembering them. In any case, her book, *Progressive Education*, was translated into English in both America and England. One American translator, Almira Phelps, took Necker de Saussure's recommendation to write down everything about her baby's development, including first words. Phelps noted that at the presence of the cat, her son has "tat, tat" as "among the first accents he is heard to utter."

You might be wondering: *How many more historical first words can he surface here?* The answer is, not many. Even literate parents in societies where verbal fluency and eloquence were prized, or who had ample material resources to pursue them, wrote down few specific first words, at least in the archives I could access. There's always the possibility that first words were noted but only orally, thus leaving the most fragile of traces. However, what I've found seems enough to conclude that we associate parental love with attention to linguistic achievements at the peril of historical accuracy. Such attention is better considered a cultural practice bounded in time, nourished by material circumstances. The conclusion is that you shouldn't judge parents' fitness, nor their love for their children, based only on how they use language with them.

This point is relevant to contemporary discussions of the so-called word gap, which refers to the notion that low-income children in the United States hear far fewer words than higher-income peers, which negatively impacts their school readiness. To fill this "gap," experts have created interventions they deliver with the confident assumption that directly speaking to young children and interacting with them from infancy intensively is *normal*. Anthropologists have rightly critiqued the ethnocentrism of this view, which gains further perspective from a survey of the historical evidence. Even elite, highly educated parents of the past didn't necessarily interact with their children (that task has often been delegated to domestic help), and the mainstream middle-class American norm of interacting with babies as if they were individual persons is a recent development, only a bit more than a hundred years old, and more of an effect of that achievement than its cause.

§

Why did noticing a child's first words go from an idiosyncratic practice to something more mainstream in the affluent, industrialized West? For this there's a clear answer: because experts told parents to notice.

When I poked around in the parenthood literature of the nineteenth century, I saw parenting experts, psychologists, and reformers in numerous countries clearly communicating to parents how important it was to pay attention to their child's development. Once children were recognized as important social resources, they became the objects of private and public efforts to improve their lives. Campaigns for children's health, orphanages, experimental schools, and "milk depots" for decreasing infant diarrheal diseases spread widely, and laws requiring compulsory education and limiting child labor were passed. In the late nineteenth century, infant welfare organizations were founded in Denmark, Germany, Italy, Luxembourg, the Netherlands, Norway, Romania, Russia, Spain, Switzerland, the United Kingdom, and the United States.

One effect of all this was the child study movement of the 1890s, which promoted the scientific observing of children in order to generate universals of development that could be tracked, measured, and promoted. After all, expanding societies needed better information about whether their efforts were working. Mothers also needed to be instructed in these principles, in order to raise the next generation of healthier, "better" babies. The result was "scientific motherhood," in which mothers' receptivity to expertise was braided with an expectation that they would observe their babies in a manner akin to scientists.

I've been interested in when and how scientific motherhood emerged because it transformed noticing and recording first words from a relatively rare practice to something more common, even expected. An English-language periodical of the 1890s, *Babyhood*, devoted several articles in 1891 to instructing mothers to make detailed observations of their babies. In one issue, a psychology professor listed the scientists (all male, by the way) who had observed their own children as scientists would and written down what they saw. Yet parents, even mothers, could be recruited for the same. The mother "should feel that her opportunity has come, that her love and her intellect might unite in accomplishing the work that science calls for and that lies at her threshold," wrote the author. In another issue, a doctor named Elizabeth Stowe Brown instructed mothers to keep a record of their baby's mental growth. Brown recommended what mothers should observe, including language: "descriptions of sounds made, vowels and consonants, syllables, moods, parts of speech."

This observational imperative took a concrete form in commercially printed baby books, which had four main uses: recording gifts for the baby (which had long been done in the middle classes), tracking developmental milestones, recording religious ceremonies, and collecting physical items such as photos, birth announcements, locks of hair, and hand and palm tracings. An early baby book appeared in Denmark in 1831, when a collector of folktales named Just Mathias Thiele (1795–1874) commissioned a book binder to make a beautifully gold-embossed book with blank pages; in them he wrote about his daughter Ida's life until she was five years old. (Yes, he notes her first words: baby versions of "father" and "mother," for which she said "baer" and "boer," and an adult form, "mad" for "food." Ida also labeled the peat they burned "törre" for "törv" and the soldiers she could see in front of their apartment.)

It's not clear whether or how this sort of record caught on in Europe. In America, commercial books with pages prompting certain types of information about baby began to appear in the 1870s, eventually becoming popular. Some, like Francis Galton's *The Life History Album*, were exceptionally so. As historians Janet Golden and Lynn Weiner posit, this popularity "reflected the perception that babies were increasingly likely to survive," thanks to the improved resources for infant welfare. Organizations that promoted such welfare disseminated their own baby books; so did doctors and companies selling baby-related products to parents, who branded their books and even prefilled answers with their companies' foods and toys.

The baby books made it easy to think that individual babies and children mattered, as did their utterances. A good mother wouldn't want a page to be unfilled. But just how visible were early language and first words in this culture?

I examined online library records for about sixty baby books from the early twentieth century in the Louise M. Darling Biomedical Library at the University of California, Los Angeles, which has 1,200 such books in its special collection, the only such collection in the United States. In this sample, I found that about two-thirds provided space for a "first word" or "first words." The most effusive, a book from 1910, asked, "What were the first wonderful words?" One asks for "baby's sayings" and another asks for "speech" and "vocabulary at 18 months."

But this interest in first words was far from consistent, so we can't presume that an interest in first words at this date was universal. About a third of the books in the UCLA collection whose records I examined prompted nothing about words or language, amid the prompts about first pictures, birthdays, Christmases, teeth, trips. For example, *The Biography of a Better Baby*, published in 1910, figures that "better babies" eat, grow, wear clothes, get fresh air, and walk. Other books prompted broader language observations. A French book from 1906, *Le Livret de l'enfant*, asked when the baby started to speak (*"a quel age l'enfant a-t-il commencé a parler?"*), and *The Edwardian Baby* from 1908 prompted more general language milestones ("should use syllables, such as ma, pa, na, ta, without any distinct meaning").

This gave me a bit of perspective on language matters. The author of the book containing the page in figure 2.1, "Mrs. Marion Vaughn," was the pen name of Stella Scott Gilman (1844–1928), a philanthropist and writer who cofounded, with her husband, what became Radcliffe College. She was also the first president of the Mother's Club of Cambridge, Massachusetts, founded in 1878, where discussions centered on what the contemporary mother needed to know—and from whom—about how to raise her children. Nowadays this sort of mother—educated, well-connected, "consumed with concern for their children's physical, emotional, and spiritual well-being"—would have all the up-to-date methods for boosting baby's language and cognition. But Gilman's distillation of parenting advice from club members has no mention of early language in a way that contemporary parents would recognize. Thus an indifference to child language can be found even in the heart of modern parenting as elites practiced it. The seeds of an obsession with language had been planted, but they weren't to bloom for decades yet.

§

The case of Mrs. Marion Vaughn shows that parents' attention to early language wasn't monolithic, given differences in geography, race, and class. It suggests that all sorts of expectations about first words, and their consequences for child-rearing practices, weren't omnipresent or even visible (at least in ways that we now have evidence about). One emblematic set of differences in the United States was observed one hundred years after *The*

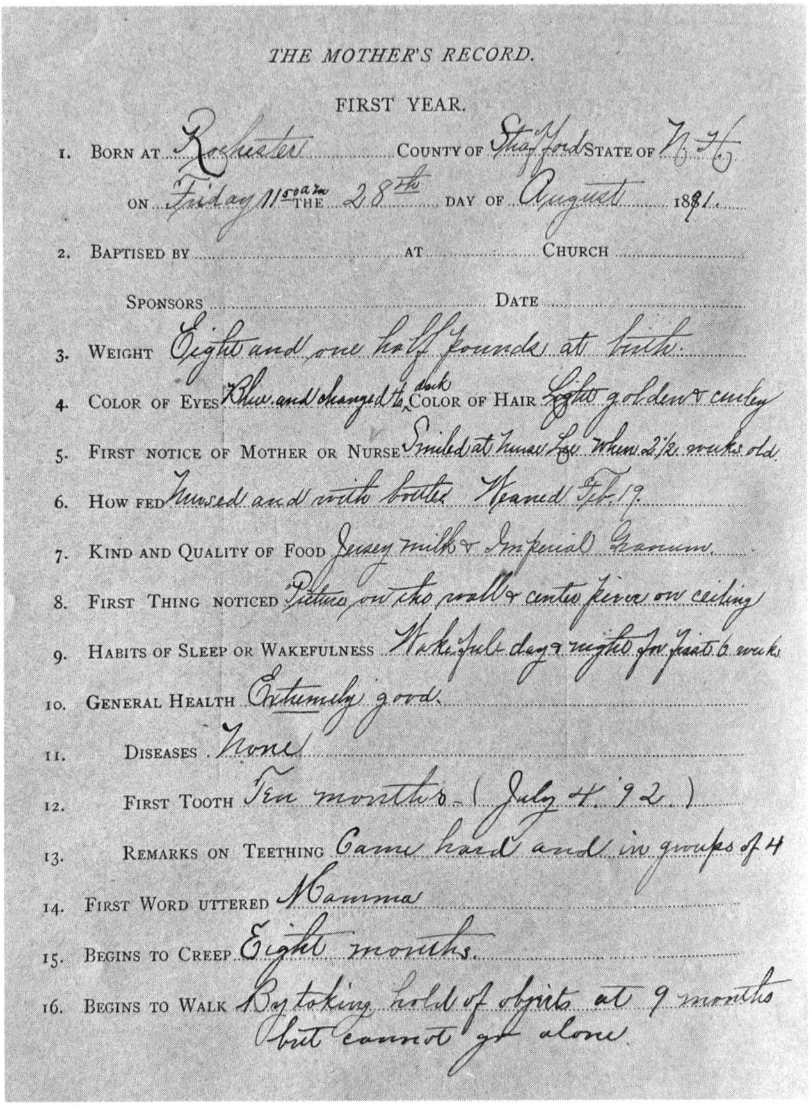

THE MOTHER'S RECORD.

FIRST YEAR.

1.   BORN AT _Rochester_ COUNTY OF _Strafford_ STATE OF _N.H._
     ON _Friday 11:50 a.m._ THE _28th_ DAY OF _August_ 188_1_

2.   BAPTISED BY _____ AT _____ CHURCH _____

     SPONSORS _____ DATE _____

3.   WEIGHT _Eight and one half pounds at birth._

4.   COLOR OF EYES _Blue and changed to dark_ COLOR OF HAIR _Light golden & curly_

5.   FIRST NOTICE OF MOTHER OR NURSE _Smiled at nurse Lou when 2½ weeks old_

6.   HOW FED _Nursed and with bottle Weaned Feb 19_

7.   KIND AND QUALITY OF FOOD _Jersey milk & Imperial Granum_

8.   FIRST THING NOTICED _Pictures on the wall & centre piece on ceiling_

9.   HABITS OF SLEEP OR WAKEFULNESS _Wakeful day & night for first 6 weeks_

10. GENERAL HEALTH _Extremely good._

11. DISEASES _None_

12. FIRST TOOTH _Ten months (July 4 '92)_

13. REMARKS ON TEETHING _Came hard and in groups of 4_

14. FIRST WORD UTTERED _Mamma_

15. BEGINS TO CREEP _Eight months._

16. BEGINS TO WALK _By taking hold of chairs at 9 months but cannot go alone._

Figure 2.1
A page from an 1882 baby book, *The Mother's Record*, by Mrs. Marion Vaughn, published by the D. Lothrop Company. The book was filled out—the first three years, anyway—for an unnamed child born in 1891 in New Hampshire. Note the first word, "mamma." On an adjoining page (not pictured here), the note-taker records that the baby says "na-na. mum-ma. da-da." The book has another "specimen" page with these items filled in. There too the first word is "mamma." Photo by author.

Mother's Record was published, in the 1980s, by linguistic anthropologist Shirley Brice Heath (who was white). She conducted nine years of extensive fieldwork in three communities in the Piedmont region of North and South Carolina, documenting how children became speakers of their community's language and how that affected their experiences in schools.

As she wrote in *Ways with Words*, now considered a classic work of linguistic anthropology, the two working-class communities, one white and the other Black, had diametrically opposed ways of interacting with babies as linguistic persons. In the working-class African American community of (pseudonymous) Trackton, Heath observed that babies were never addressed directly by adults or older children. Somehow in agreement with Rousseau's proscriptions two hundred years earlier in *Emile* ("But an abuse of an entirely different importance . . . is when one is in too much of a hurry to make them talk, as if one were afraid that they will not learn to talk by themselves"), Trackton babies weren't ever rushed into producing language by being treated as conversation partners by adults. "Trackton adults do not see babies or young children as suitable partners for regular conversation," Heath wrote. "For an adult to choose a preverbal infant over an adult as a conversational partner would be considered an affront and a strange behavior as well."

Heath confirmed for me via email that first words were rarely, if ever, noticed in Trackton. It's not that mothers weren't familiar with the practice. They certainly knew about middle-class "baby talk," a high-pitched, simplified type of language that adults use with babies; they'd seen it in action while working as maids in middle-class homes, but they didn't do it themselves. In fact, when Heath and her own children used baby talk with Trackton infants, the adults made fun of them. It seemed like a clear example of culture-making: our identity as a community is based on not doing the thing *they* do.

In her book, Heath reported that things were different in Roadville, the working-class white community, where mothers noted minute developmental achievements of their babies, such as eye movements, and were highly attuned to the range of babies' vocalizations. Only when the baby made particularly loud cries did a mother pick them up; otherwise they would leave the baby alone. They also seemed eager to listen to word-like sounds. "Young mothers often take the first 'da, da, da, da' sounds from the crib as 'daddy' and report the 'word' proudly to the father," Heath wrote.

Heath compared Trackton and Roadville practices to those in an unnamed middle-class town a few miles away populated by both races. There, too, a baby would be treated as a "potential conversationalist" from the get-go. In all of the households, the baby was treated "as an individual, a separate person, with whom the preferred means of communication is talk." Mothers also took any utterance, even a babble, and transformed it into a sensible utterance that stood for the baby's turn in the interaction.

What's a first word? Why do people pay attention to them? You get different answers if you ask that question in Trackton, Roadville, or the unnamed town. As contemporary critics point out, a white ethnographer might get different answers than a Black ethnographer. But I have a different take, one that lies in historical processes, not cultural essences. Why are infants treated as conversational partners in one working-class community but not the other (and also by the middle-class townsfolk of both races)? As Heath explained it, each community had different linguistic needs, and how they raised children reflected how they use language in church, to relate to each other, and as a vehicle for asserting their identities. It also depended on their familiarity with the types of language used in schools, town offices, and other public institutions. Yes, what Heath reported could be due to her position as a white observer. But this doesn't preclude the possibility that divergent social histories, thanks to the complexities of class and race, resulted in different attention to babies as conversational partners, in the following way:

All over the world, we're fairly certain that language development takes a similar course for children, regardless of whether it's spoken, signed, or even tactile—as long as there's daily input and interaction. However, having a child's first words noticed isn't a universal milestone on that journey—people must be socialized to their importance. So I wonder if these differences between Trackton and Roadville bear the traces of a diffusion of scientific motherhood that took two paths, determined by social factors, and became a place where two styles of expectations about first words lived alongside each other. They certainly clashed in ethnographic reports written by authors hard-pressed to explain what they'd found.

§

So this is where we end up. Engaging with child language and paying attention to first words as a cultural phenomenon emerged from the convergence of a Dutch-inspired investment in children's intellectual development in the early modern period; successful efforts to decrease infant mortality in the nineteenth century; literacy campaigns that mandated schooling for boys and girls; and in the mediascape of the nineteenth century, an international movement to turn mothers into evidence-based champions of their children's development (which mothers, to their credit, sometimes resisted). That's never been enough to make first words culturally important outside of restricted private spheres. But when they do show up in pop culture in the current environment, you clearly see what drives the engagement.

My wife and I hung on our son's squealing and muttering from his earliest days, inspecting him for signs of brilliance. We're the sort of American parents enculturated to believe that our offspring are, among other things, cognitive projects. In the parenting literature we encountered, no baby was perfect enough. They were always improvable. Our ideal was to endow him with the skills he'd need to succeed, defining "success" in the short term as trying to make sure that he got along with others, was healthy, and followed a developmental schedule that we measured partly by looking at other people's kids. I also found comfort in anthropological reports about child-rearing in other cultures, particularly on the issue of sleep. I realized that it wasn't, as the sleep experts said, that my son "needed to learn how to sleep." Rather, it was that his plasticity as a biological organism needed to line up with our culture's demands—which, based on human norms around the world, are bizarrely incompatible with the biology. I still wasn't sleeping, but it was my fault, not his.

In the long term, our ambitions became cloudier. At any sign of a predilection or tendency, we were ready to reinforce it. For two bookish people with extravagant vocabularies, an early aptitude for language topped our list of hopes.

In our eagerness to witness and record our boy's first words, we weren't so unlike similar families all across America. At the same time, early utterances by children hardly have the weight, in song and story, that last words have. However, the aura of the first word does emerge, as it would have to in a society that's so concentrated on children, in American pop culture.

I think in particular of two television shows. One, *The Simpsons*, has become, in its more than thirty seasons, a veritable encyclopedia of pop culture. The 1992 episode called "Lisa's First Word" is plotted around the family's waiting for the famously nonverbal baby Maggie to say something. The family leans forward expectantly when she opens her mouth, out of which comes a burp.

"Did you hear that?" Homer exclaims. "She said burlap!"

Friends, another popular show that now serves as a time capsule of 1990s–early 2000s culture, took on the first word issue in the 2003 episode "The One with the Lottery." The character Rachel happily announces that her daughter Emma's first word is "gleba." No adult shares her excitement—a nonsense word sparks no joy. "Gleba is not a word," the father, Ross, insists. "What does it *mean*?" Rachel looks it up, reporting that it's defined in the dictionary as a "fleshy, spore-bearing inner mass of a certain fungi."

There's a philosophical depth to this joke—if a string of sounds is credentialed in a dictionary, does that mean we credit the baby with saying a word? Does the baby have to know its meaning for it to count as a "first word," and if so, how much?

Another trope is the enthusiastic joy with which adults receive these early utterances. In a different episode, from 1996, Ross's infant son, Ben, says something that Rachel hears as "hi." "I'm sorry, what did you just say?" Rachel squeals. "Did you just say 'hi'? Oh my God!" Of course, the baby doesn't repeat this. But as Ben is being taken out the door, he says "bye," which sets off Ross in a dance of joy as he "byes" his son out the door.

At one level, the situation comedies are mining the proverbial gold that lies in that tension between the utterances themselves and what grown-ups expect (and how they react). At another level, the episodes satirize one symptom of what has been called the "post-industrial family." This is a label that anthropologists Elinor Ochs and Tamar Kremer-Sadlik gave to a constellation of behaviors by modern families, one core trait of which is child-centeredness. Families are organized around the needs of children, not adults, from sleeping to eating to education. They're also constantly busy with activities meant to boost the offspring's ability to perform in what's predicted to be a competitive knowledge economy. Thus, children's verbal creativity and expressiveness is constantly fostered by middle-class parents, and this is where the first word comes in: it announces the onset of verbal creativity and signals an opportunity for more complex interventions. It marks the direction of the child's cognitive future in the world of adult work. Hence Emma's first utterance, "gleba," prompts Ross to exclaim, "She's going to be a scientist!" when he finds out its technical meaning.

§

One refreshing exception appeared in *Knuffle Bunny*, a popular children's book by Mo Willems, published in 2004. It gives us another way to understand the plight of the linguistically less capable, whether babies or the dying.

Nominally, the story is about a wide-eyed little girl, Trixie, and her stuffed rabbit, but it's actually about her first words. Spoiler alert: they are "Knuffle Bunny," which she says at the climax of the book, when she gets reunited with her beloved toy. However, that's not the first thing that Trixie says, and it's also not the first thing she means to say. But because "Knuffle Bunny" is the first thing her father recognizes, that utterance is the first word that the book is ultimately about. We might call it Trixie's Dilemma: all along she's been saying things, intending to mean something by those sounds, but which her father doesn't recognize as such, and given her linguistic status, she's not able to use *other* words to point his attention to her first attempts of meaningful communication.

The first thing Trixie says in the entire book is an attempt to tell her father that Knuffle Bunny has been left behind. "Aggle flaggle klabble!"

"That's right," replies her father. "We're going home."

This might explain my son's giggly relief when I recognized his "round-round"—finally, we'd broken free of Trixie's Dilemma. It was as if Catherine Snow's sentence about the cultural decisions behind first words had come to life. Her son Nathaniel also suffered in the jaws of Trixie's Dilemma: What happens when someone with greater linguistic powers doesn't recognize either an intention to signal or an intended meaning? What's the less empowered language user to do? This question will resound across all the chapters that follow.

Too many people believe that attention to child language is a keystone of parental love. However, that supposedly irresistible thing that's called a "baby's first word" is really a romanticized milestone, shaped by social and economic circumstances. You have to be socialized to pay attention to it. The natural state of first words, if they have one, is to be folded into the flow of living. Selecting them to dote over isn't perverse—it's a modern, underappreciated luxury. Not all parents or caregivers believe that luxury matters, which doesn't mean their children are any less cared for or loved, but that a person can be made in diverse ways, not all of them in language.

By far the most territory of the first word's story, whether it's "ka" or "piz" or "home," has to be devoted to its evolutionary origins. Scholars used to fantasize that the *first* first word, if it could ever be reconstructed, might mark humanity's dawn.

3 The First First Words

Banal or quirky, every single first word, spoken or signed, late or on time, has a thrilling duality: it's totally new and also incredibly ancient. I'm not saying that the words themselves are old. Rather, the path to first words in the developmental sense parallels the path to first words in the evolutionary sense, which the child traverses, at least in part.

Whether it's "ball" or "bye," the events called "first words" represent a living sediment of abilities and reflexes, spread throughout the animal kingdom and accumulating in modern humans. To put it another way, if nature builds new machinery out of old parts, then a child's first words draw on very old parts. This chapter tells their story. To appreciate the timescale, consider that theories of language evolution usually aim to explain how grammar emerged. This gets you about 100,000 years ago. However, if you dig directly into that word-making sediment, you can transport yourself millions of years back. By comparison, a last word, tied to the life span of the individual who says it, is fresh faced and tender.

§

Where do first words come from? Here's an illustrative story. One afternoon in Davis, California, in the early 1980s, a twelve-month-old girl named Kate pointed at a rosebush in the garden and, for the first time, snuffled out of her nose. It was a child's version of how a parent demonstrates what to do with a flower: put it under your nose and *sniff, sniff.*

Her mother, Linda, noticed immediately. Her daughter had no spoken words yet, and no signs either. So if Linda's account can be trusted, Kate's snuffle was her first . . . something. Something deliberate. A symbol? Which Linda could see in how Kate snuffled at other flowers, whether they were in the garden, on her pajamas, or in a book. *Sniff, sniff.*

Is she labeling things? Linda wondered. Is she saying "flower"? Curious, Linda modeled other gestures for Kate. Lip smacks for "fish." Armpit scratching for "monkey." Palms up for "Where is it?"

Over a few days, Kate picked up the invented signs, which she used with her mother. A window into Kate's mind had been opened for Linda. "We had a lot of fun," Linda remembered. Over the next five months, the child learned to use twenty-nine signs, thirteen of which she invented herself. Her first spoken word was "kitty," and by seventeen months old her spoken language exploded, her signing dwindled, then stopped.

Their garden scene provides a hint about where and how the very first word might have arisen among ancient humans. The precise details are less important than what gets sparked in the imagination when you think how amazing it all is. The story, whatever shape it takes, should provoke wonder and awe. The first word, as an inheritance of the species that's bestowed by the community, emerges along the evolutionary path of the species' development at the moments that the thing called "community" stabilizes. That community has to remember how things are done, which it passes down across generations, creating rules about doing them again. This sequence of achievements is so wobbly with contingency that we can't know for sure how many forking paths led away from the cognitive and social precursors of language. That mother and baby sniffing flowers in the garden might have a timeless beauty, but you should also feel the lurking presence of a specific terror: none of it might have come to pass at all.

Happen they did, some first first words. So too "mowuh," "round-round," and "ka." Looking for a definite, defining instance is bound to be a frustrating project. Yes, there's a timeline for the endless becoming of wordness; no, there's no zero moment on this timeline that distinguishes before from after. The word marks no definite point, only one region of a cline. (Which is often true, as we will see, for last words as well.)

This shouldn't be disappointing, not at all. It allows us to enthuse about a great many things, actually. Take nothing for granted here: Linda's garden was safe, free from predators, so the child could try a symbolic innovation without distraction. The mother was free to be struck by the child's innovation, enough to make her notice and respond in a novel way. They used their whole bodies: looking with their eyes, pointing with their fingers, hearing with their ears, standing on two legs. A mother and child would be swaddled in oxytocin, a hormone that encouraged the socialness that proto-conversations like these require, because if you don't want to be together, you won't interact in these extended ways.

You'll note that Kate's snuffle wasn't a word, not in the way that we usually talk about "words." Also, the snuffle and the point happened at the same time. This matters, as does the point directing her mother's gaze. Wrapped together here are the arrival of an important ability in Kate's life and the communicative history of the species: the ability to direct someone else to pay attention to something and to recognize, because of what they signal, that they're doing so. As I wrote in the previous chapter, this was also the story of "ka," which marked the beginning of my son's symbolic communication. Some linguists have been insistent that, in order to count, a first first word must refer to a thing, and they have been reluctant to admit that it might be a cluster of sound, gesture, and eye-gazing that means "look at that" or "here it is"—a demonstrative, in so many words. But the rest of us can be tantalized by that possibility.

Also key: Kate imitated her mother's sniffing, as well as the later signs, which were iconic. Recall the importance of iconicity in children's language learning, as well as the role of imitation. The point is that these first words—or, in this case, the gesture—wasn't solely something that Kate produced, uttered in a vacuum. Neither was Linda seeing the possibility of a meaning to the snuffle that she reflected back to her child. Rather, mother and child did it *together*. The first word was a co-creation. It takes two to sniff and mean "thing with petals with a pleasant odor."

§

Where do first words come from? A genetic perspective leads to a different answer. Here, first words' deepest history isn't about creatures with important meanings to get across yet have no way to do it. It's about protohumans, generations of them, interacting in rich, myriad ways and fumbling to get each other understood. This is the conceptual gulf between "Adam's first word" and "Adam's first word to Eve," because Eve had to somehow have learned what he was communicating. A gulf that protohumans crossed with their eyes, brains, jaws, fingers, even hormones—their whole bodies, which language is intimately linked to (as we see, too, with last words).

The first first words came about because of a patchwork of mutually reinforcing genetic changes—and not many of them, according to most accounts—that created the assemblage that linguist Steve Levinson refers to as the "interaction engine." He defined this as "a loose assemblage of various abilities, instincts and motivations, which work together to make possible the miracle of human communication." (There's more about this assemblage in the Interlude.) Interestingly, and contrary to what you might expect, these changes weren't aimed at altering how these hominids *communicated*.

Recall how Kate pointed at the rosebush as she snuffled. The first words trace their lineage to hand and fingers, which point. (So do lips.) Arms and faces are also employed for gestures. In most likelihood, language began with gesture—but not, as one might think, because naming things was the first use for language. Rather, pointing is how infants manage the attention of other people in order to make sure that they're all looking at the same things. Once they achieve this, learning and producing words can happen. "For the child to understand a word as a piece of language she must understand it as something the adult is using to direct her attention to some referent in the environment," wrote Michael Tomasello, "in a way that she, the child, could do in reverse toward the adult if she so wished." A word *is* a pointing. (Or some words are.)

Around the world, regardless of culture or language, nine-month-old babies begin pointing with their whole hands, then their index fingers. Indeed, it often precedes the first-word stage (or in Kate's case, the first-symbol stage). Thus, the observer interested in the first word ought to keep an eye on pointing behavior. Somehow I remember a point of my son—his first? I don't know—an enthusiastic, full-armed arrow at the wheel of an old War of 1812 cannon in a park. Well before "ka," by the way. But the point isn't perfectly unambiguous either. Was he aiming at the wheel or the cannon? Given his later interests, retroactively we chose "wheel."

Predictably, pinning down when pointing in primates might have emerged remains an area of debate. All of the great apes reportedly have large repertoires of gestures—primatologists say orangutans have sixty-four, chimpanzees sixty-six, bonobos sixty-eight, and gorillas 102—and many of these gestures are common to all of them, including humans. Some scientists maintain that only humans point in a way that suggests they know that others are also looking, but primatologists say that wild chimpanzees can (and do) gesture deliberately to change the behavior of a specific individual. This overlap among the gesture repertoires of the great apes (including humans) suggests that we're dealing with innate behaviors, shared by the human primate as well and thus incredibly old. Innate does not mean, however, that they don't involve a substantial amount of learning as well.

First words also trace their lineage to eyes, because creatures look at each other and then at the objects of shared attention. Not until a creature can understand and participate in a triad of "me, you, and that thing over there" can they manage the other participant's attention.

Another part of the interaction engine (and therefore a precursor of language) is the back-and-forth, often rapid, exchange of expressive behaviors. When humans talk or sign, they trade signals in bursts, first one person, then the next. They take turns. This volleying is such a fundamental part of the architecture of interaction that it has been noted across phyla of the animal world. Chimpanzees do it; frogs do it. Even cicadas and katydids do it. This suggests that in evolutionary terms, turn-taking is very old. It's the first social thing that the newest of newborn babies learn to do, whether it's with eye gaze or gurgles, as early as two months old. (The beautiful but unremarked-on symmetry is that this pattern also unfolds at the other end of life, where one's turn-taking ability might be the last social power one will have.)

Where does these creatures' willingness to interact in these sustained ways come from? One current idea is called the self-domestication hypothesis, which posits that protohumans mated mostly with less-aggressive partners, or those who could manage their emotions. Over time, groups became less prone to convulsions of violence, which meant they could collaborate, seek food and shelter together, and become reproductively more successful than other groups. Through this self-selection, protohuman groups became oriented toward (more) peaceful social life. Your child's first word is, in a sense, a distant descendant of the protohuman discovery of tameness. Thus, "hi!" makes perfect sense, as does "no!" (at least it's a word and not a smack or bite).

This discussion about self-domestication, of which the above paragraph is the slightest sketch, is ongoing, and it remains just a theory. What makes it attractive for understanding first words' origins is how it enrolls not just the body but the relationships among those bodies. When you consider the evolution of certain neural mechanisms that underpin language, you also have to acknowledge the role of hormones, specifically oxytocin, which sustains the strong emotional attachments between parents and infants, in a feedback mechanism that underlies communication. In songbirds,

oxytocin supports social motivations for learning songs, and most importantly the specific brain activity associated with learning the calls of adult
members of the species (such as stimulating synapses to retain memories).

Oxytocin triggers something in humans too. In her reminiscing, Linda
told me how she felt more emotionally attached to Kate after they shared
signs, which made me recall how I felt more connected to my son after
"round-round." The reality is that he and I were already so bonded bio-
chemically and socially entrained, I didn't need a spoken word from him to
know what he needed. However, "round-round" opened the door to more
complex connection and play. The resulting burst of oxytocin reinforced
the miraculousness of it all.

§

Where do theories about first first words come from? In the beginning was
the obsession with the word. Beyond the fact that the Western mind has
relentlessly pursued questions about origins, the first word played a significant conceptual role in the European mindset's view of humanity. *In the
beginning*, as the Gospel of John begins, *was the Word*. This concern with a
prime mover Logos was foundational.

For centuries, European intellectuals were fascinated with the search for
the oldest human language. In the book of Genesis—not an orally transmitted epic, I must note, but a written text—the story of the Tower of Babel
explained the world's linguistic diversity as a defensive maneuver by God,
who was threatened by the unity of humanity. If one could go back to that
moment, if we could find the first word (as if there were only one, incanta-
tory and revelatory), we would be that much closer to Paradise. Humanist
curiosity joined with Christian worldview in speculating that whatever language preceded Babel would be closest to what God bestowed on Adam in
the Garden of Eden. Some admittedly bonkers claims arose along the way.
To choose just one of them, there was the theory by Flemish physician Jon
van Gorp (1519–1572) that his variety of Dutch, despite its obscurity, had
to be the most ancient language on earth, because it had more short words
than Latin, Greek, or Hebrew. He bolstered his argument with the claim
that the Flemish word for *baker*, or "becker," was close to the ancient Phrygian word *bekos*, or "bread." (You will remember that "bekos" was the first
word those unfortunate, hungry Egyptian children spoke to the shepherd.)
Finding the oldest language became more important after the discovery of

the "New World," which put into doubt the Europeans' conception of the world, since evidently they hadn't known the half of it. In the King James Bible's version of the book of Genesis, Adam first spoke about naming the animals of creation, while his first quoted speech was a reaction to God's creation of Eve: "This is now bone of my bones, and flesh of my flesh: she shall be called Woman, because she was taken out of Man."

The Koran takes a different approach. There, Adam's first words were to praise and thank Allah, which came about when Allah joined Adam's soul to his body. The human sneezed, then said, *"Al-hamdulillah."* Many Muslims still say this today. (A good Muslim's last words are also supposed to be a confession of faith, the same one whispered in their ears as newborns—more about that later.) Unlike the Bible, the Koran also gives first words to Jesus—which are also fuzzy. The clear ones arose when Mary, who had just given birth, was confronted by villagers about this unexpected baby. She gestured to the baby to answer them. "How shall we speak to him, who is an infant in the cradle?" they asked. According to the Koran, the infant Jesus defended her with a couple of sentences, starting with "I am truly a servant of Allah. He has destined me to be given the Scripture and to be a prophet." The ambiguous first words occurred a few verses earlier, where Mary complained about her situation and was consoled by a voice telling her where to find food and drink. Some say this voice is from Jesus; others say it's from the angel Gabriel.

Other traditions propose other first words for the first human: a Vedic text, the *Brihadaranyaka Upanishad*, holds that the first words uttered by the first man were "I am myself," and that, when addressed, he answered, "I am he."

Wasn't my son saying this too with "round-round"? At a basic level, he was referring to a ceiling fan, but the subtext was *I am he who notices fast-moving round things.*

The European obsession with Adam's language led to scholarly comparisons of old texts, then inspection of human speech, arguably motivating many of the human sciences, from geography to anthropology, and of course linguistics as it's known today. Unsurprisingly, from these founding preoccupations, linguistics has grappled more with themes of origins, growth, and change in language than with decline and demise. More recent attention to the issue of how languages "die" or how individual speakers lose their language doesn't erase how durably linguistics has been committed to first things. This is my best explanation for why linguists don't deal with the matter of last words or language at the very end of life. Even though they've ventured opinions on speaking in tongues, speaking while drunk, and languages spoken in a previous life—none of which have been central to theoretical concerns in any scientific epoch—and even though they've stood up for endangered and dying languages, the field is pulled to beginnings like the Moon orbits Earth.

Most language scientists would probably find it absurd to imagine the language of this lifetime presaging what occurs in an afterlife, beyond the individual's biological life span. But quite a lot of modern linguistics is built around debates about what aspects of language and learning *predate* the individual's biological life—what's innate in the human species, as opposed to what comes from an individual's experience. This gives contemporary linguistics the flavor of an intractable religious war over irreconcilable metaphysical views, but about the before-life, not the afterlife. But there's nothing theoretically at stake, apparently, in looking at ends.

§

One of the most powerful arguments for God's existence had been the deity's power as Creator of Life. But as the early modern European religious worldview crumbled and the dominant paradigm of the Enlightenment flourished in the nineteenth century, science dispensed with the hypothesis of a divine creator. So where had the natural world come from? Darwin's theory of natural selection provided a powerful alternative. In it, humans were no longer treated as the pinnacle of God's creation. Rather, they were creatures who were subject to the same material processes as any other living being. This, of course, repositioned the way that scholars talked about humans. If the hierarchy of humans and nature were not founded in God's design, the markers could be moved to what characterized the human species most: their language.

As German philologist Friedrich Max Müller (1823–1900) famously asserted, "The one great barrier between the brute and man is *Language*. Man speaks, and no brute has ever uttered a word. Language is our Rubicon, and no brute will dare to cross it." That irrevocable crossing of the Rubicon would have been marked by the appearance of first words, which thus represented the threshold of humanity. (And spoken words, I might note.) For this reason, first words became the focus of early theorizing by philosophers and language scientists who imagined those primitive words, "the actual first utterances," as nineteenth-century American linguist William Dwight Whitney (1827–1894) put it.

For parents like me, the baby's first word flags another momentous arrival of a fuller person. Yet for scholars in the nineteenth century's human sciences, the first word marked the rise of humanity out of the savage muck of natural life. Other intellectuals proposed other first first words in the primordial languages they speculated about. For instance, in his *Essay on the Origin of Languages*, Rousseau proposed that humans in warmer, southern climates invented language. Their first utterances were "Love me!" (in French *Aimez-moi*) while northerners' first words were "Help me!" (or *Aidez-moi*). First words, in other words, were expressions of emotional need. Meanwhile, Italian historian Giambattista Vico (1668–1774) imagined primitive humans frightened by everything, so their first word was "thunder!" One notes that these words, for all their supposed drama, were to no effect without a community that shared what they meant.

One theory, contemporaneous to Whitney, held that early words were onomatopoetic, so that the meaning "cat" was manifested as "meow." Some argued that the earliest words must have been exclamations ("oh!") or interjections ("pshaw"), or that they stemmed from vocalizations that created rhythm for people working together. Müller, channeling a linguistic Romanticism, ventured that some human ancestor, miraculously struck by the ineffable essence of things, somehow discovered a way to express it linguistically.

A range of arguments can be made for and against each of these proposals, which were abbreviated with a flavor of mild derision as the "bow-wow," "pooh-pooh," "yo-he-ho," and "ding-dong" theories of language origins. I'm not about to referee another wrestling match between these theories, which others have refereed so well before. But I observe that these utterances were posited as emanations, as expressions or exclamations. Unlike *sniff, sniff*, they don't arise in the context of a communicative exchange or interaction but are broadcasts from a language producer.

These proposals also assume that first first words arose directly from animal calls. Let's call this the Extended Hoot theory of first words. Some language evolutionists have argued against this, on the basis that monkey and ape calls are specific only to certain contexts. They don't refer to objects or entities that aren't present, and they don't label things or events that multiple individuals can pay attention to all at once. The conclusion seems to be that "the earliest words had little in common with primate calls, apart from probably using the vocal/auditory modality."

However, let's give the Extended Hoot theory some credit—animal calls served as easily accessible evidence for scholars. What was the other available evidence? Well, children's first words, which began to be exploited for this at the end of the nineteenth century but which opened a controversy that soon was dropped, in light of a broader diminishing of scholarly discussions about language evolution. As a result, first words by children weren't scientifically exploited as much as they could have been. By the time an interest in language evolution was resuscitated in the 1970s, a raft of additional evidence had become available, leading to new crops of hypothetical "actual first utterances."

Could they have been syllables of repetitive baby babbling that took on meaning? Maybe they were rhythmic, singsong vocalizations, connected first to emotion. Could they have been cries? Babies do a lot of crying. Could they have been single utterances packed with meaning, like Shirley Jackson's son's first word, "dewey?" In evolutionary terms, these meanings would have been later parsed out as individual units. Again, if these hypothetical "actual first utterances" seem familiar, it's because human baby behavior had retained its relevance as data, thanks to diary-keeping parent scientists. Thus, the Extended Coo theory of first word origins was born.

Unexpectedly, modern children's first words have come to matter less, not more, to evolutionary discussions. This is in part because there is so much other evidence from primatology, archaeology, genetics, and game theory. Far more can be known today about language and communication through observations of primate behavior in the wild; raising nonhuman primates in language-rich environments to see what happens; studies of vocal learning in songbirds, elephants, bats, and seals; fieldwork in communities that have created, entirely on their own, spontaneously appearing local sign languages; fieldwork in communities with diverse approaches to raising children; innovative behavioral experiments with language-making games; new statistical techniques; and genomic analyses of the genetic basis for the biological foundations of language, including expression of the FOXP2 gene. All of this evidence has transformed language evolution into one of the most fertile—and complicated—topics in the language sciences. Amid this ferment babies' first words are a small part of the puzzle.

But I still revere them for helping to tell the evolutionary story of the settings in which interactions between individuals took a symbolic turn, like that sniff in the garden.

Who gets credit for producing the first words, babies or adults? For a long time, this role was granted to male adults. To take one example, in the 1980s linguist Derek Bickerton's theory of language imagined an ecological niche in which the human ancestor *Homo erectus*, living in Africa two million years ago, ate meat acquired by "confrontational scavenging." This involved following herds of large herbivorous mammals, waiting for speedier predators to take one down, then scaring the predators away. Bickerton argued that the seed of language sprouted from what happened next. As he put it, "band members who had located a carcass would have had to use sounds, gestures, or mimicry to inform potential recruits of what they had found."

Until some primordial inflection point, individuals had what Bickerton deemed "a typical animal communication system." But if a group of cunning scavengers had been able to change that system in one crucial way, they could have gotten calories more efficiently, thereby ensuring their reproductive success. Bickerton called that change "displacement." It involved adding a single, stable meaning to one of those calls, a meaning that wasn't bound to a single context and which could refer to something that wasn't present. Semantics had arrived. As Bickerton wrote, displacement was "the wedge that broke the walls of the here-and-now . . . potentially allowing free reference to anything in the world, past or future, real or imagined."

Others, in addition to Bickerton, gave credit to adults (also assuming they were heroic male hunters, which must have been a comforting thought to thinkers of a certain generation), but more contemporary thinking credits babies and female caregivers, like Kate and Linda, as the fundamental drivers. For several decades, Kim Oller, a psycholinguist at the University of Memphis, has been recording and tabulating the squeals, growls, gurgles, and raspberries that babies make. He contends that these so-called protophones entered the evolutionary story of first words in a crucial and formative way, which he developed in his 2000 book, *The Emergence of the Speech Capacity*.

From the time they're born, babies produce protophones four to five times per minute, over three thousand times a day while they're awake. (By the time they're six months old, these vocalizations can predict the words they can say at twelve months—more protophones, more spoken words.) Oller argues that protophones from human babies have served as fitness signals—basically, helpless human babies make lots of quasi-vowels and other sounds to tell adults that they're worth caring about. Early hominid parents, along with other adults in the group, paid attention to these signals, and here we are. He also argues that this dynamic doesn't exist among bonobos, who are humanity's evolutionary cousins. He has recorded bonobo infants and reports that they produce much fewer and qualitatively different sounds than human babies, ones that don't lend themselves to what happened next.

How did protophones become words? Oller explains that the first genetic change on the pathway to first words had to connect the voice to the organism's "seeking system," giving the brain conscious control over the larynx. Once in control of their voices, infants could explore with them flexibly.

"They explore the vocal world and the sound-making world in much the same way that they explore objects with their fingers," Oller says.

The vibrations of the voice outline the cavities of the body, for one thing: the space of the mouth, the inside of the skull, the chest. The voice distinguishes inside from outside. You can also (if your hearing provides reliable feedback) understand your surroundings. Are you in a large space? A warm space? What other information can you gather this way? In this humans are different from the nonhuman apes, who use their hands and eyes to explore—but not, curiously, their voices. This exploration led to fluidity and flexibility that infants could alter at will, so that the speechlike vocalizations could sound curious, sated, or angry.

Another development—not necessarily preceding, probably parallel—was a change in how infants look at faces. Many mammals look at each other's faces. Chimpanzee mothers and infants do too. But only human infants sustain a gaze with a caregiver's eyes and vocalize at the same time, which the caregiver gives back. This seems to differ from what other primates do; even ape mothers who interact face-to-face with infants don't vocalize in response. This might be the evolutionary origin of the interaction window, a concept that I'll explain in chapter 7.

Then, argues Oller, another thing happened. Protohumans somehow got the ability to recognize a sequence of objects or temporally occurring events —like strings of gestures or sounds—then try to make something of them.

In Oller's scenario, infants are responsible for all of the innovations involved in first words. Imagine the family tree of first words that begins with protophones. Babies who produced them would have been noticed by parents and were more likely to survive, so their offspring would have been likely to have this trait too. Along the way, they learned to use their protophones when they're mad, sad, or happy—"performative protophones," or just "performatives," in Oller's terminology—that spread because they were successful. Some of them were canonical syllables ("ma," "ta") that became ways for the infant to negotiate a care situation with the caregiver.

In this scenario, it was the protohuman babies who first gave their performatives a stable, intended meaning that the two parties could recognize. This was their contribution to the birth of the meanings of utterances. The argument is that in order to have semantics in adults (which was Bickerton's scenario), children had to have the precursors already (which is how Oller's works); children grow up to recognize them well enough to be engaged in proto-conversations, creating and replicating further semantic bonds. In short, "the reason that adults can do these things is because the babies had the foundations that were developing into the things that adults could do," Oller says.

I remembered that my oldest son's language trajectory paralleled the sequence that Oller describes. His earliest call was "eh," always made with a pointing gesture. Then came the puzzling "ka." That word wasn't displaced; it was overplaced. Then came his earliest stable semantics, the word "round-round."

I also can't forget that "round-round" happened in an interaction: me looking at him, him looking at me, him venturing "round-round, round-round," maybe several times, me listening, then recognizing his efforts to mean something intentionally. Like Linda and Kate's interaction in the garden, this differs from the common thread between Extended Hoot and Extended Coo theories, which seem to make the first word an emanation in a communication vacuum. There's no listener or receiver; the message is just broadcast.

The fundamental scene is the proto-conversation, where the infant and caregiver (maybe the mother) trade bits of vocalization and eye gaze as a first social contact. In this way, the first first word wasn't a production of only the adult or only the infant, but both of them together, as in Linda and Kate's experience in the garden. It's not just the vocalizing, hand babbling, touching, or lip smacking that matters, it's also the recognizing. It involves the eyes, the ears. *The togetherness.*

Was there a single, fully formed first word or did it slowly appear? Theories of language origins vacillate on whether changes leading to language were sudden or gradual. I look to the way that a modern baby's first words emerge for an answer: things were fuzzy for a long time, until they weren't. Probably an adult found something compelling but didn't know what to make of it, then by the time they realized something had changed, that moment was long gone. Modern human babies also produce utterances that show up in different arrangements, fade, then return as the child "learns" the word.

With no previous models of language to learn from, protohumans might have used word-like vocalizations of various shapes for hundreds of thousands of years, with simple forms bootstrapping more complex ones at a glacially slow pace. All that before a fully crystallized language appeared.

When were the first first words produced? According to the fossil record, humans did not have the shape of the modern human vocal tract until about one hundred thousand years ago. As a result, most reconstructions of the origin of language place the appearance of grammatical structures, words with semantics, and intonational conventions around the same time. What existed before that? If you're willing to consider a simpler language system, then you'd be looking at *Homo erectus* two million years ago. They had sophisticated tools, the ability to create fire, and probably the cognitive and social capacity to make symbols. For them, having a protolanguage would certainly have provided an advantage.

Where were the first words produced? It depends what you mean by "words," and it depends what you mean by "first." If the *Homo erectus* story is correct, this particular hominid group migrated from eastern Africa to occupy a huge swath of the planet that included Africa, the Middle East, southern and western Europe, India, stretches of interior China, and Indonesia. That would imply multiple origin points as a part of multiple protolanguages. How many such origins? At the language evolution conference Protolang in 2021, Sverker Johansson presented a calculation that around 3.4 million languages had existed at one time or another in the hominid past (compared with about seven thousand extant languages currently). More than 50 percent of these were protolanguages, meaning they possessed small sets of conventional symbols but rudimentary grammars, if any at all.

One implication is clear: there might have been incalculable *millions* of first first words, not a single one, occurring in geographically diverse parts of the planet.

What were these first first words about? Even that putative millions of first words in all those protolanguages probably took only a few forms and a confined set of meanings. It's been argued that they must have been concrete nouns, referring to distinct objects. This gets support from the observation that nouns predominate among the first words of modern children, given what appears to be a cognitive bias for delimited, discrete objects. Basically, babies label things as they perceive them.

Others have argued that the earliest words could have been clumps of meaning wrapped into a single word, call, or phrase, such as "bana," meaning (for instance) "Give me that stick; it's my turn" or "The river is too high to cross." This is the holophrase notion. These earliest words could also have been commands, warnings, or exultations. Possibly first words weren't used for description but rather emerged in getting people to do things together: playing, singing, gathering food, even attempting to correct a miscommunication. Oller's view is that they were performative-centric, not referring to things. Indeed, language evolution experts have compared these protowords to utterances from modern babies like "yes," "no," "hello," "ouch," "oops," "wow," and "hey," which follow rules particular to a language about their form and meaning but don't have any syntax. Indeed, many children's first words (remember the dauphin's *hé*?) have such words counted among their first ten. Primordial referential words that found a place in the signifying repertoire of a community might have been a point, then a point and a mimicked moo of an animal, then just the moo, then a point, then a look in a certain direction, all of which added up, on the fifth or tenth try, to a meaning that could be recognized as "there's a buffalo."

These first first words may not have been discrete in the way that most people think of words, which depends on which language they use and whether they can read and write it. No matter what, the first first word was probably a shambling, charades-like process involving varying modalities, levels of iconicity, puzzlements, and multiple attempts. It was the target that moves, not the arrow that flies.

Were the first words spoken or gestured? One way in which these millions of first words weren't diverse is how multimodal they were. By "multimodal," language scientists mean that language can be spoken, signed, written, or even felt. They also mean that when a language user produces a signed or spoken utterance, they always use other parts of their body to provide accompanying information in the visual mode. In her work, linguist Aslı Özyürek stresses the "multimodal expressibility of language"—to express meanings, people use their voices, writing, and parts of their body, like their lips, eyes, faces, hands, and body posture.

"No language community uses speech only," she told me. "We haven't discovered a language community that only uses speech dominantly—it's always accompanied by some type of gestural expression." Protolanguages probably also had a mix of utterance types, labels, and ways of communicating that deployed the visual and the vocal alongside each other, but in different ways.

Because language is typically (but incorrectly) understood to be a spoken phenomenon, the Extended Hoot and Extended Coo theories typically imagine that the first human words were solely spoken too. Many contemporary arguments insist that vocal cord control was essential to the origin of language. On the other hand, arguments for a gesture-first language capacity have been around since the eighteenth century.

As of 2024, as I'm writing this, the leading edge of theorizing is that not only did the vocal and visual modality evolve together, but they still operate that way. The first first words of protohumans were multimodal; so were the last words you spoke yesterday before going to sleep. Another way to say this is that linguistic meaning can be expressed via multiple, simultaneous modes that are welded together so tightly, they look whole. It might help to think of language as laminar. What we see at the end of life is that the welds loosen, and the modalities delaminate. How they do this and in what sequence still needs to be explored.

Why do spoken first words take the forms they do? One afternoon in 1999, I left my apartment and crossed two lawns to the house of my friend Christina Gildersleeve-Neumann. A television crew was shooting B-roll video of her daughter, then about a year old. The occasion was that Peter MacNeilage, an esteemed phonetician, and Barbara Davis, a language acquisition researcher and speech-language pathologist, both professors at the time at the University of Texas at Austin, had published a paper in *Science* about the structure of baby babbling. Christina had contributed data from her fieldwork in Ecuador and was loaning her baby to the publicity effort.

Their paper was groundbreaking inasmuch as the authors tabulated the babbles from six babies and first words from ten babies in several languages. The team found that the babbles had four patterns of sounds, as did the children's first words. These were labial consonants with central vowels (which results in sequences of sounds like "mama" and "papa"), what are known as "coronal" consonants with front vowels (which gives you sequences like "titi" and "didi"), what are called "dorsal" consonants with back vowels ("googoo"), and a labial stop consonant, then a vowel, then a coronal stop consonant ("pot").

I had taken MacNeilage's phonetics course, so I knew his theory: the infant's babbling stems from basic open-close movements of the jaw; the result is the basic canonical syllable. MacNeilage and Davis called this cycle the "frame," and suggested that the evolution of speech began here. The frame, along with an expiration of breath, allows the speaker to produce basic consonant-vowel combinations. The most basic frame, the first pattern they described, produces strings of sounds like "mamama" and "dadada." Babies grow up to produce more diverse, complex consonants and vowels—which they called the "content"—as lips, tongue, velum, and vocal cords come under conscious motor control. MacNeilage and Davis argued that a baby's first words take their shape from the increasing sophistication of the phonetic content within the frame. First words, they might claim, are Extended Coos.

The relatively later emergence of vocal babbling in deaf babies suggests that all babies need to hear themselves too. When deaf babies are raised in families that sign, they also mostly babble with their hands. So do hearing babies raised in signing families. All babies gesture, but the babbling of the deaf babies is faster, more repetitive, and more constrained than that of the hearing babies; they also babble in the "signing space," the space from the head to the lower torso where most signing occurs. Like spoken first words, signed first words also draw from the motor patterns most frequent in the manual babbling. First words take their shapes in part from the practiced movements that precede them. In that sense they don't emanate from nothing; it's just that the seeming disarray of that something disguises an underlying order.

What can we tell about ancient first words from children's first words? The connection between modern children's first words (and other patterns of language acquisition) and the linguistic innovations of protohumans is an old one. The assumption was familiar to Hippolyte Taine (1828–1893), an influential French critic and historian, who published "Note on the Acquisition of Language by Infants and the Human Species" in 1876. In his essay, he related some of his observations on how his daughter Geneviève developed language, arguing that her process must have followed the same stages as adults in the past. Thus, a child's actual first words would parallel the first human words.

I cannot overstate how intellectually consequential Geneviève's first words were, not so much for her but for the study of children and development. Her utterances were certainly more visible than the dauphin's nearly three hundred years earlier, thanks to what her father made of them. At nearly fifteen months old, she said "papa" and "tem." This second word her father called "one of the most remarkable and one of the first she uttered." It was, he noticed, a demonstrative, at first to get her parents to give her something, or to draw attention to herself. But then she developed many meanings for it, sometimes "give" or "take" or "look," which she herself developed on her own. (It may have been a baby version of French *tiens*, which has a mood of insistence, my French-speaking friends report, though not those specific meanings.)

If Taine were an ancient Roman, he might have headed at that point to the temple of Farinus. He wrote, "It seems to me rather a word that she has created spontaneously, a sympathetic articulation that she herself has found in harmony with all fixed and distinct intention. . . . It is a natural vocal gesture, not learned."

From his description, he clearly adored Geneviève's inventiveness, writing also with palpable sadness when "tem" waned. This occurred because "we did not use it with her and therefore she left off using it herself," probably because "we did not choose to learn it, for it did not correspond to any one of our ideas." With their wide meanings, such words resembled those used in "primitive civilisations," in the same way that "the human embryo presents in a passing state the physical characteristics that are found in a fixed state in the classes of inferior animals."

Taine didn't pioneer this notion; he simply extended to language an idea already prominent in natural history discussions about embryology and morphology. (As for what Genevieve's first words spawned, chapter 5 has more.) The idea was that modern organisms represented accretions of evolutionary change, and that those stages, layers, or levels visible in the young of a species were signs that evolutionary forebears had them too. If human embryos have tails, it's because their ancestors did. This idea was immortalized in the phrase "ontogeny recapitulates phylogeny," coined in 1866 by German scientist and philosopher Ernst Haeckel (1834–1919). Taine held this idea along with Sigmund Freud, Friedrich Engels, many child development experts, and other nineteenth-century thinkers, who used it to justify, among other things, colonialism, in which Western countries took on parental roles relative to the "childish" cultures they conquered.

Linguists have a mixed relationship with this recapitulationist idea. They merrily draw from it when it suits their arguments, but they dismiss it otherwise. In the latter case, linguists who want to discuss language evolution on its own merits reject what children do (how they learn and what they say) as evidence for what protohumans did. As Berkeley psychologist Dan Slobin argued in 2004, when modern children learn language, they always get some sort of input from an existing language, not creating it entirely de novo. There is no influence-free *before time* when babies operate in a vacuum, free from linguistic or cultural input in their environments.

This echoes Max Müller's position in 1861. "I fear [using children's language as evidence] is as useless to watch the first stammerings of children, as it would be to repeat the experiment of the Egyptian king who entrusted two new-born infants to a shepherd," he argued. Because modern children don't invent language but learn what they see and hear being done, they can't be models of the distant human past.

Kim Oller countered this by saying that when children develop first words, they follow the same natural logic that he thinks the evolution of first first words did. It's not exactly that ontogeny recapitulates phylogeny, but both have to follow a certain order—the drive to vocal interaction must precede vocal imitation, which must come before semantics. Each complex innovation requires a prior, simpler innovation (though of course the simpler innovation isn't driven to complexify per se).

So, if Oller is right, human babies and protohominid babies acted alike —but it's not advisable to put modern baby words into ancient adult mouths. Admittedly, it's tempting. In their *Science* article, MacNeilage and Davis matched their four babbling patterns with a list of twenty-seven reconstructed protowords, themselves controversial (a long story for a different time), where they found some of the same patterns of consonants and vowels appearing together. They offered these correlations as evidence that all of the world's linguistic language must have derived from a single ancient form.

It followed that one word in this ancient language, perhaps even its first, was the word "mama." Among the arguments enlisted for its status as one of humanity's earliest words have been the default jaw oscillations that MacNeilage and Davis posited as the motor basis for speech. "Mama" is thus a "pure" repeated frame, easily performed by hominid infant mouths and thus protohominid ones too. Such primordial sounds must have been recruited for that most primordial of social and emotional attachments, that between a mother and child. A few years later, anthropologist Dean Falk cited MacNeilage and Davis's work as evidence for a primordial "mama."

In her 2009 book *Finding Our Tongues*, she argued that language must have had its origins in interactions between babies and their caregivers—not in male domains like hunting. So far, so plausible. And Falk's argument is a refreshing departure from the adult-centric, heroic hunter theories of language origins. But she takes the argument quite too far into "mama" territory. As she wrote in 2004, "It does not seem unreasonable to suggest that the equivalent of the English word 'mama' may well have been one of the first conventional words developed by early hominins." In her book, she expanded on the thought: "I love the thought that one of the earliest words invented and shared by our ancestors might have been the equivalent of 'mama.' After all, wouldn't babies then, as now, have been inclined to put a name to the face that provided them with their earliest experiences of warmth, safety, and love?"

The sentiment is certainly attractive. How nice to think this could be true. However, as we'll see in the next chapter, the notion of a primordial, universal "mama" meaning "mother" is more language ideology than science.

4   The Truth about "Mama" and Other Cultural First Words

What follows is an exploration of the cultural first word and the *laissez parler* mode, which may not immediately seem to belong together. The tour begins in a hut in the French Congo in 1893, where a white American man holds a grubby young chimpanzee named Moses on his lap. It ends more than a hundred years later, with a baby sign class in North Carolina. On the way we'll pass through Papua New Guinea, Samoa, Ottawa, and ancient Rome.

The American man was Richard Garner (1848–1920), who aimed to teach Moses to speak, starting with four human words, one of which was "mamma." That's how Garner spelled it in his reminiscences, where he also reported that no matter how many corned beef rewards he doled out, Moses could move his lips for "mamma" but not produce the sounds. It was a damning fate for a word that Garner chose because it "may almost be considered a universal word of human speech."

Here was a confident American schoolteacher-turned-primatologist who had captured the calls of monkeys in the Cincinnati Zoo with a version of Thomas Edison's phonograph, then claimed to have distilled a "monkey language" from them. In 1892, he'd traveled to Gabon to investigate primates in the wild for the first time, then made his way upriver to Lake Fernan-Vaz (where today there's a reserve protecting gorillas). Hypothesizing that wild monkey "language" was more primitive than that of the sophisticates at the Cincinnati Zoo, Garner bought a chimpanzee and named him Moses, because he'd been found on his own in "a wild papyrus swamp of the Ogowe River," as the biblical Moses had been found in the bulrushes. The name encoded a promise: perhaps Moses would lead Garner to the promised land of animal speech. They became roommates in a hut, where Garner threw himself into the project of trying to teach the chimp to speak. Moses performed the best with the French word for "fire," *feu*, making it the first human word ever spoken by an ape (though it's no more a word than the French dauphin's "no," because it had no semantics attached). For his achievement, Garner wrote, Moses should live on in history, but a year later the chimpanzee died from pneumonia.

I'm going to leave aside the tales of myriad other talking animals for the sake of brevity and focus on this one phonetic trick that humans have made apes perform. In 1909, a captive chimpanzee named Peter was brought to psychologist Lightner Witmer at his clinic, dressed in top hat and wearing roller skates, mainly so he wouldn't escape. Among his tricks, Peter spoke a single English word, which you might have already guessed. Forty years later, Keith and Catherine Hayes home-reared a chimpanzee, Viki, treating her like a human child to test her developmental capacities. After training her to grunt on command ("Speak!"), the Hayeses taught her to vocalize "mama" by manipulating her lips.

"She soon learned to make the proper mouth movements herself, and could then say 'mama' unaided—softly, and hoarsely, but quite acceptably." Her other three words: "papa," "cup," "up." Eventually she could say "mama" and "papa" to address Catherine or Keith, though inconsistently.

The reason the first word was "mama" is obvious: to adult humans of certain cultural backgrounds, it has magical powers of person-making.

§

"Mama" has an enduring role in these talking ape games because it's a "cultural" first word—a prescribed verbal form that human babies must produce as the threshold that grants them personhood. They now count as social actors (though not necessarily competent ones) in human society, through bestowing a label on the person equipped to satisfy their needs. Fortunately, parents who expect to hear "mama" and "papa" can easily find it in baby's spoken babbling, where it inevitably occurs, thanks to how young children's speech motor abilities develop.

If I were talking to parents, I'd be careful to say that "mama" deserves every one of our emotional reactions. Wrote Heather Armstrong, who blogged about her experiences as a new parent in the early twenty-first century, "When people ask me about my week or my day, instead of complaining like the old me would do, I say, 'She calls me Mama now.' I never knew

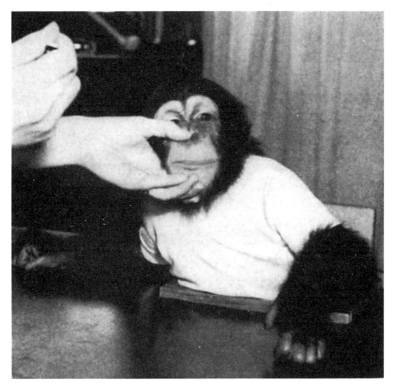

Figure 4.1
At fourteen months old, the chimpanzee Viki was taught to vocalize "mama" by
Keith and Catherine Hayes. In the photo her lips are manipulated by a human.
Reproduced with permission from the American Philosophical Society.

that word could be so amazing." This amazement is why people whose
children develop speech late or who are nonspeaking grieve the fact that
they'll hear it on a delayed schedule, if ever.

But I'd want to point out that pediatric researcher Herbert Goldman successfully primed dozens of parents to hear "mama" in the protophones
of their babies as young as two weeks old. Sounds were directed solely to
mothers a quarter of the time, but three-quarters of the time to mothers
along with fathers, grandparents, brothers and sisters, and in one case the
family dog. Thus, "mama" is no reliable early label for "mother." Yet, as
I showed in previous chapters, eager parents are quick to find affection-
ate words in the protophones, and one they inevitably, confidently find is
"mama." If you ask someone what their first word was, and if they have no

specific family story or record, "mama" is often the default reply. When a Stanford University research team surveyed parents about their children's first words, 67 percent reported "mama" or "dada," either because it was easiest to supply in hindsight or because they were accurately recalling what they heard.

Why do parents perceive "mama" so readily? For the same reasons that it's reportedly often spoken by people who are dying, which is the same reason that comedian Jimmy Kimmel's 2015 book is titled *Your First Word Will Be Dada*, and which is why some linguists and anthropologists consider "mama" to have primordial primacy. It's the same reason that Mrs. Marion Vaughn prefilled "mamma" on a sample page in *The Mother's Record*.

The reason is this: "mama" as a first word reflects core cultural beliefs about a child's intrinsic attachment to their mother and the enduring power of that bond. It has a ritual quality. It reflects the value placed on the domestic sphere and the family in it, reproducing that sphere and supporting its reason for existing. As it reflects the gendered division of labor when it comes to caring for babies, it would be fascinating to associate the rise of "mama" with a sexist insistence that women's place is in the home. The baby's first word makes its world. The playful competition over "mama" and "dada" as a first word is certainly connected to gender dynamics in society.

None of these ideas will diminish that powerful moment when the baby reaches for you and says "mama." I just think it's important to know this ritual from the outside too: adults have been socialized to expect a first word of a certain form, which is something that can be resolved from a string of babbling or is easy for a baby to imitate. The baby animates the utterance, supplying a string of sounds or handshapes as a developmental reflex, while the adult, the author, supplies the meaning. *The first word is an inheritance of the species, bestowed by the community*. The baby is the animator of the utterance "mama" but doesn't author the adult meaning, yet still gets enormous social credit for wanting and loving their mother (and, perhaps more importantly, a mother gets social credit for being loved).

§

One vector for the mama-first meme has been psychoanalytic thinking that reflects dominant ideas from European cultures. Sigmund Freud, Carl Jung, and others left behind the idea that the child's personhood is a gift from its bond with its mother (or, as Freudians would argue, the product of that bond's tensility and rupture). Therefore, it can only make sense for "mama" to be the first word.

Moreover, it's the breast that begets "mama," as some explain, because it supposedly contains the only sounds that babies can make while nursing. Thus, another deep-seated layer to the mama-first meme gets exposed: the assumption that every mother nurses her own baby, and every baby is nursed by their mother, or that every baby feeds from the breast, which is more normative than historically accurate.

Sabina Spielrein was a Russian psychoanalyst and physician who argued for "mama" along these lines in a 1922 essay. She's famous for being a patient of Carl Jung's, before becoming his student and then a romantic partner, then having a decades-long career in psychoanalysis and education in Germany, Austria, Switzerland, and Russia. Among the people she analyzed during her Swiss period in the early 1920s was Jean Piaget (1896–1980), who later quit the sessions, unmoved by psychoanalysis. It's tempting to think he influenced her interests, but she had already begun looking at child psychology from a psychoanalytic perspective. She asserted in her essay what she called the "common belief that 'Papa' and 'Mama' are the child's first words," finding it "remarkable that according to general opinion, it is always the same words, Papa and Mama, which are seen as the child's first words."

Then she offered psychoanalysis as a way to resolve the question—if "papa" and "mama" are indeed the first words that a child speaks, they must be inventions of the child's subconscious. Therefore, they "are imbued with a magical, wish fulfilling quality." This might be reasonable, if one agrees with the Jungian idea that "the ancestor sleeps within the child, and the child within the ancestor."

However, Spielrein's confident theorizing faltered once she inquired what babies actually say. Her essay embodies the friction that this rigid style of attention to first words has with the more flexible observational one. It's easy to imagine what happened: she'd been telling people she was writing about "mama" as a first word, then they told her about *actual* first words, which obviously imperiled her argument, because the reports didn't fit her mold. One girl said *"dida"* (for "clock"); another said *"lululu"* after hearing running water. The first meaning that another little girl knew was "a-a" (an adult euphemism for defecation), but her mother didn't mention the first word she said and understood herself.

After she listed these examples in her essay, Spielrein ducked: "Are Papa and Mama really the first words for all children? This question is very hard to answer because as well as the observational material being sparse in itself, there is in addition the difficulty of distinguishing between the word and meaningless babble." Maybe, Spielrein pondered, "mama" and "papa" are truly the first words but go unnoticed and unreported.

Eventually she abandoned the phonological parsing and returned to psychological theories about babbling as pleasure and nursing, doubling down on the babiness and the mother-child bond as immediate, irrevocable, and universal. That's another sign of the cultural first word: people's beliefs resist any evidence to the contrary.

§

Another way to reveal "mama" as the result of cultural decisions is to examine these cultural first words in other language communities.

"Is your child talking yet?" the linguistic anthropologist asked the mother.

"No," she replied, "they haven't said nɔ or bo yet."

About one hundred people lived in Sulibib, a small village in Papua New Guinea, mostly in a large communal longhouse but also in separate small houses, all made of sago palm, fronds, black palm, and vines. They were Kaluli, a horticulturalist people who spent their days working in gardens, checking animal traps and fishing, and preparing food. In the late 1970s, linguistic anthropologist Bambi Schieffelin went to Sulibib to study how young Kaluli children become Kaluli speakers. The puzzle was: How did they learn language? And what did they learn language is for?

For her project, Schieffelin followed two boys and two girls, talking to their parents, siblings, and family members as well. That's how she inadvertently discovered Kaluli first words.

Other mothers said the same thing about their children: without /nɔ/ (the vowel is the same as in the American pronunciation of "thought"), which means "my mother," and /bo/, which means "breast," they didn't consider the children to be speaking. Schieffelin found this odd—some of those young children were already saying words for dogs, foods, and their brothers and sisters. She'd even heard that child say words like "pig," "dog," and "this." But those words were "to no purpose," the parents told her, because the children hadn't said "nɔ" and "bo" yet. Schieffelin had discovered that the Kaluli first word was neither a child's early discernible utterances nor "mama" or "papa," but rather words that (to the adults) marked the beginning of explicit language instruction. Once a child said "nɔ" and "bo," they could be taught to say things in specific ways, the goal of which was to "make language harden" in the child.

Though the Kaluli adults noticed a child's first word, they didn't often engage children in conversation. Parents greeted their babies by name and cooed at them, but they rarely said much else to them. "This isn't to suggest that children don't get attention," Schieffelin said, "because they get a lot of it, but the organization and multiparty nature of most social interactions creates a different set of foci. The small child is always in the mix, observing, contributing, but not the center of everyone's attention."

Kaluli parents also don't use baby vocalizations as the basis for an interaction, as Shirley Brice Heath said she was laughed at for doing in Trackton. For the Kaluli, as Schieffelin wrote in an email, "there was no valorizing of precocity, rather everyone, including kids, did things when they were ready. There was often talk about not pushing anyone, especially a child, to do something they were not ready to do." Moreover, in societies like this one with socially distributed caregiving, there aren't any primary love objects, like a single mother or father, who need the recognition that an early kinship word like "mama" confers.

As with the errant example of the Aztecs, it's tempting to infer that if parents love their children, they surely expect some first words and might even recall them. But this is wrong. Maybe it's more accurate to say this: first words are more likely to be known by parents who need to know that their children love them. Though it's easy to associate adults talking directly to young children with noticing first words, this doesn't seem to be the case. Just as the recognition of children's language differs among cultures, so does the status of the first word, whose salience as a milestone is neither natural nor universal.

Another linguistic anthropologist, Don Kulick, who has done field studies in Brazil and New Guinea, found first-word beliefs similar to those in Sulibib in Gapun, an isolated Papua New Guinea village of about two hundred people. There, villagers use a language called Tayap along with Tok Pisin, the creole language. As Kulick describes in his book *A Death in the Rainforest*, Tayap is spoken by fewer and fewer people, bringing into view the shrinking distance between the first word and the last word of a whole language. (Even Kulick never learned to speak it, he admitted, though he could understand it.) In Tayap, a child's first word is generally held to be /ɔki/, pronounced something like "okuh," a word that means "I'm getting out of here."

"Attributed to infants as young as 2 months," Kulick has written, "this word encapsulates the adult belief that babies 'do what they want' . . . and go where they want to go regardless of the wishes of others."

For the Gapun, a baby is emotionally bristly and defiantly antisocial, traits summarized in the Gapun concept of *hed*. Their *hed* is further indicated by a couple of other Tayap first words: "*minda*," or "I'm sick of this," and "*aiata*," or "stop it." These all stem from protophones that parents label as words. "The villagers don't notice sounds like 'Mama' or 'Papa,'" Kulick wrote. "They pay them no attention. Instead, from a baby's incoherent babbling, villagers extract those three words—oki, *minda*, and *ayata*—that they reckon express a baby's way of engaging with the world." We know from MacNeilage and Davis that indeed these strings of sounds appear in infant babbling.

For about a year and half after this threshold is crossed, any child speech is ignored or derided as "rubbish talk," "nothing calls," or "bird talk," partly because it's in Tayap, a language associated with irrational, backward qualities that the villagers are obsessed with overcoming, so after those three words, no other babbling is resolved as words in Tayap.

Also, adults don't converse with babies, "which is nonsensical, since a baby can't hold up its end of the conversation," and don't use language to teach them, "since they don't believe that toddlers learn by being taught," Kulick wrote. However, children do get enough interaction to realize that everyone is constantly lying to them—in Kulick's account, village life consists of a surprisingly large amount of constant low-grade, overlapping, and mutual gaslighting—as well as enough exposure to obscenity that Kulick suggested that children's *real* first words are two Tok Pisin phrases, "*kaikaikan*" ("eat cunt") and "*giaman*" ("that's a lie").

As I mentioned in chapter 1, linguistic anthropologist Elinor Ochs has also done very influential fieldwork on how we understand infant language learning. As a young mother herself, she spent time studying children in Western Samoa in the 1970s and 1980s, carefully portraying how the baby interacts with many caregivers: not just a mother but other children and female family members (though rarely fathers). Ochs noted that Samoan concepts of natural behavior (*amio*) and socially appropriate behavior (*aga*) preside over how infants and caregivers react. Samoans tolerate behavior in children that would be considered a disciplinary problem from the Western point of view—running and shouting during church services, throwing stones at caregivers, hitting siblings—because children aren't able to control *amio* nor adequately perform *aga*.

It's in this context that Ochs related Samoans' emblematic first word, which is a shortened version of a longer curse, "*ai tae,*" meaning "eat shit." This word embarrassed the Samoan mothers, at least when they mentioned it to Ochs, even though it confirmed a socially acceptable view that children are ruffians, unfit for social interaction, and even though the children didn't actually know the meaning of *tae*. Yet saying "shit" for the first time confirmed that the young child was indeed fitting the template of what young children do.

Like "mama," these other cultural first words are extracted from babbling. They also mark a boundary of personhood that everyone crosses in the same fashion—and which people in that community have always crossed. There's a sense of gathering to these words, a timeless enfolding. Sometimes the caregivers recognize them formally; sometimes they do it only in passing. In all cases, the words themselves (and what people say about them) indicate how they view children. For the Kaluli, "these words fit into a broader sense of sociality and personhood," Bambi Schieffelin wrote to me in an email. "It's about the first relationship and giving food, central to, and culturally embedded in the expectations and obligations of the kin-based exchange system." In another echo with Rousseau, a first word holds a tremendous responsibility in giving shape to the society.

§

Another way to show that "mama" isn't so natural or universal is to look beyond spoken language. If "mama" meaning "mother" were universal, deaf infants would make it first too.

I had originally contacted Sacha Jackson, a sign language interpreter who at the time headed the Ottawa Deaf Health Care Team, which makes sign language services available in palliative care and hospice settings, to talk about signing at the end of life. We ended up organizing a video chat about first words with her mother, Charlene LeBlanc, and her friend, Beth Hutchison. Bright and friendly, Sacha is a CODA (child of deaf adults), whose first language was American Sign Language. So her first word, Charlene remembered, was "milk." This is a common first word, at least in ASL-using communities, not "mama." This is because the sign for "milk" is a grasping gesture with the full hand and all five fingers that's easy for a child to produce. A nonsigner might interpret it to mean "gimme."

Charlene was sure about Sacha's first word, because they had participated in a university linguistic study; it had been captured on video. Beth, who works as a call center manager, remembered her three children's first words as "milk." Then she invited her son Paul, also a deaf signer who happened to be at home that day, to join us on the call.

"Do you remember your first word?" Beth asked him.

"It was 'ball,'" he replied. "You're the one who told me that."

Beth said she remembered it as "milk."

"No," Paul signed (Sacha was interpreting). "It was 'ball.'"

First-word memories in many families can be fuzzy, too, and "milk" functions as something of a cultural first word for signers as "mama" does for speakers.

When she was a baby, Sacha babbled with her hands to anyone, and Charlene realized that her daughter understandably thought that everyone signed. She didn't know that deafness wasn't the norm. For her part, Charlene marveled at this openness, but wasn't so interested in Sacha speaking. "She would speak, but I wouldn't care about that, but when she would learn a new sign, I was so inspired, so excited," she said. Charlene's mother, who was hearing, happily told Charlene about Sacha's new spoken words, but Charlene was less moved.

It's important to point out that a first word as "milk" or "ball" can happen only in circumstances where the parents also sign, but not all deaf people learn to sign as children. Charlene grew up in a hearing family and didn't encounter any signed language use until she was a teenager. Prior to that, the family used ad hoc, made-up signs (usually called "home sign"). But she recalled being overwhelmed by all of the attention from other deaf students, and the astonishing speed of their signing. "They all just loved me and taught me so many signs, and I became so much happier to have that connection." When prompted by Beth, she could remember that her first sign was "group." She was seventeen years old.

§

Despite these examples from deaf signers, and despite what linguistic anthropologists have told us about the various ways that adults direct language to young children, some language scientists can't see past their own commitments to "mama." Because it's the first word that their communities bestow on babies by filtering it from their rhythmic motor activity and vocal-seeking behavior, they think it's everyone else's first word too. Some of them have bent over backward to gild their beliefs about motherhood, child-rearing, and even how parents interact with babies with science, all in service of explaining the primacy of "mama." They basically argue that since "mama" is already known to be the first word, then "mama" is what must be explained.

This is the case for one piece of evidence usually brought out for the universality and primacy of "mama." At a Stanford University seminar in 1959, anthropologist George Murdock wondered if there was a linguistic explanation for phonological similarities in terms for "mother" and "father" across multiple languages. Could it be that these terms favored sounds that were easier for babies to say? Using data for kinship names from 474 societies, Murdock later collected 531 words for "mother" and 541 for "father" and concluded that the broad linguistic pattern held. (In fact, it doesn't, as we'll see.) However, in Murdock's analysis, most of the vowels were low, and the consonants were nasal, bilabial, or alveolar stops.

Why are the words so similar? It's possible that they reflect a common ancestry of all languages. But in 1960, famed linguist Roman Jakobson offered another argument: the words reflected good phonological design. Repetition? Check. Open syllables? Check. Consonants that are easy to tell apart? Check. Moreover, he pointed out, the sounds that predominate in "mother" and "father" terms, particularly in the baby talk or "nursery" forms of those words, reflect young children's phonological abilities. Single consonants? Check. Low-mid vowels? Check.

As Sabina Spielrein did, Jakobson sourced "mama" to the "nasal murmurs," which are, as he put it, "the only phonation which can be produced when the lips are pressed to mother's breast or to the feeding bottle and the mouth is full." Yet there's no need to put mothers or nursing in the mix—these nasal murmurs are simply protophones. As Kim Oller noted, babies produce protophones consistently when they're awake, not just when they're nursing, and of course those protophones are easy for babies to produce. Implicit in Jakobson's explanation is the assumption that all mothers nurse their own babies (they don't) or that all babies nurse from the breast (they don't) or that babies can't vocalize with a bottle in their mouths (if they really want to, believe me, they can). The diversity of social and physical contexts therefore precludes a universal outcome.

To be sure, the mama-first meme has other leaks. One is that "mama," as a string of sounds, has no intrinsic connection to kinship or maternity—it might simply mean "food." Indeed, in Goldman's pediatric "mama" listening study, thirty-two of the fifty-five infants were perceived to be wanting to be picked up, nine wanted food, and seven wanted attention. It always signaled "wanting"—not a label for a person.

A bigger weakness of the mama-first meme is this: if you assume that kinship terms are frequent meanings of usual first words (which is itself an idea about first words), and if you really engage with child language, then you should notice that word forms like "tata" and even "papa" are more frequent and happen earlier than "mama." In the late 1970s, linguists Jeanne Brooks-Gunn and Michael Lewis showed seventy-one white middle-class children between nine and twenty-four months old photos of their own mothers and fathers, as well as photos of other men and women. "Daddy" was used correctly earlier and by more subjects than "mommy," while children were more likely to label photos of their father more correctly than those of their mother. Mothers were asked if their children knew kinship names; of those who said yes, half reported that "daddy" came first; only 5 percent said that "Mommy" was first. Though this study was about social labels, not first words per se, it showed that early application was fuzzy and inconsistent.

This research occurred at a time when linguists were leaving the mama-first meme behind, focusing instead on both "mama" and "papa" (or "daddy" and "dada"). Perhaps the gender consciousness of the era put more men of science in contact with their own offspring? Nevertheless, Murdock's and Jakobson's work still gets cited, as if there were a cultural need to assert that "mama" as "mother" must be a universal first word—as if the work of anthropologists such as Bambi Schieffelin, Elinor Ochs, and Don Kulick hadn't shown that cultures transform similar linguistic phenomena into their own milestones. Sure, it's tempting to dismiss the beliefs of Samoans and Papuans in favor of tables of quantified data, but the lesson from Catherine Snow rings true to me here: even scientific observations about babies' language reflect cultural decisions (as we'll also see in the next chapter).

But the discussion can't end there, because I can make Murdock's data itself give a more nuanced conclusion.

Jakobson and others didn't explain all of Murdock's data, dismissing as outliers the data that doesn't support the mama-first thesis. In fact, only 52 percent of the kinship terms for "mother" used nasal consonants /m/ and /n/. This seems insufficient for securing a universal. Moreover, 7 percent of words for "mother" have the consonants /p/ or /t/. In both cases, these consonants reflect how children's speech develops, so the words themselves may be reduced forms of the words that are easy for babies to say, then are adopted by adults.

Importantly, though, other types of consonants appear in significant numbers. For instance, a whopping 41 percent of "mother" terms use a phonetic rainbow of other consonants, like /tʃ/ (as in the "ch" of "chomp"), /dʒ/ (the two consonants of "judge"), /s/, and /z,/ and a plethora of vowels, not only the low ones. There are even words for "mother" and "father" that have sounds like /ŋ/, /l/, /r/, and clicks, all of which are consonants that children can pronounce only when they're older. That means that some kinship words can't be nursery forms. So where do they come from?

Of course, many of these forms might have been imported from other languages—Murdock wasn't clear on their exact provenance. Missionaries, colonialism, migration, and language contact between groups, which have been going on for millennia, can lead to the exchange or imposition of kinship terms. Once you introduce such deep historical forces into the mix, Murdock's survey (and any other one) becomes a unreliable portrait of the universal and primordial. However, it does tell us one intriguing thing: approximately 20 percent of words for "mother" and "father" in Murdock's lists might have arisen in communities where adults and children don't co-create the forms—you can tell because the sounds don't fit the developmental patterns like the others do. This may indicate how many language communities, at the time of the survey, behave according to the fourth mode of expectations about first words, where adults don't expect anything about child language at all.

§

So far I've established that cultures can vary in their emblematic first words—a more rigid expectation about those words actually comes itself in several forms. However, some cultures are more elastic, such that adults or caregivers notice a young child's linguistic leap from babbling but have no preconceived idea of that leap's form.

This more liberal style, in which parents pay attention to their baby's particular speech act as it comes from the individual baby, what I've called the *laissez parler*, is what we see emerging in the twentieth century. This worldview puts the emphasis on the baby's uniqueness, on the potential of each baby to be, somehow, different from the rest.

Why did this mindset arise? As I wrote in chapter 2, a range of factors influenced this, but it's not uniquely modern. Cultures of the past were similarly elastic in their expectations, in particular the Romans, with their concept of *fari*.

From chapter 1, you'll be familiar with this concept, via the word *fans*, of which *fari* is an older form, as Italian philologist Maurizio Bettini has explained. It refers to a way of speaking that is distinguished by its authority, efficacy, and credibility. Oracles and prophets speak with *fari*—the utterance is a revelation, a confession. Remarkably, for the Romans (unlike, say, the West Samoans), this authority is invested in the language that the child learns to produce. Until they do, they are *infantes*, without linguistic authority. In other words, *fari* isn't just about making sounds but about a verbal decisiveness. Words, but words that *mattered*.

"At Rome, the speech of infants was taken very seriously," Bettini wrote, "not only when a baby first uttered a 'meaningful word' (*significabilem vocem*, an act that the Romans defined in terms of *fari*), but also when it made its absolute first sound, its first *vagitus*." The arrival of *fari* was not just "vaguely meaningful babble" but a moment of considerable expressive power. There is an anecdote that when Octavian, the future Augustus Caesar, began to talk, the frogs all stopped croaking, because the baby had commanded it. Though this was undoubtedly imperial flattery, it expands on a real Roman belief about the child's speech act. The first word had so much power because it was believed to be divinely inspired by that divinity known either as Fabulinus or Farinus.

The Roman writer Marcus Terentius Varro (116–27 BCE) described how, upon the arrival of *fari*, ancient Roman parents went to the temple of Farinus to make an offering. Perhaps it was cakes, a cup of wine, a bouquet of flowers, honey, milk, or meat. A first word wasn't a signal of the child's linguistic autonomy—in fact, far from it, Bettini wrote. "Even at the moment in which a baby is said 'to now speak' (*iam fari*), therefore the 'word' that comes to his lips is somehow divinely inspired, as with the prophet or seer. In other words, the agency of the animator (the baby) is again joined to that of a principal (the god Farinus or Fabulinus), who supernaturally merged his voice with that of the child."

How many Romans made sacrifices to Farinus? Such a fact is lost to time. They were probably more attentive to aspects of childhood and their own children than modern people typically give the ancients credit for, but going to the temple of Farinus was likely reserved for elites rather than plebeians. This is a bit at odds with a classicist view that Romans didn't "discover" babies until the first century CE, well after the ancient religion Varro mentioned had vanished. For a long time, Latin had no word for "baby," with the modern connotations of a cute, helpless newborn human who inspires feelings of tenderness. Plenty of other baby attributes are expressed in other Latin words: their tiny size (*parvulus*), their nursing (*alumnus* and *lactens*), their cries (*vagiens*), their doll-like status (*pupa, pupus*), and their lack of sensible language (*infans*). However, the meaning of *infans* evolved so that only by the first century CE did it become a rough equivalent for "baby" in the modern Anglophone sense. No one tied Farinus to the first word anymore, but babies' relationship to language became central to their place in the civic order.

Nowadays, this partnership with divine agency doesn't have much currency. Nor are first words granted magical powers; yet we have a sense, at least, that those word-like utterances can augur something of the baby's character. Thinking about my own expectations for my sons' first words, I definitely used them to plot their potential futures. *What will he be like?*

The first words are, of course, not meant by the baby to confer a special status. But as they emerge from a private conversation with a caregiver, they can become status objects in public. They can also be tussled over by adults—recall the subtle competition between Nathaniel's parents and his babysitter, or Ross's reaction in the *Friends* episode. The question isn't about what the words are but who the baby privileges with them. Just as in Diné communities, the person who makes a baby laugh for the first time has a sacred bond with them, the middle-class white parent who can report a first word will accrue the status of doing the parent's role "right." That's what lies beyond my peacocking around with my kid's first steps, first words, hitting a ball, building with bricks. He wasn't just saying "mama," he was saying something compellingly full of cultural capital, like "book."

§

One predictable result of the *laissez parler* mode and its economic aspirations is what might be called first word accelerationism. Teaching hearing babies how to sign, therefore arriving at a first word precociously, became fashionably popular in America and other countries starting in the late 1990s, continuing to the present day. If you signed with your baby, according to certain books and numerous magazine and newspaper articles, it would be easier to care for them because you'd have access to their wishes and physical state.

An early researcher who set this stage was Linda Acredolo, the developmental psychologist we met in chapter 3, whose experience of seeing her daughter, Kate, mimic sniffing a rose began her quest for a vocabulary of symbolic gestures that would let parents communicate with their preverbal babies. Despite her published research with a collaborator, Susan Goodwyn, parents were resistant to signing.

"We kept finding that a lot of parents thought the signing would impede verbal language development," Acredolo said. "They thought, If you let kids use their hands, why would they bother to do the hard work of learning to talk?"

Consequently, much of their early research was aimed at proving early sign's positive impact on language, even though the original impetus for the gestures was connecting parent and child emotionally.

"We always pushed that in our talks and classes," Acredolo said. "We'd say, 'Our goals are emotional development. Yes, signing helps with language development, but what we want you to get out of this is the sense that you and your child are on the same level.'"

After several years of research, including a grant from the US National Institutes of Health, they published *Baby Signs: How to Talk with Your Baby Before Your Baby Can Talk*, in 1996. Much to their surprise, that book took off, leading to the best-seller lists, television appearances, and speaking opportunities. These two scientists had walked right into an American mini-boom of the late 1990s, in which educational materials targeted parents of children under three in order to optimize the cognition of the youngest Americans. Notable was an American-produced video featuring music and words in several languages, colors, and shapes called *Baby Einstein*, followed quickly by humanities-ish titles like *Baby Mozart*, *Baby Bach*, and *Baby Wordsworth* (featuring a sign language component with actor Marlee Matlin). Anxious American parents turned the Baby Einstein company into a $200 million a year business. By 2003, a Kaiser Family Foundation report noted:

> an explosion in electronic media marketed directly at the very youngest children in our society: a booming market of videotapes and DVDs aimed at infants one to 18 months, the launching of the first TV show specifically targeting children as young as twelve months, and a multi-million dollar industry selling computer games and even special keyboard toppers for children as young as nine months old.

A few years later, an observer argued that international capital searching for new profits had created a market by "redefining babies as solely learners, which has implications for relationships between babies and adults." Babies, in this view, were rather like the newly notable software that people had just begun downloading on their personal computers: you had to tinker with it before using it. Adults pushed symbolic gesture in order to force a "first word" moment and jump-start language development—which Acredolo and Goodwyn's research had promoted, showing that babies who learned sign had longer sentences and more words than their peers. Down the road, they also had higher IQ scores than non-signing peers, Acredolo and Goodwyn claimed. Other companies promoting baby sign language sprang up, making grander claims, which are largely dismissed by academics. Baby sign may improve emotional connection, but it has negligible impact on verbal development.

It's also notable that babies had been gesturing forever, waving "bye bye" and shaking their head for "no" and nodding for "yes." When Acredolo and Goodwyn interviewed parents, many reported noticing their babies using these symbolic gestures, but they didn't encourage it. It didn't seem like a good idea—what if the baby chose to talk with their hands? (That same fear makes parents drop the baby sign when the child begins to speak.)

"Unless they're looking for the generalization of the gestures to something else, parents just think these gestures are a part of the game they're playing," Acredolo said. The parents care only about the game, not the broader application of the gestures. It was as if they were innately prone to ignoring an opportunity to connect with their child via symbolic gesture; not until it was linked to cognitive development by scientific authorities (in this case, Acredolo and Goodwyn) did they believe something significant was going on. In a 2020 episode of *The Simpsons* called "Screentime," the baby Maggie learns some baby signs. "My baby is communicating with me!" Marge announces joyfully—though notably not proclaiming the signs to be "first words," which the hearing world usually grants to the spoken.

While Acredolo and Goodwyn originally taught parents to use child-led gestures (rather than ones taught to the children), other baby sign entrepreneurs appropriated signs from American Sign Language or British Sign Language, sometimes for branded communication systems (one used in the UK is called Makaton). All this has come under fire from members of the Deaf community, who see components of their language being appropriated, then sold to hearing families for commercial gain; even the term "baby sign language" is an appropriation. Meanwhile, deaf children don't enjoy the benefits of claims that early signing creates language geniuses. Instead, they're denied access to sign language at home and in schools on the basis of the attitude that signing impedes speech acquisition, and that sign languages are somehow less, only communication tools for the disabled.

Jon Henner, a linguist at the University of North Carolina at Greensboro, recalled taking his baby daughter to a baby sign class at the local library in 2008. The instructor, who claimed to be certified in baby sign, began with colors but named them incorrectly. Henner knew they were wrong, because he is Deaf and fluent in ASL. When he talked to the instructor, she told him she doesn't know ASL, only baby sign. "And that set my perspective about the whole business," he said.

To Henner, baby sign is an unnecessary shortcut. "Babies talk to us the moment they come out. We spend a lot of time trying to understand each other. People have this idea that if only their baby could use words, things would be easier. Baby sign is a panacea." We don't sell baby-fied English, he added. The larger problem is a societal one: caregivers don't get sufficient support, so they feel desperate. "Baby sign exploits this. I dislike that," he said.

Indeed, many parents hope for language to alleviate day-to-day concerns of care. A first word's appearance suggests things might get easier—that when you ask the screaming baby, "What do you want?" you might get an answer. "Mama!" "Yes, I know you want, but what?"

Such objections haven't halted the spread of commercialized baby sign around the world. As a 2007 study concluded, "The very populations who are most likely to use baby signs are those with a large presence on the internet and high visibility to the media, making their behavior socially influential beyond their numbers." Acredolo and Goodwyn's book has gone through three editions, the third of which has been translated into fourteen languages and sold 400,000 copies. Their organization, Baby Signs, has certified instructors in over forty countries, who have also translated materials. "I'm sure together we have trained thousands of instructors around the world and reached hundreds of thousands of families, professionals and child development centers," said Michelle Cromeenes, who acquired Baby Signs from Acredolo and Goodwyn in 2014 and has international partners in seventeen countries. I checked to see where those countries ranked in the Organisation for Economic Cooperation and Development's rankings of parental leave support. About half of them ranked high, which makes it hard to assess Henner's claim, at least internationally. However, baby sign was popularized first in the United States, the only country in the world with no national parental leave system. And some research has shown that parents who go to baby sign classes have high levels of stress—and that attendance does not, contrary to the promises, reduce that stress. So Henner's criticism is borne out.

In a cultural history of first words, "baby sign" represents the apotheosis of the *laissez parler* approach to first words. Now I can open up new territory worth exploring: if children, in their caregivers' view, don't produce a prescribed "mama" as the first word, then what first words do they actually make? This is the topic of the next chapter, where the most expansive attempt to understand children's early vocabulary across dozens of languages and cultures provides a fascinating look at who we really are.

5 The Normal First Word

For all the children's early words in the scientific literature, one never gets their perspectives about being observed by their parents and scientists. Imagine what one of the first subjects might have to say:

Friedrich: He comes in the nursery and doesn't make a fuss when he writes down what I do, but I'm just a baby and I wonder why it matters. Right after I was born, he noticed when I turned my head to the light and became excited by it. Now I have a record of my first sounds too—maybe I'll do the same thing for my children. When I saw something I liked, I exclaimed "ach!" (February 10, 1782). I tried to imitate Mama saying "ma" with my lips (March 14, 1782). I pointed my finger at things to make sure people would look at them too and said "ha!" which Papa called "the natural expression of reflection and of surprise" (May 13, 1782).

My first words that he recognized came on November 27, 1782, "papa" and "mama," though he said I didn't use them to call persons, I just babbled them and they were so excited that Papa wrote it all down.

Historians (and historically minded language scientists) usually credit German philosopher Dietrich Tiedemann's efforts in 1781 as the first child diary. In contrast to Louis XIII's doctor, Jean Héroard, Tiedemann was a product of the Enlightenment: he didn't consider the immortal soul or God in his view of psychology. After he published his diary, it went unnoticed for a long time, but after his death it was rediscovered and published in translations in France and the United States, where it influenced a revival of experimental psychology. Thus, historians usually follow their nod toward Tiedemann with a book of Genesis–like genealogy of subsequent diarists and who inspired whom, an approach whose air of inevitability obscures compelling points of interest.

One such point is that the male chroniclers of language and baby life have always made a big deal of "discovering" phenomena that women have already discussed, thanks to up-close, day-to-day caregiving experiences. You can imagine that the person who was consulted in the village and the city neighborhood in the early modern era through the nineteenth century was a "wise woman," often a wet nurse or midwife. It's only slightly hyperbolic to say that men who developed protocols for noticing and writing down first words were following in the footsteps of wise women, mothers, grandmothers, sisters, and aunties. Men moved freely in the public sphere while women's role was stereotypically in the home, which explains some of this dynamic. Though contemporary language research tends to lock onto mothers' contributions, nurses, maids, and babysitters also drift, mostly unacknowledged, through the diaries. In the feminist history of child-language studies that will someday be written, these nameless women, hovering in the background, will get more than passing mention.

Such a history would also note that prominent women kept diaries about their babies and children before men did. Among the British upper classes in the early nineteenth century, it was a common practice. Two of Charles Darwin's cousins, Elizabeth Gaskell and Sophia Holland, began child diaries in 1835 and 1837. Probably many of their peers did too. Gaskell had been inspired by Albertine-Adrienne Necker de Saussure's 1828 book, which urged mothers to keep diaries of their babies' growth to track the emergence of their soul. Necker de Saussure even has a chapter on first words and on learning to speak.

Thus Charles Darwin began his diary of his son William in 1839, noting his first word, "mum." He published the account in 1870, responding to Hippolyte Taine's notes about his daughter Geneviève's tem when they appeared in English. Darwin's diary, which is credited with making babies into legitimate objects of natural historical interest, differs from those of his cousins, as "it is not a record of parental anxiety," noted historian Sally Shuttleworth, "but rather a precise observational study of the physiological processes of development." But observation of children ran in the family: Darwin's wife, Emma, had her childhood observed and recorded by her father, Josiah Wedgwood, who kept a diary from 1791 to 1799.

An oft-overlooked point is that this diary-keeping didn't bloom in a vacuum. Rather, it occurred within a broader European embrace of self-oriented writing. Historians note the explosion of so-called ego-documents—written memoirs, autobiographies, personal letters, and diaries, either published or kept in family archives—around 1800. People in greater number, especially literate people living in urban areas, begin to record all sorts of ephemeral events from ordinary daily life. In the 1990s, Dutch historian Rudolf Dekker inventoried all of the extant, accessible Dutch language ego-documents from 1500 to 1914. A subsequent analysis by historian Arianne Baggerman found that people in the Netherlands (and elsewhere in northern and western European countries) produced more ego-documents during the upheavals of the Napoleonic era, from 1770 to 1830.

This explosion was long explained by pointing to the discovery of the self's interior, a private realm that people wished to explore and commit to paper. However, introspective, personally intimate writing didn't predominate in the ego-documents that Dekker and Baggerman surveyed. People didn't pour out their souls on the page, detailing their dreams, wishes, ideas, or sins, but rather listed household expenditures. Where the local army was fighting. New imports in the shops. What they read, but not what they thought of it. In fact, most ego-documents contained no personal reflections whatsoever. People had become their own recording angels, writing for a future person, often an unknown descendant, or sometimes their child. Elizabeth Gaskell dedicates her diary to her child, "as a token of her mother's love." I can't help but notice that the diaries by Tiedemann, Necker de Saussure, and even the Darwins date to the boom in ego-documents.

From this, Baggerman concluded that people wrote things down in order to orient themselves in time. They needed to recognize a past that was distinct from a future, and above all connect private experiences of time at the family scale to public time at the turbulent national scale. "People felt that their world was no longer a given, but an experienced phenomenon, replete with expectations, uncertainties and possibilities to mould both their personal lives and the society they were part of," Baggerman and Dekker wrote. Writing things down was a personal practice that preserved the smooth, continuous flow of time by ensuring that one's personal present could become a future reader's sense of the past. This overly concise statement of an extraordinarily rich (and contested) period in European intellectual history will have to suffice here. But child diaries are undoubtedly connected to this era. It may also explain why there aren't *more* such diaries: the world is big; there's lots someone might want to record.

§

Hildegard: What are you always writing down, Papa? I asked him.

Oh, Hildegard, he said, I'm taking notes for my work. He wrote down so much of what Karla and I said. Four whole books!

He liked to tell people that my first word was "bild," for "picture." Traditionalists would have predicted "mama," he liked to say. But Papa was no traditionalist. In fact I said "papa" two and a half months before I said "mama," which I used for the maid before Mama.

"Dr. Leopold, do you remember why you decided to invest your time in studying the language of your daughter?" an interviewer once asked him.

"I can't remember," Papa said. He thought it was something he got from the Sterns. But Mama knew. "When I brought Hildegard home, you were immediately fascinated by the sounds that she was making."

"Many a doting parent writes down for safekeeping his child's first baby words," a January 1, 1940, *Time* article began, "but Dr. Werner F. Leopold, a professor at Northwestern University, outdid most parents."

Until the 1930s, linguists hadn't studied child language; most of the interest came from psychologists and educators. Along came Werner Leopold, who looked at his two daughters' language from every linguistic angle—how it sounded, how they formed words and made sentences, and how they negotiated meanings. Leopold was an unlikely source: he had just migrated to America from Germany via Costa Rica, where he'd been a high school teacher, and found a job in Wisconsin teaching Spanish, then moved to Northwestern University. In an interview from the late 1980s—around the same time that Catherine Snow was publishing about first words—Leopold compared his close observation of his children to scientists who study the behavior of ants and bees. (Charles Darwin had sanctioned exactly that activity when he published his diary of William, sending natural historians who were otherwise more comfortable in the jungle or the zoo into the nursery.)

Why was Leopold studying his daughters' language acquisition in English and German? Because he wasn't a linguist. Though he'd taken some phonetics, he was mainly a Germanist, and he knew that only three other studies of bilingual children existed. But he had in front of him his two daughters' language, which he described as he encountered it, without shoehorning it into a theoretical framework. This made his subsequent diaries rather special.

In some reflections on the history of child-language studies published in 1947, he tackled first the mama-first meme, calling it one of several "speculative interpretations" and "sweeping generalizations" about how babies come into language. In a spicy paragraph, he assured the reader that "mama" is indeed produced early. However, by no means is it the earliest, nor always among the first words, he wrote, noting Hildegard's preferences. He criticized linguists who fall into the same trap as "fond mothers" who take "mama" to refer to them when, in fact, that particular syllable sequence results from "mere muscle exercises" that come to mean "food." (Leopold points to *mjammjam*, also spelled as "yum-yum," calling it a phonetic variant of "mama.")

As Leopold alluded in his interview, first words weren't significant in linguistics for most of the twentieth century, even after Noam Chomsky made child language acquisition central to theories of grammar, starting in the 1950s. The central question was how grammatical structure emerged, especially if children had supposedly spotty input. Because "structure" was thought to have arrived when children produced two-word sequences, not much about what happened before was theoretically relevant. In fact, that beloved first word marked the lack of language.

Yet other researchers, such as Catherine Snow, coming from a psychology perspective, explored what occurred before grammar's arrival: Who interacted with babies, and how? What else were babies learning, and learning to do, as language sprouted? Perhaps other information about meaning and the structure of language came attached to single words. From that perspective, children seemed to be assembling important elements of the languages that surrounded them by using cognitive mechanisms that were apparent well before the first-word stage. Those insights led to theories of language acquisition called *emergentist*, distinct from Chomsky's innatism.

Numerous academic battles have been fought between supporters of these theories, and other writers are better suited as tour guides to these battlefields. As for myself, I'm interested in first words and last words, and since data-driven emergentists deliver the interesting insights about early vocabulary—the lexicon and its growth is at the core of some emergentist approaches—my story turns in their direction. I'm not dismissing all innatist ideas, but an approach that makes room for the interaction between parents and babies has more to offer an attempt to understand the first word.

Between Leopold's time and the work of the anthropologists of the 1980s, a curious thing happened: the more closely scientists looked at children's early utterances, the more crumbly the first word became. By the 1980s, linguists had given up trying to find William Dwight Whitney's "actual first utterance," or any such bright line between one linguistic state and the next. For example, Alan Cruttenden, a phonetician in England, tape-recorded his twins and found himself in fuzzy territory, unable to find a singular, monolithic first word. First words were revealed to be processes, emerging over time, not discrete events. "Indeed," he wrote, "I found it extremely difficult and perhaps rather pointless to pin down the occurrence of the first word."

Another linguist, Alan Kahmi, called the first word "the most common and pervasive of the myths about language development." He criticized parents for naively calling any string of sounds that sounds like an adult word a word. "It should be clear," he wrote, "that parental reports of first words are generally not accurate." Kahmi's own bias for scientists' dispassion was clear.

Catherine Snow reflected on these developments in her 1988 essay, "The Last Word," noting that first word-iness retained a status of theoretical import. But instead of continuing to search for a single Rubicon-crossing moment, scientists opted to identify the fourth word, or the first ten, or the first fifty. Eventually they resolved to look at a first-word *stage*, marked by babies starting to understand words, later producing them. That's when the science really took off.

I'm delving into these developments because they're all part of the story of the observational style, particularly the way that scientists skeptically poke and prod at the objects they're interested in. As is the case with many stories in science, as observations become more exact and the tools for making them become more sophisticated, the object of interest begins to complicate. In the case of first words, this process has a lot to tell us about how we came to our contemporary sense of how a "typical" or "normal" baby learns language, and how to judge the normality of the infant. Science proceeds by disputes that make battlegrounds of certainties, but what if the choice of battleground causes us to ignore other aspects of what babies do?

§

Allison: Mama said she wasn't going to pay attention to my language or write anything down. I want to be a mama, she said, not a researcher. So nobody remembers what my first words were. But of course she watched me and wrote some things down, like "wida." A nonsense word. Nobody could figure it out. I would just stick it onto other words. I'd say "babywida" or "mamawida." It lasted for about twenty days, then I stopped doing it, I don't know why. Mama always said it was evidence that kids could keep two words in regular order.

Despite their enthusiasm for observing children, scientists occasionally rebelled when it came to their own. One American child-language expert in the 1970s, Lois Bloom, vowed that she was going to enjoy her daughter's language. "I wasn't going to pay attention to her language, I told myself, I was just going to enjoy it and not do anything with it," Bloom told me. "I wanted to be her mother, not a researcher." Consequently, Bloom can't say what Allison's early words were, though she remembers the first time Allison said "ma." Bloom herself argued that the one-word stage isn't a unitary stage of development, and the more revelatory performance came from two-word utterances—which is indeed one way to solve the first word's fuzziness.

For nearly two centuries, diary-keeping mothers and fathers had been the main source for facts about child language, collected in English, French, German, Chinese, Russian, Polish, and other languages. But in the 1930s, parents and their diaries fell out of scientific favor, thanks to the philosophy of science of the times, which favored a scientific rigor and objectivity that parents marred by their involvement. This extended even to the scientist-parent, apparently, "who, it was presumed, was necessarily biased in what he chose to record in his notes and in what was overlooked as well."

That meant children had to be carted into laboratories and observed by emotionally distanced experts behind mirrored glass, not at home. But no one grows up in a laboratory, so children didn't act much like themselves in the small, inevitably windowless basement rooms that serve as university child-language labs. Plus, children come to understand words over days or weeks in a variety of contexts. A lab is a less than ideal place for capturing that.

One advantage of the lab-based studies was the ability to gather data about a group of children at the same age, akin to taking a core sample of the local child population. By the late 1950s, studies were enrolling 430 children at a time. Starting in the 1970s, recording equipment, first audio and then video, had an impact on the investigations. Devices became cheap and relatively portable, so people were able to gather real data from children at home. An early study by Katherine Nelson involved tape-recording eighteen children in their homes, visiting each one every month for a year.

These gains created new bottlenecks. Children had to speak clearly enough to be captured in recordings. And each hour of tape required several hours by one or more humans to transcribe. Eventually tens of thousands of such transcripts, aligned with common data standards, were collected in a single repository, the Child Language Data Exchange System (CHILDES), created in 1984 by Brian MacWhinney and Catherine Snow. It has data on twenty-six languages, which seems expansive, except there are an estimated seven thousand languages on the planet; researchers have dealt with only 1.5 percent of them.

You can readily grasp science as a practice by watching how its practitioners transform a phenomenon of interest—chemicals, bursts of electricity, babbled sounds—into charts and graphs. Two social scientists, Bruno Latour and Steven Woolgar, noticed this while embedded as fieldworkers at the Salk Institute in the 1970s. You can also map the maturing of a science in the way its practitioners collapse more data points into increasingly sophisticated graphs. Child language study illustrates this trajectory perfectly. Diaries on individual children became diaries on multiple children within families, then the diaries were aggregated. Slowly, the diversity of languages and home environments increased. Babies and children were observed in laboratories, their language behavior measured, then recorded at home; the resulting transcripts were made searchable, then aggregated. So far so good, Latour and Woolgar would say. Then, in the 1980s, someone took the next step.

§

Julia: I was referential. That's what Mama called me. When I was thirteen months old, I could say thirty-four words and understand eighty-four of them. Most of them were nouns—that's what referential meant. I was oriented toward the world of objects. But that's because Mama was. But when I was twenty months old, we spent a summer in Italy. *Piano!* The babysitter used to say. *Silenzio!* Her dad took his nap after lunch, so we had to be quiet, especially the dog, who was often told *sta zitto!* Mama said that when I spoke Italian I wasn't referential but expressive. Everything I knew was oriented towards people and relationships. Maybe that's because the babysitter was that way?

Anyway, Mama said she didn't want to write stuff down about me. She wasn't organized enough! She ended up writing 100,000 words of notes. I was eleven weeks old when I started vocalizing back-and-forth with her, up to 12 turns! Then she was amazed when I stopped doing it for months. She shouldn't have been—I didn't need to practice this anymore, I understood it.

> She was changing my diaper when I picked up a shoe and tried to say its name. "Yes, that's a shoe," she said. I tried again and again. Every time it came out sounding different, but at least I was trying, and Mama knew from the context what I meant. I used to say "mamamama" when I wanted something but not for her, then Papa came to pick me up and I said "dada!"

As Elizabeth Bates (1947–2004) wrote in her notes about her daughter, Julia, "I continue to be surprised by the 'now you see it, now you don't' nature of Julia's accomplishments, since the beginning . . . Are all those protowords and gestural schemes still 'in there,' underground, when they disappear for weeks on end? Or have they genuinely decayed in some way?" Elsewhere she wrote, "Julia's language comprehension continually comes out like the sunshine, and then goes back behind the clouds." She was already looking at the trajectories of individual children, puzzling out how there were so many routes to fluent knowledge of a language.

Bates and her legacy remain strong within child-language studies, although she's unknown to most nonlinguists, which is incommensurate with the impact her work has had on their lives. Born and raised in Kansas, she spent a year in Rome as a college student and fell in love with the country; she counted Italian as one of the four languages that she spoke. As a professor at the University of Colorado and then at the University of California San Diego, she collaborated with Italian child-language researchers, spending enough time in Italy that Julia, born in 1983, could learn some Italian. Over her career, Bates would impress people with her brilliant, relentless energy. "You always knew when she was in the room," said Virginia Marchman, a child-language researcher at Stanford University who collaborated with Bates. "If there were a nuclear holocaust and the world was destroyed," remembered a former postdoc, Barbara O'Connell, "Liz would claw her way through the rubble to her computer terminal so she could keep writing."

By the time Julia arrived, Bates had already embarked on scaling up the scientific study of early words by returning to the oldest method for collecting them. For her PhD research, she had pioneered the use of parent reports, including interviews with mothers; the word-like thing was important to capture, but so was information about the interaction where it arose.

"The thing about parents is their breadth of exposure. They see the kid when they're happy, when they're in the bathtub, in the car," said

Marchman. "So what parents might miss or lack in expertise, they make up for with breadth—they see and hear things that no researcher can."

One of the first discoveries was that children in this stage were unlike one another to a tremendous degree. They learned to understand and produce words at vastly different rates, and also different sorts of words. That is, some kids tended to learn lots of names for objects, which made for a noun-heavy vocabulary. Meanwhile, others tended to learn whole phrases ("come here") and words for managing social interactions. The first group, dubbed "referentials," tended to be firstborns (like Julia) and also males (at least in the early studies), while the second, the "expressives," tended to be born later. Researchers also noticed that some children imitated more than others. Some kids labeled things, while others engaged in long stretches of meaningless talk with the rhythms of adult sentences. Clearly the referentials, the word babies, learned other parts of language more quickly, while those intonation babies learned a bit more slowly. The question was, how did these patterns play out in the whole population of language-learning kids? And above all, what was *normal*?

§

The work on what would become the MacArthur-Bates Communicative Development Inventory, or the CDI, started with a phone call in 1982. Larry Fenson, a professor of psychology at San Diego State University, took a call from a colleague who told him that the MacArthur Foundation was soliciting proposals for studies on children between two and five years old. Did Fenson have any ideas for research projects? When he got off the phone, he called Bates.

She was quiet for six or seven seconds. Which was striking, Fenson said, because Bates was almost never quiet. Then they met and put together a two-page proposal for studying child language from infancy to toddlerhood. That became a longer proposal to the MacArthur Foundation, ultimately accepted. They called themselves the San Diego group. (Another MacArthur-funded project was MacWhinney and Snow's CHILDES database.) Eventually, using some preliminary work from Bates, the San Diego group hit on what the CDI became famous for: establishing norms of language development in children one to three years old, sampling pockets of the linguistic knowledge that young children might have. Up to that point, the topic had been treated too vaguely for doctors, teachers, and parents to make clear determinations about individual children's developmental progress. The method that the San Diego group proposed was a back-to-the-future mode: instead of getting kids into labs to play, setting up experiments, or using standardized tests, they proposed that the kids should be observed at home, where they felt most comfortable. Bates suggested just asking parents what's going on. Until then, most language scientists had worked mainly in labs. Controlled conditions, trained observers. "We were skeptical of how well parents could report," Fenson said.

To deal with potential objections, Bates had developed some guidelines. "Yes, we know parents are knowledgeable," Marchman, who became part of the research team, remembered. "But we could ask them in the wrong way. So let's not make them look bad, let's make them be good reporters."

This meant that parents should only be asked about what their kids did now as opposed to recollections, and they should be asked to focus on skills that were just showing up, "with enough frequency to be noticed but still within the limits of a casual albeit intimate observer," as Bates wrote in a 1988 book. Importantly, the parents wouldn't get open-ended questions, like "What words does your child know?"—this would produce only biased answers. (Nearly all studies of things people say at the end of life rely on such a methodology.) Instead, parents would get a checklist of words that sampled what American children might say (which is exactly the way to do it at the end of life—I have been developing just such a thing). Later versions of the checklist were adapted for people living elsewhere and learning other languages, but the earliest one was seeded by Julia's earliest English words. Eventually the team developed a form with checklists of words and gesture types. The idea was that parents would mark what they thought children could understand, and what the child could understand and produce on their own.

§

You may not have heard of the CDI, but if you have a child, it's undoubtedly touched your life. Since it became widely available around 1990, the CDI has become a crucial tool for teachers, clinicians, and researchers for determining whether a child's linguistic development is on track. It's been adapted for several varieties of English and Spanish, Hindi, American and British Sign Languages, and nearly one hundred other languages, from Arabic to Yiddish. (As a joke, the list of adaptations includes Klingon.)

At the center of the CDI is a checklist (one version has around four hundred words; another has about seven hundred) of nouns, verbs, adjectives, and pronouns that parents check off if children say or understand them. Parents also note how their children use gestures, parts of words, and grammar. The CDI asks, *Does your child tend to say "doggie table" or "doggie on table"? Does your child say "blockses"?* This allowed researchers to capture the full range of first-ish vocabularies, how they grow, and how they link to other language abilities, such as syntax.

"The prevailing view at the time was that vocabulary development wasn't interesting," Marchman said. At the time, linguists were focused on detailing grammatical universals, and not on how individuals differed, though small-scale studies suggested they would. An early CDI study with two thousand eighteen-month-olds showed that "normal" vocabularies had an enormous range, from fifty to six hundred words. It also showed that the average number of words that a twelve-month-old could produce is fifty, with a range from zero to 140. Everyone knew there was variability, but that much "was big news," Marchman said.

In 2016, Michael Frank, a Stanford professor, approached Marchman in the hallway. "I've got a bunch of CDIs in my filing cabinet, and I bet others do too," he said. "Wouldn't it be great if we could build tools for people to access all that information?" The result is Wordbank, which is the next step from Bates's advance. It now consists of over 94,000 CDI reports in thirty-eight languages. An initial analysis of Wordbank data was published online in 2019, and a book by MIT Press came out in 2021.

If the CDI showed how variable children's early vocabularies are, Wordbank revealed remarkable consistencies across that variability in multiple languages. Most strikingly, infants talk about more or less the same things, no matter what languages they learn. Across fifteen languages, they prefer to say and understand words about sounds, games and social routines, body parts, and important people in their surroundings. Words learned early in one language tend to be learned early in other languages as well. In American English, the most frequent first ten words were "mommy," "daddy," "ball," "bye," "hi," "no," "dog," "baby," "woof woof," and "banana." Seven of these words—"mommy," "daddy," "ball," "bye," "no," "baby," and "woof woof"—are frequent in other languages as well. In Hebrew, the earliest ten words are the equivalents of "mommy," "yum yum," "grandma," "vroom," "grandpa," "daddy," "banana," "this," "bye," and "car," and in Kiswahili, it's "mommy," "daddy," "car," "cat," "meow," "motorcycle," "baby," "bug," "banana," and "baa baa." One conclusion is that no matter what languages they use, children tend to understand and produce the same sorts of words. Why?

Such words rank high in a trait called "babiness," which simply means they're words that have to do with babies, their immediate surroundings, and important concrete things. Clearly babies encounter a lot of bananas! These are also words that babies hear frequently (though not all—"mommy" and "daddy" are in all first-ten-word lists in fifteen languages, even though they're not heard all that often). And they also reflect the concreteness of the thing the word refers to—"ball" will be learned before "idea." They're also brief—the number of sounds in a word predicts how early it's said, but not how early it's understood.

Another reason for their similarity: interactions with parents and care-givers are important to babies. It turns out that we don't learn words for purely utilitarian reasons, such as to get fed; we learn words, even about food, to interact. "Kids want to share things, they want to be part of the social mix," Frank said. "Hi" is the first word for a lot of kids (and in American English, more frequently first for girls than for boys). "No" as a refusal is also a frequent first word. In an earlier study, Frank found that "no" was often a first word for later-born kids.

Obviously, another big reason is the checklist itself. It comes with assumptions about what babies will say; since Bates had to start somewhere, she drew partly from Julia's first words.

Even with the checklist, though, Wordbank results display different cultural norms and parenting practices. For example, sounds (like "vroom"), body part names, and words for games and routines are unusually frequent from English-speaking babies, while Kiswahili- and Kigiriama-speaking babies produce many words for places to go and words about the outside. (Frank suggested this reflects how CDIs are tailored for where kids live—urban, rural, or semirural.) However, some patterns are difficult to account for. Take the high proportion of words for vehicles, clothing, and animals learned by infants who are learning northern European languages as well as Korean. What explains that?

Across languages, Wordbank also reveals curious demographic differences. In twenty-five of twenty-six languages, girls produce more words than boys, particularly in Australian English, Croatian, German, and Czech, while in sixteen of twenty-two languages, girls understand more words than boys, an effect that's notably stronger for Korean, Latvian, and Hebrew. There are also gender-related differences in the kinds of words. Across languages, boys and girls know sex-appropriate words for genitals, while more boys know words for vehicles and sports than girls do, and more girls than boys know words for stereotypically female clothing and toys.

It also appears that one-year-olds in most languages tend to say and understand more nouns than verbs and many fewer function words (like "the" and "and") than either, even though function words are far more frequently heard. Two exceptions are Mandarin and Cantonese, where children say more verbs, probably because those languages allow you to use a lone verb ("run") to stand for clauses that in other languages require nouns as subjects or objects ("he runs").

Almost as striking as these regularities is how much individual kids varied, even those learning the same language, in the same cultural frame. No one child anywhere is exactly the same as any other. This makes the first words a fairly poor way to establish the child in their uniqueness. To put it another way, if you're opening the black box of one baby's mind, you're opening them all. "It is very clear," Frank and Marchman write, "that variability is the norm!" (That exclamation mark is theirs.) Over time, however, children do become more like each other, in the grammatical structures they possess and the number of words they know. Yet for a short period in the earliest months, they're idiosyncratic. This suggests that no culture, no family structure, no social environment has some special sauce for turning out language learners of a single type or trajectory. Everywhere, kids are "taking different routes to language," as Frank puts it.

The father of two children himself, Frank finds this variability liberating. "We obsess as parents about small decisions in parenting as though they were immensely consequential, but it turns out that the effect size of any single parenting decision, in the context of a stable family life, is quite low."

§

Liz Bates would have loved Wordbank, Marchman said. It's open source, and she always wanted to publish it for free. "She had a communistic streak," Fenson said. "I wish she could see what we're doing. She'd probably come up with things we haven't thought of yet." At the age of fifty-two,

Bates developed pancreatic cancer and died four years later, in 2004. Fenson visited her at home the day before she died and held her hand. "I'm sorry," Bates said.

As powerful as the CDI is, its design reflects the scientific battles it had to pick. To improve the reliability of parent reports, it uses the checklist, not a free-form list. To some contemporary critics, this seems to bias the list in racial, linguistic, and socioeconomic terms. Linguist Megan Figueroa looked at the words on the CDI checklist and knew that she rarely encountered them. "I would have done quite poorly as a child on this," she said. (Her first word was "button.") "But I knew 'union' very early because I was a union kid. I knew 'scab'—did you?" Surely "beans" and "tortilla" were early words, she said, but these aren't on the list. "They say the CDI is standardized, but who is it standardized on?" (Technically, it's not standardized, it's "norm-referenced.") Though the list has hundreds of words, it seems to promote the idea that some first words are "right" while others aren't, and that having an ample number of "right" words is key to school readiness and other future activities.

Figueroa's concern about bias is a reasonable one, said Frank. "Because of that, we've done extensive work to address it." Which words in the CDI lists were biased by the family's race, the mother's educational level, and the child's gender? Frank knows exactly which ones. A couple of queries to the Wordbank database turned up fifty-nine words on the CDI with "extreme bias"—twenty-two on the gender dimension (all but one of which were nouns, many of which are stereotypically associated with one gender over another, such as "fireman"), twenty-seven on the mother's education dimension, and twenty-one for race (only eight were easier for non-white children). Interestingly, white children with highly educated mothers knew more animal names and animal sounds; children with less-well-educated mothers knew "candy," "soda/pop," "and "gum" before others. You might notice that the instances of bias don't sum to fifty-nine; that's because ten of the words ("tractor," "grrr," "quack quack," "uh-oh," "moo," "daddy," "walker," "gum," and "so") are biased in more than one dimension. One item—"vroom"—is biased along income, race, and gender lines; it's more likely for higher-income white boys to know and produce. If these fifty-nine "extreme bias" words are taken out of the analysis, the distinctions created by race and maternal education shrank slightly, while girls' advantage (they typically learn to say and understand more words earlier than boys) actually grew.

"Thanks to Wordbank," says Marchman, "we have the tools to understand our biases." They say there aren't plans to remove the words from the CDI lists themselves.

The checklist is also built to capture phonologically recognizable and semantically endowed words, but not protophones. As Frank and coauthors write in their book, "The CDI as an instrument is simply not the appropriate tool for asking every kind of question about child language development." One such question would be, When do early, idiosyncratic wordish things that do word-like work (at least for a child) emerge? Something like symbolic gesture like *sniff, sniff,* or my son's "ka" and "eh"? In retrospect, these performative protophones (as Kim Oller put them) were the most fascinating aspects of my oldest son's development, and I could see the long runway of his creative experimentation. "Round-round" simply marked when the plane lifted off. Here I should acknowledge another truth: by the time he said "round-round," we'd communicated so much in other ways, via smiles, eye gaze, waving, and pointing that his spoken words, when they actually arrived, felt somewhat superfluous. The person who needed the words was me, not him.

It's inescapable that before every first word is a protoword; before every protoword, a gesture; before a gesture, what? The desire to interact, I suppose.

When I interviewed Mike Frank via Skype, he was sitting on a light-colored couch in his home while, it turned out, his newborn son slept in a bassinet nearby. He was in the process of telling me how, before he had kids, he too focused on the discrete emergence of things like first words until he learned—then the baby squawked.

"Hey, dude," Frank cooed, "you okay there?"

The baby's protophone worked just as Kim Oller had posited: as a signal that the infant is alive and healthy.

So scientists may never probe the deepest questions about how early communicative efforts by humans might have left a mark on human genes. Do children who point earlier or have more protowords make up a distinct genetic profile? Are there genetic markers for these early, fuzzy first words? Perhaps even for the timing of performative protophones? Alas, genetic studies require enormous samples, so scientists often reach for CDI data, which provides language data at scale. One finding is that genetic variation partly explains how many words young children can produce. But because the CDI wasn't built to capture that fuzzy in-between territory where word-like things emerge, those inchoate protophones on the edge of semantics, the results have been inconclusive. And because the science has been provisioned in one way, this aspect of human becoming will likely remain a mystery.

6 Ritual, Sincerity, and the First Word

Early in the twenty-first century, a religion professor, an anthropologist, a psychiatrist, and an Asian studies scholar took a new look at a very old phenomenon: ritual. In their book *Ritual and Its Consequences: An Essay on the Limits of Sincerity*, Adam Seligman, Robert Weller, Michael Puett, and Bennett Simon argued that these aren't only religious activities; they're also civic, secular, even interpersonal and mundane. Saying "thank you" is as much a ritual as a graduation ceremony is. But this wasn't the heart of their redefinition.

Yes, a ritual is a more or less fixed sequence of actions or words that participants are taught to perform in a particular way. But why is ritual needed? To draw a line around fragmented, disordered social relationships and other phenomena. The result are "as if" universes, playful but temporary realms in which the world can be as it's hopefully imagined. Here's the heart of their reorientation: ritual doesn't reinforce order as much as it brings it into being.

What does this now-classic work of ritual theory have to do with first words? I'm proposing that first words are received with undeniable ritualistic elements, at least in societies that pay attention to such things. When you mark a first word, a number of things become possible. It's as if a child can now play by the linguistic rules, as if adults can interpret them perfectly, and as if linguistic meaning itself is uniformly stable and accessible. In this "as if" world, Trixie's Dilemma has been banished. All is *fari*.

A linguistic threshold doesn't preexist the ritual; the ritual calls the threshold into being. That's why linguists have been frustrated in their search for a sole first word, by babies or prehistoric humans—a discrete, concrete threshold proves very slippery. As far as first-word rituals go, people are required only to accept that they tame the seeming chaos of profuse protophones and babbling, the zigzagging acquisition of semantics, the words to no purpose, the coyote language.

Of course, even after the first word has been negotiated, a lot of zig-zagging gobbledygook and Protozoic muck remains. But designating a first word makes it seem as if the threshold has been crossed. If you have to apply the first-word label in retrospect, the boundary still holds. Thus, it's not a matter of "now we'll do the ritual," it's "we find that we've already done the ritual, we're living in the world it created."

Such "as if" qualities appear strongest in the case of cultural first words, like "mama" (in some spoken languages) and "milk" (in some signed ones), as I described in chapters 1 and 4. In the world that the cultural first word creates (and in the communities that don't care about early language users), all children possess the same sort of membership in their community. And fittingly, because rituals must be repeated, the world continually remade, children past and present will be seen as inevitable sources of such words. However, people get tangled in their cultural models, which leads some lin-guists and anthropologists to go too far in making evolutionary arguments for "mama" as primordial.

By the same token, there's much less "as if" world-making invoked in the *laissez parler* and observational styles, as I described in chapters 2, 4, and 5. So little, in fact, that these modes stand within an alternate framing of human activity. The four authors of *Ritual and Its Consequences* called it the "sincere."

Sincerity is a prominent feature of modernity that encompasses a "total-istic, unambiguous vision of reality 'as it *really* is.'" This "as is" perspective looks upon ritual as hollow and robotic, ultimately a form of magical think-ing, and thus an offense to objective ways of knowing. Note that just as ritual isn't specifically religious, the sincere isn't necessarily secular—many religious reform movements, including Protestantism itself, are rooted in sincerity. But the sincere "as is" has, over several centuries, squeezed out the ritualistic "as if."

Let me bring this back to first words. The last two hundred years or so has witnessed the rise of the sincere first word, as a function of a desire and a hope. The desire was to uncover what children actually do; the hope was for each child to have a unique first thing to express, as a beam of light shines down the obscure tunnel of their becoming. Much as the ritual first word is a form, the sincere first word is a content. In fact, it often follow no predetermined template of form, only one shaped by the person who produces it. In the case of "round-round," it wasn't difficult to perceive that my family was sailing into new linguistic waters. But the truth is that sincerity would have allowed me to set it with any linguistic moment I wanted. And it only occurs *once* in all of time—only my toddler said "round-round," not yours.

One powerful reason for the emergence of the sincere first word is that the sincere dominates so much of modernity, starting with the modern liberal order, in which the individual expressive self is the basic unit of society. It's not surprising that the sincere's antipathy for the ritualistic has filtered into parenting practices too. This expressive self also mattered in Protestant communities, where believers looked inward for the divine, then professed what they found—unlike Catholics, who all performed the same confessions of faith. An individual's ability to make their own professions of faith was prized, so an early first word might have been treated as an auspicious sign of future sincerity. I see this conflict reflected in my own baby book, prepared by a Catholic nun, which had a space for my first prayer—not my first spontaneous words. How this all works in other worldviews I hope to continue to learn.

Another current of sincerity comes to the fore in the history of ego-documents. As I discussed, historians have argued that people began producing journals, diaries, and autobiographies in larger numbers in Europe during a period of political upheavals and other profound changes in the social order. The impetus seemed to be anxieties about one's individual place in the passage of social time in the public sphere. One form that this anxiety took was a fascination with one's own childhood. I find it easy to imagine that nostalgic adults, after making the usual country-to-city migration, returned to their home village and looked up the local school, the fishing spot on the river, their parents' home with its nursery, and other relics of childhood. All this might have stimulated them to wonder about how they began to talk or write, and they swore to notice their own children's first words, writing them down for the offspring's future enjoyment, perhaps in a family journal, perhaps in a commercial baby book. As an author wrote in the nineteenth-century parenting magazine *Babyhood*, "Probably no more acceptable or valuable present could be given a child who has just attained his majority than a little book containing a record of his life from babyhood."

As *Ritual and Its Consequences* points out, ritual and sincerity are inevitably in tension with each other. They crop up now and again to resolve each other's perceived excesses; they're also tangled up together. For the matter of first words, the "as if" hasn't been eradicated completely—it lives quite comfortably alongside the sincere take. A great number of people still claim "mama" as a first word, for instance. Or they claim (for themselves or their children) two first words, "mama" and another singular utterance. Recall Sabina Spielrein's essay, in which her ritual take on the first word "mama" wrestled with her observations of children's utterances as they "really" are. She couldn't sustain it, though, and her desire for maternal magic won out in the end.

This is just as well, because no first word can be purely sincere—the signifying self that produces it can't authentically confirm it as a form, a meaning, or an intention. And then the observational style provides us with huge collections of first words (as in the case of Wordbank) whose insights betray the dichotomy in even newer ways. Yes, there's an enormous variability not only in what young children learn to produce but about what they produce, at what rate, and in what combination with other linguistic abilities. Though children are singular at these levels, at other levels they're alike, given that they share a path of development. Experts call this "normal," which is really another "as if" designation.

As I'll show next, numerous parallels can be drawn between first words and language at the end of life. As with first words, social, cultural, and biological mechanisms drive how people perceive last words and other communicative behaviors at the end of life, but we struggle to come to grips with those mechanisms and how they influence an individual person's signifying in extremis. There's a shift from the ritualistic to the sincere in expectations about last words, too—and not necessarily, I would argue, for the better.

Interlude: A Year at the MPI

One morning in the kitchenette of the research institute, you strike up an unexpected conversation while waiting for the electric kettle to heat. She's a researcher and has just given a presentation in the crowded meeting room downstairs about the genetics of Neanderthal brain shape. You were somehow taken by her finding that modern humans with less globular brains have fragments of Neanderthal DNA in their genomes, something you never expected to know about the world. Chatting further, you learn from her that 4 percent of humans have some form of synesthesia, which she also studies. None of this you anticipated when you awoke.

Beyond the sleek counter of the kitchenette, a wall of glass looks onto a lush pocket forest, many trees of which were saplings when the institute was founded forty years ago. Another researcher comes by for her cup of tea, one of the last she'll enjoy before heading to Rossel Island, in the Pacific Ocean. On her previous trip sailing from Papua New Guinea, she and her supervisor were threatened by actual pirates. In her luggage, she's packed a portable laboratory that will help her perform experiments aimed at revealing more about how the island's children learn their mother tongue, one of the more complex languages on the planet, called Yélî Dnye, which is spoken exclusively by the six thousand people on Rossel. It's unrelated to any other in the world, has sounds unknown in any other language, and possesses a rare grammatical property known as "syntactic ergativity." Her research may someday show that language learning doesn't proceed as universally as we've thought.

Later in the week, you might wander into a seminar about vocal learning and FOXP2 gene expression in 1,400 bat species. You might attend an inaugural reception for a high-tech lab for linguistic experiments with bilingual children. Or you might close your office door and write. I did all these things and more at the Max Planck Institute for Psycholinguistics in Nijmegen, Netherlands, where I was writer in residence in 2017 and 2018.

Everyone there called it "the MPI," which is incorrect, strictly speaking, because the Max Planck Society operates over eighty such research centers, most of them in Germany. By reputation, this institute has been the home of cutting-edge language research for decades, while in lived experience, it's full of treats, both intellectual and otherwise. Unlike other places where I've worked, it has a cozy canteen, whose pot of soup infuses the lobby with a delicious domestic scent, one that is incongruous in an aggressively modern steel-and-glass building with high-angled staircases and abstract art on the walls, soundproof labs in the basement, and brain organoids growing in a wet lab on the third floor.

Some of this activity goes into articles that can be read anywhere, but spending time at the MPI makes its researchers' stunning range of intellectual enthusiasms immediate and concrete. Language as neural oscillations. How individuals vary in their language abilities, including early words. How the size of people's social networks affects how they learn language. The rhythmicity of seal barks. How reading changes cognition. The genetics of vocabulary acquisition. How brains process sentences. All are threads of an emerging story about how language-ready brains evolved, a story that language scientists at this MPI and elsewhere are weaving together.

That language is for interacting is obvious, but MPI researchers are also exploring how features of interaction have shaped brains, languages, and human evolution itself. Interaction isn't an epiphenomenon of language or a synonym for communication; rather, languages in all their diversity are themselves the products of long processes of humans doing things together with language, and vice versa. Moreover, interaction doesn't happen only in a single channel (speech, sign, or touch) but in multiple modalities that humans are able to coordinate. We humans do language with our bodies, not just our minds.

It may seem surprising that the language sciences haven't always been oriented toward interaction or how people use their whole bodies. Why study language at all, if not to map its potential for connecting people? In the linguistics graduate program that I attended in the mid-1990s, the classes, seminars, and random hallway chats were deeply rooted in Chomskyan views on the structure of language, and particularly which structural elements might be innate, therefore preceding any individual's life span or their experiences in it. The brains that made and received such signals were considered in passing, the social uses and cultural contexts of language barely acknowledged. Communication was a fortuitous by-product of language, which had been designed for something else, perhaps for thinking, perhaps for no practical purpose, probably arriving (it was argued) in one fell swoop of a genetic mutation or two. This version of linguistics hewed to the distinctions that French philosopher René Descartes (1596–1650) made between mind and body, placing language in the mind. This meant that language learners and users had no physical presence in a material world. They were unencumbered by bodies, in all their difference and frailty. These models of language put speakers (always speakers, rarely signers) in the center of the stage, while listeners, receivers, and interlocutors waited in the wings for the spotlight of theory to warm them. I grew accustomed to hearing mockery of any language topic that couldn't be theorized within the Chomskyan framework of that decade.

That was then, in America. The contemporary language sciences, as they're pursued in Europe and at the MPI, are engaged in a more expansive, compelling perspective along these lines: the genetically coded brain is situated in a body, and that body in a dynamic social and material world, in relation to other bodies. Coordinating those bodies requires language (speech, sign, and gesture) as forms of action. The ranges of action and coordination, along with cognitive constraints, produced a tool kit for interaction. Each individual human organism receives that tool kit as a genetic endowment. You could study how items in that tool kit worked across animal species, within evolutionary lines of descent, and across the human life span. You could also see how those tool kits shaped, and are shaped by, languages. Is the tool kit for Yélî Dnye the same as for Hindi, German, or Yoruba? Once I settled in at the MPI, this wide-ranging language science, with an ambition to trace connections between the gene and the society across biological taxa and massive expanses of time, came as a life-changing revelation.

Over the last seventy years, when scientists have debated language acquisition, most of the time it's been about which aspects of language and cognition preexist the biological life of the individual human, mainly as innate mechanisms unique to the human species. At the MPI, that debate was being carried further: how did aspects of language preexist the biological

life of the individual because they were generated by gene-driven developmental processes that resembled those in other animals? Which aspects
of language and its precursors predate the evolutionary existence of *Homo
sapiens*, or any species of *Homo* at all? One candidate receiving intense scrutiny right now is turn-taking, the same back-and-forth that people do in
their conversations, and how participants mutually attune themselves to
what they need in that situation. Another one is vocal learning, which
refers to the need for young members of a species to learn their calls (songs,
if it's birds, or barks, if seals) from mature members. The evolutionary story
about language is one in which a set of layered innovations like turn-taking,
vocal learning, rhythmicity, and others accumulate across tens of millions
of years. Centrally and crucially are mutually reinforcing adaptations that
appeared over hundreds of thousands of years between languages, genes
(and through them, brains), and social interactions.

First words bear the traces of those processes, as I addressed in the first
part of this book. They emerge from interaction; they're multimodal; and
they reflect cultural decisions. It occurred to me that last words might bear
the same traces—in fact must bear them. While I was in Nijmegen, I wrote
and published several pieces of journalism and was free to follow my interests, and language at the end of life seemed ripe to explore, especially in
light of these new ideas about language. How do humans deploy their language abilities to care for the dying and the dead? How and why do the
dying express themselves?

All I knew about last words were the distillations of deathbed scenes cir-
culating in books and conversations. They were crafted to seem eloquent or
witty, even if apocryphal (Oscar Wilde's reported last words as he lay dying
in a shabby room in Paris, "either those curtains go or I do," though an
inevitably competing source offers "I am dying, as I have lived, beyond my
means"). The view seemed to be that people's language begins with their
first word, which they don't remember, and ends with their last, which they
presumably can't remember either—forming a certain linguistic corpus. But
do they close the loop reciting jokes or moralisms? That can't *literally* be
what happens, can it? In a lingering death, people would moan or speak
gibberish. How much fresh, spontaneous talking goes on, and at what point
does it stop? What other expressive behavior accompanies this decline, and
can you account for its inevitable disintegration in the same ways? This
made me wonder about the medicalization of dying, and especially the rise

of sedation, and its impact on the culture of last words. Might one expect fewer last words in the future than in the past?

I asked researchers at the institute about this, but although I was pointed to work on consciousness under anesthesia and classic sociological studies of dying, nobody knew of any research on language and dying per se. I gave a talk full of questions, futilely hoping to attract answers. Then I searched for information in published sources, abstracts, theses. I searched PubMed, the world's largest database of research in the life sciences. I made requests to the MPI librarians, who had shown superhuman competence at retrieving obscure texts. But the results were all the same: the end of life was invisible to scientists descended from intellectuals who sought Adam's first word.

When this interest formed in my mind, I had about as much experience at the deathbed as any nonmedical civilian living in an industrialized country. Which is to say, not much. My parents were alive. I'd been at the deathbed of one grandparent. I'd had no other experiences to dispel that outdated model of communication in which the language producer was a sort of signal emitter like a TV set, and in which a last word is simply the thing that's playing right before the machine gets unplugged.

But the expanded world of the language sciences that I encountered in Nijmegen offered exciting new prospects. If language is something that people do with their whole bodies, then language doesn't end with the last phrase or vocabulary item, which means the person doesn't either, if we grant that the use of language can be one mark of personhood. The person persists beyond the point where verbal behavior ends. That means, among other things, that the entire existential drama around last words has been misplaced—it exists, even more intensely, in correspondingly more subtle expressive behaviors. The question is, Does the society that surrounds us make room for that?

For another thing, the lastness of the word wasn't in the utterance. It didn't exist in the signal. What you find, in most cases—excluding the death of infants or of those with severely impaired language capacities—is that the last word is a scene or a social practice, an activity that people do together, and an activity that we're linguistically prepared for, as lifelong users. If you're dying, you might be flummoxed by brain failure; your fading consciousness might witness the breakdown of your language system that's been so reliably there. And if you're surviving, you may extend a pragmatic generosity toward the dying person's language, one that would allow them to go out on a note of making sense. It's very hard to not frame things so that they *matter*.

I found it possible to transpose Catherine Snow's quote about first words into the key of dying, making it as illuminating as her original: "The *last* word is a reflection of the culture's decisions about many matters—the status of *dying person* versus *the survivor*, the attribution of intentionality, language socialization beliefs and practices, and beliefs about the social and communicative capacities of *dying people*, as well as theories of language and of meaning."

This flexibility made me love that quote even more.

§

Thinking about last words as a reflection of a culture's decisions, as bound in an interaction, all at a certain biological limit, has fascinating implications.

It puts the authenticity of last words in new light. When we're told an anecdote about famous last words, we're used to asking if that really happened. Did Oscar Wilde really quip about the curtains? Or were the reports, for whatever reason, made up? A healthy suspicion about the supposed last words of famous people is warranted, given the motives for sharpening them as they're transmitted. But perhaps that suspicion could also be informed with a sense of the linguistically possible. A linguist may have good reason to doubt that "succotash" or "flamingo" could be a baby's first word, and perhaps you could inform your suspicion of last words on the basis of what a dying person's linguistic abilities are likely to be.

It gets us reconsidering accounts of famous deaths. Take the death of the German poet Johann Wolfgang von Goethe. Traditionally, his last words were said to be *"mehr licht,"* or "more light," and rather famously, too, because even people who know nothing else about Goethe will be happy to quote *"mehr licht"* at you. A sizable subfield of Goethe studies exists to referee competing claims about other candidate last words, such as "Open the shutter in the bedroom so that more light can come in" and "You didn't put sugar in the wine, did you?," none of which are versions that people quote at you.

These debates about veracity overlook that Goethe apparently had more to express—just not in words. George Henry Lewes, in his 1855 biography, *Life of Goethe*, describes how Goethe, even after saying something about light or sugar, "continued to express himself by signs, drawing letters with his forefinger in the air while he had strength; and finally, as life ebbed, drawing figures slowly on the shawl which covered his legs." In that era (and even up to the present day), the spoken last word was privileged, and so "*mehr licht*" became enshrined as (one of) his last phrases.

But what was Goethe doing with his hands? Expressing something, maybe himself—but about what? These tracings in the air have been rendered invisible, even meaningless. His last attempts at signifying, if that's what he was doing, have been muted by his own last words. To whom, if anyone, and about what, if anything, was he gesturing?

It highlights how people make meaning and how they connect with each other. Language doesn't end with last words for its witnesses; neither does connection or meaning. A friend of mine described sitting with his dying grandmother. He spoke her name, her eyes opened, she looked at him, then she expired. That plain description omits that moment of mimicry, when he paused in the story and widened his eyes just as she had.

Someone else told me that he'd accompanied his mother to hospice, explaining to her where she was, who he was, who else was present, even though she wasn't responsive. He swore he saw the muscles in her face relax. I was moved by his tremendous sensitivity to her potential disorientation, and also by his attention to her response. She never spoke again, but he felt as if he'd received her message.

What should be done with this glance, this moan, this flicker of a cheek? How do we keep from being mesmerized by the words, and our need for them, instead of the whole scenario of signifyings? Can satisfying stories be told about articulations of consciousness that take different forms? You can't transcribe a silence. I think of Goethe's plucking hands. I think of the observation by a Victorian-era physician that "sometimes, immediately preceding the very act of death, the eyelids are raised, and a look of recognition of those around seem to be permitted to the dying man." (The author assures us that this is a physiological response, not an emotional expression as such.) These moments are fascinating not only to the Victorians, who punctuated their huge novels with such scenes, but to us, too, for the way these subtle interpersonal textures and their emotional impacts are so frail, pass by so quickly, and seem to leave no more trace than the faintly enlarged eyes of my friend's grandmother. A look, a change in muscle tone, a gesture, overwritten by the monumentalism of wordness.

I know someone who needlepoints last words as a hobby: "Put that bloody cigarette out" (H. H. Munro), "Is it really meningitis?" (Louisa May Alcott), and "What's that? Do I look strange?" (Robert Louis Stevenson). Could you needlepoint a final glance of the eyes?

It offers new insight into deathbed practices from other cultures. People are socialized to behave the way they do, and the dying person who produces some language or interacts hasn't escaped those norms. Nor are the people who keep vigil with or care for them. However, not every culture prizes expressions of individual consciousness at the end. In some cultures, there's a ritual in which you're supposed to make a specific, prescribed utterance when you die—sometimes at the moment of expiration—in order to smooth the way to the desired afterlife. Some of the power of this utterance comes from its timelessness. Presumably these have always been last words, and always will be. So what happens when people are too weak to produce what's ritually required?

§

Along the way to seeking more answers, I met Mira Menzfeld, a German anthropologist whose boundlessly sensitive ethnography of dying people in Germany and China—among other activities, she spent days in a hospital bed to experience things from flat on her back—introduced me to a global perspective and a new set of terms. We met in a café in Cologne, where she told me that most of the dying people she encountered were silent. A friend of my wife's, an end-of-life doula, said the same thing.

This presented a challenge: how to square this with the work of Lisa Smartt, an American woman whose book about last words, *Words at the Threshold*, made dying seem relentlessly talk-oriented? I interviewed Smartt and found her alert to the possibilities of collecting utterances and looking for patterns of grammar and meaning. But I had trouble aligning her approach to death and what comes next with my reconfigured view of language. (There is more about her work in chapter 7.)

I knew I wanted to approach things in a different way. At a conference on the political lives of dead bodies, to which I'd contributed an essay about finding Toina Hanson's remains, I found myself at dinner next to medical historian Thomas Laqueur. His new (at the time) book, *The Work of the Dead*, was a wide-ranging account of attitudes about death, particularly the ideas and practices around mortal remains over several centuries in the United States and Europe.

Fate couldn't have provided a better dinner partner than Laqueur, an incisive thinker and a captivating storyteller. I explained that linguists and psychologists have produced so much knowledge on how babies and children learn to use language, it's easy for the average person to find out what happens. You don't even need to be around a child. But unless you've attended a lot of deathbeds (very rare today), there's no way to check your intuitions about what really happens. Perhaps there's an emancipatory or therapeutic side to understanding these dynamics, as there's a theme in the literature on bereavement that stresses the healing power of the exchange of last words. (It's more important, actually, than being present in the final moments.) One friend's father died in a car accident; another friend's mother died of Alzheimer's, her ability to produce language long gone. Maybe their experience of leave-taking was closer to the norm than they knew.

To go further, I needed data.

Laqueur had a suggestion. At the dawn of the twentieth century, a Canadian doctor had observed hundreds of deaths for a study of the dying process. Laqueur told me that the doctor's papers were cached in an archive in Montreal, including the data from that study. "I'm sure they have something about language in them," he said. He didn't need to convince me—I was already mentally planning my trip. "These files," he told me, "you should go see them, they may have something to tell you."

7 How Do We Really Communicate at the End of Our Lives?

How do people really communicate at the very end of their lives, in the last week to several days? That's the question I try to answer from here on out. As we'll see, the answer has several parts.

Consider what happened in America in the 1970s, when a social trend around dying called the "happy death" movement arose, a full story (which includes the ascendance of figures like Elisabeth Kübler-Ross) that I won't tell in favor of noting one of its linguistic ramifications. Among the tenets of this movement, as University of California, Los Angeles, sociologist Lyn Lofland noted in her classic study *The Craft of Dying*, was a focus on "expressivity." Dying people were being instructed to say things, in other words; last words didn't (and don't) happen in a cultural vacuum.

Wait, wait, you might be saying. *Let's stop with the history, let's have some last words, and lots of them! Why can't you just scoop some up, like Wordbank did for first words, and crunch the top five things that men and women say at the end of their lives in Japan, France, and Nigeria?*

Believe me, I'd love to be able to do that. But reliable databases of final utterances don't exist—despite all the corpses, there aren't any corpora. I'm not dodging the undeniable interest in last words by pointing this out, but it's important to first get a handle on how these matters reflect cultural decisions.

Yes, yes, that's all fine, but what about all those anthologies of famous last words? Well, they're much better reflections of cultural decisions than they are of linguistic facts. They aren't universal, dating only to the seventeenth century or so, at least in Christianity-based Europe. They're overwhelmingly focused on last words by men. More importantly, they're not transcriptions from the bedside. That hasn't kept people from using them as data anyway. One analysis from a 2016 compilation looked at 2,515 last words in English (or translated from other languages) and found that 30 percent predicted or foreshadowed death; 8 percent called attention to the dying act; 7 percent were expressions of feeling; and 6.6 percent mentioned a name. (The rest of the topics are predictable: expressions of love, proclaiming innocence, asking for mercy.)

An even older attempt (and perhaps the first) dates to the early twentieth century, when Arthur MacDonald, an American social psychologist who once called for "a systematic and scientific study of the dying hour," mined last-word anthologies in hopes of assessing people's "mental condition just before death." MacDonald's idea is by no means unique to him—the notion that last words divulge secrets about the experience of dying is quite engrained. To get at this, he divided people into nine occupational categories (statesmen, philosophers, poets, etc.). There was another category for women, who totaled seventy out of 794 entries—for some reason, he wouldn't include them in the occupational groups. MacDonald then coded their last words as sarcastic, jocose, contented, and so forth. He found that military men had the "relatively highest number of requests, directions or admonitions," while philosophers (which included mathematicians and educators) had the most "questions, answers and exclamations." The religious and royalty used the most words to express contentment, while the artists and scientists used the fewest.

Unless your goal is some sort of perverse entertainment, analyses like these produce useless results, because they lump together executed criminals, soldiers killed on the battlefield, and those dying of illness. They also mix offhand comments, prepared speeches, and woeful queries ("Is there anybody in the room?" asked John Abernathy [1764–1831]). They glory in the "lastness," whereas I want to revel in the "wordness." The underlying data are rife with bias, pulled from sources meant to confirm the most conventional of truths: great people (usually men) have great truths to articulate at the end, and, to a lesser extent, what an absurdity it is to die.

For another thing, the psychological and emotional valences of final utterances aren't easily mappable. Even if they were, you can't so readily analyze the moans, pointing, other nonverbals, and silences that are so clearly also relevant. Which is the final *final* articulation of consciousness that we should pay most attention to? And if you analyze the plethora of behaviors and chart their course toward death, the story would still be incomplete, because you must also explain what creates the conditions by which interacting with the dying and perceiving their last words is desirable—and achievable—in the first place. After all, dying people also bear these ideas themselves. So what did people think they were doing together, and what were they actually doing?

Recall the roots of Wordbank. That massive collection of first words reflected a societal interest in preparing children to participate as citizens and economic actors. By identifying the path of normal child development, educators and policymakers could determine what resources might be needed to turn the majority into productive citizens. Indeed, the previous two centuries of studying child development, from Rousseau onward, reflected similar civic priorities, with some philosophical questions, such as how humans differed from animals, sprinkled in. By contrast, there's no corresponding economic or political imperative, no compelling public interest, to collect language at the end of life at scale. That doesn't mean it shouldn't be done. But it might explain why it hasn't been done *yet*.

§

Like first words, there may be a diary tradition for last words, too, but it's remained resolutely private—and for good reasons. One striking example of a privately recorded sequence of final utterances comes from over a century ago, from Leoš Janáček (1854–1928), now regarded as one of the most famous Czech composers. His avant-garde compositions, including several operas, drew from Moravian folk music as well as human speech patterns, whose musicality so fascinated him that he painstakingly cast them into musical notation. Each one of these "speech melodies," as he called them, was meant to capture a person's unique expression of themselves in that place and time.

Observed musicologist Paul Christiansen: "[Janáček] claimed to be able to divine the emotions, motives, and moods of people based solely on their intonational patterns, irrespective of the specific words they spoke." Over his lifetime, Janáček created over four thousand notations of speech and other phenomena, such as birdcalls and train whistles.

Janáček and his inspirations are relevant here because he captured the speech melodies of the most intimate sort: the things that his daughter Olga uttered as she lay dying in 1903. Though she was twenty-one years old, his record was still a sort of child-language diary, in a grim yet deeply

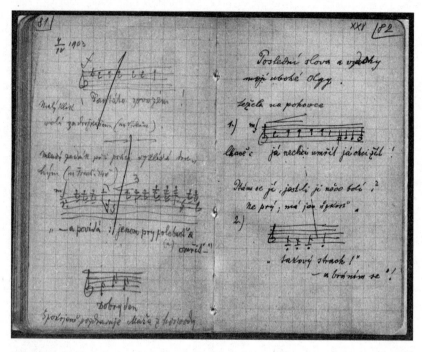

Figure 7.1
From Janáček's notebook. "The last words and sighs of my poor Olga lying on the
sofa." The notation on the top is the one for "I don't want to die, I want to live!" and
on the bottom "Such fear!" Reproduced with permission of the Moravian Culture
Museum.

moving form. "It may seem ghoulish to us that during his daughter's last
moments, Janáček was recording her last words and phrases and some of
the corresponding intonational contours," Christiansen noted. "But he
couldn't do otherwise." I checked an online database of his speech melodies; it doesn't appear that he recorded her first words.

As a young adult, Olga Janáčková had light, wavy hair and a wide, gentle
face. She'd fallen in love with a medical student, the son of her mother's
former piano teacher, and was sent to St. Petersburg to escape his threats
after she broke off relations. But she contracted typhoid and had to return
home, her fragile health further damaged. Her parents, Leoš and Zdenka,
were estranged, but they cared for her together. Olga was their only child—a
son, Vladimir, had died as a toddler thirteen years earlier—and the one
remaining bond between them. Through notating her utterances, Janáček

attempted to deal with his intense grief by preserving, with the aesthetic tools he'd mastered, what he could of her soul.

His notations can be found in the Janáček Archive of the Moravian Museum in Brno, with the title "The last words and sighs of my poor Olga lying on the sofa." Among the utterances he notated was, "I don't want to die, I want to live!" This is the most poignant, the one most likely to be called her "last words." But she also repeated, "I am dying, I am dying," until her speech became unintelligible. After receiving an injection (he noted her response as *"jejda,"* or *whew*), she regained some energy, saying, "That was some walk we took!" and "A person should have so much to say and then she speaks such nonsense." On February 25, Janáček notated her final sighs, *"a-ja,"* and finished the page with his own words, "God be with you, my darling."

Janáček's wife, Zdenka, recalled other utterances in her memoir (which suggests that she didn't use Janáček's notes for her reminiscence). On Wednesday, the day before Olga died, delirium began. When Leoš leaned over her, Olga said, "Daddy, it's so beautiful there, there are just angels there."

"And you're the most beautiful angel of them all."

"Just say that to them there, they'd laugh at you."

She was restless and said other things, like "It's already eleven, so I must go now" or "They still won't let me inside there." Olga's final utterances that Zdenka noted were single syllables: *"Kuk. Tak. Tak. Tak. Pryč, pryč."* Then a sigh or expression of pain. *"Jeje."* The editor who compiled a definitive version of Zdenka's memoir noted that *tak* means "so" and *pryč* is "away," and that *kuk* and *tak* might relate to Olga's obsession with a cuckoo clock. After sighing, she stopped talking and was unresponsive, dying the next day.

Christiansen noted that one might expect Janáček to have used these notations in a memorial composition, but there's no evidence of them in his choral and piano cantata "Elegy on the Death of Daughter Olga." His daughter's last words over those few days and his notations apparently were too intimate and private, even sacred, for any public piece of music. He could only manage to make a fair copy in a bound notebook (as in the photographs). It seems unimaginable that he would have discarded the pages with the original marks, given how close they were to those moments.

There was no single "last word," no poetic closure, no rainbows. Only a crumbling, a linguistic angling toward silent repose. Even if Olga saw

Figure 7.2
At the top of the left page, Olga said, "I just remembered that I am supposed to die," and below that her father notated, "I am dying, I am dying." He added: "She repeated this until it was incomprehensible." In the other notated utterances, she said (from the lower left across to the right), "A person should have so much to say and then she speaks such nonsense," "So I announce to you that I am feeling better now," "wait," and her final sighs. Reproduced with permission of the Moravian Culture Museum.

angels, the linguist has to reckon with the crumbling. Janáček had traced its trajectory, as well as the diversity of her utterances, through her delirium right down to the moans and sighs, with a poignant frankness. One wonders what comfort those pages gave the composer, revisiting them over the years, and if he ever played those notes on a musical instrument, and what he heard in them.

§

Let's pick up again in 1970s America, when "expressivity" in dying had become an important value. This was the notion that "whatever the emotions engendered by dying and death, they *should* be expressed" as talk from the dying person. Lyn Lofland stressed that expressivity "calls not simply for talk but for *talk about one's varying emotional states, which talk 'authentically' expresses those states.*" A happy dying presumably meant a talkative one, all along the journey as well as at the very end, punctuated with some last words.

At the time, hospice care was still an unfamiliar practice. The first hospice opened in 1957 in London, thanks to a medical social worker-turned-doctor named Cicely Saunders. She intended to serve the specific needs of the terminally ill: pain control, social and emotional support, spiritual perspectives. Her hospice movement spread to the United States in the 1970s, and one of its effects was to put nurses into more extended contact with the dying. After several years working in hospice, two nurses, Maggie Pflaum and Patricia Kelley, noticed what they called "a special type of communication" coming from patients. It was clear these strange and mysterious things had to *mean* something. "Jumbled and rambling as they may be, these final communications often hold important meaning for those who are leaving this world and those whom they've left behind," they wrote in a nursing journal in 1986.

During a lunch conversation with colleagues, Pflaum (whose last name changed to Callanan) and Kelley realized that they were having similar experiences. "Everyone had a different story about some patient's attempts to get across a point; on one particular day, these stories suddenly seemed to come into focus—linked to one another by patterns of speech or gesture." They collected two hundred cases, in which "someone had something to say," and analyzed them, turning the result into *Final Gifts*, a book published in 1992.

Could all this talking have been prompted by a new social value wrapped up with expressive happy deaths? Or was it the result of some new pain relief technique or another knock-on effect of modern ways of dying? Was it more a function of nurses' attention than communication by the dying? Such questions don't come up in the nearly universally positive reviews of the book by laypeople and professionals, who often recommend it as a guide to dying. Though it's thirty years old, it has tremendous staying power. As someone told me, it's not too sentimental, it's clear-eyed, and it's based on experience. Not everyone likes it, however—some find it too New Agey, and it distorts some of the realities of dying, particularly delirium, as we'll see. Yet it's not overtly religious, but rather denominationally beige, like a chapel in an airport, which also feels comforting. Perhaps its greatest appeal lies in how it's intensely relational, full of emotionally sensitive, poignant vignettes about people who are dying and how they communicate special messages—the final gifts of the title—to their loved ones.

I bring up *Final Gifts* because, in the story of what the dying person's linguistic powers are expected to be, it seems to signal a new (for its time) sort of attention to their language, especially this "symbolic language" that's unique to the dying process. "In the final hours, days, or weeks of life, dying people often make statements or gestures that seem to make no sense," Callanan and Kelley wrote. "It's time to get in line," a dying woman named Laura is quoted as saying.

The book instructs the reader how to respond. "Tell me more about the line," the author asks Laura. "Is there anybody there you know?" It turns out that Laura's friend Susan is in the line too.

These symbolic messages appeared not only in words but in smiles, reaches, and gestures, all of which needed to be recognized, weighed, interpreted, responded to, because they might be meaningful. This, too, was new. Callanan and Kelly urged family members to "pay attention to *everything* the dying person says." (Their emphasis, not mine.) "Remember that there may be important messages in *any* communication, however vague or garbled." What were the messages? Often they're expressions of feeling about dying or an aspect of a personal relationship that's holding someone back.

And so, just like an early-twentieth-century text on scientific motherhood encouraging mothers to take notes about their babies, *Final Gifts* counseled family members to have pens and paper handy to "jot notes about gestures, conversations, or anything out of the ordinary produced by the dying person." Nothing should be lost, in this invaluable resource for the future, especially as one grieved the loss of that singular person. When they were gone, would you scour your notes for some hidden truth they'd told you? As in the ego-documents of yore, such notes would anchor their existence in time.

Above all, they urged people to consider the importance, to the dying person, of delivering these messages. "When dying people aren't allowed to talk about what's happening to them, they become lonely, even amid loving, concerned people. They may feel isolated and abandoned, and in turn become resentful and angry."

The conventional wisdom about emotional expression has vacillated since those days; what I hear from practitioners now is that no one should be forced to talk about dying if they don't want to. As one observer put it, happy death groups risk "alienating the very people they so eagerly want to help through non-stop ultra-upbeat expressive death talking." This is an issue I'm going to step back from in order to pursue beliefs and practices about language at the end of life and how they square—if they can—with the actual behaviors and linguistic powers of the dying person.

I admire how *Final Gifts* moves away from words as the sole vehicles for interpersonal meaning. For so long, last words have almost dutifully been *words*. Otherwise, the book is linguistically rather sanded down, in the sense that everyone speaks, everyone speaks English, and a standard variety at that. It could be much more linguistically sincere. No one uses a signed language or is deaf or hard of hearing, and no one appears to have a preexisting communication impairment. No one is affected by neurological diseases, dementias, or scleroses. And nothing mediates their linguistic agency: no interpreters, no technologies, no divinities. Everyone makes sense.

All this makes for a paradox. On one hand, people have to authentically express themselves, in the logic of the book, in order to die well. On the other hand, certain linguistic and cognitive facts about a person—either ones they've lived with for a long time or which have recently cropped up—may limit their expressive abilities. How are we supposed to deal with that? Different traditions and societies have solved this in different ways; *Final Gifts* does it by offering the survivors an interpretive tool kit. You may have to watch a loved one stop making sense. You might have to see them go. You may not be able to control this loss of linguistic and cognitive powers. But you can control how you interpret it. You can frame things differently. You can make an "as if" world. People behave as if they're producing a message. As if they intend a certain meaning.

It's the gift, at the end, of control.

All of this is the proper place to start a discussion about last words. After all, losing control is a constant theme in people's fears. Something you might gain back by writing everything down.

§

Mort Felix, a California psychologist, had always believed that his name, read as two Latin words, meant "happy death." Over three weeks in 2012, he lay in his study at home and dwindled away, his seventy-seven-year-old body besieged by cancer and cradled by morphine. "Enough" was the last thing he told his wife, Susan. "Thank you, and I love you, and enough." The next morning, she discovered that Morton had died.

As he dwindled, he had talked. "There's so much so in sorrow," he said at one point. "Let me down from here," he said at another. "I've lost my modality." He told his secretary, "This is very interesting, Alice. I've never done this before." To the surprise of his family members, this lifelong atheist also began talking about angels and complaining about the crowded room—even though no one was there.

We know what Mort said because his daughter, Lisa Smartt, wrote it all down. She'd been a linguistics major at the University of California, Berkeley, and was an adult literacy teacher, so she knew the possibilities. In a photo from those days, she's seated next to her father, turned to her lap, intently writing with a pen on an unseen surface, while he lies back under a red blanket, eyes closed. After he died, she was left with pages of notes—what would she do with it all?

After unsuccessfully knocking on the doors of academics and hospices to help her make sense of her notes, she discovered *Final Gifts*. "It was very anecdotal, beautifully written and confirmed and built upon what I had wondered about in terms of metaphor and also the occurrence of visions of the predeceased," she wrote me. "However, the book did not focus on all the many other aspects of language that caught my attention in my dad's final days."

Eventually, after a seminar with death studies pioneer Raymond Moody (whose wildly popular book about near-death experiences, *Life after Life*, appeared in the death-focused decade of the 1970s—it's also cited in *Final Gifts*), she decided to write her own book, built around her notes as well as solicitations from other survivors to relate their memorable final words. It has since morphed into a website, The Final Words Project.

In her book, published in 2017, *Words at the Threshold*, she described how Mort's pronouns like "it" and "this" stopped clearly referring to anything. One time he said, "I want to pull these down to earth somehow . . . I really don't know . . . no more earth binding." What did "these" refer to? Also, she noticed that his prepositions hinted at how his sense of his body in space seemed to be shifting. "I got to go down there. I have to go down," he said, even though there was nothing below.

He repeated words and phrases, often ones that made no sense. "The green dimension! The green dimension!" (Repetition is common in the speech of people with dementia and those who are delirious.) Smartt found that repeated language often expressed some predictable themes, such as gratitude and resistance to death. But there were also unexpected themes like circles, numbers, and motion. "I've got to get off, get off! Off of this life. I'm dying. I'm dying," Morton had said. As in *Final Gifts*, nonsensical language can't be nonsense. It must have meaning. So it's reframed as the expression of a soul that's undergoing transition to another realm, a place where directionality is meaningless because bodies have been left behind. Notably, these expressions all occur in a stage, not a singular threshold moment—as with the science of first words, chasing the actual boundary-marking utterance proved too challenging.

During my year at the MPI, I interviewed Smartt and wrote about her project for *The Atlantic*. This article has been viewed online over a million times, and Smartt sold more books; both developments indicated that the public hungers for a more sincere take on language at the end. Afterward, I felt torn. On one hand, something had sparked in Smartt the desire to notice and record, a page seemingly taken from the child-language diary tradition in linguistics that had achieved so much, in a heartfelt project that kept her connected to her father, whom she clearly grieved. On the other, it seemed more in line with the anthology tradition, collecting extraordinary utterances, the emotionally memorable, as evidence of the "as if," rather than an "as is" mapping of what's typical. The ordinary language of ordinary dying. And if you're going to collect only the extraordinary, as *Final Gifts* recommended, how can you know how frequent the extraordinary is?

It seems cruel to dangle such a prospect in front of people. After all, rainbows don't happen every time it rains. We're glad to see them, but we don't plan our days according to the likelihood of rainbows. We know, for the most part, there's only rain. We need to know more about the rain.

This could be done by accounting for a range of other interesting linguistic conditions. What happens with someone who knows multiple languages, for example? What's the linguistic status of delirious language? What do the dying expect of themselves linguistically? These weren't just academic questions—the answers could be used to train care workers who don't share cultural backgrounds with their charges, among other practical uses, such as knowing when to begin scaffolding communication and with what sorts of tools and mindsets. I still had no idea how common these phenomena were, or when they occurred in the course of dying. Smartt's project, like *Final Gifts*, seemed to confirm the "as if" world that was needed for managing grief, rather than describing language, communication, and interaction at the end of life in a way that create more "as if" opportunities.

I couldn't stop admiring her for finding that *something* about language at the end of life was worth examining in closer detail. I just wanted that something to be about language, not beliefs about death.

§

Language is a function of the brain's cortex, that fragile sheath of woven neurons a few millimeters thick that covers the human brain. Neuroscientists now model it as activity across networks of neurons that crisscross that cortex, sometimes extending below it. Learning to use a language means developing those networks, whose structural integrity weakens when neurons are stressed, disconnected, or damaged. Injury can do that; so can aging.

And that's as far as language scientists can really take you; to go any further, you need neurological expertise from clinical situations. As someone approaches death due to an illness or medical condition, their resulting brain function fluctuates, decreasing steadily. One contemporary research team called it a "neurochemical commotion."

The metaphor of a collapsing house may be useful for illustrating the process. The structure doesn't come down all at once but in bits and pieces. Some parts may seem intact, but this actually reflects their isolation. After all, a door can swing in its frame even in a house with no roof. What remains will be foundational elements as well as automatic processes.

Which means there's a patchwork quality to this commotion—it doesn't affect entire language networks all at once. Imagine looking down at a city undergoing a power outage. At first, it affects random individual households, then blacks out whole neighborhoods. The neurochemical commotion means that a person might not find the right words as easily or keep their place in a conversation; they have a harder time staying on topic or remembering who they're talking with.

But its patchwork quality also means they might remain available for stretches, with some people but not others. Reliably, that commotion also produces delirium, in which grammaticality remains intact while the person loses touch with reality, and their access to the context that gives meaning to utterances collapses. Hallucinations intrude. People stop inter-acting in any way, then they lose consciousness. Though we know about near-death experiences (which are different from delirium), and though some people with delirium (say after surgery) can recover and tell us what it was like, the experience of the self spiraling downward to its final end is one we must imagine. The dead person isn't around to help us reconstruct it.

This fluctuating decline of the brain was explained to me by Daniel Kondziella, a critical care neurologist at Denmark's Rigshospitalet, the national hospital in Copenhagen, who researches the neurology of coma and death, especially in relation to near-death experiences. Some might find the bluntness of his biological and clinical account distressing. I hap-pen to find it refreshing. It provides a framework for understanding what happens (and what doesn't) and how we can plan accordingly, and it also opens the door for venturing "as if" understandings that also involve what happens with the body and the brain.

The brain is an organ, he explained, and organs fail. The sign of any organ failure is a trend toward deficient functions, and the brain is no dif-ferent. Decreasing cerebral function is a sign that neurons are failing. Why are they failing? Oftentimes because there's less oxygen in the tissues, as a result of a weakened heart, which can't pump the same volume of blood through the body. The result are metabolic changes. Less oxygen, less oxi-dation of glucose.

The first parts of the brain to suffer are the ones that consume the most energy, meaning neuronal cells in the cortex and hippocampal cells. This is why dying is associated with decreased mental capacity, and why one symptom of this decrease is the decline of language fluency. (Thus, those with the closest linguistic experiences to the dying aren't dreamers or drug users but high-altitude mountaineers running out of oxygen—more on this in a bit.) Communication impairment has been identified in over a quarter of hospice patients. In the rare instance that hospice patients are given tests of memory, verbal fluency, motor control, and sentence com-prehension, nearly all of them show problems, mainly in comprehending sentences—only two of the eleven patients in one study were anywhere close to normal. All are signs of a neurochemical commotion, as well as its patchwork quality.

Along the gradient of failure, cortical function goes first, Kondziella explained. No one has yet mapped how this failure proceeds precisely, but the human powers of authoring and animating utterances diminish on this gradient. This is perhaps why Goethe's ability to gesture with his hands outlived his ability to speak. Some other language patterns might be explained by the weakening of the left hemisphere's function before the right's, but this is speculation. One could say with more confidence that the pace of dying affects language considerably. Perhaps a rapid decline, one in which the brain fails catastrophically, is what enables the stereotypical last words. In that situation, the brain is otherwise healthy. However, the longer, slower declines that characterize contemporary dying might leave people incommunicado. But this is speculation and likely not so neat in reality.

At a certain point, the dying person is left with only their working limbic system. This is a group of brain structures that supports emotion, motivation, long-term memory, and learning, as well as behaviors essential to human survival, such as sexual arousal, emotional bonding, and panic. For everyday uses, the limbic system also connects to the cortex, but when a person is dying, a palliative care doctor told me, it works unchecked. Thus instinctive cries and moans, as well as their gestural analogues, might be expected to happen more. Here we come back to the evolutionary roots of language. As some have argued, cortical control of vocalization, especially of the larynx, was a critical turning point in the evolution of speech. Under normal conditions, the deeper brain structures, such as the basal ganglia and the brain stem, are more resilient in the face of lack of oxygen. But they must eventually fade too.

At the lowest point on the gradient of failure, people lose consciousness, you lose contact with them, all electrical activity in the brain ceases. Prior to the invention of machines to keep blood moving and supply oxygen, a person would be considered dead at this point. It was a unitary deadness, not a modular one. These days, the brain can die while cardiovascular function remains, which creates a space in which researchers like Kondziella can explore signs of consciousness in comatose and unresponsive patients. (It also creates cultural conflicts in hospital wards, where medical interpreters must explain alien concepts to grieving families from other places.)

When I visited Kondziella's team at the hospital, his PhD students explained how they employ a clinical protocol that involves giving tasks to comatose patients: move your eyes, squeeze my hand. They take measures of pupil dilation in unresponsive patients to whom they've given challenging math problems; someday, this might be a way to determine an existing degree of consciousness. One researcher found that some patients who aren't able to perform other tasks can still thrust their tongues. This makes sense, given that a relatively large portion of the brain is devoted to tongue control, so this may someday be another method.

After meeting in a conference room, we walked to lunch. I had told Kondziella and his students what I had planned for this book, so when one student asked this question, it wasn't unexpected. In fact, I was relieved that someone found it credible to ask. "What if," they said, "you could show that people lose their abilities to communicate at the end of their life in the same order they acquire them as babies?" *What if indeed.*

§

What is that neurological commotion most akin to? Perhaps the experiences of high-altitude mountaineers who are running out of oxygen. "The sky was nearer black than blue," begins phonetician Philip Lieberman's account of some of the more unusual linguistic research ever conducted. "At 24,000 feet on Mount Everest, Dr. Mike keyed his radio and began to speak. Far below at the Khumbu Glacier Base Kamp, I punched the record button of the digital tape recorder . . ."

Several times in the 1990s, Lieberman went to this base camp in the Himalayas to study the effects of high altitudes on climbers' cognition. (In addition to being a professor at Brown University, he was also a photographer, specializing in people living in Tibet.) His analysis of their speech showed indeed that they lost control of some aspects of pronunciation. They also had a harder time comprehending sentences, needing 50 percent more time to understand sentences that their children, back at sea level, wouldn't have been challenged by. Why? Lack of oxygen to their brain, or hypoxia, limited their cognition, including their language abilities. Lieberman claimed that these findings supported his theory about language in the brain—that motor control was linked to thinking—but he overlooked an opportunity to make another connection: as far as language goes, dying is a lot like living unsupported at very high altitudes.

One might wonder if a psychedelic trip also resembles dying. After all, disordered language reflects a disordered mental experience, and, a psychedelic trip, like the experience of dying, is inaccessible to others. The language of psychedelic experiences is disordered, too: people express more but have less diversity in their vocabulary, and they jump from topic to topic. One hypothesis says that psychedelics increase neural entropy in the brain. Picking up on this, Enzo Tagliazucchi, an Argentinian brain scientist, posits an "entropic tongue," in which the semantic coherence of speaking dissolves as people become unpredictably hyperassociative. However, that associativity seems to be its own thing. Psychedelic users report generating mantras that guide their trips, like "No way out but through" or "This is the era of radical abundance." These are semantically compressed semi-profundities that aren't high frequency in any language, and though they have some appeal as last words, they're opposite to the templated character of actual last words, as we'll see.

Hypnagogia, the imagery that happens near sleep, is also an appealing comparison, evoking a long-standing cultural trope in which death is compared to sleep, as in Hamlet's soliloquy: "to die, to sleep; to sleep: perchance to dream." Anecdotally, watching someone die is often compared to watching someone fall asleep. They drift in and out of awareness; at one moment they're available, at the next they're not. But like psychedelic experiences, falling asleep doesn't share any underlying physiological mechanisms with dying—otherwise we wouldn't wake up in the morning.

What causes the brain failure that Daniel Kondziella described earlier? Normal brains function thanks to what's called a neurovascular unit: a cooperative cluster of neurons, clusters of brain cells called astrocytes, and vascular cells. This unit produces neurovascular coupling: when neurons are activated, they draw more blood (and oxygen). But these neurovascular units can uncouple too. When cerebral blood flow goes down, neurons aren't able to activate, then they die. This leads to groups of neurons shutting down because they can't maintain the necessary balance of electrical charge. This electrical destabilization can spread, and it eventually takes over the whole brain. The effect of lowered blood flow to the brain is hypoxia.

Which is exactly the phenomenon that Philip Lieberman climbed Mount Everest to study.

§

Not everyone who dies is old, but for those who are, one must account for the effects of normal aging on their linguistic powers. Statements, expressions, and politenesses that that people frequently produce aren't affected as much, and words and their meaning are easily recognized. But people have a hard time producing and comprehending complex sentences. So does their ability to retrieve words, most notably if they are less educated. For those who hear, reducing hearing acuity impacts their abilities as well. In other words, language degenerates at many levels before someone dies, even decades before they're diagnosed with dementia or have a stroke.

In other cultures, this decline is received, and conceived of, very differently than in industrialized societies. To take one example: among the Lihirians of Papua New Guinea, it is thought that an aging person gradually resumes characteristics they had as a small child, then as a baby. They lose their mobility as they become unable to walk, and their cognitive abilities decline, sometimes to the point of eliminating speech. In the local language, such people are referred to as *zik mandion*, which literally means "unripe" or "not yet ready child," and the process of aging is *zik mandion miel*, "to go back to being an unripe child." To paraphrase extravagantly, they conceive of the life span as a cycle of unripeness and ripeness.

By contrast, anthropologist Maurice Bloch describes how, among the Zafimaniry people of eastern Madagascar, no one is surprised how older people speak: more quietly, and also "using formalised and fixed language which is highly decorated and full of quotations and proverbs." In this stage of life, people merge with their actual wooden dwellings, which contain the ancestors. They become drier and harder, when they would have started out as "soft and bendy" children. Here, the life span is a linear process of becoming more solid.

Ripening or solidifying, this is one of the trajectories that intersect with the end of life, bringing changes associated with neurological disease, cancer, or even normal aging. Conceivably, it proceeds on a steady course, even if someone isn't dying, where it will inevitably affect a person's linguistic repertoire. We all have this waiting for us—distressingly, our brains begin to degenerate decades before any changes become apparent. If we're lucky, those changes are gradual enough that they have the lightest of impacts on our daily lives. We may even die without noticing them much. However, in some diseases, the slope of change is so severe, as in the case of advanced dementias or stroke, that people will be entirely nonverbal by the end—though perhaps not silent, if they are moaning or crying out.

The second trajectory involves changes associated specifically with the dying process—the effects of hypoxia, medications, and even aspects of the environment, such as the presence of familiar communication partners or noise.

Then there's a third trajectory, in which the first two combine to influence each other, which hastens the decline.

This means that any question about declining abilities should be answered in terms of how the three interact. This is a matter for further research that would try to synthesize these factors, which are often allotted to different fields of study in a way that obscures their relationships. One thing is certain: as death approaches, the frequency and likelihood of verbal communication declines, and the ability to interact crumbles.

§

If these ideas and considerations seem to tie me to biomedical models of causes and effects, I can untie myself and go a bit further. The brain is in a body, which is in relation to other bodies, orienting to each other not only with what's heard but with what's seen. This seems obvious, but you'd be surprised how little this is accounted for. This body houses a self, which by necessity is in relation to other selves, and the drive to interact with those selves is foundational for language, as I learned at the MPI.

People do this through what might be called an interaction window. Words, signs, gestures, and facial expressions flow through it, part and parcel of the ongoing human project to coordinate actions, communicate information, and connect emotionally with others. The metaphorical window has a size, which determines what flows through. It also has a resilience—how, for instance, do people fix things if they don't understand each other in a manner appropriate to their culture?

This window also determines the timing and coordination of interactions, as people have to predict quite rapidly (on the order of several hundred milliseconds) when it's their turn in the conversation and what they'll do. Some of these constraints come from the brain's ability to process information; some come from culture. In our everyday lives, it doesn't matter which is which, because we use the window so automatically.

Babies are innately drawn to experiences through this interaction window, via an enduring, seemingly innate instinct for interaction that humans possess (though not uniquely). They immediately search out faces and quickly develop the ability to mimic. Eventually they become communicatively competent, which is one way to say that they acquire the know-how to engage through the interaction window with many different people. At the end of life, it's hard to tell if the self is receding from an open window or if the window is collapsing. The deaths that Kondziella's students deal with—from illness, the worsening of chronic conditions, and other forms of organic failure—are characterized by the radical diminishment of this window.

This interaction window concept was introduced to me by Kathryn Mannix, a British palliative care doctor who draws from decades of clinical experience to write books and advocate for open discussions about death and dying in society. She focuses on the importance of understanding "ordinary dying," which is the physical process of the body slowing down and the management of those symptoms. In other words, dying isn't an extraordinary medical event but something more social, emotional, and even spiritual. Her term was actually a "conversation window," but I've modified it to make room for the signifying that people do with their bodies.

She described the window at about a week to three days before death like this: "As people are gradually losing consciousness, there's a period during which they're swinging between awake enough and not awake enough to communicate, and the communication itself becomes progressively more simple in that eventually it isn't even words anymore. It's the squeezing of a hand, or it's the moving of an eyebrow, and you see families saying, 'I don't think he's really awake anymore, is he?' And then you see the eyebrows going. Okay, so they're not awake, but they're listening."

I wanted to know more about the timing of this decline, and how it affects a range of people. Unfortunately, only a few studies have looked at it, and their results are mostly too vague. Until there's a CDI-like instrument for collecting behaviors, and until there's a Wordbank-like project for aggregating them, we're far from being able to say. Also, most of what's known is about cancer patients, perhaps because the pace of their illness makes it more convenient to study them. (Some, however, is known about patients with amyotrophic lateral sclerosis [ALS], as I'll discuss.) But enough information exists for a rough sketch of the matter.

For example, an Australian hospice reported that 60 percent of their patients (all but one of whom were dying of cancer) could "speak lucidly" in the last three days of life, even though they'd been given a range of drugs to control symptoms of pain, lethargy, dyspnea (or shortness of breath), terminal agitation, and others. This contrasts strongly with the findings from another study of cancer patients in Japan, which found that those who could achieve "complex communication" declined steadily, from 43 percent at five days before death, to 28 percent at three days, to 13 percent at one day. Here "complex communication" simply was defined as "the patient can voluntarily express him- or herself with clear meaning, even when the theme is complex."

Not only that, but 63 percent of all patients were incoherent one day before death, with unsedated patients slightly more available than continuously sedated ones (57 percent of the former group were incoherent as compared to 73 percent of the latter).

In a practical sense, the implications are clear enough. Yet you might find "speak lucidly" and "complex communication" as frustratingly vague as I do. Lucid to whom? What is "clear meaning" (and when are human language users ever reliably clear)? Is it as clear to a stranger as to a friend? And what is a "complex" theme? Those researchers also looked at something they called "clear, simple communication," in which the "patient is able to voluntarily express him- or herself with clear meaning, but the contents are limited to simple matters." The researchers defined "simple" as utterances only two or three words long (which also suggests they only considered spoken language). But this is frustrating—surely the length of an utterance has little bearing on the complexity of its meaning, at least in absolute terms. After all, the single word "no" can contain a universe of ambiguity; silence a multiverse. And communicating a refusal for a particular treatment, which a patient might be using their remaining linguistic powers to do, is far from a "simple matter."

Given that simplicity was measured in number of words, it's certain that the researchers in all these studies only considered spoken language. Yet from other research we know that people are able to, and do, switch modalities to make themselves understood. In other words, they take advantage of some of the flexibility of the interaction window. For example, there's some evidence that, at the end of their lives, people with ALS use hand squeezes at a consistent rate until they die. Not all of them remained communicative, though, and about one quarter in one American group weren't able to communicate at all in their last one to two days. But the communicative resilience of the rest, particularly in the face of that particular disease, might stem from long experience (unwanted, to be sure) with adapting to a shifting interaction window. Their experience has myriad lessons to offer the rest of us.

My point is, this ready availability of other modes of communication isn't portrayed in most of the medical literature. Keep that in mind when you read that 30 percent of patients can achieve this "simple communication" at five days, 20 percent at three days, and 24 percent at one day before death—numbers that would be higher if nonverbals were counted. Thus, even the existing research has been skewed. It's not given us an adequate sense of the rain.

Either way, it comes to a close in a mostly uniform fashion, as Mannix explained. "There's a period of also what we consider to be deep unconsciousness, with some retention of auditory awareness. What we see at bedsides is the person who was agitated becoming more deeply unconscious. Certainly, fewer restless movements going on when certain voices are in the room, or when the news that everybody's been waiting for is announced, that the baby's been born in Australia, or the grandson has proposed to the long-term lover, or whatever it is." (There's more about the preservation of hearing in chapter 11.)

I feel grateful to Mannix for providing this portrait, which is good to have in the back of one's mind. The gradual closing of the interaction window, and the need to adapt to this fact, is an essential part of a mental shorthand for language at the end of life.

But there is more to chip away at. Because many societies are oriented to literacy, "last words" usually means spoken or signed actual words. In actuality, what people do with their eyes, their hand gestures, and their body postures can be sources of meaning, as *Final Gifts* indicated. With these two concepts in hand, the failing brain and the closing interaction window, it becomes readily apparent what linguistic behaviors the dying might display—and why and how other people respond.

8   William Osler and "The Study of the Act of Dying"

The sun was bright, pouring through the high windows of the octagon-shaped hospital ward, which smelled of bleach, coal smoke, a lingering hint of pine—that scent coming from a cutting-edge disinfectant. In 1902, Johns Hopkins Hospital was a state-of-the-art facility, the biggest in Baltimore, founded over twenty-five years earlier by a wealthy businessman. Some male patients resting in chairs watched a man shuffling weakly to a window, then a nurse crossing the ward and standing at a bed with a man in it. Patrick Henry had lain there for days, awake but immobile. As the nurse checked the clipboard, Henry stirred. "He's got me now—took advantage while I was asleep," he muttered, to her, to the room, to no one. An hour later, he expired. That was the last thing he said.

Only those patients and the nurse knew why Patrick Henry was in the hospital and what he was dying of. For patient information, all that exists is his age, his name, and his nationality: "American." (This also implies he was white.) Thanks to some nurse or doctor, we know he stayed conscious until he died, as well as that last utterance. What did that mean, *someone got him now*? Who was "he"—the devil? Maybe Henry had words of a hymn or sermon in his mind—even today Christian preachers will warn against letting Satan "take advantage" of you if you go to sleep angry—in the same way that many last words are echoes of one's lived life. In any case, all that's known with certainty is that they were captured in medical history's first clinical study of dying.

Nowadays, there's a vast world of research on death and dying by doctors, psychologists, sociologists, and others to draw from, but it has all accumulated fairly recently. By Patrick Henry's time, dying had received little systematic, scientific regard. Published works in the English language about medical aspects of dying, scattered and anecdotal, were mainly produced by retired doctors. No one had ever tried to describe the process of dying in a single population, in one institutional setting, in one period of time. No one, that is, until Sir William Osler (1849–1919).

If you've ever seen a scene in a movie or TV show in which a senior doctor grills medical students at a patient's bedside, you're already familiar with one of Osler's innovations in medical education. He joked that he wanted his gravestone to read "Here lies the man who admitted students to the wards."

Born in Canada's backwoods to an immigrant Anglican minister, he became one of the most famous doctors of his time. Dark-haired, olive-skinned, he stood barely five and a half feet tall, and possessed a consider-able charisma and an appetite for pranks and cheery ribbing.

"Everyone knew Osler, and almost everyone loved him," wrote a biographer. "A few disciples literally worshiped him."

After graduating from McGill University, he trained in Europe for a few years, then returned to teach at McGill, where he spent a decade. He was recruited to the University of Pennsylvania in 1884, then became one of the four founding medical professors and chief physician at the Johns Hopkins Hospital in 1889. He remained at Hopkins until he became Regius Professor of Medicine at Oxford University in 1905. Famous for a landmark medical textbook, *The Principles and Practices of Medicine*, first published in 1892, he also wrote 1,500 articles on a range of medical topics. He was renowned for his keen powers of clinical observation as well as his belief in the healing power of optimism, and he had many private patients, which made him relatively wealthy. Osler has such a solidly positive reputation even to this day (there's an American Osler Society, the William Osler Society of Aus-tralia and New Zealand, the Osler Club of London—you get the idea), it's almost as if he's still among us.

For all that, Osler wasn't moved to become a pioneer in the study of dying during the first part of his career. His biographers say that his views on death were complex. Given his upbringing, he could quote Scripture extensively, which made people think that he believed in heaven. But he was demure about his own religious beliefs and unforthcoming about his feelings—given the opportunity, he'd avoid painful topics.

He was also a scientist, given to wondering how far the physician's powers actually extended. Did dying not mark the failure of medicine to

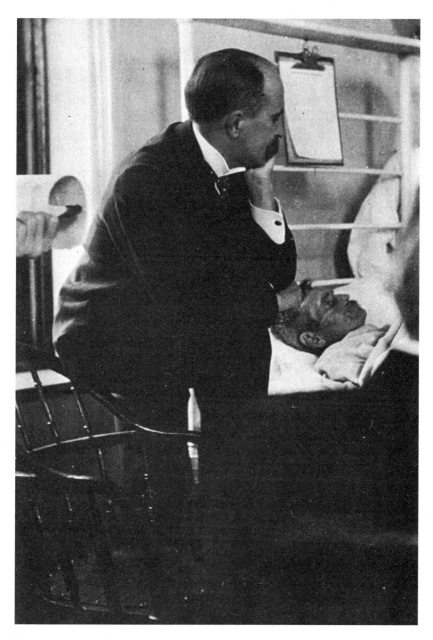

Figure 8.1
William Osler observes a patient at Johns Hopkins, circa 1890.

restore health in those who were dying young? Penicillin and other antibiotics were decades away yet; in that sense, he was right. He had probably attended hundreds of deathbeds, and a physician is never far from the reality. In one photo from his time at Johns Hopkins Hospital, he's perched on the side of a chair, contemplating a prone, gaunt male patient. Another photo from 1886 shows him seated at a table, his sleeves rolled up, wearing a crisp white apron over a dark shirt, hunched over a mass of tissue in one hand and an undiscernible tool in the other.

But in 1889, when he moved to Baltimore, Osler stopped doing autopsies, which was unusual, given that pathology was a major source of his medical knowledge. One reason for the shift seems to be that once he turned forty, he realized that he was perilously too close to the limits of his own mortality to know so much about corpses but so little about the human experience of dying.

§

I'm describing all of this in detail because I'm fascinated by Osler's motivations as well as the contours of his life. One thing is clear enough: His birthday milestone inspired lifestyle changes. He married, and he and his wife, Grace, had two sons, one of whom died at birth, the second of whom would later die in World War I. He also began to collect books, building a section he jokingly called the "Death, Heaven, and Hell" corner, which contained books on "spiritualism (with which he had scant patience), dreams and ghosts, on witchcraft, on immortality, longevity, premature burial, preexistence, resurrection, 'self-murther,' euthanasia, embalming, cremation, and similar subjects." Many of these books became part of a library he curated for his alma mater, McGill University, which today holds his original copies.

Notably, he didn't own any anthologies of last words, though he did appear to have an interest in the phenomenon. One utterance in particular seemed to have caught his imagination so much that he used it in several letters and publications. It was from Dr. William Hunter (1718–1783), who apparently had whispered to a friend right before expiring, "If I had strength enough to hold a pen, I would write how easy and pleasant a thing it is to die."

Osler might have found it in the book *Euthanasia*, published in 1887 by British physician William Munk (1816–1898), which was an important source of inspiration for Osler as well as palliative care experts in the next century. Favorably received in medical journals of the time, *Euthanasia* was "the authoritative text on medical care of the dying for the next thirty years." Munk wasn't writing about assisted suicide but used *euthanasia* to refer to "dying well" or "having a calm and easy death," as in the ancient Greek meaning. Though Munk argued that the dying process wasn't naturally anguished or painful (though disease processes might be), he also sought to show how the physician, providing proper medical care, can "smooth the bed of death." Death itself didn't represent a moral failing, or a failure of medical science, but took a natural course that ought to be calm, even pleasant. In fact, Munk wrote, "the process of dying, and the very act of death, is but rarely and exceptionally attended by those severe bodily sufferings, which in popular belief are all but inseparable from it."

This has been the comforting message from studies of near-death experiences, starting with Raymond Moody's 1975 book, as well as surveys of dying people. At one hospice, 98 percent of patients died peacefully, and 60 percent had been peaceful for the last twenty-four hours or longer. At another hospice, 91.5 percent died peacefully, and 64 percent were so in the last twenty-four hours. In these studies, "peaceful" was defined as having no pain, dyspnea, nausea, confusion, or other physical symptoms. Keep in mind that such surveys involved dozens of trained professionals and hundreds of patients, who were likely the beneficiaries of the modern pharmacopeia: morphine, other opiates and analgesics, antidepressants, anticonvulsives, and antibiotics. As a physician, Munk had opiates, alcohol (as in sherry), ether, ammonia, and copious home remedies; as a writer, he had only his own experiences (albeit fifty years of them), quotes from other physicians, and anecdotes from revived near-drowning victims, who—foreshadowing Moody—reported feeling calm as they slipped away. He even marshaled a few last words as evidence, among them William Hunter's poignant advertisement.

Osler wrote a positive (though not glowing) review of Munk's book in 1888, which presaged what he would undertake next. "We speak of Death as the King of Terrors," Osler wrote elsewhere, "yet so rarely does the act of dying appear to be painful." How could he demonstrate this?

There's no indication that he doubted Munk's description, but he wanted to obtain stronger evidence for the assertion. He might also have been inspired by the late-nineteenth-century British movement "collective investigation" to collect self-reported health data across populations of people. A similar observational urge permeated many layers of society on both sides of the Atlantic, in order to reduce infant mortality and ensure healthy families. (I discussed its impact on first words in chapter 2.)

And so it was that twelve years after publishing his review, Osler organized the research project at Johns Hopkins that captured, among other things, the last words of that thirty-eight-year-old Baltimorean. Now known as "The Study of the Act of Dying" (or sometimes "The Study of Dying"), Osler described it as his "collecting data for some years on 'this business of death,' as Milton terms it." He seemed to think he could get individuals to describe their own dying, and through that say something conclusive about what dying was really like.

Osler's study is often mentioned in medical histories and ethnographies of the later twentieth century as a pioneering project, but curiously his biographers don't highlight the innovation, probably because they followed his contemporaries, who didn't exult about the study either. Arthur MacDonald, who mined last-word anthologies in the 1920s, seems not to have heard of it. One of the two women physicians who interned at Johns Hopkins in 1900 and 1901, Dorothy Reed Mendenhall, mentioned the study in her autobiography, which contains the only other contemporaneous description of the study that I've found. Hers is also rather neutral: "One of the interests of Dr. Osler at the moment was just what happened during the final moments before death came," she wrote. "We were all given a sheet to fill out at or immediately after death, covering a number of different observations. All I now remember is heart and respiration—which stopped first—and how long before neither could be determined. Also last remarks and especially premonitions and fears." (Of course, Mendenhall might have been nonplussed because as one of the few female doctors at the time, she was innovating every day.)

As we'll see, the study isn't perfect. In fact, by modern standards, it's badly designed. But for Osler to undertake it set him apart. Why am I using it, especially if he didn't set out to look at language? Because when people deliberately look at language at the end of life, they seem to find what confirms their ideas about death and dying. So could the linguistic things that turned up in Osler's net incidentally tell us something different? I'm not interested in recuperating the whole of this study, but if you want to know more about final articulations of consciousness, then it provides an invaluable, if unconventional, key. It gives us a specific place and time, whose values can be mapped. The actors are knowable; we can see the effects of the built environment.

To check out the details of Osler's study, I happily went to Montreal.

§

The city's concrete jungle was so hot and humid that week, I wasn't prepared for the frigid air inside the university's library. When the archive librarian, Mary Hague-Yearl, delivered a clamshell box about the size of a collegiate English dictionary to my desk, I was shivering from the chill—or was that nervousness that Osler might have no surprises for me?

"The Study of Dying" was printed in golden letters on the side of the box. Unlike many archival materials, it had no smell. I opened the lid, then lowered the front, revealing the hard edges of 486 data cards, also odorless, separated into two neat piles. Very matter-of-fact, not dramatic at all. Each card, slightly gray-yellow in color, measured fifteen by seventeen centimeters and had printed on it, in a crisp serif font, prompts for this information:

> Name, hospital number, date
> Age, nationality, religion
> Length of illness
> The act of dying:
> If sudden
> Did respiration stop before pulse—how long
> Coma or unconsciousness before death—how long?
> If any fear or apprehension, of what nature.
> Bodily, i.e., pain
> Mental
> Spiritual—remorse, etc.

The bottom of each card added some lines. "This card is not to be filled out unless done within twenty-four hours of the death of the individual," it read. Then:

> NB: the object of this investigation is to ascertain, the relative proportion of cases in which (1) the death is sudden; (2) accompanied by coma or unconsciousness; (3) by pain, dread or apprehension. Prof. Osler requests the intelligent cooperation of the members of the medical and nursing staff. Please note fully any other special circumstances connected with the act of dying.

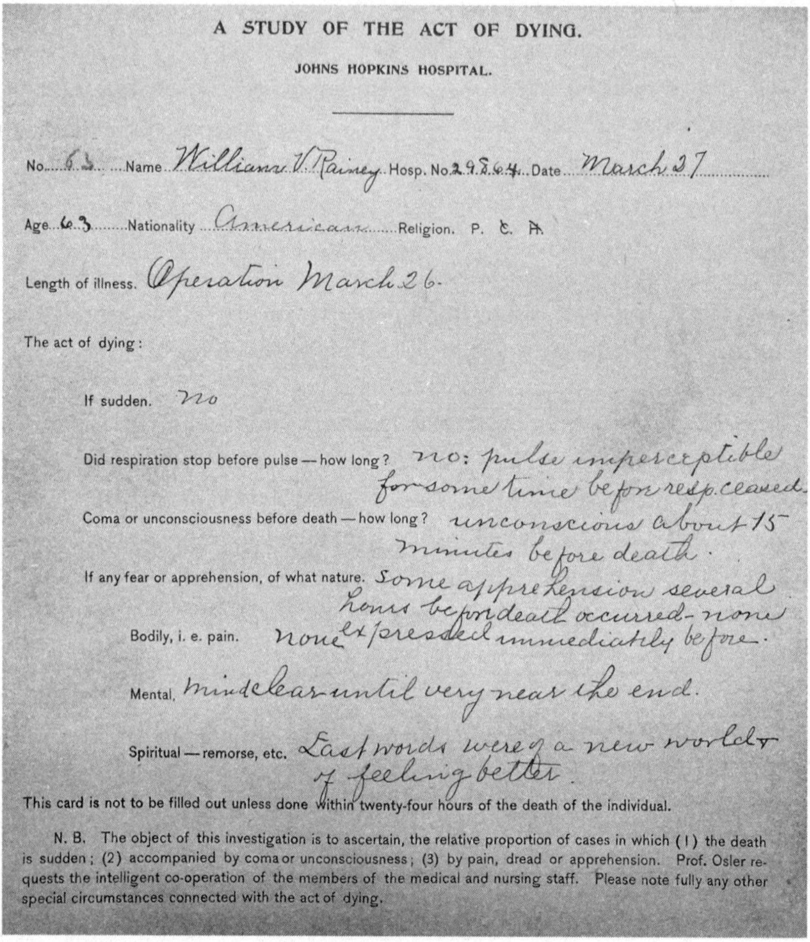

A STUDY OF THE ACT OF DYING.

JOHNS HOPKINS HOSPITAL.

No. *6 3* ....Name *William V. Rainey*..Hosp. No. *2 9 5 6 4*...Date *March 27*

Age *63*........Nationality *American*......Religion. P. E. A.

Length of illness. *Operation March 26.*

The act of dying :

If sudden. *no*

Did respiration stop before pulse — how long ? *no: pulse imperceptible for some time before resp. ceased.*

Coma or unconsciousness before death — how long ? *unconscious about 15 minutes before death.*

If any fear or apprehension, of what nature. *Some apprehension several hours before death occurred — none*

Bodily, i. e. pain. *none expressed immediately before.*

Mental. *mind clear until very near the end.*

Spiritual — remorse, etc. *Last words were of a new world & of feeling better.*

This card is not to be filled out unless done within twenty-four hours of the death of the individual.

N. B.   The object of this investigation is to ascertain, the relative proportion of cases in which (I) the death is sudden ; (2) accompanied by coma or unconsciousness ; (3) by pain, dread or apprehension.   Prof. Osler requests the intelligent co-operation of the members of the medical and nursing staff.   Please note fully any other special circumstances connected with the act of dying.

Figure 8.2
A data card from Osler's study. Nothing was written on the back. The document is held at the Osler Library of the History of Medicine, McGill University. Photo by author.

I noted that there was no explicit request for last words. Yet given these prompts, I anticipated finding more than a few. As I examined the cards, it became clear that they'd been filled out with varying attention to detail. Two-thirds were signed by nurses. Understandably, most wrote the bare minimum. I imagined them annoyed at having to interrupt their duties in busy wards to make these observations. Some, mainly doctors, wrote longer notes. Were they trying to impress their chief when he inspected their work? Language barriers might have kept people from talking or being observed. Some patients were German, Polish, or Russian speakers. Under "apprehension," one observer had written: "could not tell—pt. did not speak English."

So much death, card after card. So much data about dying. A couple of months earlier, I'd interviewed Robert Gramling, a palliative care doctor in Vermont, who was studying the conversations between doctors and their terminally ill patients. One day, he had found one of his research assistants crying as she listened to recordings of those conversations in order to mark the silences. (Which were, Gramling posited, indicators of emotional connections between doctor and patient.) She felt guilty for turning a sensitive moment in someone's end of life into a piece of mere data. It seemed to her cold, inhumane. So Gramling asked the hospital to allow him to bring in a singing bowl, used in meditation. Now at the beginning of every lab meeting, a researcher reads the name of a patient from a database, then rings the bowl twice. The commemoration calmed them, this form of caring for the dead.

I wished to ring a singing bowl for each card I touched.

The cards were also historical documents, opening a window onto the segregations and biases of the American past. Under "nationality," a patient was listed as "American," presumably if they were white. If not, they were listed as "colored," "American negro," "or US-colored." How did such attitudes affect the study? I later learned that Johns Hopkins, a Quaker-born railroad investor, had built his hospital to serve people who couldn't afford private care, meaning laborers, immigrants, African Americans, and the poor. The facility had been designed under the direction of the well-known hospital consultant (and former Civil War surgeon) John Shaw Billings (1838–1913). By housing patients in large, well-ventilated rooms in separate wards and pavilions, Billings aimed to minimize infections while centralizing heating infrastructure and food services. Most of the patients were arranged in large common rooms (not hotel-like suites, as in modern hospitals). Presumably, such open space would have made a death easy to observe. Yet the architecture also separated people by class, gender, race, and disease. There were only three common wards, two private or "pay" wards, an octagon ward, and an isolating ward for patients with infectious diseases. There was a separate "colored" building with two wards, one for men and another for women. All this would have influenced what was observed and by whom.

It appeared that most of the patients, about two-thirds of them, were male. They were also young, with a median age of thirty-nine years, at a time when the average life expectancy was 47.8 years for men and 50.7 for women. The youngest patient was nine months old, the oldest eighty-three years. Yet the cards reveal little about patients' medical conditions. For some reason, it wasn't until 1902 that Osler bothered to ask about the "nature of illness" on the cards. By that time, 288 deaths had already been recorded. After this change (and from clues from notes before it), we know that sixty patients died of infectious disease, thirty-three of cardiovascular disease, twenty-one of cancer, sixteen of renal failure, and thirty-one of postoperative complications, which caused the most deaths of women. It may not reflect the way people die today or at the time, but that's how people were dying during those years in Baltimore, at that hospital.

§

Clarifyingly, only four cards contained directly quoted final verbal articulations of consciousness. The first I found (working backward from patient #486) came from Patrick Henry, patient #398, who died in 1902. The record also stated that he was mentally uncomfortable and afraid of having been caught.

A second example came from a twenty-four-year-old woman who had just given birth and was probably hemorrhaging (though no cause of death was mentioned). "Am I dying?" she asked.

There was also a forty-five-year-old woman, with no diagnosis marked, who said she was "afraid to die" twenty-four hours before she died. She was unconscious for eighteen hours prior, so it's conceivable she said something else in those intervening six hours. Yet nothing had been noted. Then there was a sixty-three-year-old whose gender and condition weren't marked.

They had just had surgery. The card noted, under the space for noting any "spiritual discomfort," that their "last words were of a new world and of feeling better."

That didn't make for many directly quoted last words. Out of 486 deaths, four speakers, twenty-three words in total, each utterance in its own brief way about the act or experience of dying. I thought about this—perhaps other utterances weren't recorded because they didn't speak to the question of death's peacefulness. Then I recalled Mendenhall's report that observers were supposed to be alert for last remarks in general. Shouldn't the cards contain more? But the nurses and doctors were busy; people may have spoken out and been heard only by others in their wards. Or by their gods.

However, these four weren't the only speakers. In twelve other instances, an observer referred to something a patient had said, paraphrasing the content rather than quoting it directly. Reading these is a moving experience—there's wishing to be taken home, begging for a chance to get well. Patients asserted that they weren't ready to die. Others announced that they were. One twenty-four-year-old man asked the doctor to stand beside him and hold his hand. One man felt he was suffocating. Another man said his heart hurt.

None of it communicated the ease that William Hunter had. Nor did it seem pleasant.

In total, sixteen patients had some preserved ability to utter something that made sense to listeners, and the facts of their speaking got written down. The verbs used to describe this speaking: answered, asked, complained, cried out, expressed, groaned, made, moaned, rambled, said, uttered. But verbal linguistic powers were not, on the whole, very evident.

§

As I recalled from my time at the MPI, language happens in more than one modality. What if the dying also communicated, as preverbal toddlers do, in a spectrum of gestures and postures? What if the end of the signifying self, like its beginning, happened somewhere beyond spoken words?

The cards contained incidental mention of these behaviors too. For example, an attempt to rouse someone meant that the doctor had wanted to interact with the patient, probably to diagnose them. This wasn't recorded often, though it was noted that one patient was a forty-six-year-old man dying of kidney failure, who "could be partially aroused by frequent shaking and responded fairly intelligently to questions."

There was also a range of behaviors pointing to the fact that the deathbed is a place where biological ability (can someone signal?), communicative intent (can someone mean to signal?), and interactive instinct (does someone want to signal?) become unraveled, at the same moment that linguistic and interactive behaviors become tangled up in the social and personal expectations of an interlocutor (is that a signal?). It's a vicious variant of Trixie's Dilemma, vicious because there's so little time left. For example, two other patients were observed gesturing, indicating that they intended to communicate something, but before they could do so, their hearts or breathing stopped. Both were men in their sixties, one dying of inflammation of the heart muscle, the other of pneumonia. In the first case, the man stretched out his right arm and "uttered an inarticulate exclamation or two," then expired.

The second was more poignantly dramatic. Of all the deaths described in these cards, this one haunted me, and it's the one I most want to ring a meditation bowl for. The man had been in a coma for six days, and his daughter, the only family member mentioned in any of the cards, was at his bedside. A contemporary of Osler's wrote that coma amounted to a "complete loss of consciousness, from which a patient cannot be roused—except by themselves, perhaps." So did he know his daughter was there? Perhaps not. Yet right before he stopped breathing, "his eyes opened widely." He suddenly awoke from the coma without prompting, then turned toward his daughter, "with [an] apparent look of intelligence." Maybe he could feel in his body what was happening and wanted to tell her, but ultimately he couldn't. "He made no sound nor did his lips move," the card read. Then he expired.

Later I found a poem by a British palliative care nurse, Mel McEvoy, "The Lightness of Self," that captures threads of this moment. He is watching a patient awake after brain surgery.

. . . Then I witnessed
her surfacing,
into being

Vulnerable like the powder
that comes off
butterfly wings.

'Hold me
Be gentle.
Make me safe.'

Quicker than thought
turned in on herself
and descended

To where
we all are
adrift like dust

in sunlight
in the absence
after the words.

In that moment of surfacing, did the father recognize his daughter? Was that "look of intelligence" (as the nurse interpreted it) his puzzling out who she was? Or was it simply a physiological response into which people will read intent and intelligence? That flash of whatever it was, too fleeting to gather a sensible response by other people, gives me a start whenever I think of it. Yes, it's true that the scene is cinematic, the deathbed recognition that appears in movies and poems (like McEvoy's), so it's recognizable in a fashion. But the naked humanity of that irretrievable connection missed for inscrutable reasons speaks to wounds that we all carry, or will carry, being mortals born of mortals. The man, his daughter, a scene, a bedside, a window, a nurse—not where any of them wants to be. There doesn't need to be an utterance—that look in his eyes, it meant everything. *After the words.*

§

Two patients showed that they could be addressed but couldn't respond. The first, a twenty-four-year-old woman, was suffering in great pain from an unrecorded cause. "Up to the moment of her death she understood when addressed," reads the observation. In other words, she may not have been speaking, but she continued to be interactive. The second, a thirty-one-year-old man, marked as dying of typhoid, looked at a nurse or doctor (the note is illegible here) "as tho' he understood questions." He was unconscious for four days before he died, and there's no indication that his comprehending happened before those four days.

In total, nineteen Baltimoreans were observed to have some degree of preserved interactive ability near to or even immediately before their deaths. More might have gone unrecorded in those who died suddenly or were comatose shortly before they died. Yet even this isn't everything on the record that symptomizes the collapse of the interaction window. For instance, five other patients, ranging in age from thirty-eight to sixty-six, could be roused from an unconscious state or coma. One had "an occasional lucid interval" amid three days of coma, and another was the forty-six-year-old dying of kidney failure. A third was "dazed," while a fourth could be roused from his coma for twenty-four hours, but was unrousable for two to three hours before he expired. Another was in a coma for twenty-four hours but would still rouse to his name. All of the cards indicate whether or not people were comatose, but fewer describe rousability—the interaction window, in other words, could be pried open a bit.

In five other instances, people vocalized but seemingly involuntarily. They might have been limbic vocalizations. Indeed, people with brain damage have been known to laugh, scream, or groan even if they have lost the ability to speak, while patients with dementia often scream, sing, chant, hum, and grunt at late stages of the illness. Some patients with primary progressive aphasia eventually produce only laughter-like vocalizations. At Johns Hopkins, a thirty-five-year-old with amebic dysentery "groaned often," while a fifty-one-year-old groaned constantly. A ten-year-old "moaned as if in pain," a thirty-five-year-old groaned whenever they were moved, and the sixty-one-year-old with myocarditis had an "inarticulate" exclamation or two. These groans weren't the only ways that people expressed pain. A forty-nine-year-old made facial expressions that the observer said came from pain, as did a seventy-two-year-old.

These expressions or behaviors could be organized according to the amount of cortical control they require, starting with the latter expressions—the moaning, the facial expressions—as products of the limbic system. If you went looking for the last word, you might easily ignore these behaviors as irrelevant since they don't seem to be intentionally communicative. Yet the competent language users on the scene, given their intact drive toward the interaction window, may treat these behaviors as intentionally meaningful somehow, demanding to be interpreted. In fact, family members "tend to see purposefulness in small movements and to think that the conscious person that they knew before the crisis is still there," wrote medical anthropologist Sharon Kaufman.

§

As with William Munk's caseload, many of the Johns Hopkins patients were delirious as they died. In the dying process, Munk wrote, "more often some delirium is present. Such delirium is generally shown in quiet talkativeness, which becomes later on a low muttering." Contemporary research about patients who recover from a delirious episode (after surgery) say that their reality was distorted and contradictory, the real mixed with the unreal, waking life infused with dreams, and past events filtered into the present. They felt angry, afraid, panicked, and insecure. In the Johns Hopkins group, sixteen patient records were marked "delirium" or "delirious," while nine more records referred to patients as "irrational." One patient was described as "raving." (Delirium is discussed further in chapter 10.)

The most frequent—and most cryptic—description was that deaths were "quiet," thirty in all, more than all the speakers, vocalizers, rousables, and moaners combined. What does "quiet" mean? Had they deliberately decided to stay quiet or withdrawn, or was there simply an absence of vocalizing? A general peacefulness? It's impossible to know if vocalizations happened in those cases and were unheard, or if the patient was too young, didn't speak English (there were about a dozen of these), or had been unconscious for a long time.

It's also not clear to what degree "quiet" was caused by opiates, as such information wasn't requested. We might assume that it was used, as Osler himself was an advocate of opiates for pain management; people associated him with their use. A few years later, he received a letter describing the death of a friend, who had asked for "Osler," meaning morphine, and sighed when the injection was given. "Ah," he said, "Osler has come." And as Osler himself lay dying at age seventy after complications of chronic bronchitis, his painful fits of coughing were eased thanks to opiates. "Shunt the whole pharmacopoeia, except opium," his biographer Harvey Cushing reports him writing in a letter. "It alone in some form does the job. What a comfort it has been!" On the other hand, it's not a medication described in Mendenhall's unpublished account, and at a public hospital, opiates may not have been so freely dispensed, if people were considered undeserving or to have different experiences of pain (as white male doctors thought about women and African Americans).

§

I was surprised first by the small number of speakers in Osler's data cards, then by the larger amount of silence and delirium. My original impetus was to understand how much language was produced. I hadn't expected so much silence. *In the absence, after the words.*

But this is what the rain is like. Very few rainbows.

But even this glimpse of the rain raises further questions. One puzzle is why the deaths of 401 patients weren't described in any linguistic terms whatsoever—apparently, they neither talked nor gestured nor moaned nor even were quiet. Maybe it's just that not all the nurses and doctors were fully on board with the study. Nowadays, they would be directed by strict protocols; in Osler's day, these were looser. In fact, in all of 1903, only two deaths were observed, and the last patient was recorded on March 29, 1904, barely two months after a fire devastated significant portions of the city of Baltimore, and shortly after Osler had been invited to Oxford.

Osler has been such a monumental figure that, even a century since his death, it seems crass to point out that this study, a curious footnote to his illustrious career, had no discernible impact on medical care. If he recognized that his study could have been executed more effectively, he didn't indicate this in letters—perhaps it was one of the emotionally painful topics he avoided. He mentioned the study only in the famous lecture series, the Ingersoll Lecture at Harvard, which he gave in 1904. It was titled "Science and Immortality," and its publication was the only printed mention of the study's results. "I have careful records of about five hundred deathbeds," Osler said, "studied particularly with reference to the modes of death and the sensations of dying." He claimed that 104 patients suffered "bodily pain or distress of one form or another." The discomforts included pain, dyspnea, convulsions, weakness, fever, fear, anxiety, irrationality, mental distress, or depression. The great majority of the deaths were peaceful, thus supporting his long contention. "The great majority gave no sign one way or the other; like their birth, their death was a sleep and a forgetting," Osler famously wrote. But in his prepared talk, his argument that beliefs about immortality were largely pointless to pursue wasn't well-received, and the only part of the lecture that met the approval of Harvard's president, Charles Eliot (who had invited Osler in the first place), was the part about the "careful records."

Yet if these findings were so definitive, why didn't Osler publish them? At one point, he had planned a book about death, to be titled *The Inevitable*

Hour: A Discourse on Death & Dying, which would have made a fine home for the study. Yet he didn't write such a book, nor did he mention the study in a 1911 letter that he wrote to *The Spectator* disputing Belgian writer Maurice Maeterlinck's assertion that dying experiences were painful. Osler wrote only that "the truth is, an immense majority of all die as they were born—oblivious. A few, very few, suffer severely in the body. Fewer still in the mind." Only someone of Osler's stature could have gotten away with such an unsupported claim, or with conducting a four-year study without reporting the results.

One clue to Osler's disavowal emerged about one hundred years later, when his results were revisited by Paul Mueller, an American doctor who became fascinated with the study after dropping in at the archives at McGill. He tallied all of the discomforts reported in the data cards and compared them to Osler's spreadsheet (which is also held at the archives). He was shocked to find that where Osler counted 104 patients with discomforts, he counted 186, mostly in physical pain. "Rather than supporting a conclusion that dying patients rarely suffer during the dying process," Mueller wrote, "the data instead support the conclusion that a substantial number of patients experienced discomforts."

Osler's raw data isn't out of line with what's seen elsewhere—about the same proportion of patients in a New Zealand hospice experienced difficulties in the last forty-eight hours, mostly due to pain, noisy breathing, and restlessness. But the bigger issue concerns the discrepancy. "Do you think your study challenges Osler's reputation?" I asked Mueller one day on a Zoom call. By way of a reply, he lifted his laptop so the camera caught the two framed photos of Osler hanging on his office's far wall, implying that the very premise of my question was off target. Mueller had been the president of the American Osler Society and saw the discrepant tabulations as a sign of Osler's all-too-human flaws, while the conduct of the study itself reflected the undeveloped state of clinical research over a century ago.

I tend to think it reflects the strength of "as if" commitments, particularly at this stage of life, even in the hands of someone otherwise committed to the "as is." In the end, Osler couldn't allow the observable facts to challenge his beliefs. I'm not ruling out that having this data also challenged Osler's view of death in some other way, perhaps by raising doubts about a role for medicine at the deathbed. The central notion of palliative medicine, that you could treat the symptoms of dying, even if there was no hope of a cure for the underlying condition, was still far away. Perhaps Osler glimpsed a possibility for that approach, yet it was one he couldn't ultimately call more fully into reality than supplying opiates. There were extenuating circumstances too: In February of 1904, the great Baltimore fire destroyed 140 acres of central Baltimore and came within two blocks of Osler's house, prompting the family to flee. The terror of a fire would have erased thoughts of peaceful death. At that point, the study was finished; Osler rushed to tabulate things for his Harvard lecture that May.

You may think it ill-advised to use these data, given these limitations, but I think they show us a variety of the behaviors that stand to be transformed into "final articulations of consciousness." The data may still be biased, but they're not overtly biased toward ideas about death. The important point is that Osler—like Arthur MacDonald before him, among so many others—seemed to think that language at the end of life, in the form of last remarks, might help him open the black box of the dying person's experience. Where did this resolute belief in linguistic powers at the end of life come from? The story of last words, it turns out, must also be the story of the linguistic agency attributed to the dying person.

9 The Linguistic Powers of the Dying

One clear difference between first words and last words is that a person brings ideas about what last words should be, if anything, to their deathbeds. A baby has no such programming. So what are ideas about the linguistic powers of the dying to which people are socialized to bring to their own deaths?

Pandemics will bookend my inquiry: I'll start with the medieval European scene that birthed Christian ritual last words and the emergence of a preference for individual, unscripted expressions. Then I'll take a brief but tantalizing look at a few of the surviving ritualistic last-word traditions, not so exotic or distant, and equally as fascinating from a linguistic point of view. I'll close by looking at the new publicness to last words that's emerged thanks to omnipresent smartphones, and how the coronavirus pandemic dashed expectations about final conversations.

A good beginning is in 1414 CE, when hundreds of cardinals, bishops, other clergy, and scholars converged on a lakeside town in southern Germany for a conference on holy church matters. At the Council of Constance, a nameless person, so inspired by devotional debates and other texts, composed a how-to guide in Latin about who should say and do what at the deathbed, laying out the death of Jesus Christ as the model for everyone else's.

Given the era's catastrophic epidemics, a guide to required prayers filled a true lack: with so many people dying outside the Church's ability to reach them, and with so many priests dying (making the Church's shortfall even worse), communities often lacked experienced priests within reasonable distance of hard-hit areas. When the conference closed in 1418, attendees seem to have taken this text, called the *Tractatus artis bene moriendi*, back to their homes all over Europe, where it became, in a historian's words, "exceedingly popular." The *Tractatus* existed in three hundred manuscripts, both in Latin and vernacular languages, including English (the first by William Caxton, in 1490, who was possibly motivated by his wife's death a year earlier). Thanks to new printing technologies, it kept spreading all through Europe and even to the Americas, thanks to missionaries. This explains how this guide and others derived from it, known collectively as *artes moriendi*, provided guidance for Christian deaths for the next 250 years. Despite powerful waves of secularization, it remains a powerful model for linguistic agency at the end of life.

A nineteenth-century doctor like Osler had probably experienced many deathbeds conducted according to the cultural influences of *artes moriendi* as "a complete and intelligible guide to the business of dying, a method to be learned while one is in good health and kept at one's fingers' ends for use in that all-important and inescapable hour." Not surprisingly, Osler had two versions of the *Tractatus* in his library. What the *artes moriendi* meant to psychologically and spiritually prompt for the participants was complex, but I'll take a linguistic perspective on the most relevant sections, the third and the fourth.

The third part lays out questions about faith, or "interrogations," to which the dying person must reply "yes." (These interrogations are routine in other sacraments, such as confirmation in the Catholic church and baptism in Protestant churches—a dying person wouldn't be encountering them for the first time.) The fourth part dictates how a person must pattern their dying on that of Jesus's. This included crying out at the appropriate time and saying certain prayers. These instructions contain the seeds of the Western last-words tradition, whose expectations are simple: the person must speak, well enough to say prayers and to cry out to God, as Jesus did, and they must comprehend enough to answer the interrogations about faith, saying "yes." (Martin Luther's last word in 1546 was "*ja,*" in response to the question of whether he was dying in the name of Christ.) Other later works prescribed that one's last words literally be the same as the dying Jesus's, "Into your hands I commend my spirit," or a variation thereof. All of this speaking is a way that the survivors confirm that the dying person has successfully combated the devil's temptations and is eligible to enter heaven.

The modern temptation is to take the *Tractatus* and subsequent *artes moriendi* as scripts, but they're something more than this. They're also

Figure 9.1

An illustration from the *Rohan Book of Hours*, painted by an anonymous artist, known as the Rohan Master, between 1418 and 1425. In these very early proto–speech bubbles, the dying man is speaking Latin, while God is speaking French. Reproduced by permission of the Bibliothèque nationale de France.

models of how people should behave at the closing of the interaction window—when you die, you're to vocalize, just as Christ did. In the Gospel of Matthew, in fact, Jesus cries out loudly before expiring.

Some *artes moriendi* amount to frank guides for communicating with the dying in more flexible ways, as in *Final Gifts*. For instance, the *Tractatus* acknowledges that a dying person may not be able to speak or might lose their reason. In that case, the prayers will be said for them or to them. "So a sick man, that is in point of death, he should pray," one English text reads, "namely in his heart, if he may not with his mouth." Other texts refer to the importance of crying out "in the heart"—you must animate your crying, but silently. Similarly, later *artes moriendi* texts offer the option for the dying person to use some other sign or gesture besides speaking to indicate "yes" to the interrogations and communicate about battling with Satan. As one text puts it, "and if he be so sick that he has lost the use of speech, and has his knowledge whole and entire, he ought to answer to these things [statements about his sins and remorse] by some outward sign." It acknowledges that people who have lost the power of speech may still be mentally available.

This points to considerable flexibility around the observance. It wasn't required to be oral, for example, though evidence of ad hoc signing or gesturing is sparse. I came across one story from seventeenth-century Italy, where plagues and wars had made death inescapably frequent, causing a surge of interest in the *artes moriendi* and a rise in spiritual death consulting. In 1648, a Jesuit priest in Rome founded the Bona Mors Confraternity ("happy death confraternity"), whose motto distilled the age's definition of a good death: to help its members withstand the devil's temptations on the deathbed, offer up one's suffering, and be welcomed into heaven.

One such consultant was the priest Francesco Marchese, the nephew of the celebrated Baroque sculptor Gian Lorenzo Bernini (1598–1680), who engaged Marchese as confessor and advisor for the foreseen spiritual struggles of the deathbed. They came up with a communication method involving signs and gestures, a sort of ad hoc, multimodal, single-use manual pidgin. Whether it was inspired by Marchese or Bernini isn't clear, though one can certainly imagine a deathbed specialist inventing such a system for a client who feared being incommunicado.

As Bernini's son wrote, "Assuming also that, as is usual, words would fail him at the extremity of life, and he would suffer the anguish of one who cannot make himself understood, they worked out a special way in which he could be understood without speaking."

Scant but intriguing details about their pantomimes have been left behind. Apparently they involved "gestures and external motions," wrote a biographer, noting that thanks to a "inflammation in his head" (a stroke), Bernini could indeed only "speak brokenly," before losing the ability entirely. He was able to point with his left hand (his right was paralyzed) at some equipment used for lifting heavy objects, joking with his assistants that it might be used to clear his throat. With this signed system, Marchese apparently had no problem understanding Bernini, who "gave such suitable replies to his proposals that they sufficed to lead him with admirable calm to his end."

Despite Bernini's florid example, it would be a mistake to romanticize sign language at the end of life. In fact, signers aren't necessarily more communicatively enabled at that point. In contemporary times, people who are deaf or hard of hearing face numerous challenges, including poor access to medical interpreters and ignorant medical staff who have strapped down the arms of signers, mistaking their movements as delirious flapping. Meanwhile, deaf people who can read lips find themselves unable to see faces clearly, because lying down in a hospital bed means you look up at darkened, backlit faces. Another challenge: some deaf people of a certain age are themselves uncertain signers, given that they learned sign language relatively late in life (because they didn't have access to deaf education). Not only does signing provide uncertain advantage, but the deaf and hard of hearing might be less communicatively resilient in the face of medical challenges.

§

The practices around attending to a dying person might have an evolutionary history. Scientists have observed chimpanzees, both in the wild and in captivity, displaying surprisingly familiar patterns of behavior around dead and dying individuals. Chimps pay close, silent attention to a corpse. They also have some leave-taking behaviors, such as a "moving-off-and-glancing-back" gesture or lingering for a final touch, again with corpses. If you're compelled by the search for evolutionary roots of religion, you may find these (and other) behaviors fascinating, though it's also been noted that nonhuman apes might not naturally show leave-taking behaviors of any sort, even with the living.

Under such conditions, I'll keep my investigation closer to my own time. Over subsequent centuries, the cultural influence of the *artes moriendi* waned, as the Enlightenment encouraged skepticism about the afterlife, and the Protestant Reformation broke the shackles of ecclesiastic power on everyday life. The ritual last word was giving way to a *laissez parler* mode.

As one historian observed, "Objecting to the impression that a death-bed confession could compensate for a reprobate life, the Protestants eliminated the sacramental value of the rites altogether, left confession to the initiative of the dying person, and substituted the support of godly friends for the priest."

How diverse Protestant traditions transformed the Catholic *ars moriendi* is beyond the scope of my story, except for one important point. For Catholics, a person's performance of the deathbed rituals was how they gained God's favor, while for Protestants those performances were proof that one already enjoyed God's favor. Thus the "art of dying" morphed into a more general "art of living," but it also opened the door to abandoning the script altogether. What was the dying person supposed to do, then? A humanistic paradigm made its appearance in the hands of Michel de Montaigne, whose *Essays* Osler had in his library. In one essay, "That to Study Philosophy Is to Learn to Die," Montaigne confessed his fascination with death: "If I were a writer of books, I would compile a register, with a comment, of the various deaths of men." He wanted to know the manner of their deaths, "their words, looks, and bearing." A hundred years before this statement, there could have been no reliable interest in actual last words that differed among people, because no one uttered any distinct, individual words. The decline of the *ars moriendi* ritual makes me wonder what the first last sincere word might have been. It wasn't Montaigne's. He himself was unable to speak for three days before he died, because of an attack of quinsy, a bacterial infection of the throat, forcing him to write down what he wanted.

For the next two hundred years or so, the only accounts of individual last words came mainly from religious martyrs, criminals, or infidels—all outlaws from social institutions and not beholden to any template for a good death. (Renaissance drama in English, on the other hand, was full of dramatic death speeches, an innovation by English dramatist Christopher Marlowe [1564–1593], to make a dramatic death a moment of character development.) People could read about remorseful or vengeful criminals on the scaffold, while partisans, theologians, and polemicists sought affirmations or recantations of faith, pulling from deathbed descriptions any evidence about who experienced either painful or exalted deaths and even dividing deathbed scenes in anthologies between "infidels" and Christians. Their last words told what their gods were like.

Later in this chapter I'll write about last words during the COVID-19 pandemic that began in 2020. For now, I'll note that the role that last words played in the religious "deathbed wars" of early modernity came back to life during the pandemic, in the form of videos taken of COVID-19 denialists and anti-vaxxers on their deathbeds. In the videos, dying patients begged for a vaccine, or they renounced their previous anti-mask or anti-vaccine status. Captured on video and circulated widely on social media platforms, these gripping statements were the deathbed conversions of the twenty-first century. Also making news were similar testimonies of doctors. Said one quoted in a news article, "The fact that I have patients begging for a vaccine when they're taking their final breaths is obscene." Said another, "One of the last things they do before they're intubated is beg me for the vaccine. I hold their hand and tell them that I'm sorry, but it's too late." Both sorts of videos were hungrily consumed and disseminated by people who supported public health institutions and their science-based recommendations, in whose view living as an anti-vaxxer was a sure way to die unhappily.

§

In his library, William Osler possessed extended accounts of the deaths of various British royalty, Napoleon, Edgar Allan Poe, and others, but as much as he might have been captivated by William Hunter's final paean to dying, there's one last-words book that he somehow didn't include in his Death, Heaven, and Hell corner: a prominent anthology of last words, *Last Words of Eminent Persons*, compiled by Joseph Kaines, a London lecturer, published in 1866. Maybe Osler passed it over because some contemporaries found it distasteful—one reviewer chided Kaines for passing down "second-hand information" and not bothering to subject the contents of his compilation to any scholarly inquiry. The reviewer also noted that Kaines makes no effort to moralize about his "alphabetical eminences." But Karl Guthke claims it was the first book to realize Montaigne's vision—Osler would have seen the value of that. And because Kaines's title denotes the eminent person, not the saintly or the sinful, it was marked as a testimony to the secularization of death, which made Kaines a pioneer in the sincere, *laissez parler* last-word literary genre.

"The last words of dying persons are always interesting," he swaggered, and so his reader learns about the deaths of monarchs and philosophers, doctors and officers. (Therefore mainly men.) "Am I blue?" asked Dr. Adam Clark (1762–1832), dying of cholera. *"Mais quel diable de mal veux-tu cela me fasse?"* ("How the deuce can that hurt me?") wondered Denis Diderot (1713–1784).

Kaines's work signaled a shift in views of the language of the dying, marking a side effect of a print culture that was creating a celebrity culture. For one thing, the characters in Kaines's book reflected on many topics, not just the experience of dying, and not just of their souls (and therefore their status in God's eyes). Also, as if channeling the Roman writer Marcus Varro, Kaines wrote that the dying gained *fari*-like linguistic powers from their proximity to not one god but all of them. If I can pull Erving Goffman's framework of animator, author, and principal back into view, we can say that the dying person may be the animator and the principal, meaning they physically produce the utterance that they also get credit for, but it's the gods who author the message. Which isn't so different from the *artes moriendi*, putting holy words in the dying person's mouth.

Karl Guthke, a Harvard scholar, had probably read all of the last-word anthologies, analyzing them for his relatively compact landmark book, *Last Words*. (By the way, it appeared in 1992, the same year as *Final Gifts*.) His definitive tour of the literary genre of the last word has been widely cited by literary and cultural critics. He surveyed the cultural moments in which their meanings are constructed and the controversies surrounding them. It's not that the utterers of last words are consciously crafting them, yet survivors do have a tendency to style final utterances in the literary fashions of the moment. Last words are the ultimate bon mots. He respected the uncanny charismatic force of the dying articulation while bringing an understated but cosmopolitan mordant style, which serves to blunt the melodrama and mess of the death scene. As he wrote, "Kings of Sweden tend to murmur 'Sweden' when the curtain falls, according to usually well informed Swedish sources." He made it seem so lively, so literary. It was also a probe: if you're chuckling at his wry takes, you're still alive.

One thing I've borrowed from Guthke is his reliably durable definition of the last word, as a "final, self-validating articulation of consciousness in extremis." It also alerted me to the need to link the form of last words to cultural decisions, to harken back to Catherine Snow's interpretation of first words. At first, this seemed to make possible a history of dying entirely on the basis of the utterances themselves, which Guthke ventured. But the history of last words reflects such a history only if you account for the relationship between the way that people of an era and a community are socialized to be linguistically capable and attentive at the interaction window with a dying person, and if you account for the ways in which they tend to die. A true history of last words, as of first ones, must be about bodies.

To Guthke the attention to last words is obvious: more than curiosities, they reveal the stakes of life's limits. His tour of this narrow slice of language experience at the end of life is quite enjoyable, relating the last words of French presidents (as from Paul Doumer, "How did an automobile get into the book sale?"), Russian novelists (Tolstoy: "How do peasants die?"), Mexican revolutionaries ("Don't let it end like this," Pancho Villa said to the gathered journalists, "Tell them I said something"—though this turns out to be apocryphal, as Villaologists say he died immediately), Soviet inmates ("Stalin"), battlefield casualties ("I die happy"), obscure murder victims (the murderer's name), cartoon characters, along with multiple famous personages (Leonard Bernstein, Hapsburg Emperor Francis I, Julius Caesar, Gertrude Stein, among many others). A massively enduring cultural institution devoted to last words has been assembled through biographies, anthologies, Trivial Pursuit clues, commercial taglines, song lyrics, comicstrip punchlines, and other cultural employments, including parodies of that institution. It's no wonder that contemporary people expect to leave behind *some linguistic thing*. Never linguistic rubble, never silence. As if it's *fari* to the end.

Guthke's career with last words began, he retells, when he was invited to lecture on Swiss scientist and writer Albrecht von Haller (1708–1777) on the bicentenary of his death. Were the 1970s a more fruitful era for new perspectives on death and dying than others? Sometimes it seems so. A dutiful biographer, Guthke sought meaning in Haller's last words, which turned out to be as slippery as Goethe's, Wilde's, and others. One source reported that Haller died with "an appropriate confession of faith on his lips." Another source had Haller renouncing any religious belief whatsoever, and yet another reported that Haller simply said, "I'm calm," while a fourth had him reporting, Edgar Allan Poe–like, on his own arrested pulse

("It's beating . . . beating . . . beating—it's stopped"). There was even a fifth version, recorded by a minister who was at the bedside, in which Haller muttered, "My God! I am dying!" (apparently not an uncommon exclamation of surprise). Now captivated, Guthke took on the project of researching the varied high and low literatures of mortality, and in the process became a last-word hound and probably a more-interesting-than-average dinner guest.

From his book I learned that last words have appeared in numerous pamphlets and anthologies, such as the ones that Arthur MacDonald mined, in English, French, German, Italian, Swedish, Danish, Russian, Hebrew, Arabic, Japanese, and Chinese dating back to the seventeenth century. "One does come away with the feeling that last words are part of the legacy of mankind to itself, that they are, or have for some time been considered, a valuable part of our civilization, an element of our cultural self-awareness and our humanistic tradition," he wrote. I'm reminded of Rose Macaulay's assertion in her compendium of ruin-seeking across time, *Pleasure of Ruins*, that "the human race is, and has always been, ruin-minded." This seems to be particularly true when it comes to language too. The connecting thread between language and architecture appears to be the attempt to construct a monument from miserable finitude and its remnants. "Finality commands attention," Guthke wrote. "Last words, unlike all others, cannot be taken back."

§

To understand what Guthke was doing with all this, it's useful to return to the distinction between the ritualistic and the sincere. (The ritualistic multiplies "as if" worlds; the sincere insists on reality as it actually is and is rooted in individual expressive selves.) *Last Words* tours the relatively recent and culturally circumscribed phenomenon of sincere last words, the ones in which individuals leave an unscripted, self-defining mark on history, as if you could sign your life like an artist does in the corner of their painting.

Of course, these last words aren't truly sincere—there's hardly any acknowledgment of nonverbal communication in this tradition, nor the interaction window. They tug at the heartstrings but aren't as brutal as Olga Janáčkova's *ritardando* melodies, and they (mostly) make sense. These last words are Cartesian in that they're emanations from a mind that's somehow insulated from the depredations of the body it's connected to. For this reason, the anthologies aren't concerned with how people actually die, so there's no accounting for what's normal about language and communication at the end of life or what lies outside any cultural transformations and decisions. In this sense, you might say there's never yet been a *truly* sincere description of language at the end of many lives.

Such accounts of sincere last words don't accommodate how ritual ones persisted along with the *ars moriendi*'s demise. As it turns out, ritualistic last-word traditions in Islam, Buddhism, Hinduism, Judaism, and even Roman Catholicism—and the accompanying ideas about the dying person as someone who produces spoken language—are still alive. (Ritual last words also appear in literature—in Philip Pullman's *His Dark Materials* fantasy trilogy, witches call to a goddess of the underworld, Yambe-Akka, as their last words.) Someday, someone will dive into all of these more deeply, but I want to briefly sketch them from a linguistic perspective.

They're interesting because they push to the forefront the matter of *words*, especially the work they do, over the existential glory of *lastness*. Ritual last words are similar to cultural first words—different traditions have more or less rigid or flexible expectations here for the form of the performances. This is because the ritual marks the threshold. We arrive in the place where semiotics and speech act theory have to lend a hand: What happens, for instance, when individuals aren't able to perform the rituals? Can an incomplete form have the same ritual authority as a whole one? Does it have the same effect if it's said unintentionally? To whom is one directing one's final utterances, anyway? The ritualistic also helps manage this—it constructs the behavior as if it's the whole.

In ritual last words, the agency of the language user takes an entirely different shape. Take the ideal Hindu death, for example, which prizes the speaking of the name of a god. Religion scholar Anantanand Rambachan wrote that the preference is for Krishna, but also Rama, Shiva, or Durga, "depending on family traditions or personal preference." A Hindi funeral hymn expresses such a wish: "I pray, O lord, that when the breath of life departs my body, you enable me to utter Your name, Govind." The death of Mahatma Gandhi is held up as one model; he died saying, "Ram, Ram," the name of God as Rama.

I was surprised to find that the Hindu one models the dying person more as a *listener* than as a speaker. "What you generally find is that family members try to focus the dying person's mind, thoughts, and emotions on the divine, on the divine reality," Rambachan told me. "They will try very assiduously to make the chanting the last thing a person hears." They want to help the person transition to a new state of existence that is closer to the divine. However, this can be a bit complicated in the case of teachers, gurus, or leaders like Mahatma Gandhi. "There may still be a recitation of sacred sounds and chanting, but the disciples of a person would be more interested in the last words of a guru for their didactic significance," he noted. Such last words might also be collected in books.

In a surprising turn, even *unintentionally* saying a god's name can have powerful results. A story from the seventh century's *Bhagavata Purana* tells about Ajamila, a priest who becomes a social outcast after taking up with a prostitute, drinking, and stealing. He fathers many children, the youngest of whom he names Narayana, and to whom he calls on his deathbed. It just so happens that "Narayana" is also a name of Vishnu, so the power of speaking it secures Ajamila a place in Vishnu's realm. Also powerful is hearing the names of gods—in the holy Indian city of Varanasi is a home for the dying, Muktibhavan, where the names of gods are chanted twenty-four hours a day via a loudspeaker, "which ensures that no resident dies without the opportunity to hear the name of God."

This practice is enabled by someone like Shivam Bhatt, a man in his early forties. On his lunch break from his tech company marketing job, he agreed to talk to me about his other job, that of lay Hindu priest. Some Brahmin priests perform rituals in temples; others perform rituals in the community, like weddings and death rites. His family has played this role for thousands of years, most recently in San Jose, California, where his entire family clan relocated in the 1970s.

When a person's death is anticipated, the family will gather to make sure certain rituals are followed, including chanting a mantra from the Rig Veda called the *maha mrityunjaya* mantra, or the "death-defeating mantra." The Sanskrit chant goes, "*Aum Tryambakam yajaamahe sugandhim pushtivard-hanam / Urvaarukamiva bandhanaan-mrityormuksheeya maamritaat,*" which can be translated as "we honor the three-eyed one [Shiva], the increaser of prosperity; just as the cucumber is freed from the vine, may I be released from mortality." This mantra expresses the essential Hindu hope of freedom, called *moksha,* from endless cycles of death and rebirth.

Depending on who a person's patron deity is, you may hear them say "Rama, Rama" or "Krishna, Krishna," but Bhatt said that the *maha mri-tyunjaya* is "universal at this stage of your life, because it's fundamental to this part of your life." Though the dying person might repeat the chant if they're able to, it's more critical that they *hear* the chant. It's one of several chants that Hindu children learn early and repeat often; Bhatt said he learned to chant it before he understood it. I told him I suspected that the Western tradition of unscripted last words has had negative consequences, in that people who are expecting a truth or secret uttered with a dying breath ("Rosebud," muttered a dying Charles Foster Kane, the famous first word in *Citizen Kane*) will instead encounter silence or hallucination. This contrary material will be difficult to incorporate into the redemptive memorial stories that help grievers cope.

"Exactly!" Bhatt replied. "Your last word should be something that comes naturally to you, that you innately want to express. Otherwise it seems really forced, and there's no value to that, spiritually or personally."

§

In a similar fashion, some sects of Islam, at least in the contemporary world, prescribe last words for the dying person. It's said to be a cherished hope of every Muslim that his last breath should be accompanied by the Arabic recitation of a prayer called the *Shahadah*, or "*laa llaaha Illa Allah*" ("There is no god but God and Muhammad is the Messenger of God"). This practice is by no means uniform, as Islam contains huge variations across regions, languages, and eras. But as religion scholar Pieter Coppens noted, there's no widely accepted *ars moriendi*–like guide for Islamic chaplains in hospitals. According to a modern funeral guide for Muslims that I found online, people should gather to recite the Koran if the person isn't able and to perform *talqin*, or to remind the dying person to say the *Shahadah*. The guide continues:

> When the end nears, the dying person's breath quickens, the knees become so weak that they cannot move, the nose becomes bent and the temples subside. By these signs understand that the person is nearing their end. The *talqin* should be read before the dying person takes their last breaths, the *muhtadar* must not be asked or ordered to read the *kalimah*, but must be helped to recall it. i.e. those present should continually repeat it aloud, in front of the dying. Once the departing person utters the *kalimah*, all who are present should remain silent.

It's also imperative that the dying person not be drawn into a conversation on other topics, otherwise the *talqin* must be repeated. An Islamic scholar is quoted in a fatwa: "If he regains consciousness and says something like 'give me water' or anything else, then the person with him should again ask him to say the Shahadah." The prayer operates as a sort of sacred threshold even on this side of actual expiration, a transition from the mundane. Yet Islam's fourteen centuries have produced variation and color, its own sincerity waxing and waning: a scholar named Salih Kuftaru, who died in 1936, said, "Prepare yourself to meet God all alone, safely," while his brother, Muhammad Amin Kuftaru, who died in 1938, kept repeating "O God, the Highest Companion."

I spoke with Taqwa Surapati, the only Muslim inpatient chaplain at a hospital in California, who told me about some of the affordances in the tradition. For instance, Muslims face the direction of Mecca when they pray, but doing that might be problematic if someone is lying in a bed. "Prayers are connection with Allah, daily. If you cannot stand, you can do it lying down and do the most you can with the movements and sequences," Surapati said. If you can raise your hand, you raise your hand. Even if people can no longer speak or move, and they can only move their fingers to say their prayers, they can raise the index finger to represent a belief in the one true god.

Nowadays, saying the *Shahadah* is an ideal, Surapati said, but in modern contexts, because of medication or other medical intervention, someone might not be able to articulate the words. "But we believe that he or she will transition to the afterlife, because the goal is not to make things difficult. The goal is to have this one-on-one time with God. God did not invent hardship for you; God wants peace for you." Yet if a dying person can repeat the *Shahadah* back to you, the other prescriptions hold: once they say the prayer, they shouldn't talk about anything else. The *Shahadah* it meant to be the last thing they say.

However, crafty people try to exploit this as a moral loophole. "I've heard stories of people saying, 'I can live however I want, and in the end I can just say the *Shahadah*, and I'm guaranteed paradise.'" But they're underestimating the value of a life's worth of *Shahadah* practice—given the neurochemical commotion of the end, the *Shahadah* should be as automatic, as firmly engrained in the brain, as possible. Surapati was blunt: "You have to put in the work to be able to say it at the end of life." She continued: "You have to strive to be upright, to be a good Muslim. What we're hoping for is ease, from God's mercy, in that moment, because it's going to be hard, this transition between life and death."

Some Buddhist teachings also contain advice about language at the end of life. One constant in the varied teachings about dying is the stress on promoting a positive, compassionate state of mind at the moment of death. Sometimes this is achieved through meditative exercises (as in Theravada Buddhism), sometimes through ritual chanting (as in Mahayana and Vajryana Buddhism). A monk named Genshin (942–1017) compiled the first set of instructions for deathbed practices in Japan, including contemplative exercises and the chanting of the *nenbutsu*, or the Buddha Amida's name (*"nama Amida butsu"*). These chants initially worked as meditative aids, then became significant for someone to utter in their final moments.

Among the esoteric offshoots of these teachings was an emphasis on one's bodily posture at the moment of death, preferably sitting as if in meditation, facing a particular cardinal direction. Another teaching concerned a one-vowel mantra, a "seed" syllable, called the "A-syllable." I would identify it as a vowel that sounds like "ah." In Sanskrit, this sound is "the primordial vibration from which the universe arose" and "is associated with the origin of things," denoting "the universal or all-pervasive." Another Japanese monk named Kakuban (1095–1143) stressed how "a" is a constant sound throughout nature and in human life ("there is not a single occasion when you do not say 'A'!"). Though understanding the full meaning of "A" required access to high-level Buddhist teachings, the A-syllable was thought to be a widely accessible key for accessing the "pure land" in which one would be born as a buddha or bodhisattva after dying in this life. The *nenbutsu* eventually merged with A-syllable practice, so that a single recitation of "A" could stand for the whole six-syllable *nenbutsu*.

A blog account of a death related the importance of chanting: "Suddenly, when I was chanting sutra halfway, grandfather started saying 'Ah Ah.' He looked very peaceful and wasn't suffering. I encouraged him by chanting a few times of Amituofo to him. He was smiling and went on to 'Ah Mi,'" as he struggled hard to move his mouth, though he couldn't really speak."

Two days later, the writer's grandfather passed away. Wrote the devout grandson: "I can't tell if grandfather was reborn in Pure Land for absolute certainty, but it is likely that he did."

This A-syllable practice strikes me as an example of a linguistic fallback with which communities with strict prescribed last words manage the rubble of language at the end of life. After all, from a phonetic perspective, reciting the soul-saving sound would likely be as easy to produce as—and indistinguishable from—a moan. Modern Islam has a similar fallback for the *Shahadah*: during a Muslim's lifetime, they hold up or tap the index finger of the right hand while saying the *Shahadah*, as a gestural representation of the monotheism that the prayer asserts. If the dying person is unable to speak, they are allowed to hold up this finger, which "counts" as satisfying the ritual. And if the person is even unable to do that much, someone else is allowed to hold up their finger for them.

In this fascinating territory of ritual last words, cultures are wrapping cultures are wrapping a similarly sacred frame around a range of communicative behaviors. Moreover, what an individual is capable of doing as a language producer matters far less than in the Western stereotypical last-word tradition, whose sincerity emphasizes a dying person's individual expressions. It echoes how "mama" and other cultural first words are sometimes more preferred. The problem is that survivors and loved ones must confront the reality of fevered, restless delirium or even outright silence. Other religious traditions have solved this problem by keeping the dying person linguistically occupied. The person who utters the chant, prayer, or name of a god is on the verge of being absorbed into the existential collective. So it makes sense that they would produce a repetitive form on this side of the threshold.

Most importantly, it sadly suggests that the *laissez parler* last-word tradition launched by Montaigne and celebrated by Kaines (among others) has set a high bar, both for the dying and for family members. Raised to believe that dying people normally exit with a quip, a teaching, or a personal moment, you're left with no framework that accounts for the fragmented, the nonsensical, the delirious, or the silent. You expect to raise a monument to the mortal self; what you trip over is rubble.

§

The last words of a dying man from 2020 show something of their power, as they took on a public life spraypainted on walls, markered on protest signs, flown on banners behind airplanes, printed on T-shirts. You know the one I'm talking about, that unmistakable marker of the times and a powerful slogan for a new political era: "I can't breathe." These words became an event as I was drafting this account of last words, which makes me want to note a couple of things about George Floyd's utterances, and before him Eric Garner's, both of which were captured on video.

"I can't breathe" were for a time the most famous last words on the planet, gaining visibility almost immediately after the police officers killed the men. Last words are usually remembered by people who were present, who retell what happened. The words, the sighs, the smiles. This process of memorializing a final interaction is important for people who are grieving a death. Last words must be transported via memory in this way because they're usually uttered in private, in intimate emotional settings, though they can also be semipublic (if uttered in an emergency room, for instance). But in 2020, smartphones and social media make for public deathbeds, whether any one wants this or not, providing scenes can be repeated ad infinitum, contextualized for a variety of motivations from the forensic to the indignant to the racist. Deaths are accidents, suicides, mass shootings, private homicides, state murders, all of them offered up for consumption by global audiences, and you can barely avoid people discussing them on your social media feeds, much less seeing the scenes themselves.

Indeed, intrinsic to the publicness of Floyd's last words—and eventually their political impact—is the fact they were recorded, then posted to Facebook, where people viewed them from a range of motives, some questionable. A seventeen-year-old bystander named Darnella Frazier had the fortitude to record Floyd's killing by police for ten minutes, even as they threatened her and the other witnesses with mace. Her video was widely credited for the criminal conviction of police officer Derek Chauvin, Floyd's murderer, because it proved the police account was false. Eventually Frazier received a Pulitzer Prize and an award from PEN America. This wasn't scientific observation; it was justice. As University of Southern California journalism professor Allissa Richardson noted, Frazier's use of the smartphone is a distinctly Black form of witnessing. But as Richardson also pointed out, internet-available footage of violence and deaths of white people is routinely scrubbed, while footage of Black people's deaths is relatively easy to find. She urges people to view such videos not casually but instead "with solemn respect."

Death is a constant, but 2020 was the year of last words: when people confronted their ideas about language and the "good death," when last words rose from private intimacies, became political slogans, or became inaccessible altogether. It was a strange time to be drafting this book about a soft, even frivolous thing like language, when the topics of the day were so hard: cell membranes, supply chains, tear gas, batons. And yet life continued. It went on amid the turmoil of lockdowns and protests, and so did deaths and dying, sometimes to a lesser degree (fewer suicides, fewer motor deaths, for a while, and fewer homicides), but mainly in highly visible, publicized ways. Thousands, then hundreds of thousands, then millions were taken by COVID-19, usually after struggling to breathe but also of massive organ failures. The infectiousness of the virus meant that these people often died in isolated circumstances, unable to be visited in person by family members. Chaplains found themselves tele-chaplains. One chaplain in Minnesota told me that ministering via Zoom forced him to adapt, especially in circumstances where patients were nonverbal, because he had to become more comfortable with silence. Rather than being able to say his words and then leave the room, he had to sit looking at the patient on a screen, waiting for a staffer to turn off the device. Patients were intubated, then heavily sedated in order to make the breathing tube's discomforts bearable. Both things meant that the expected deathbed interactions and last words were now, thanks to hospital protocols, endangered or eliminated entirely, as though they'd become technologically outmoded. There was a new, nightmarish way of dying: silent, cut off from family, interrupted only by the buzz and ping of arriving text messages, or via remote channels.

"Patients and families have been very angry," another American chaplain told me. "In the eighteen months of social isolation, they forgot how to socialize. There's an immense amount of floating rage. There is a lot of second-guessing, a lot of unresolved loss, because people didn't have any rituals for death."

Restrictions on visitors to hospitals meant that millions around the world died alone, traumatizing their grieving family members who were restricted from visiting their nearest kin or partners. Said a widower in Kashmir, "There are many things a person tells to her/his family members when she/he is close to death. Maybe my wife would have also desired to talk with anyone of us about anything. I would always be in a dilemma about what would have been her last wish." The solitary deaths seemed undignified, making it difficult for survivors to accept the loss. "Coronavirus is robbing people of the opportunity of a final farewell, stripping the dead of their dignity and worsening the grief of the living," wrote two Spanish scholars. Both the media as well as the academic literature are full of reports from around the world about traumatized grievers.

One recommendation that came out of these experiences runs counter to both traditions and intuition. As some grief researchers observed, "Healthcare professionals had the impression that relatives would benefit from having the opportunity to visit when the dying patient is conscious and responsive and not just the hours before death." In the context of the pandemic, nurses and social workers had to go out of their way to offer this option and then facilitate it with video-enabled devices. Among all of the ways that the pandemic changed us, I wonder how durable this one will be. If we can remember to focus on the words, less on their lastness.

At the time that this was happening, I thought of myself as putting all this in a broader historical and linguistic context. Never had the verbal self and its ethereal traces seemed so pertinent: the canonical life of the signifying subject, from first to last, represented in speech, sign, touch, gesture, and text. And then someone would tell me a story that ripped me apart and cast a shade on my obsession with language in the book of life. I thought of Bob Gramling's singing bowl, how healing that must have felt to those researchers. The subject of first and last words would seem irrelevant, an escape from reality, even though hiding from the news of the world by researching language at the end of life did seem a perverse form of escape—if that was what I was doing.

10   Death Resists

Earlier in this book, I described four types of expectations that different communities and eras have about children's first words. As the previous chapter made apparent, last words can be mapped in a similar way. Some communities have fairly rigid expectations about the forms that final utterances should take, scripting them but also allowing for flexibility. Others have looser expectations, a *laissez parler* mode, that suits hopes for individual expressions; this also dovetails with an observational mode (though it's unclear how widely this gets practiced for language at the end of life). Finally, there are societies where a final articulation of consciousness isn't noticed or valued at all.

Yet on its own this taxonomy misses a crucial aspect of last words that doesn't apply to first ones. One of death's powers—indeed, one of its cruelties—is its ability to evade cultural transformations. Even as it defines the last-word game, it interrupts and frustrates it, as William Osler found, denying the living their usual participation. Dying people lie unconscious, delirious, too weak to interact, despite what their loved ones, heirs, lawyers, pastors, or anyone else may expect. Such physical challenges show up the cultural ideal and challenge theological understandings of existence and what happens when it ends. What might be more salient is the level of surprise that greets them—who finds that they've escaped death's cruelty? One might also anticipate a final message only to find it barbed and poisonous. I've also heard more than once that some last words can never be repeated because they were too dark, too cutting. One person, who told me she refused to repeat or analyze what she encountered, regretted that she heard them at all.

It's so easy to get twisted up in your own cultural models.

William Brahms is a librarian in New Jersey who assembled an anthology of last words, *Last Words of Notable People*. When it came out in 2010, he encountered readers who entertained themselves by speculating what their last words might be. Initially, Brahms said, they would propose something witty and profound, later admitting that they'd likely express appreciation and love, or something spiritual, if they even have enough control over their verbal production, when lucidity and intelligibility become hurdles— which Brahms saw at the bedside of his dying mother. Even though she'd spent years helping him edit his book, they'd never discussed what they thought their last words would be.

It didn't matter, because the reality was quite different.

"In her case, due to debilitating illness, it was not a clear punctuated statement," Brahms told me in an email, with evident surprise. "It was more of a slow and fading dialogue."

This gap is a dominant theme. On one side, what the neurochemical commotion and closing interaction window leave of language. On the other, people's expectations and cultural ideals. Sometimes the neurochemical commotion is so severe, sometimes the interaction window won't budge, and it becomes impossible to make any "as if" worlds at all.

I am struck, however, by the counterintuitive idea that the more rigid expectations might be more forgiving, and that *laissez parler* modes can easily be frustrated. Take, for instance, the emphasis placed on last words among evangelical Christians in the Victorian era. As literary historian Pat Jalland wrote, "The last words of the dying had special significance for Evangelicals, who believed that conduct in the final hours was a vital test of fitness for salvation." People learned acceptable forms of last words from *artes moriendi*, religious pamphlets, and anthologies of last words, ranging from what Jalland described as "the sublime to the mundane." It seems that a specific utterance wasn't prescribed, as in the original *Tractatus artis bene moriendi*, but modeled for people to adapt themselves. There were still acceptable things to say for one's "godly friends," but the expectations had loosened.

This ideally sincere last word had to promise not only a linguistic form but also a spiritually flavored content. However, after examining dozens of private deathbed accounts in letters and diaries by Victorian Evangelicals, Jalland found something unsurprising: death had its way. In fact, "few dying Victorians actually succeeded in producing the required testimonies to their readiness for heaven," she wrote. In fact, most of these private accounts mentioned "bland or banal last words" at the very end, "or more often, none at all." Many lives ended after long days of unconsciousness or delirium.

When final moments didn't match the publicly available models of sincerity in death, they were probably kept private, retained only for family memories (though many more people attended Victorian deathbeds, where they likely encountered the truth). It's hard to imagine a first word having such a fate. If dying people were able to speak—for instance, when they briefly came to consciousness—they typically asked for food, liquid, or other care. When he died in 1804, Immanuel Kant waved water away. Sir John Gladstone's last words were remembered apocryphally as "Get me some porridge." (His son William found more meaning in his father's raised forefinger: "It was a striking symbol for us, the finger of a dying Father pointing up to heaven.") When Osler died in 1919 at the age of seventy, from an internal hemorrhage during a bout with pneumonia, his last spoken words were to his doctor: "Hold up my head." (A reviewer of Kaines's book sniffed that Lord Byron's last words, "I must sleep now," were the "natural expression of a patient.")

A stark rendering of a death was captured by Canadian farmwife Susanna Vickers in 1866, when her long-ailing husband, John, died: "When I had fixed his pillows and made all quite comfortable, I kissed the broad, noble brow, and bade God to bless my old darling, and give him a good night's rest. And he put up his dear arms and pulled me down to his breast, and said 'My dear dear *Auld* wife, may He bless you.' Those were the last words of love and tenderness, he would ever say to me."

Her attribution of the last words was in retrospect, because the night held further chaos. Early in the morning, she was woken up by his crying for her, asking for water.

> I lit my lamp and gave him some water, but he could not drink it, but he begged me to open the window and get him over the bed as he wanted air. This difficulty of breathing lasted about half an hour when he closed his eyes and died as peacefully as a child. I begged him to speak to me, to send some word to the children, but he waved his hand solemnly in farewell, the power of speech was gone.

We can imagine that Susanna passed along his loving words, not his cries for water, as his "last words." But we can also ask: Where is the final articulation of consciousness here? We must admit the possibility that there are several, though if there must be only one, it's his waving hand. The image chokes me up every time I imagine it.

This tension between the poetic and the banal has been another constant in the history of Western stereotypical last words. In his book, Joseph Kaines included a long account from Sir Henry Halford (1766–1844), the most distinguished physician of *his* day (as William Osler was of his), to emphasize the rare status of a sensible last word. Halford, amply quoted by Munk in *Euthanasia*, describes dying in starkly clinical terms. Either the nervous system gives out or the "oppression" of the lungs leaves "black venous blood to circulate," creeping its anoxia up from the cellular level to the brain, where "its energies appear to be lulled thereby into sleep,—generally tranquil sleep,—filled with dreams which impel the dying lips to murmur out the names of friends and the occupations and recollections of past life: the peasant 'babbles o' green fields'; and Napoleon expires amid visions of battles, uttering with his last breath '*tet d'armée.*'"

Not surprisingly, Kaines himself saw last words as unreliable measures of the authentic self. "When the faculties have become dimmed, the senses numbed, memory a wreck, the system broken and the soul incapable of thought, the man is not intact;—it is not himself that lies dying there," he wrote. *It is not himself*—the person has already departed, so the words don't reliably allow access to the dying experience of that person. This invalidated deathbeds as sites of spiritual struggle, the places where a person displays religious conviction or spiritual health. For someone to say anything sensible (and often anything at all) was less a miracle than a physiological freak. The deathbed wasn't any place to be searching for sincere truths.

This is what doctors like Munk and Osler might have found themselves explaining to families: the dwindling of linguistic agency wasn't a sign of the absence of God's favor; it was merely the body giving out.

"We hear and read of persons retaining a clear and vigorous intellect up to the moment of departure; but in truth such ideas and statements rest upon very shallow evidence," said William J. Savory in 1863 in a lecture about death. Perhaps Osler learned this too: his Hopkins patients were, at the end, mostly comatose, and therefore unavailable to comment on their experience.

In the nineteenth century, many doctors advocated across a range of matters, whether for urban sanitation or attitudes toward the dying. For instance, in 1850, a devout Christian doctor in England, Samuel Beckett, warned people of high expectations for "manifestations of gracious feelings" from the dying, especially if they are locked in fevers or dying painfully. Doctors sometimes assisted with interpreting nonverbals as elevated religious expressions. "In many such cases, it is only in half-broken accents, or by the significant movement of the head or of the hand, that we can arrive at the assurance of the Divine presence and support," Beckett wrote. As with Gian Lorenzo Bernini, the gesture had its connoisseurs as much as any abundantly meaningful last word.

§

I note these two opposing ideas about language at the end of life: the insistence on a dying person's glowing linguistic powers—producing sincere expressions that will go to work on behalf of the living—and the skepticism that these utterances can't, in fact, accomplish such work. This contradiction hasn't vanished. Take, for example, the way that modern legal commentators have attempted, unsuccessfully, to undercut the special legal status of statements made by dying people by pointing to the profound cognitive effects of bodily harm.

Such statements, because they're made by dying people, have long been believed to be more truthful than statements by those who aren't. We might find it anachronistic if someone said the proximity to the gods improved a dying person's ability to produce language. Yet this is precisely the idea that survives in all of the legal systems that are descended from the English one. A "dying declaration" is a form of legal evidence that's considered to be more truthful than other speech solely because it comes from a dying person. "The tongues of dying men/enforce attention like deep harmony," wrote William Shakespeare in *Richard II*. "Where words are scarce, they are seldom spent in vain; for they breathe truth, that breathe their words in pain." "Tell mother good bye," said one person. "I am going to die. What are my children going to do after this?" said another. "No. No. Tom shot me," said a dying man. "Tom. Tom."

Dying speeches had probably been used for centuries to identify perpetrators of crimes, the locations of valuable objects, or family secrets. But in 1202, a medieval English court enshrined the notion formally as *nemo moriturus praesumitur mentiri*—no person about to meet their maker would ever die with a lie on their lips. This principle inaugurated last words' "as if" powers of truthfulness, at least in the courtoom, where last words became admissible as evidence "as if" the usual evidentiary rigors of the courtroom gauntlet had already scoured them. For obvious reasons, the person who said them can't be sworn in, nor can they be cross-examined (as the accused has the right to do). Despite their tangled legal history, the idea that last words' truth value is divinely sanctioned has proven remarkably stubborn. It may also lend itself to dramatic purposes, for if the words are true, then they should appear in a style suitable to the person. Which is why famous last words often have the air of being *too* perfect.

Until 1803, dying declarations served as evidence in civil and criminal cases alike, but then an English court ruled that they were admissible only in homicide cases. From then on, the dying declaration's special status has been whittled down but not completely eradicated, as legal historians have traced. The ritualistic, as we've seen, can be rugged. For instance, a person must be declaring the cause of their own death, not someone else's, often out of necessity, as the only other party present. Also, in some jurisdictions a person must be aware of their imminent, certain death, even though it's not clear how a layperson could know such a thing, especially with no medical expert to tell them. Chief justice of the English high court Alexander Cockburn ruled that a dying laundress's cry to one of her assistants—"See what Harry has done!"—wasn't admissible because there was no evidence she knew she was about to die (even though Harry had slashed her throat and she was bleeding in the backyard).

Despite these whittlings, the dying declaration retains in the eye of the court and in popular opinion a kernel of unassailable truthfulness. It preserves an aspect of medieval Christianity, in which on the other side of dying lies judgment by God and his representatives, mainly Saint Peter, who bars liars from entering the gates of heaven. The truth value of dying declarations increases the closer they occur to the moment of death. Perhaps this is why the most frequent criticism lodged at stereotypical last words (even those not involved in legal cases) is that they might not be true—thanks to conceptual traffic with the legal sphere, their evidentiary status must be questioned, supported, attacked, and sustained. It may also be preferable to get benevolent words from dying people with whom we've had complex relationships. In either case, the pragmatic uses of last words are for the living.

Legal commentators have pointed out that Christian worldviews, while still powerful in some societies, don't dominate the diverse moral universes that people live in anymore. As a result, the dying declaration might be undergoing the same crisis of legitimacy that has subjected many other Western assumptions to the acid test of criticism. This hasn't annulled its legal status yet—when it comes to their truth, everyone who produces a dying declaration is implied to be close to the Christian God.

Even as such medical knowledge is fairly well represented in the media, the exceptional legal status of the dying declaration remains. Even if you assume someone who knows they're about to die will always be honest, "there may still be problems with perception, which tends to plummet when one is bleeding to death," legal scholar Aviva Orenstein wryly observed.

§

Another debate simmers about delirium, which poses the knottiest of the deathbed phenomena for a host of reasons. On one hand, there's a very good chance that a dying person, like a good number of the Johns Hopkins patients, will be delirious at the end of life. In fact, in palliative care and hospice spaces, 58 to 88 percent of cancer patients are delirious in the last week to hours before death. In Osler's study, twenty-eight patients out of the total 486 were described as delirious, with his observers using words like "irrational," "mind wandering," "demented," and in one case "raging."

"I don't want to call it a nearly universal feature of the end-of-life experience," David Wright, a Canadian medical ethnographer, told me, "but as you die, unless you die very suddenly in an instant, your various bodily systems start to work differently until they stop working at all. And that includes the way that you think, and that includes the way that you communicate."

Ancient medical writers distinguished between two types of delirium: *phrenitis*, the restless variety, and *lethargus*, an inert, dull state. Modern researchers keep this distinction, describing delirium as either quiet, listless, apathetic, and "pseudo wakeful," or as a restlessness in which patients are "muttering" and "talkative." Delirium was one of the first medical conditions ever described by Greek and Roman writers almost two thousand years ago. The Greek philosopher Celsus introduced the word *delirium* in the second century CE; the word came from the Latin *delirare*, which means to go out of the furrow (*lira* is Latin for "furrow"). The delirious plow leaves the furrow of sense. A modern person might think that leaving the planned track is a desirable thing, until they familiarize themselves with a single-bladed plow and realize the inconvenience of an errant ox-pulled plow skittering across the field's surface.

Despite this pedigree, the exact biological mechanisms behind delirium aren't well understood, but it appears to stem from neuronal dysfunction, probably due to neurotransmitter fluctuations. Neurons in the brain aren't dying (which is why sometimes people can recover from delirium) but disconnecting from each other. Basically, delirium is the result of a neurochemical commotion. Now clinicians look for three types of delirium: a restless, hyperactive form, a listless form, and a mix of the two.

Delirium is very common among the dying, particularly in the later stages, where that lethargic type shows up most often. As a diagnosis, it covers a complex of symptoms and isn't a single thing. Despite its prevalence, doctors don't reliably recognize delirium. It's often mistaken for dementia, depression, or psychosis. In a study of one hundred consecutive cases of delirium in a palliative care unit, researchers found that 33 percent of patients were classified with the hypoactive, lethargic form. They had the same impairment in cognitive functioning as patients with other variants, showing similar deficits in orientation, memory, and comprehension on cognitive test scores. This variegated presentation makes it hard to tell when someone is delirious. Though clinicians want to take it seriously, they don't have a uniform method for recognizing delirium or dealing with it therapeutically.

On the other hand, delirium also outstrips an ability—and the willingness—to grasp a phenomenon as simultaneously biological, emotional, and social. It has what David Wright called a relational dimension, in the sense that any individual's delirium impacts other people's perceptions of the relationship. Some find it traumatizing and distressing, others less so. In either case, what seems to help is when delirium is described as a normal part of dying, in the same way that baby babbling is described as a normal feature of language acquisition. Some medical staff try to normalize the delirium as part of the natural process of dying, and they encourage family members to enter the hallucinatory world—or at least not to fight it. Many hospices recommend the latter as well: "Do not contradict, explain away, belittle or argue about what the person claims to have seen or heard," reads a short text that a hospice provides about the dying process. "Just because you cannot see or hear it does not mean it is not real to your loved one. Affirm his or her experience. They are normal and common."

By itself, the brain explanation isn't soothing. What does help is taking advantage of the interaction window that remains. Or you open another window, as if that's the one that the other person wants to operate with. You might respond, "So you say you're going on a trip. Who do you think will be waiting for you?" Or, "Tell me some nice things you remember about your mother." Family members might be told that the patient has already undergone a sort of social death; though their body is present, the previous person they is gone, so a new relationship is required. So while your father's brain is the author of some insult, and his body its animator, your father as you knew him isn't the principal of that offensive utterance.

Some families take it better than others—some want to deny what's happening, while others roll with it ("Oh, you're seeing bugs? What's it look like?"). For other family members, some meaning needs to be made from the delirium. "It can be very meaningful for family members to say, 'Oh, Dad's now with Mom,' who is dead. That can be a great source of comfort," a doctor who often treats delirium told me.

I faced this with my own grandmother. I'd known my father's mother, Norma, from childhood. A bright-faced, cheery woman, she'd fold me in her arms, say that she loved me, then laugh chirpingly and say that she prayed for me, that unmistakable Irish grandmother code for "I want you to go to Mass." Now I was no longer a child, and now she was dying. The gray skies on our visit to the hospital will be forever seared in my memory. When my wife and I entered my grandmother's room, I told her who I was. Her eyelids fluttered open, and her eyes focused on me, her gaunt face lit up, she reached out her arms, I hugged and kissed her. "Michael-Jean, you're an angel!" she exclaimed. "You're an angel!"

At first I was concerned—*does she know it's me, not an angel?* Apparently so, she said my name, then repeated joyfully, "You're an angel, you're an angel." Delirium? Maybe. But when your beloved grandmother calls you an angel, you reach for the interpretation that feels most loving. She said what she said; the words, they're right there, her last ones, as far as I'm concerned. She became unresponsive shortly after and died two days later.

My father remembers this differently. He maintains that she roused to a saying of the Lord's Prayer. But I won't argue—from both of our stories, we end up with some morsels of closure, and that's what feeds us.

§

One phenomenon of note is the dying person's brief return to lucidity. This behavior, which can seem mystical, is known as "lightening up," a homespun label invented by William Munk, or the more clinical "terminal lucidity," invented by biologist Michael Nahm to name "the unexpected return of mental clarity and memory shortly before death." I mention it here because this phenomenon might actually be a form of delirium. The interaction window flies open; people have unusual mental clarity, even returning to their old selves so vigorously they seem to have left the precipice of life. It's possible that some stereotypical last words, as discussed by Guthke, occurred in moments of terminal lucidity. British physician Richard Lamerton presented the case of Mr. B, "who, when I went by to say good-bye, suddenly opened his eyes and said to me, 'I'm joining your flock now, Doctor. I hope the coffin is ready. Cheerio!'"

Such a last-chance opportunity to connect with a dying loved one sounds welcome. It makes for a wonderfully redemptive story, with a graceful arc toward optimism. But don't depend on this actually occurring, no matter what the television shows depict, because it's fairly rare. New Zealand hospice director Sandy Macleod witnessed only six instances of "lightening up" out of one hundred hospice deaths. What seems more reliable is what happens next: these instances occurred in the last forty-eight hours of life. They're a sure sign that the end is near.

§

From a linguistic perspective, delirious language is unhinged and incoherent. This is one way it's been described:

> The verbal activity consisted of more or less incoherent speech, speaking continuously and without addressing anyone nearby, and changing rapidly from one subject to another. The patients returned in their speech to the same subject several times. These areas were seemingly associated with what was happening around them or to other things, unknown to the observer. They spoke about various events, experiences, places and people. The patients hovered between "now" and "then" and between "here" and "there." The tone of their speech was somewhat speeded-up and the voice was normal at the beginning but the intonation became sharper and louder or mumbling. Some patients cried, shouted, wailed and groaned, called for a person, whistled or laughed. They asked questions without waiting for responses. The subjects were reflections on the current

situation and/or reflections on events of a seemingly historic nature. These reflections were about the confusion, expressions of needs and discomfort, searching for help from others, expressing the need to be alone, not to be disturbed, talking about the injury and/or surgery. In addition they misinterpreted people, objects or events, misplaced themselves in the situation, tried to regain orientation, and commented on what happened around them.

People who are delirious after surgery and then recover can sometimes relate their feelings of being briefly outside the furrow of sense, which reduced them to a state of abject terror. Osler might have been surprised. "I remember that everything changed to me," reported one patient. "Suddenly I was a prisoner in a Nazi camp, and I thought that the nurses were the Nazi camp guards . . . and I wondered whatever happened since the nurses had become so unkind to me although they were so nice before." They reported seeing things that were beautiful, awe-inspiring, and pleasurable. They saw fragments of past events mixed up with the present. And they heard people talking to them but didn't know what they wanted, nor could they communicate with them.

As with all these phenomena, delirium involves experiences at the edge of the interaction window, or far beyond it. In many instances, that window has been shut, perhaps not forever. In the case above, family members who knew the person in a "normal" state were also shocked at losing emotional and cognitive access to their loved one. They missed knowing about the other person's interior life and struggled to figure out if the person with delirium was comfortable or distressed. To deal with this, the advice seems to be: Don't engage in the main interaction window, because your loved one's not there; instead, open another interaction window on their terms. That will allow you to be present without expectations or demands.

§

Of course, another option is to deny the existence of delirium altogether, as *Final Gifts* does. "Health-care professionals and families may assume that what they're hearing and seeing is confusion . . . unfortunately, dying people are often labeled 'confused' without adequate assessment," Callanan and Kelley wrote. The only reality is the special symbolic language of the dying, and the brain-based understandings of delirium diminish those messages or their meanings. (They don't have a monopoly on this, by the way. Nearly 40 percent of Indian family members said that delirium was the cause of supernatural beliefs, emotional stress, or a failure of religious observance—and did not have biomedical origins.)

Given the documented prevalence of delirium, it was a bold position to take. However, in a 1998 interview, Callanan walked the rejection back. "I'm not here to say that everything a confused patient says has great significance. It's often very hard, even paying close attention, to find exactly what the person is saying. Seventy percent of people dying of illness, at some point, have some confusion; that's a lot of confusion. However, our point is to always listen specifically to the words."

Several years later, on a speaking tour to Chicago, Callanan reversed again, telling the *Chicago Tribune* that delirious behaviors aren't the product of mental confusion or drug mis-dosing. "The confusion is ours," she said. "The patient knows what's going on."

The newspaper reporter also quoted, in contrast, the views of Joel Frader, a palliative care physician, who identified the source of hallucinations and other unusual behaviors as the failing brain. "There are some fairly characteristic changes in brain chemistry that people have documented as death occurs, whether it's lack of oxygen or high levels of carbon dioxide or changes in nutrition getting to the brain," he told the newspaper.

His take was not only frank and sharp, but it reiterated what Victorian doctors also warned: the existence of God or the afterlife won't be proven with people's dying words or their hallucinations, because they are "matters of faith." The organic response of the brain to the body's failure, on the other hand, is a matter of physiology. Implicit is the idea it works that way for everybody.

"I do understand people trying to get some meaning out of everything they witness, but delirium is real, and it happens a lot," Romayne Gallagher, a palliative care physician in British Columbia told me. She didn't recommend *Final Gifts* to people because of its unrealistic view of delirium. "Certainly the misperception of reality plays a role in delirium—people seeing ants on the ceiling (spotted ceiling tiles) and seeing a bowl of rice (a glowing white lamp globe)—but if delirium goes beyond that, it seems to empty the limbic system's treasure trove of horrors, which doesn't seem to relate to the person's experience. By that I mean people seeing a train coming at them or seeing a loved one on fire just outside the window."

My speculation is that the interpretive control promoted in *Final Gifts* reflects a cultural adaptation to the *laissez parler* approach to language at the end of life. That is, if no one gets a clear model about the language they should produce at the end of their lives, except that it be pithy, poignant, and meaningful, then a lot of it risks ending up delirious and nonsensical (if it exists at all), which survivors must interpret.

Meanwhile, other religious practices keep dying people occupied, authoring for them what to utter, chant, or pray. Sharing linguistic agency in this way looks like a wise cultural adaptation to the prevalence of delirium. Only the prescribed words matter—everything else becomes noise, harmless and inconsequential.

§

Perhaps the biggest bunch of last words to challenge cultural models are the ones that are most normal: the ones that don't occur, that aren't perceived, that are overlooked. How people die, where they die, and what medications might be involved are relevant causes of this. In Osler's study, this invisibility befalls the largest group of patients, 401 of them, about whom no final articulations or terminal signifyings were recorded. It's a reminder that the number of possible scenarios for death are limitless, but the circumstances that narrow the possibility of coherent last words (if that's important to you) are finite: your age, sex, community, access to health care, and medical condition, and of course the presence of other people. If you die behind the wheel of a car, you'll be more alone than if you're surrounded by your family. Maybe your family gets called, but they won't make it to the hospital in time. Maybe you'll die in an unfortunate way, like Toina Hanson. Any final utterances, if they occur, are for the record of the gods.

Yet not all human communities place the same emphasis on gathering around a dying person (though they all appear to have special funereal rites for dealing with a corpse), because a person's biological and social death don't necessarily co-occur. Even the same society can have different emphases across social classes or professions. For instance, the history of medicine shows how medical schools in the United States and Europe encouraged young doctors to protect themselves from the suffering of patients, while in the same period nursing students were taught to not be emotionally invested in patient outcomes. That didn't keep doctors like Osler or Mendenhall from showing sympathy and compassion to patients, but such values can be difficult to employ at institutional scale.

In that sense, the place of death strongly influences whether, and how, others are present. Worldwide, about 18 percent of all deaths occur in long-term nursing facilities and 54 percent in hospitals. Location has a sizable impact on whether or not a death is attended and by whom. "I've spent more time to talking with people in palliative care and hospice than nursing homes, and those scenarios lead you to believe that people may not be talking, but at least they're attended," a chaplain in a large American city told me. "But intensive care units and nursing homes are different. Oftentimes, there isn't anyone from a family there."

Another American chaplain told me, "If people are in a nursing home, more than half of them are there because they don't have a good relationship with their family or don't have a family." She provides spiritual care if it's indicated but often doesn't encounter any family or friends at bedsides. No interaction windows, no last words.

The values of the medical institution also matter. As far as I can tell, Johns Hopkins Hospital doctors were as attentive as their schedules allowed, though they were motivated by medical interests. The fact remains, however, that they worked in a hospital that served a wide range of otherwise underserved people. In the 1960s, sociologist David Sudnow spent nine months at a public institution serving mostly lower-class patients, which he dubbed County Hospital, in order to make observations about dying as a social affair. He also did fieldwork for five months at Cohen Hospital (also not its real name), a private institution that served mainly middle- and upper-class patients. His observations and analysis were put into *Passing On*, a landmark study about dying in America, which uncovered some uncomfortable if unsurprising truths. I realize that more contemporary investigations exist, but I employ Sudnow's book here because it's closer to Osler's Johns Hopkins.

One truth was that care for the dying, despite advances, wasn't equitable. Compared to Cohen Hospital, County Hospital was a "peculiarly impersonal environment," where three people died per day, mostly on the medical and surgical floors. Most of these deaths weren't attended by doctors or nurses, nor were relatives around at the time of death. It was common for people to die in a solitary fashion, though relatives may have visited earlier. (Sudnow relates a humorous incident in which a family patriarch was prematurely declared "about to die," then visited by repeat rounds of family members, increasingly puzzled at the patriarch's durability.) The presence of visitors was not welcomed by management due to the fact that it required "more constant vigilance" by nurses. Because County Hospital was a medical institution, if someone was assessed as dying, they became medically less interesting to doctors, who were concerned with curing the living, and thus an incipient burden for staff. Subsequently, patients who were expected to "terminate" were moved to private rooms or curtained areas in wards, subjecting them to a "pattern of infrequent scrutiny." (The euphemism "terminate" was often used to talk about death in front of dying patients. Sudnow quotes the following exchange: "She'll probably terminate this week," a doctor said to a nurse. "Am I all right, doctor?" the patient asked. "Yes, Mrs. K., you're doing just fine.")

However, certain patients, and their deaths, came to have special status at County Hospital: children, middle-class people, and the intoxicated or psychotic. "In key instances, patients' external attributes operated to alter the institutional routine in significant ways, causing vehemence, disgust, horror or empathetic dismay," Sudnow wrote. These became special cases, invested with meaning. For the most part, at County, there was a "decided phasing-out of attention given to 'dying' patients," and comatose patients were treated as "essentially dead." (This has changed since the 1960s—in contemporary medical practice, extended attention is paid to gauging the possibility of rehabilitating a comatose person.) Many deaths were discovered by other patients, not by staff. On their rounds, nurses checked on patients with a long glance from the door to make sure they were still breathing. This wasn't so much a concern about the person, Sudnow observed, as their need to start managing the corpse.

One could reasonably say that people died at County Hospital and Johns Hopkins Hospital in the same ways: "Most patients die unattended at County," Sudnow wrote, "largely because of the nature of the care accorded them when they reach what is considered to be the 'dying' stage." He stopped short of explaining this impersonal dynamic, pointing briefly only to a "medical ideology toward the nonpaying patient" that might explain it, but because it wasn't the goal of *Passing On*, he left it alone.

The cultural history of the unattended dying person would be vast; it could be a large subchapter in the history of impersonality as a medical style. Here's where it becomes useful to know something about the institution where one's data about end of life comes from, because at Johns Hopkins, one likely factor that created this impersonality was the medical condition of the patient. Those with an infectious disease like typhoid, for instance, would have been isolated in private rooms, for hygienic reasons that can be appreciated much more in the age of COVID-19. Thus, patients were overheard less and probably not visited much, as visitors were discouraged. In his famous textbook, Osler had recommended "a moderate degree of isolation" for typhoid patients, while people with diphtheria, meningitis, smallpox, and scarlet fever should be fully isolated and put under the care of "an intelligent nurse." Another factor was the training that medical personnel received. The principles of the era mandated that doctors and nurses learn how to remain emotionally distant from all patients, not just the dying ones. As medical historian Emily Abel wrote, "dying [in hospital] remained an extremely lonely and dehumanizing experience."

Yet another factor arose from the prejudices and social biases that Johns Hopkins doctors and nurses brought from their experiences in society. They might have held biased attitudes about the poor, immigrants, and the racially marginalized. The data cards leave us no information about which ward patients were in, but African American patients were kept in one of two "colored" wards, which the white intern Dorothy Reed Mendenhall headed from 1900 to 1901. She described being on the ward often and experiencing the deaths of patients, which shook her. She signed twenty-one cards herself, but she couldn't have been at the bedsides of everyone.

Last words cannot be repeated by the person who produces them, because they are dead. Thus, we have to depend on the testimony of an observer, who is, in turn, strongly influenced by their attitudes and relationship to the dying person. All of these aspects impinge on the one who is attending to the interaction window as it closes.

11   Beyond Last Words

What can be expected from language, interaction, and communication at the end of life? What might be considered ordinary and what extraordinary? Osler's data cards tell us about some phenomena that have to be dealt with, and not just words, but silence, delirium, perceiving, moaning, and nonverbals. These are other raw linguistic materials that will be transformed into a wide array of public and private meanings, and the data cards give us some sense of their relative frequency (at least in that period, at that institution, so they're not generalizable). In the previous chapter, I discussed delirium; here I discuss moaning, silence, perceiving, and nonverbals, as much as possible through the experiences of people who must make sense of them. Though these phenomena are rarely discussed in one swoop when it comes to language at the end of life, they all trigger an interpretive imperative: *Should we stay at the interaction window or not?* That makes them worth the effort.

Moans and groans are frequent phenomena among the elderly and the dying, and there's a surprisingly large literature about them, particularly among people with advanced dementia. Though you may not think of a moan as part of language, the imperative to interpret its meaning is certainly linguistic, and here's where things get messy. I found a troubling discussion on a contemporary online nursing forum, where a nurse described her puzzlement at a patient who began a "constant rhythmic expiratory moan" during her last twelve hours. The patient wasn't responsive, and her moans didn't stop if her body was adjusted. "What is that vocalization?" the nurse wanted to know. "I never felt it was pain, although I treated it like pain because frankly I would rather err on the side of kindness."

Such moans, it turns out, are called "expiratory vocalizations." (The expiration here refers to breathing out, not to any association with the dying, who are also expiring.) They can be distressing because they're weird and otherwise, and some sound like expressions of pain.

But that wasn't the troubling part. It was that nurses had been left to their own interpretive devices for making sense of the moan, and if they decided it was an expression of pain, they said they gave larger doses of sedatives, which silenced the patient. Here a frankly awful deathbed version of Trixie's Dilemma raises its head. What if the moan is actually an attempt by a person who can't summon words to see if anyone is there? What if it's a delayed response to an earlier stimulus, like someone saying their name? This scenario comes closest to my darkest fear. It's a version of being buried alive, communication-wise, my signal taken as mere noise.

A speech pathologist told me that sometimes her patients moan after she talks to them, because she's made it clear she has time to wait for a response. What does the moan mean?

"It's never just a moan," said Leelo Keevallik, a Swedish linguist who studies nonlinguistic vocalizations. A moan can have many different meanings, depending on the activity and who is there, and so, in the linguist's judgment, the moan is something to be made sense of, not tossed aside. Doctors may interpret moans one way and nurses another, and family members and friends may interpret them differently still. Nurses on the forum described the rhythmicity of the moaning as indicating that the patient isn't expressing pain, perhaps recognizing a limbic quality to the expression.

A few people were noted as moaning in the Osler study, credibly too few, given the likelihood of delirium and the prevalence of dementia. Among the elderly, especially those with dementia, moaning is frequent, so it's likely this happens at the end of their lives as well. Visitors to facilities like nursing homes and other patients don't like moaning, particularly the kind called "calling out" or "disruptive vocalization," which may also include verbal utterances, like "Help me!" "Oh my God!" and "Let me die." Medical caregivers struggle to stop these vocalizations, so it makes them feel helpless. As a result, disruptive vocalizers receive lower-quality care (even though some of them may be deaf and not even aware that they're vocalizing). Unfortunately, moaning happens a lot. Among seventy-four dementia patients observed in one study, about half vocalized this way. Probably there was more moaning in the hospital than Osler's staff reported in the study, not necessarily from dementia patients, which wasn't reported.

A linguist who had noted the two instances of moaning in the Osler data cards might wonder what was being described. An ordinary word, spoken loudly and with vowel elongated? Or a nonword, perhaps a single vowel, also elongated? If a vowel, which one? Did its pitch change? All humans moan the same way, the capability controlled by circuits in the brain stem. In this way, moans connect humans to their mammalian evolutionary history, along with cries; our primate cousins all produce their emotional cries from the limbic systems of their brain.

Linguists who study moans and other nonlinguistic vocalizations note that perceivers can ascribe fourteen to sixteen emotional states to moans, including ones indicating pain. They're marginally linguistic—people make meaning with them, yet they're not words. Here, a curious example is the Buddhist A-syllable, which at the end of life might be easy to mistake for a moan.

One use of the moan seems obvious: as an indication of pain. Some have suggested that a person moaning from pain isn't likely to stop if a third person speaks, yet moans as a part of "disorganized" vocalizations can be interrupted. But expressions of pain are highly variable and even culturally graded, so you can't directly link certain types of vocalizations and pain. We might think they're iconic, that someone in pain will "sound" hurt, but this isn't the case; expressions of pain often parallel the language a person speaks. Multicultural settings—say, emergency rooms in large cities—complicate matters, even in situations where people speak the same language. How to recognize expressions of pain that don't match your own?

A moan may not even count for most observers as a last word, but it can count as a turn in an interactional back-and-forth, allowing the dwindling self to be chased a bit farther down the path. In Sean Day-Lewis's account of his father Cecil's death, he relates how his stepmother announced Sean's arrival. "By intention or coincidence he responded to this with a kind of conversational groan," Day-Lewis wrote in the biography of his father. It seemed, for the son, like enough.

The point is, some subtle but critical matters surrounding care for the person can get swept aside because their behaviors have been considered peripheral to the core enterprise of language and communication.

§

The most frequently noted phenomenon in Osler's study was that the deaths were "quiet." What does this mean? That nurses and doctors expected to hear sounds but didn't? Because it was the easiest thing to write, the one that wouldn't lead to further questions?

Maybe it meant that a patient's dose of morphine was correct, or that the act of dying was indeed as calm and peaceful as Osler thought. Perhaps "quiet" referred to an inability to vocalize because of fatigue or unconsciousness. This does befall people. About one-fifth of advanced cancer patients in one Japanese study were "obviously incoherent" (meaning unresponsive) three days before they died, as were one-third of patients one day before death. In an Australian study, about two-fifths of patients—also with advanced cancer—were unable to speak in the last three days of life. And more than 90 percent of people dying from stroke were unable to communicate in the last forty-eight hours of life. Here, more precise terms are needed—does this incoherence or inability to speak mean they were entirely incommunicado?

If so, perhaps it's because they'd been given drugs like propofol or midazolam, sedatives that were invented in the 1970s. The history of dying is marked by inventions like these: the hypodermic needle, invented only in 1857, delivered substances such as morphine, commercially produced starting in 1827. By relieving pain and altering the experience of dying, doctors would also have constrained the possibilities at the interaction window. Before medical professionals learned to adapt the timing and doses of injections so that people's desires to communicate could be accommodated, some patients eschewed the drugs, particularly if the lucid mind (and resulting statements) were prized. Nowadays, when they offer sedation, doctors always explain that it diminishes a patient's capacity to communicate, partly because it degrades a person's ability to process the meaning of words. But light sedation may merely slow conversation, not eliminate it, and even heavily sedated people can be roused, albeit with difficulty. About half of the sedated palliative patients in a German hospital were able to ask for help or answer questions about their pain level, comfort, or thirst. You might say, on one hand, that sedation doesn't necessarily cause silence, but on the other hand, only half of the patients were able to communicate. *Only half.*

The future of last words is thus linked to the future of palliative sedation. Recent research in Europe showed that it increased from 2000 to 2020 in

Switzerland, the Netherlands, and Belgium, and possibly other countries. In 2002, a German team found that 19 percent of palliative care patients in one hospital had been sedated until death, up from 15 percent only seven years earlier. Internationally, the reasons for palliative sedation have shifted: originally it was to control pain, delirium, and other uncontrollable symptoms, but it's increasingly prescribed to relieve psychological distress. No longer is sedation seen as a last resort. Now it's standard to the palliative care tool kit.

Silence isn't always due to lessened mental ability; it might well be a conscious choice. What if there's no one to talk to, or if you don't want to talk to the people who are there? The real earthshaking possibility is that dying isn't so much of a disaster for the individual, hence there's nothing to communicate about.

This is the point that Allan Kellehear, a death studies scholar from Australia, tries to get across in his study of the experiences of dying *from the perspective of the dying*, not from caregivers. "Most of what we know about dying doesn't actually come from medicine, but most of what we know about the awful side of dying comes from medicine," Kellehear told me. "They'll tell you how much suffering there is, but not how hilarious dying can be, and how happy most people are during their dying period." His perspective led him to see that verbal communication at the end of life isn't universally important. "If you're middle-class, educated, your ability to communicate in words is terribly important to you, but it's not important to everybody."

Silence reflects social background. Not everyone likes to hear themselves talk as much as many middle-class folks do (who also like to hear their babies and children recognize them through language, for similar reasons). And silence doesn't mean that language isn't happening—someone who is silent can be perceiving language and, in the case of a signer, might be signing. It might even be a communicative choice. Poet Mel McEvoy recalls in a poem visiting a patient whose wife saw a need to talk. One excerpt: "When the door closed behind her I sat and asked how you were doing. You looked out on the garden: we never spoke a word for twenty minutes. No splash of noise disturbed the hush. When she returned you spoke first and said: we have had a long chat and I feel ready."

Silence is also a feature of delirium; people with delirium in its hypoactive form can appear withdrawn, unwilling to talk.

Then there's silence when someone doesn't want to be available. Naomi, an end-of-life doula in the United Kingdom, can tell which is which. "It's just the *eyes*," she said to me. "Their body might be tired, but it's like you can feel they don't want to let you in." They look away or shut their eyes. Sometimes they use drugs to hide themselves. A decade ago, Naomi's best friend, dying of cervical cancer, would dose up on morphine when Naomi visited. "Not so much of the pain," she said, "but she needed to emotionally disconnect from me. She used the morphine to hide in that fuzz."

She's encountered positive silences too. A homeless man became a patient in a hospice where she worked as a nurse. Straight from hard living on the streets, he had difficulty adjusting to the calm, caring environment. Deep talks weren't his thing. He didn't want to have a big cry. He just wanted to be quiet. To be left alone in the safety of his room, perhaps for the first time in a long while. In this case, silence represented a radical economy of expression. "It was his way of coping," Naomi remembered.

At a more complex level, people can also be silent on important topics while communicating nonetheless. Diane, another end-of-life doula who works in a hamlet north of London, related the story of her sister, who was dying of liver failure. "Don't tell her she's dying," her husband told Diane. At her final visit, she didn't—in so many words. Instead, when they embraced, Diane told her, "Say hi to Dad for me." Her sister looked at her with understanding, or so Diane thought.

Their father had died years earlier after a massive stroke. Diane's mother didn't want him to be told he was dying. When she visited him, she listed the name of everyone in the family, said what they were doing, and that they'd be okay. After each name, he nodded his head.

"What did you take that to mean?" I asked. "Yes, I hear you? Yes, you're right?"

"More like 'Thank you, thank you,'" she said. *He knew what was going on.*

There's also silence because someone doesn't know they're dying—they haven't been told. So they don't feel the urgency of expressing things, if they tend that way.

There's also silence because verbalizing thoughts or emotions has lost its value. "Some people just don't ever say the bits they've carried for years," Naomi said. "I wonder if it just becomes not important to say, not in that very end stage."

Finally, there's silence on the part of family members, which can help people die. "Sometimes people need space to die. And quiet," said Emma Clare, director of End of Life Doula UK. She had recently experienced the death of a family member, with whom she'd sat, along with others, for six days. Still he lingered.

"You know, I think maybe he needs some space, maybe we should all just go away for an hour and come back," she said. In that hour, he died.

"I know that's just anecdotal," she said, "but we hear that so much from families. A lot of what we do as doulas is sort of reassuring and saying, 'Just because you weren't there at the exact moment doesn't mean that you weren't there.'"

§

And even if a dying person is silent, it doesn't mean that family members keeping vigil at bedsides have to be. They're often told by doctors and nurses they can, and should, keep talking to a dying person, even if there's no sign of recognition. The reason is that "hearing is the last sense to go," a truism that I heard over and over from care workers, like spoken language interpreters and chaplains, who treated it as something worth acting on, even if was little more than folklore. Yet it's also important for some religious traditions that concede to the dying person a role as a listener or perceiver of language.

"It is usually considered that hearing is the last of the senses to fade, and many religions have accordingly provided special prayers to be read quietly into the ear of the dying man," wrote a hospice doctor in 1973.

"Even though people can't vocalize, they can still hear things, and it might provide peace to them," said one chaplain. "If you go into an ICU and they're sedated or intubated, they still deserve pastoral care." I asked how she did it. "You stand there and you communicate verbally," she said, acknowledging that people may still have their sense of smell or feel the heat of another's body. Other chaplains as well as family carers talk about the comfort from holding hands, even in silence; during the COVID-19 pandemic, families were distressed to be kept from doing even this. Thus hearing may not be the *ultimate* last sense, but it persists,

Only recently has science caught up with this folk belief.

In 2017, Lawrence Ward, a cognitive neuroscientist at the University of British Columbia, received an email from Romayne Gallagher, a local palliative care physician, who was curious to know what her unresponsive patients were hearing or feeling. She'd often witness the patient relaxing when someone they knew spoke to them. She wanted to know what this corresponded to in the brain.

Ward's first suspicion was that the patients were comatose, and that there would be little brain activity. He had modified an existing experimental method developed by cognitive neuroscientist Stanislas Dehaene for detecting consciousness in people with brain injuries and recording any brain activity. Over the next two and a half years, he worked with a graduate student, Elizabeth Blundon, who was on call with a local hospice. As soon as a suitable person was admitted, Blundon rushed over (it helped, she said, that her boyfriend was a medical student used to inconvenient schedules) to get their consent and record baseline brain activity before they became unresponsive. When they stopped responding, she recorded again.

These weren't research subjects but people, each one etched in her memory. She'd never seen what someone looks like at the end of life. "No one looks more frail," she told me. "That seems stupid to say, but when they're unresponsive and they're dying, it's clear. This is the end." It was also surprisingly physically demanding—studying babies isn't that demanding. Wheeling out the electroencephalogram (EEG) recorder and setting it up took thirty to forty-five minutes. To put the sixty-four-channel EEG rubber cap on, she had to lift the patient's head, often with a nurse's help. Heads are surprisingly heavy.

Sometimes family members objected to the cap. Early in the study, one man had been keen to participate in the study, but when his ex-wife saw him with the EEG cap on, she tried to stop Blundon. This dying person wasn't so much of an individual; he'd come to hospice with his pack, who protected him. After that, the researchers took a photo of the person during the first recording session, when they were still responsive, then showed them the photo. Usually the patient had no problem with the way they looked and said it wasn't uncomfortable, and the photo helped the pack—the family—understand their loved one had agreed to this activity, that it wasn't an intrusive medical overreach. It helped some staffers accept the research too.

Blundon understood their resistance—it can be hard to have a dying person looking like a science experiment. "A big part of being in a hospice is that you have a comfortable, naturalish death. To have the full sixty-four-electrode cap hooked up . . . that doesn't jibe with the culture," she said.

I'm describing the research process to show that research with dying people is in fact possible, and that it can be done respectfully. If we're going to understand all aspects of the human experience, including dying, then researchers on communication and consciousness have a place at the deathbed, if the dying person wishes.

The second person Blundon recorded made a big impression on her. This was an older person who explained what it had been like to live in and out of cancer treatment for seventy years. This person told Blundon they'd just broken their leg. Because of a fall? "No, it's cancer, honey."

Blundon had no idea cancer was like that. That your bones just break. Because some of the patients had faced their mortality for years, the prospect of dying wasn't scary. Neither was the experimental setup—they were easy to recruit. "Some of the most extraordinary people I met were our participants," Ward said. "It takes some extraordinary strength to not think about yourself at that moment but consider what others might learn from that experience." Sadly, Blundon didn't get a second recording from this patient, who died one night in their sleep.

Of course, not all eligible patients wanted to participate in the research. "A lot of people weren't ready to really think about what's going to happen to them. Some were in total denial. They were like, 'No, I don't want to talk about death. I'm here to get better.'"

In those exhausting two and a half years, she'd made only thirteen recordings. She often felt overwhelmed by the twin tasks of learning to do research along with learning how to work with the dying. "The emotional toll that it takes to be present with these people, in their families, in this very delicate moment with a lot of emotions running high, and also remembering, 'Crap, I gotta put this cable in here and I gotta remember to actually press record.' There were definitely days where I was like, I don't know how I'm going to finish this."

§

In the first experimental task, patients were played a string of beeps that went on for twenty minutes, then there was a pause. A recording instructed them to lie there and let their mind wander. Then they were asked to imagine walking through rooms of their house, to activate their visual cortex, or sing "Happy Birthday" to themselves, to get the auditory cortex going. Between those trials, they were played a musical excerpt and asked to identify the dominant instrument. Over the next twenty-five minutes, the experimental stimuli alternated between imagination prompts and music.

The brain data from the imagination exercises didn't turn up a consistent pattern—people did the task in their own ways. But the patterns of brain activation from the listening exercises showed that acoustic processing in their brains remained as active as in the brains of healthy volunteers. Though the sample was small, Blundon had come up with the evidence for the popular notion that the ability to hear continues.

Even more surprising were patients' reactions when the music began. Their brains showed different patterns of activity during the beeps than the music, which matched the switch that the brains of healthy control subjects made. "To our vast surprise," Ward said, "this showed evidence that people were listening to the music."

Ward and Blundon also found that the brains of unresponsive dying people did a similar thing as healthy control brains when they weren't engaged in a task at all. When they were idling, perhaps letting their minds wander, doing what's known as inner-directed thought, their brains were prepared to be active in a way that resembled the control brains. (Neuroscientists call this the default mode.)

This means that the unresponsive state before dying is unusual but might be its own state of consciousness. Ward called it a "palliative active dying state"—a state of the brain, though we don't know enough to characterize it as a conscious state. "It's different from unresponsive wakefulness, because they're not awake," he said. "They don't have the same brain-stem arousal, but they're in a very low arousal state."

The results of these experiments seem to say that the auditory system still worked and maybe even allowed people to switch their attention. The default mode network of the brain seems to be active and connected, which might indicate internally oriented thought (if we assume people were daydreaming). That third experiment indicates that people are actually actively listening to music, which indicates there might be a conscious level of processing going on.

What are the implications? One seems obvious but requires repeating: Never talk about someone as if they're already dead. Include them as a social person in the exchanges. Another practical point is that even if a dying person is nonresponsive, don't take out their hearing aids, Blundon said. If their brains are still able to process sound, their ears need to get the sound. People should also in advance indicate what sort of auditory environment, including musical choices, they'd like to die in. At a certain point, they won't be able to indicate what they want. This leads to a more phenomenological matter raised by the experiments: How do you describe this unresponsive state? Gallagher compared it to being almost asleep, but so far, based on what's known, it's more accurate to say it's a state where someone can receive information from the outside world but are unable to respond to it.

Another implication is more speculative. "There's a reasonable probability that when you're talking to those people, they might be getting some information," Ward said. "It won't be detailed. If somebody's telling their loved one that that argument they had two years ago didn't really mean anything and I love you anyway, I think the unresponsive person is probably only getting 'I love you.' Or some kind of feeling of comfort or warmth from those words. I don't think they're getting the full intended meaning." He added, "And, of course, there's no way we can find out."

The conclusion: while people can hear, they get a gestalt, a gist. It's worth pointing out that this is analogous to newborn hearing. Both dying people and infants hear tone of voice, volume, and pitch. They also recognize voices and presumably which spoken language is used. The adults, who have spent a lifetime using words ever since they learned their first ones, will have brains that can recognize them. Some of those words, like names, will be more salient than other words. All of this suggests ways that the giver of palliative care, whether professional, family member, or friend, can use sound to reach the dying person, if they would have indicated that's what they wanted.

§

Finally, there are nonverbals: hand gestures, facial expressions, eye gazes, and blinks. A few descriptions of the dying process, as well as deathbed scenes, acknowledge these phenomena, and even the stereotypical last-word genre, as Karl Guthke discusses, contains a few examples. For instance, Queen Elizabeth I's (1533–1602) last word is often given as "I told you my seat had been the seat of kings, and I will have no rascal to succeed me!" (A successor had not yet been chosen.) Yet like Goethe, Elizabeth's actual final articulation of consciousness was a gesture. (Unlike Goethe's, her meaning was clearer.) She was begged for clarification about the matter. Show some sign to us! Elizabeth obliged. "Suddenly heaving herself upwards in her bed, and putting her arms out of bed, she held her hands jointly over her head in manner of a crown," it was remembered. Like Gian Lorenzo Bernini, she made herself understood with a Herculean effort of moving her body. The next day she died.

Perhaps it's only eminent persons who get less social credit for their gestures than their words, because medical professionals often mention the nonverbals. An interpreter told me about a man in the palliative care unit, dying from lung cancer, whose adult children were yelling at him, cursing him for his life. But he couldn't answer because he was coughing severely, unable to speak, so he gazed at them desperately. "The patient seemed to me," she said, "that he was trying to apologize to his kids with his eyes."

Romayne Gallagher recalled a man dying of cancer, unable to speak any longer, whose gaze lingered intently and meaningfully on each of his daughters in the few seconds before he succumbed. This story had clearly moved her; she got choked up when she retold it. You end up with a vast lake of feelings doing this work, she explained, and some stories threaten the dam you've built. That was such a story.

This man's intentions were clear. But what happens, I wondered, when the intention is ambiguous while the linguistic form is clear? Or if the intention is obvious but there's no reliable vehicle for a message? Of anyone in a medical setting who can mediate, it's speech-language pathologists, because they know how to help people send messsages and structure interactions using any tools that work.

One sunny day in Melbourne, Australia, a young, dark-haired speech pathologist knocks on a hospital door. A nurse pops her head out. "This is a palliative patient," the nurse says. "You don't need to see them."

The speech pathologist is puzzled. "Do they not speak?"

"They're still conscious," the nurse assures her.

"Do they need any help communicating?"

"Thanks, we're okay—we don't need your help." The door closes.

This was the scenario that Laura Chahda, a speech-language pathologist now at Victoria University, faced when she tried to visit palliative care patients at her hospital. Maybe someone has had a stroke, maybe a neurological disease. Maybe they're disoriented, maybe confused or delirious.

Lots of patients need help with communication, perhaps in the moment, maybe transiently. "Given those needs, why are you rebuffed?" I asked Chahda.

"The ability to communicate, I don't think it's valued very highly at the end of life," she said. Amid the work of taking care of physical needs, she said that "communication falls to the wayside."

Speech-language pathologists (SLPs) are trained to confront these dilemmas, because they understand how to scaffold a message and can discern an intent to communicate. When Chahda is welcomed into the patient's room, she tries to assess if they can hear her and if they can respond somehow, with their voice, a blink, a hand squeeze. Which channel of communication remains open? That's her first step.

"We start an assessment as soon as we walk in the room," said Wendy Kinton, another Australian speech-language pathologist. "Is the TV on? Is the light shining in their eyes? Have they been asleep? Are they more cogent in the morning or the afternoon?" SLPs are simplifying messages, pulling apart the grammar of sentences. They are trying to see what medication does to their cognitive abilities. They're looking for attempts to give a message. If medical staff or families expect that to come in the form of verbal language, they might miss the cues. They'll miss an opportunity to make the environment more conducive to communication. The SLPs can remind them to close the door or turn down the television.

The SLPs are brought into patients' rooms to assist with conversations about funeral arrangements, wills, or disputed assets. "If they're having word-finding difficulty, we know how to help them do it without putting words in their mouths or assuming things for them," Chahda said. Other conversations concern medical care. Does the patient want to be put on a feeding tube? What other wishes do they have—and can they express them?

A minority of doctors and nurses, at least in Australia, know these strategies, such as holding up an object at the same time they ask a question ("Would you like a drink of water?" while holding up a glass), but they often don't have time to deploy them. Seventy to 80 percent of doctors don't know the strategies or don't think to use them. Mostly, Chahda said, they just talk more loudly.

But she has the luxury of time. She can linger, ask a question, then wait for a response, as long as it takes. This will sometimes draw responses out of patients who have been labeled uncommunicative but who need time to fight to consciousness. This is key to understanding a few of the Osler findings: people are roused to interact only if someone makes it a priority to rouse them. Sometimes, Chahda said, a patient will moan—which they do because she's made it clear that she's listening. Or that's what she believes, anyway. The bit of language they repeat may be the only thing they can say, and it may have no more meaning than the person is signaling their presence and trying to connect. *I am here, is anyone there?*

To put this in context, I return to linguist Roman Jakobson, who was last seen arguing for the primacy of "mama." In the 1950s, he famously laid out six functions of language, only one of which is about the transmission of information. When someone moans to signal their availability in the inter-action window, that's a language function called the "phatic." This isn't a message in itself, it's more of a check into the communication channel, like tapping a microphone to see if it's on. Small talk and ritualized greetings are also phatic—the North American Anglophone greeting "How are you?" is a purely social gesture, not an invitation to divulge one's state of mind. The speech-language pathologist can distinguish phatic utterances from other signals, intentional and unintentional.

This role for language professionals in palliative settings was pioneered early in the twenty-first century by an American, Robin Pollens, who had been working in hospices for ten years. Often called in to help patients with swallowing (another usual job for speech-language pathologists), she encountered people struggling to communicate. Once she created a let-ter board that a patient could point at with a laser pointer attached to a headband. Another time, she helped a man dying of a brain tumor express himself to his wife, which calmed him down. It turned out he wanted a spe-cific soft drink with a special meaning from their lives, not just to quench his thirst.

Pollens hadn't been called to these situations very often, since the SLP role is often considered only a rehabilitative one, and no one wants to pay for such services for a dying person. However, Pollens recognized that goals of hospice often involve communication problems, such as getting the patient to freely express their symptoms, participate with care planning, and express psychological and spiritual needs. People with aphasia and ALS need help that professionals like Pollens and Chahda can provide.

The SLPs are scientists of interaction windows, and artists of their nar-rowest remaining gaps. Thus, there's a broader role for them, which they're beginning to embrace. "Depending on how close to end of life a person is, we're still talking about loss of consciousness, confusion, dips in acuity, and drowsiness," Chahda said. "Even just talking can take a lot out of someone who's nearing the end of life, so the question is how to get a message to them in the quickest, simplest way. Having the SLP there to organize things is useful because the amount of life is short. We've got to get right to the point."

There is an irony to that point, if the goal of connecting with a person is so they can help make decisions about ending their care. A physician asked a critically ill patient if he wanted to go on a ventilator. "Squeeze my finger," he said. There was no response at all, indicating the patient's wish. Thus the final utterance, in whatever mode it appears, smoothed the path to dying. This patient was eventually able to vocalize a final wish. "It's time to be comfortable," he said. There may be no greater purpose for the things people really say at the end.

12   A Linguistics of Last Words

As I've reiterated, popular depictions of death scenes as well as books about last words, from anthologies to emotional guides, leave one with the distinct impression that dying people can and do actively produce spontaneous language. They're in control of their linguistic powers, at least for one terminal push. Their utterances *matter*. Many people seem to believe their own path will be the same. "When you talk to people when they're well, they sort of expect there to be this cliff edge, where they're having perfectly great communication with their family right up to this second where they have this dramatic dying," said Emma Clare, the end-of-life doula. However, "unless it's a trauma, it just doesn't happen like that. It's a slow slide, really."

The power of these final, verbal articulations of consciousness in extremis is often explained in spiritual, philosophical, or relational terms. I want to cast a bit more light upon them in *linguistic* terms. How are they shaped by the closing interaction window and the neurochemical commotion? How do our lives with language prepare us—or not? And what might the future of our last words be?

§

Will I die *infans*? Guthke's overview of the sincere last word highlights something that, from a historical perspective, is a durable fantasy: that the dying person can, in certain cases, author, animate, and get social credit for their communication behaviors. In other words, they possess *fari*. The stereotypical last word—clear, eloquent, apt—is the fantasy about *fari*.

But based on my sources, this doesn't match most end-of-life scenarios. In truth, people find it difficult to author utterances—that's why they might

rely on familiar phrases (and more about this in a bit). They also find it hard
to animate utterances, given fatigue, dry mouths, shaky hands, medications. Their dentures have been removed; they can't see faces clearly; hearing aids have been taken away. If they're delirious, they won't be treated
as someone who takes responsibility for what they say, though loved ones
seem to want to interpret circumstances and tell stories in such a way that
retains the image of the dying person as the person they've known. In a
sense, the stereotypical last word grants a remaining shred of social credit
to a person after their authoring and animating powers have disappeared,
"as if" the language were theirs.

**Perhaps the question is this: When I'm dying, will I express myself as I
usually have done?** There are competing notions concerning the continuity
of the individual's signifying.

On one side is the idea that dying people continue communicating as
they used to, hewing to lifelong social conventions about how to be a user
of their languages. How you've lived your life is how you'll be at the end.
This matches the idea about the stereotypical last word as a moral capstone.
Thus, people try to remain communicatively competent for as long as possible. They might be dying, but "they don't back away from their interactional responsibilities," said linguist David Gramling.

For a project with his brother, palliative care physician Robert Gramling
(the one who instituted a singing bowl at lab meetings), Gramling analyzed
thousands of hours of transcribed conversations between palliative care
patients and their doctors. These patients don't interrupt; they cede the
conversational floor. Linguistically, they're polite. They tell jokes, they use
the private lingo of their families. They don't necessarily turn philosophical either. "Sometimes clinicians would love for somebody to come to some
insight about what they're facing, being so close to death," Gramling said,
"but frankly a lot of these folks have other priorities." (He recalled a former
businessman from the study who was pitching a doctor on buying a mini-
golf course even as he was receiving news about a terminal prognosis.)

More broadly, unless there's an underlying neurological problem, the
grammaticality of what they say remains surprisingly intact, perhaps
because grammar is such an "overlearned" skill. Even delirious language,
though it may not make sense, continues to be grammatical. People may
use the wrong words, and their utterances are shorter and simpler; they have
a harder time understanding what's said to them. However simple, their

utterances usually follow the formal rules of the language, which became automatic so long ago. So do social rules about how to interact. (This is unlike first words—young children haven't yet internalized those rules.)

If someone has been living with a dementia or aphasia for a long time, then "who they are" (and who others recognize them to be) has probably shifted already, so the dying process won't, in fact, mark the biggest shift. (There's a growing literature on anticipatory grief of family members for someone diagnosed with dementia.)

On the other side, language undergoes observable changes, related to neurochemical factors in the brain and medications. Given the confusion of delirium, people won't interact as they used to. As their executive functions deteriorate, they'll say things that they would have previously suppressed. It can also show up as the breaking down of word-finding abilities, staying on topic, and recognizing other people. Their ability to communicate about complex topics will recede; they'll rely increasingly on other modalities of communication. These are the linguistic facts which then undergo cultural transformation. For instance, such changes are attributed to dying as a new and unique experiential stage of life, expressed in a special symbolic language, as *Final Gifts* relates. They may also be incorporated into the anthropomorphizing of disease, as in "that's not Dad talking, that's the cancer."

Another operative belief about dying is that each instance of death is, as an event, idiosyncratic. Thus, you can't generalize across them. Indeed, every death represents the loss of a unique, individual person, the breaking of a mortal thread that could only have been woven in the way it was. However, there must be shared linguistic patterns across types of dying. One lesson from child-language studies is the sizable amount of variability in how many words children learn and how they acquire the structures of grammar. But these individual differences never deterred scientists from discovering the proper scale of generalizations. That's what science is built to do.

That's not to say there aren't mysteries or puzzles that families wrestle with. A friend told me that when her ninety-three-year-old grandmother died, her last words were "Ferko, amen," as she tightly gripped her daughter's hands. Ferko: that was the name of her husband, dead forty years, yet it was also the name of her son. He had recently passed away himself, though the family had decided not to tell her. "There remains this ambiguity," my friend said, "though I tend to believe she meant her son, the one she was worried about, the one she cared for her entire life, since he was single and never moved away." Each family member interpreted this their own way, and rehashing the puzzle over the years was one way to keep the person present.

Will approaching death change the shape of my utterances? A linguist is less attentive to what people communicate about than to the forms that utterances take. Do people produce full sentences or phrases? Do they use only single words, and if so what types? How intact are their word-shaping powers, given the rules about this in the language?

Anecdotally, people say a range of things, much of it ordinary and some of it banal. As Osler's data cards showed, only sixteen people out of 486 were observed and noted to be speaking, all in English. When people do speak, they call out: people's names, curses, religious phrases. They state the obvious ("I'm dying"). They ask questions with sadly obvious answers ("Am I dying?"), as happened in the Osler study. They direct a carer to do something mundane ("Take off my mask"; "Lift up my head"; "Water"); these utterances resemble the action schemes of first words. Sometimes they bid farewell ("I'm done") or demand release ("Let me out of here"), as they're leave-taking in the literal sense. They can be unfailingly polite ("thank you"). Yet from a doctor I heard that Anglophones often say, "Oh fuck oh fuck." This is because cursing has a well-documented analgesic effect; actual vulgarities relieve more pain than made-up ones. Yet vulgarity and transgression are culture-specific, so the experienced person might encounter a variety of curses, to be matched with Samoan babies' first words ("shit!"). As to whether or not a dying person swears more (or does any other linguistic behavior), the only way to tell is if you know how often they swore before. Which is something few of us are able to say with objective certainty.

Even if they aren't curses, the utterances have an expletive quality. They're short, sharp, *exclaimed*. "Tak. Tak," said Olga Janáčková. People say the names of wives, husbands, sons. "A nurse from the hospice told me that the last words of dying men often resembled each other," wrote German writer Hajo Schumacher in a September 2017 essay in *Spiegel*. "Almost everyone is calling for 'Mommy' or 'Mama' with the last breath."

Hospice nurses have told me a variety of things, such as the prevalence of terminal lucidity. "I've seen it so many times, it doesn't surprise me," said one retired American nurse. (Evidence says it happens infrequently.) She went to visit her unresponsive father on his deathbed. Her sister had accused her of visiting for selfish reasons—"He won't recognize you"—but when he heard her voice, his breathing changed, he turned his head to her, he knew. It was her version of terminal lucidity. She found what she needed at the interaction window. "It's okay, Dad, go see your mom, tell her that we miss her," she told him. He died later that night.

But the reliance on anecdotes as evidence about these behaviors is vulnerable to cultural norms about what can count as a last word. It's vulnerable to people's memories, and therefore to what they find salient. An American World War II veteran recalled his battle experiences in France, presaging the observation by Hajo Schumacher. He observed a young soldier who'd been hit with a mortar; his only words were "Mom, Mom," then he died. He also reported shooting a German soldier, who also said "*Mutter*" over and over.

Despite their emblematic nature, these occurrences do make sense, in that the brain reserves a special place for words with emotional associations, something that the names of loved ones and curses both share. The question is, what's to be done with the unremembered utterances, the ones that might unstitch our dearly held ideas?

Will I use more metaphors? Metaphors, whether they come from the living or the dying, are often considered to be extraordinary instances of language. Given that our regular lives are full of them, however, their use by the dying (which *Final Gifts* asssures us is considerable) may not be so remarkable. One of the insights by George Lakoff and Mark Johnson in *Metaphors We Live By* is that much of everyday language is metaphorical, in the sense that it maps its conceptual structure from experiences in other domains. One implication of this is that purely literal statements are much less common than you think. The true nature of the figurative and literal is a matter for language philosophers, I realize, so I opt to use a more widespread definition of metaphor as casting one experience in terms of another, more familiar one. In that sense, for a dying person to use a metaphor is understandable, given that we only die once, and thus have this new experience that we can only communicate with reference to a familiar aspect of the world. People who have recovered from delirium also describe their experiences after the fact using metaphors, say of being in suspended animation or a coma.

In another sense, metaphors seem to be a form of language magic, so in them people find some expression of the liminality of dying. This is similar, in fact, to the way that adults find in the earliest child language the traces of their inscrutability: Hippolyte Taine mentions a young boy, twenty months old, who used *téterre* to refer to potatoes, meat, beans, and other solid food that he liked to eat; milk he called *lolo*. As Albertine Necker de Saussure once wrote, infants, even our own, are strangers. Their funny babbling, the patois of another land, confirms this.

In *Final Gifts*, Maggie Callanan and Patricia Kelley note travel metaphors as characteristic of the special symbolic language of the dying: packing bags for a journey, needing to catch a bus, needing to find a car, going home. This is often noted by other end-of-life workers.

My linguist's eye has two notes about these metaphors. For one, we shouldn't claim these journey metaphors as universal expressions from the dying experience, when they will vary among cultures. To take one striking example, from a Middle East expert I learned that nomadic people use metaphors of stasis and immobility, rather than journeying, to relate experiences of dying. And Susan Long, an anthropologist who studied dying in Japan, told me that dying people often talk about meeting their ancestors, who exist in the mountains or across a body of water. Yet these aren't journey or travel metaphors as much as a reflection of life's stages, described in geographic terms. (I know this sounds like journeying, but Long assured me it wasn't.) Elsewhere, sure, metaphors of journeying happen. But they're not intrinsic to dying.

For another thing, if you consider that dying is a sort of ultimate leave-taking, then these people may not, in fact, be using metaphors at all; they might literally be making statements that anticipate having to depart. If I can offer one prescription: when someone uses these metaphors, pay attention and participate in their leave-taking rituals. It would be rude to do otherwise.

Does where I die affect the language I produce? Consider that children's first words are more likely to be recognized by parents when they're in familiar settings. Likewise, where people die also has a major impact on those final articulations of consciousness, as does what they're dying of.

In the United States, many people define the good death as the one that occurs at home, even though the hospital was where most people died; now the trend appears to be going the opposite way. This is a good thing for last words, because medical environments, at least in the United States and Europe (where most of my research took place), pose many unexpected barriers. An obvious, well-known impact on the interaction window will be palliative sedation. Another is intubation—patients cannot vocalize, and often they are sedated. Less well-known is how medical staff restrain the moving arms of patients, concerned about delirious gesticulations that knock tubes and cannulae lose, thus insensitively silencing deaf patients who have actually been signing. Acoustically speaking, hospitals are stressful, which can trigger delirium, along with constant intrusions by medical staff. Another barrier is the lack of access to medical interpreters, who help caregivers communicate with patients who use different languages. To the degree that all this is included in "the medicalization of dying," it suggests that the interaction window may be highly attenuated, particularly for the linguistically marginalized.

In turn, where people die is often linked to how they're going to die. In the emergency room or intensive care unit, a patient may not have an opportunity to have a conversation. If they do, it's not going to be a reflection on their life, but will be information related to the team trying to save it. They may get asked a few things, and they may be able to answer a bit, then they lose consciousness.

Will I make sense? One of people's biggest fears seems to be that they won't make sense, or that they'll be unhinged, vulgar, or incomprehensible. Given the prevalence of delirium, that isn't an unreasonable fear. It's certainly going to be exacerbated for those who have had traumatic experiences around communication in medical settings before. However, I wonder if it's the right thing to be afraid of.

What does "making sense" mean? It's always relative to the social frame that people bring to a situation. So it's worth asking what frame people will bring to your dying.

If you have a purely biomedical sense of what causes delirious language, you might think it's unrelated to the complexities of the person, the life they lived, or their current state. You might also use a relational frame: Who do you need the person to be to you, right now? Books like *Final Gifts* or *Words at the Threshold* offer a spiritual frame. It's in the key of the "as if." While statements in "this world" may seem nonsensical, they make sense if you can posit the existence of an afterlife. That is, after all, the destination implied in the journeying metaphors. These frames, the relational and spiritual, have the welcome effect of neutralizing the potential discomfort of delirious behavior.

To address the fear more simply: one way or the other, leave some instructions about how you'd like to be interpreted. You'll have no control over what your brain authors for you anyway. That way, even when the interaction window has closed, a usable interpretive frame might remain.

How does the modality I use affect what happens? Speech, sign, writing, and even touch are modes of language that people use at the end of life. (By signing I don't mean gesturing.) People who use them may have different experiences. For instance, speech quality is affected by phonetic factors. Speakers lack physical strength, and even lung capacity, for long, well-articulated utterances. "People will whisper, and they'll be brief, single words—that's all they have energy for," said Maureen Keeley, a communications scholar. Medications limit communication. Dry mouths and lack of dentures impede clear articulation. Using a laser pointer on a board of letters can be tiring for long utterances. An eye tracking system can't work if you want to close your eyes.

Anecdotally, signing ability seems to be more durable than speaking—signers can animate their utterances longer than speakers can, probably because they don't need to sustain sizable breaths needed for vocalizing. This durability was reported to me by an American medical sign language interpreter with decades of experience. "I feel like when I've seen hearing people at the end of life, at a certain point their ability to produce speech relies on their ability to do fine-motor-skill things. At a point, that drops off. But you can still move your arms or your fingers or hands. So I felt like I've been able to communicate with deaf people for a longer period of time." However, signs with complicated hand shapes get reduced to a simpler form. "It's like when you're drunk or you're injured and you can't do the sign as you normally would, but you find ways to get around that. Say a person can't lift their hands—maybe they can sign a little on their chest. That's enough."

But the sad fact is that deaf people are more likely to die in circumstances where they have to be around people who don't sign. "I've heard untold stories of deaf people dying without any interpreter," he said. "The scenario in which an interpreter is present is a luxury. If someone is dying at home, there's no one who is required to pay for that, and it's expensive."

More often than not, he said, a hearing person, or some structure within the hearing world, is often deciding whether a dying person gets an interpreter. And even if they do, sometimes it's a new interpreter each day, sometimes it's just a person on a tablet or smartphone. "As much adaptability as deaf people have to have, it's a Jenga tower that could collapse at any time, because of decisions made by hearing people." So in the abstract, it may seem as if the dying signer can communicate until closer to death, but any advantage (if one can call it that) may be overshadowed by aspects of the environment that always favors those who hear.

What if I use more than one language? Anecdotally, multilingual people may revert to a single language, but which one? The earliest acquired, the one most often practiced, or the one the person feels most emotionally attached to? A professor at a Dutch university told me that her father had spoken several regional languages, but with her he only spoke Dutch, until he was dying. "*Loat mich goon,*" he said to her in Limburgish, the language of his youth but which he'd never taught her. "Let me go." It was the last thing he said to her. She replied in Dutch: "*Natuurlijk, pap.*" "Naturally, Dad." And then he died.

A German man generously supplied another curious story in this vein, though it's overshadowed by heartbreak. With his wife, who was Estonian, he spoke English. But immediately after she gave birth to their baby, she suddenly began speaking Estonian, or that's how he recognized it. But he couldn't figure out what she was saying. The sudden eruption of Estonian alerted medical staff that something was wrong—indeed, the so-called foreign accent syndrome is a well-known sign of stroke. Shortly after, she became unconscious. She was rushed to a brain scanner, where they discovered that she had undergone a massive brain hemorrhage, which ultimately took her life. Thus, her last words were unrecognizable to him. He was left with a newborn to raise and a last-word-shaped hole—an inaccessible meaning, an unknown intention.

It's not uncommon for people who are confused or delirious to use their mother tongue exclusively, even if they're very proficient in additional languages. An American neurologist told me that he remembers "countless" cases in which delirious bilingual patients suddenly needed a translator—their English was no longer available. However, once the delirium resolves, their bilingualism returns.

Interpreters can play a role in some of these situations. Without interpreters, people who are dying and their families have worse experiences, which underscores the critical role that language plays at the end of life. In the United States, hospital patients are required by law to have access to language services, so they are flagged upon admission as needing an interpreter. Whether that interpreter is a live person or a video-linked resource depends on the language, the resources of the hospital, and even the perceptions of medical caregivers about patients who use interpreters. Even so, people with limited English who are dying in American settings, even if they have access to interpreters, often refuse palliative care services that would help them die peacefully. One reason? The lack of a way to interpret or translate "palliative care" into their languages in a way they understand.

Hospital interpreters told me that conversations in medical settings occur well in advance of someone's death, but they've encountered their share of dramatic utterances. One interpreter remembered how one patient couldn't catch her breath and showed irregular heart activity. Because of a nursing delay, her move to the trauma bay was rushed. "I can't breathe, what's going on, can I breathe?" the patient said. "We're going to help you breathe," said the interpreter. But despite their intervention, the woman died of a stroke. Her last utterances were about breathing: What are they going to do with me? Can they give me something for my breathing?

Another man gasped, "Give me the medicine!" Five minutes later, he was taking his last breath. An interpreter told me this story because in the throes of immense pain, he'd refused morphine for over an hour because of its connotations of illegal drug use. Finally, a friend asked if he wanted some medicine to help him, which is what he begged for.

Interpreters generally had more stories about final utterances than chaplains and doulas, which reflected the fact they're more likely to be present in dire medical moments. They described chaotic scenes in intensive care units, but otherwise often aren't present when someone is dying in other circumstances, for the simple fact that when someone's dying, the interpreter gets less involved because medical staff are less involved. The dynamics that Sudnow described in the 1960s haven't dissipated entirely after all. Once the doctors have decided that someone needs palliative care or to go to hospice—or what is called "comfort care" (a euphemism so awkward to translate that several interpreters brought up their annoyance with it)— the interpreter may be called on to communicate about basic things but is generally less involved.

"Our role as an interpreter is to facilitate conversation between the health care team and the patient, and once that decision is made about comfort care, there are fewer interventions from the medical team," an interpreter manager at a major hospital system in the Pacific Northwest said. "The conversations that were happening before are happening less."

§

Though a reliable database of language at the end of life doesn't yet exist, we could make some predictions about the verbal material it might contain, given the neurochemical commotion of brain failure, the closing interaction window, and intersecting trajectories of language change. Such a database would obviously also map the nonverbal.

Final utterances are likely to be short. Without knowing what was linguistically typical for an individual, it's impossible to say what changed for them. One thing that's reasonable to say about final spoken utterances is that they're shorter than the ones a person would typically use. Curses, names, imperatives, interjections: these are all short, one or two words. So are moans (if one includes them as behaviors that can be last words) and cries. This may seem like an unsubstantial conclusion, but linguists often consider utterance length, which immediately opens the door to considering what remains of syntactic complexity.

Also, like first words, and unlike other kinds of utterances, it's not likely that they'll be about themselves. One doesn't say, "This is my last word." Of famous last words that I'm familiar with, Karl Marx's comes close. His housekeeper asked him if he had any last words, to which he shouted this reply: "Go on, get out! Last words are for fools who haven't said enough!" But the reported last words of James Joyce surely belong to this category too: "Does nobody understand?" Only the rare few might choose to use their limited remaining energies to make an observation about communication itself. The day before he died, Gregory Bateson asked his student, Stephen Nachmanovitch, "Can you speak at the end?" "Yes, Gregory?" Nachmanovitch replied, unsure what he should say. "Good," Bateson said, "Because I can't." This is unusual, however—indicating that you don't understand something takes physical and cognitive energy. Thus, an exchange like this is highly unlikely:

Person A: Am I dying?

Person B: Huh?

Person A: Do you think I'm dying?

Final utterances are likely to be disinhibited. Even if they aren't outright delirious, people who are known to be discreet or proper may say things they wouldn't have before. They might curse, comment on someone's appearance, or accuse someone of a bad act. But this is to be expected, as one of the functions of the brain's cortex is to inhibit behaviors and attention, and its failure means its inhibitory powers fall away. The neurochemical commotion in the dying brain will have less effect on the limbic system at first. Consequently, such limbic vocalizations as emotionally charged language, exclamations, and cursing have fewer impediments to expression. Someday, an enterprising research team that's collected observations about the language of the dying might conclude that such utterances are, in fact, decreasingly cortical and increasingly limbic in nature.

Final utterances are likely to be formulaic. It's likely that even the *laissez parler* last word has been used before with some frequency, an aspect of language at the end of life that has escaped notice so far. Many last words like these reported anecdotally (and also those in Osler's study) fall into the category of "formulaic language," which researchers have defined as "conversational speech formulas, idioms, pause fillers, and other fixed expressions known to the native speaker." In English, these are utterances like "I love you," "Thank you," "Can I go?" "I'm going," "Cheerio," "My dear wife," "Amen," "Oh God," "Oh fuck."

There's some beauty to appreciate in this. In one sense, the use of familiar language isn't unusual, as people's frequent use of fixed expressions is also a feature of normal, "healthy" language—as much as one-fourth of everyday spontaneous language production. The most worn-out idiom has a meaning only as a whole, not the sum of the words it contains; we store media catchphrases and song lyrics in our brains as chunks. Ordinary second-language learning involves grammatical patterns that are explicitly stored as wholes, as are early vocabularies of children, which are made up of expressive words and polite phrases that bootstrap further language learning. Thus, at the ends of our lives, it's touching that we return to the embrace of the formulaic that launched us.

Familiar expressions persist because, as cognitive scientists have shown, they have a differential status in the brain. People in later stages of Alzheimer's often have only familiar expressions, which are also well-documented in people with aphasia, who can recover their idioms before they can produce utterances with some propositional content. We might wonder if, at

Continuum of familiar language

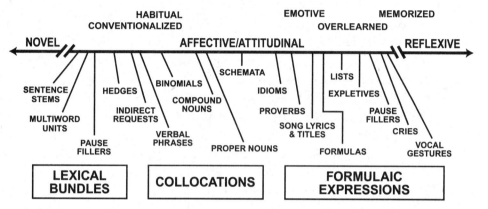

Figure 12.1

The graphic shows types of familiar or formulaic language identified by Diana Van Langacker Sidtis. Many instances of last words are recognizable as one of these types. Reproduced with permission from Wiley Publishers.

the end of life, no matter how brief the interval, familiar expressions are easy to access. Yet this persistence of automatized actions hasn't typically been accounted for in the discussions of last words; instead, the cultural focus is often on their amazing novelty.

Recall that Patrick Henry, the man from Baltimore who died at Johns Hopkins, said something that echoed a sermon or a song. The point is that if dying people aren't filling a prescribed speaking role, as in the *artes moriendi*, they don't automatically choose from their usual repertoire nor use it with the flexible creativity that's taken as the hallmark of language. Thus, a novel analogy, like the *Blade Runner* replicant Roy Batty's "washed away like tears in rain," is unlikely for mere humans.

Alison Wray, a linguist who studies formulaic language in dementia, put it this way: "If you put people into new situations, they will use the formulas that are appropriate to that situation. Changes in the brain will also alter the ease of processing, and if it's harder for someone to do cognitive processing, they will tend to call on more formulaic language, because it's easier to process."

In order to work at the upper limit of our cognitive capacity, which we tend to do, we often choose an amount of formulaic language, Wray said. The more you have to communicate, the more you need the formulaic, and the reverse is also true. Formulaic language works as a pressure valve for balancing cognitive capacity and communicative need. The deathbed is one place where cognitive capacity is waning, possibly quickly, while communicative need is high.

Thus, at the end of life, formulaic language shows up as prayers, other religious language, expressions of affection and relationship, and other words or phrases a person might have used a lot in their lives, including names and curses. In *Euthanasia*, William Munk related the last words of a British aristocrat who had served as a judge. "And now, gentlemen of the jury, you will consider your verdict," he said. Prior to this, he had been muttering incoherently, but seemed to "recover his composure" and raised his head from the pillow, as if he were intoning from the bench. Immediately afterward, his head fell back. A few minutes later, he was dead. Setting aside for a moment the length of this, it's still worth pointing out that if you want to have a prayer, a sacred phrase, or a deity's name on your lips in your final moments, *it helps to practice well in advance of the deathbed, ideally for most of your life*. Indeed, some religious traditions seem to be organized around preparing over a lifetime in order to perform successfully at the moment of death.

Some of these linguistic remnants can be fairly sizable. When I spoke with Kim Oller about his work on protophones, he told me a story about his father-in-law, who came to the United States at the age of sixteen from Poland and became a labor organizer. This meant giving speeches in Yiddish, his native language, often risking political violence to do so. At the end of his life, he stopped speaking English and began spouting long streams of Yiddish. His wife eventually identified it: it was part of the labor speeches. Oller found the experience moving.

Even if these persistent chunks are called "formulaic" or "familiar," it's important to underscore that the emotional feelings they generate are genuine. In other words, calling them formulaic is a linguistic definition, not a relational one. They will still touch the hearts of the person who receives them, they will still make for good stories, and why not? We have no problem finding pleasure in encountering (and retelling) when a baby says "bye bye" or "uppy."

They can also serve as scaffolds for profound communication. In the United States, end-of-life workers sometimes promote five key phrases for the dying person and any family members to say: "Thank you," "I love you," "I forgive you," "Please forgive me," and "Goodbye." In those settings, staff try to figure out which phrase or phrases might be most important and pertinent. "Someone might want to say, 'Forgive me,'" said an American chaplain, "but it might be more healing to be more specific and say, 'Forgive me for this event and that reaction.' Specificity matters." Only one of these phrases, "I love you," is powerful without much elaboration. Among the relatively more reserved people he works with, someone may never have heard a person say that. "I asked if saying 'I love you' fits, and they said, 'We don't say that.' In those cases it's even more healing for loved ones to hear those three words before a person dies." The healing occurs, not in spite of, but because of the formulaic phrase.

These and other formulaic, familiar pieces of language have a sociolinguistic dimension as well. People pick them up in the course of their gendered, enclassed, encultured, and racialized lives. Jackie Guendouzi, a psychologist who studies dementia, said that American women of a certain generation use language formulas that make the other person the conversational focus. This effectively masks the impact of the disease. She remembered several people in a support group. One was a physics and engineering professor who could speak seven languages but had probably never done much small talk. "When we had coffee, he would remain silent," she said, "but when there was a quiz show with trivia, he became very engaged." By contrast, the women were more accustomed to small talk. "They could keep a conversation going for twenty minutes: I say something, they say something." Guendouzi said she didn't see that among the men, except one— a politician.

Finally, people will communicate differently with different partners. Earlier I mentioned findings about communication at the end of life by people with ALS. This fascinating study was done by Alisa Brownlee, who worked as a manager of assistive technology services for a local US chapter of the ALS Association, and Lisa Bruening, a speech-language pathologist with another US chapter. Normally, Brownlee makes sure that patients have access to speech-generating devices and can use them. However, over time, she saw that in the last week of their lives, people tended to stop using the technology. "I was frustrated that we weren't teaching people how to use letter boards and laser pointers," she said. "People want to say things as they depart the earth, but how are they going to communicate if they can't speak?"

The problem was that physicians didn't believe this happened. Brownlee and Bruening sent a survey to six hundred bereaved people about the communication strategies of their loved ones from two to six months until one to two days before they died. Did they speak? Use a letter board?

Though the survey relied on people's memories, the result added up to a remarkable portrait of their closing interaction window. Of course, Brownlee was well aware that 95 percent of them lose the ability to use speech before death. Over the course of their disease, most of them had begun to use augmentative and alternative communication technology, such as devices for generating speech.

As she'd suspected, they stopped using their speech devices, as well as flash cards and writing. But that didn't mean that communication stopped—hand squeezes remained just as potent, as did sounds, while the use of letter boards actually increased. Brownlee acknowledges that more sophisticated technology exists today, more than a decade after her study, so the outcomes of more contemporary research might be different.

What probably isn't different is that the communication tools can differ, depending on who the patient is communicating with. In general, family members and close friends can understand each other better than outsiders, an oft-noted dynamic at the deathbed and with first words too. Thus simple and complex communication may decline less precipitously for close relations than outsiders. (The Japanese study that I cited earlier did not account for these partners.) Indeed, at the very end of life, Brownlee and Bruening found that people used more gestures with children and health aides than with friends, doctors, or strangers—they also used eyeblinks, letter boards, and hand squeezes less often with strangers. Likely such communication methods require context and pragmatic generosity that strangers and the young can't muster.

One implication is that everyone should prepare to use multiple forms of communication—we can learn that from people with ALS and their families, and also from the deaf and hard of hearing. This resilience—if it is important to you—comes from preparation and practice. Another lesson is that the interaction window may have many types of participants. First words are products of the same dynamics, and as Elizabeth Bates realized, parents can decode their children's speech or signing more easily than strangers can.

In practice, however, there's a paradox to this familiarity, pointed out Mary Beth Happ, an American nursing researcher who developed tool kits to aid communication with intensive care unit patients who've lost the ability to speak. When language interpreting is needed, American health facilities must provide it, by law. "Yet when people can't speak, we think it's okay if families be the interpreters. But this isn't the game of charades they played at Christmas—the stakes are higher, the emotions are higher." It shouldn't be their job.

However, families can help interpret an idiosyncratic gesture or facial expression, Happ acknowledged. I recalled an anecdote about a woman who had to explain her dying sister's vocalizations to a doctor. "The doctor said to me, 'Your sister is not in any pain,'" she recalled. "I replied, 'Yes, she is.' The doctor questioned 'How do you know that? You just got here.' I answered, 'By her moans, groans and 'oh me's.' I explained to the doctor that we grew up in a family of 12 and that in order to be heard, you had to make a lot of noise to get attention, whether you were sick or well."

A chaplain from Texas recalled how a man dying in her hospice was visited by his son and his wife. The man, a Korean War veteran, was nonresponsive, even though the son was holding and squeezing his hand. which made the son distraught, though he kept holding his hand. "I guess there's nothing we can do," the wife said, uncomfortable at how distraught her husband was becoming. She was ready to give up. It was almost as if they were going to leave. "I know something we can do," the chaplain said, and they held hands in a circle around the man and prayed. That's when the patient opened his eyes and looked right at his son, who began happily talking to him for some moments, then the man closed his eyes and never opened them again.

The point isn't the effectiveness of the prayer. It's that the interaction window became more resilient with the stamina of the chaplain, whose persistence gave the son one last comforting moment of connection.

Could your last words be predicted? Setting aside a debate over a cultural obsession with predictions, I'll consider this question seriously. In 2016, data scientist and designer Nathan Yau posted a data visualization on his website, Flowing Data, with the title "How You Will Die." The visualization used Centers of Disease Control and Prevention data to map the causes of death that had befallen men and women of three races from the age of 0 to 100. Yau billed it as a predictive tool, but more accurately it indicated the percentage of people at any age who have died from one of twenty causes, including cancer, infections, and cardiovascular disease. It didn't include suicide or homicide, and because the visualization was prior to 2020, it didn't include COVID-19 deaths.

Okay, I thought, *I'll play*. My stats: white, male, age fifty-three. According to the simulation, when I'm sixty, 88 percent of my cohort will still be alive. Of those who've died, 28 percent will have succumbed to cancer and 39 percent to circulatory causes (likely heart disease). Translating this to end of life, we could say that about 20 percent of people in that age group won't have last words, assuming that half of deaths from coronary heart disease in the United States are sudden, while 5 percent to 15 percent, those with cancer, will be unable to speak or incoherent three days before they die. Assuming they'll die in a hospital, nearly all of them will be delirious. That's a snapshot of the likely linguistic behavior of this population's cross section.

By the time I'm eighty, things don't look much different. About half of the deaths in that cohort will be from causes that eliminate the possibility of stereotypical last words (such as heart attacks), promote delirium (such as cancer and frailty), and increase the likelihood that someone will be a receiver rather than a producer of language (again, cancer) at the very end.

While you can't predict *what* someone will say, you can get a useful overview of *how* and *when* they might say it. For instance, for deaths by cancer we know that if you're not sedated, about one-fifth of patients will be using short, two- to three-word utterances when they're five days from dying. Contrary to what you might think, those who are continuously sedated (in the Japanese study I'm quoting from, anyway) actually talk more—one-third of them at five days and one-fifth at one day. It's only at doing complex communication that continuously sedated patients are most limited—only about one-fifth of patients can do it three days before dying. Here is something very eye-opening: *a very small group, only one-sixteenth of all patients who were studied, could do this one day before they died.* I find these sort of calculations a satisfying, if idiosyncratic, pleasure for the patterns they reveal and the decisions they enable.

To go one step further, I propose a benefit to looking at the broad linguistic profile for three of the four trajectories of dying, which are cancer deaths (or terminal illness), frailty and dementia, and organ failure. When does verbalizing typically become impossible and other modes, like gestures, become more important? And when do they typically fade? Mapping all this would get people organized to better prepare for their communication needs, if they're so inclined. One problem is that more is known about cancer's impact on communication than the frailty/dementia and organ failure trajectories. (Evidence shows they're not the same. For instance, a failure to respond to verbal stimuli is a slightly more prevalent sign of death within seventy-two hours among non-cancer patients than among cancer patients.) Another problem is that deaths on the fourth trajectory—sudden deaths via accidents, homicides, or suicides—are widespread and increasing. For example, the fifth-highest killer of African Americans in the United States is suicide (as of this writing in 2023), while globally the eighth-highest killer is road accidents. Even a broad look at last words leaves out something.

Yau's visualization provides some perspective on the history of dying, which influences last words. In the past, people had shorter average life spans, and Yau's visualization shows that when people die at younger ages, the causes are more often "external": vehicle accidents, homicide, suicide, even medical interventions (as in Osler's study). One needs to take care with extrapolating about the past using modern statistics, but I want to point out that until the mid-twentieth century, people (including those in Osler's study) were very likely to die from infectious diseases. In 1900, influenza and pneumonia were the most common causes of death, killing 200 people out of every 100,000 people; in 2010, they killed only 16 out of 100,000. Similarly, gastrointestinal infections killed 137 people out of every 100,000 in 1900, though by 1940 this had stopped registering as a cause of death.

One implication is that most people in the past were more likely to die with their "normal" state of cognitive and linguistic functions intact. Not in all cases—people dying of infections such as typhoid can rage deliriously. But they weren't old. Neither did they enjoy medical care that could keep them alive, albeit in a chronic state of health. I venture that prior to 1900 or so, dying people would have retained more cognitive and linguistic powers as they approached death's door, which means more opportunities for cogent last words. This means that the incidents I've been calling rainbows might have been more prevalent, because death came quickly to linguistically and cognitively empowered people. However, given the way that people tend to die now, at least in industrialized countries, the cultural model of language at the end of life that we inherited might actually work against us.

Most people who die now in affluent Western countries have multiple life-limiting diseases. "They'll probably have organ failure in motion, possibly cardiac failure, possibly renal failure, they may have a cancer, maybe not just one. Maybe a couple of cancers," explained Allan Kellehear, the sociologist who studies dying. "They may have neurological problems that could be any one of the dementias. For them, the last week of life could look a bit like renal failure. And it might look a bit like Alzheimer's. So how these people move in and out of their hospital room and how they talk to their friends and family by the bedside will be shaped not by one thing but by multiple things."

This further complicates any attempts to predict last words. It also changes the nature of what dying people expect to be able to do. "Unlike dying in the past," Kellehear said, "most dying people who you find in hospitals and nursing homes are quite experienced dying people, in the sense that they will have been doing it for some time. They will make meaningful communications well before they die and not care much about their communications in the last twenty-four hours, because they know they won't necessarily be in control of those."

Acknowledging in advance a loss of control, and leaving instructions about what to do about it, may be the true final gift.

Conclusion

The end of this book begins with a human becoming. A small group gathers in a dark room, surrounding a large man, who is dying, on a bed. It's July 2. He's interacting with members of his family, eating cheese and drinking sherry. Over the day, his breathing becomes deep and labored. In the last few years he's had a bout with lung cancer, and now pneumonia is creeping up on him. They're all at the San Francisco Zen Center, so a Zen priest visits, telling the gathered people to match their breathing rhythm with his as he drifts through the night.

The next morning, he lives. He's still speaking. He hallucinates a bit, sees people who aren't there and addresses them. He asks others if someone was present or if it was only in a dream. A lifelong atheist, he has no belief in an afterlife. When you're dead, you're dead, he used to say.

A group of people leave the room together, so he makes a joke about transmigration of souls. He also, his daughter wrote later, makes "gestures of affection and recognition, but much of what he said was blurred and unintelligible." A friend, who is the governor of California, comes to visit (the year is 1980), and the dying man "recognized him and stretched his hand out to greet him, calling him by name." Jerry. Is that the last thing he says? Maybe speech doesn't matter anymore.

July 3 comes to a close; he's still alive. In the early hours of the 4th, he's responsive, though only nonverbally. "He still smiled and responded to a hand clasp, or would draw a hand to his lips," his daughter wrote. He's still conversing, just not with words. By midmorning, he's not responsive. His pupils dilate, his breathing slows. Then it stops.

"I kept praying that he would be free from each next compulsive effort, let go, rest, and when after a time no further breath followed, we all stood, slowly relaxing with the faintest sighs, barely able to return to a flow of time not shaped by that breathing," she wrote.

Over those three days in 1980, Gregory Bateson (1904–1980), the anthropologist and philosopher, went from interacting in full spoken sentences, to unintelligible muttering to the air, to speaking only names, to responding to others and interacting nonverbally, to not interacting at all. This sequence, beyond cultural transformation, is somehow more fascinating to me than any single utterance he might have made, because it's like noticing how the rain falls, rather than hoping for a glimpse of a rainbow. Some of Bateson's writings during his lifetime concerned communication about communication, or meta-communication, and maybe he would have appreciated how the trajectory of his decline, in a way, served as a message about his abilities to message. So, too, it might be for many of us. But it prompts us to ask why language and interaction took that particular course. Several answers are possible; a good one is that the interaction window closes as the functioning of the brain's cortex declines, but there may be others. In any case, everyone must adapt, on the fly, to this closing window.

As it turns out, Gregory's daughter, Mary Catherine Bateson (1939–2021), a scientist in her own right, began her career studying a parallel human becoming: the early communicative lives of babies. As she vigiled with her dying father, her mind might have turned to her research project from a decade earlier, which had uncanny resemblances to what people experienced at his deathbed—and what her dying father might have experienced too.

§

What is shared between the beginnings and endings of our signifying selves? There are some fascinating linguistic symmetries to first and last words, if I can still, by this point, use those honorifics: they're not wholly the productions of the people who get social credit for saying them, as they're sometimes authored and animated by other entities. They're often fuzzy, which makes them dependent on the attention of those with greater linguistic powers. Multimodality is their hallmark—they can be spoken, signed, or gestured. They arise in the interaction window. In the ideal, they're spontaneous or creative. One contemporary standard is that a good first or last word is an emblem of the individual self, not just a mark of personhood, community membership, or humanity. In reality, if they happen at all, they're composed of familiar or frequently used chunks of meaning that are easy to learn, recall, and use.

In some ways, this describes a lot of language in general, which ought to come as a relief. At the same time, the phenomena we call first and last words still stand apart.

What makes a good first word also makes a good last word. Identifying, interpreting, and understanding them is often a process of separating signal from noise, and the cultural frameworks used for one are virtually the same as what we might use for understanding the other. Because each one happens so close to the limit of social and physical existence, each gets interpreted through the existential gravity of those limits, which warps and deforms and inflates them. No other things we say are altered to the same degree by both the facts of existence, the conditions of living, and cultural models or ways of thinking we have about early life and death.

Most significantly, they occur in stages of life when the people who produce them have fewer linguistic powers than they did or will, which means that this waxing and waning agency must be supplemented by others (if they care to do so) to an unusual degree. As a result, the utterances seem rather naked, whether or not they're *strictly* first or last, since they can't be clarified, commented on, or repaired by the people who produce them. In developmental terms, however, this agency doesn't need to be recognized as early or as late as some think, though in cultural and spiritual terms it might be a different matter.

Often, the context may not provide enough clarity about what first and last words mean, leaving people with intact linguistic powers to resolve the fuzziness, if they care to. Some of them will treat the utterances and other behaviors as special. Some will use their powers in service of care and connection, interpreting things in a way that makes the other person seem fully empowered. I've called this "pragmatic generosity." Basically, it's the gift of sense. It's often in contexts of pragmatic generosity that the milestones we call "first words" and "last words" emerge. This can be easy. Otherwise, people stretch. If you believe (as I did) that your dying grandmother has a message for you, then you might adjust how you frame what's going on in order to get such a message. Doing this may succeed at making your memories more positively inclined in your grief. It may help you align what's happening with your spiritual beliefs. And if entraining with a baby through face-to-face interactions is something you do in your community, then you'll shift your behaviors too.

Ultimately, people seem to deploy their linguistic powers on behalf of connection to the person (however the culture defines "connection" and "person"). That's the thing at stake.

Which is precisely what Mary Catherine Bateson had studied a decade before.

§

At the beginning of her research career, Bateson's job was to analyze films taken of mothers interacting with newborns, which had an additional poignance, as she herself was a new mother. In the films, one dyad—a child named Mackie and his mother—caught her eye, and she later labeled their interaction as "proto-conversation." (She was the first person to use this term, which is now widely prevalent.) Even when Mackie was younger than three months old, Bateson found stretches when he and his mother appeared to be conversing, the two of them less than a meter apart, the mother's face at the baby's level. The mother spoke words; Mackie cooed and grunted happily. They each seemed to get pleasure from the interaction, and both used strategies to keep it going if it seemed to flag.

As she described it, "A study of these sequences established that the mother and infant were collaborating in a pattern of more or less alternating, non-overlapping vocalization, the mother speaking brief sentences and the infant responding with coos and murmurs."

The way they preserved this conversational structure was itself a form of communication—it demonstrated a willingness to meet at the interaction window. Bateson acknowledged that it may seem strange to call this conversation, since no information is exchanged. But she was struck by how Mackie and his mother were so committed to exchanging expressions; moreover, they seemed to be regulating each other in what could only be called an oxytocin-induced back-and-forth. In this brief temporary system of entrainment, you can glimpse the connections that people spend their whole lives trying to foster—and whose loss breaks the heart. For Mackie and his mother, the lengths of their vocalizations lined up, and so did the pauses between them, Bateson noticed. And if one of the pair sensed that the other's participation was flagging, they adjusted their own behavior. It almost seemed aimed at bringing the other person back to the rhythm.

Later, she made some observations that anticipated what she must have seen at her father's side: "When we expand our attention beyond the linguistic line," she wrote, "we notice that communication is normally going on in other modalities, so that there may also be switching between linguistic and other codes (whatever their structure) or indeed switching between several linguistic codes." When the participants differed in their abilities, their conversations took on a marked ad hoc quality, as the more able one adjusted to subtle changes in the other. Bateson called this "conversation as praxis." She saw it between a baby and his mother. She might have seen her father, his visitors, and herself switching between codes too. At the end of life, we return to proto-conversation in its fullest form.

"As they slip away, the dying often become like infants again," wrote Stephen Nachmanovitch, a friend and former student of Gregory Bateson's who had also been present at his death.

He meant the way the dying are helpless and require care, and also return to an innocent playfulness. I like taking it as referring to the faint outline of proto-conversation in the exchange of a smile, the kiss of a hand, a name. As Nachmanovitch recalled in his lovely remembrance, "My goodbye with Gregory was an endless half-hour of reverberating silence, smiling, seeing, pointing."

Here's another parallel between first words and last words: conversation as praxis begins long before a baby knows how to speak. It's an ancient ability. It also persists long after a person loses the ability to verbalize. It stands outside of *fari*, that prized linguistic authority of the ancient Romans; in fact, it's the thing that enables *fari*. Then it fades. The last communicative thing that many dying people do reveals the bedrock that has sustained the signifying activity of the species and the individual all along.

This has some implications when it comes to caretaking. Some people appear to find it natural to approach the elderly and the dying as they would a preverbal child, using whatever remains of the interaction window. Osler said it best, claiming that for most dying people, "like their birth, their death was a sleep and a forgetting."

A doctor at a hospice in Roosendaal, Netherlands, told me that people often ask him how they should behave to the dying person. "I always say they're a lot like a baby. They like to be held, they can hear sounds but don't know what anything means."

Laura Chahda, the Australian speech-language pathologist, noted that many of the ways that adults interact with babies through those immature interaction windows could also be used with the dying and the elderly. "We're much more mindful with young babies—if they move, if they cry, we say they're engaging with us, but we don't do that with dying people." We do come full circle, she has observed. "There's a profound link between early life and the end of life, so we need to adopt some of the same practices. But we have to be careful not to infantilize anyone."

No one is saying that dying people should be treated like babies. But we might think about our proto-conversation skills. In that sense, when it comes to language and interaction, babiness seems to be a useful and highly apt framework for dyingness, a metaphor that might give people some directions for using their linguistic powers.

§

Some caveats are in order, because first and last words aren't perfectly symmetrical. Obviously, a dying person isn't at the end of something in the same way a baby is at a beginning. A first word has an aura of discovery—a child's quick experiment with a certain motor action (of mouth, of hands) pays off. The last word or gesture, by contrast, rings with closure and departure, occurring in a matrix of overlearned, overpracticed linguistic behaviors. And yet the first word has a primordial flavor. It's redolent of the course of hominid evolution. By contrast, the last word feels almost minted for the occasion. The first word is also sensitive to the linguistic environment— children tend to produce words they encounter more often—while the last word is no echo at all. Moreover, the last-word producer knows at some level (or knew, depending on their state) what their culture expects them to do. A child on the verge of a first word is oblivious.

And yet—the similarities keep pulling me back—the history of last words, as of first ones, is hardly one of etymologies but rather the much more slippery history of bodies, what's expected of them and what's done to them: of tongues and fingers, eyes and faces and heads; of hormones; of foods and medicines, beds and bedtimes; pain, sleepiness, hunger, thirst, comfort. A noticed first word, an identified last word—these are attempts to make a body's place in that history matter somehow.

Along these lines, one more similarity: in some cultures, such as mine, it's easy to assume that the social body cleaves along the same lines as physical bodies, that "I" begin and end where my body does. But first and last words are among some phenomena that rupture that assumption; when they appear, they make you feel that the social body's contours have been changed somehow, that the "I" is now more of a "we" than you thought possible, in the case of first words, and that the nearly invisible "we" suddenly breaks down, leaving you behind as an "I" (in the case of end of life). Which is why other humans, technology, and even gods so readily lend their agency to first and last utterances, as expressions of something more collective. Our first and last words are never ours alone.

To be clear, I'm not saying that someone's last words can be predicted from their first. However, a few threads across the life span are worth considering. For example, in Islam, the first words a baby hears are the *Shahadah*, which ideally are the last words that baby will say. Also, consider "mama." Though "mama" can be a first and last word, it happens thanks to completely different biological and social mechanisms, so it's not the same word. "Mama" meaning mother as a first word happens because an infant's motor development makes the sequence of sounds "mama" easy to babble, which parents filter from the babble because they expect to hear it; "mama" at the end of life is the name of an actual person, thus has an emotional association, which preserves it in memory and makes it more immediately accessible under cognitive duress. In the matrix of a culture, an emphasis on "mama" as a first word might make it more likely to show up as a last one because "mama" would have been emphasized throughout. At the end of life we produce what our society gives us—and because it expects us to produce something.

Other differences become clearer when you look at first word-iness in terms of last word-iness and vice versa. One curious tension: the societal wealth (and the anxieties of postindustrial life) that stimulated the obsession with babies' first words may end up endangering last words, in the following way. The richer societies get, the longer their citizens should live, thus the more frequently they'll die in medicalized circumstances from multiple chronic conditions, drastically shrinking the interaction window and reducing the likelihood of a stereotypical last word—spontaneous, cogent, intentional.

Another difference is the conceptual weight they can bear. It seems to me that in industrialized societies, it's readily grasped that a first word can be simultaneously biological, cultural, and social. Nobody claims that "mama" or "dada" in spoken language, or their signed equivalents, give you less tingly happiness if you acknowledge that those forms are also easier for young children to produce. But grasping the same subtleties about signifying in extremis is more difficult, perhaps because territories of spirit (and the sincere self) aren't allowed to mingle with those of the flesh. Perhaps this is why Osler didn't record most of his patients' actual maladies, because ultimately he was interested in an ascendant spirit that was divorced from the physical. Perhaps it's why *Final Gifts* discounts brain-based explanations of delirium. The persistent self, the ascending spirit: these send us the messages that we'll treasure, not the body and its betrayals. But so many of the documented last words, the names, curses, and familiar phrases, occur within a biological matrix. So does the nonsensical language of delirium, which is a normal part of the dying process; even more so silence. Out of all the rubble of language, the result of biological betrayals, can we build meaningful, stately ruins.

§

The linguistic symmetries of these human becomings are connected to a historical parallel, which makes most sense to me in terms of the "ritualistic" and "sincere" dichotomy. Over the last two hundred years or so, the reception of both first and last words in the surrounding society seems to have become less ritualistic and more sincere, at least in wealthy, industrialized societies. And they're going to become more so.

By this, I mean that these linguistic milestones are less likely to be forms that people learn to expect or to produce when it's their turn, thereby incorporating them into a timelessly unified community. Instead, the milestones are more open-ended, flexible, and unscripted. Catching them will involve more, not less, observation and scrutiny. They'll be shaped by expectations that the singular person will express themselves, who they are now, who they'll be (in the case of first words), and who they've been (in the sense of last ones). Fingerprints, in other words, on the passage of time.

I didn't expect to find this trend shining out so brightly from this small corner of our lives with language. My own approach throughout has been admittedly sincere: what are first and last words, in reality? How are the language facts transformed culturally? How are cultural transformations mistaken for language facts? Had I not taken this approach, I might have missed the historical arc. But what does it mean?

If I had looked only at last word-iness, I might have contented myself with an explanation about the secularization of death and thrown in for good measure the growth of celebrity culture. Maybe ventured a bit of death conquering. And if I had looked only at first word-iness, I might have repeated others' analyses of family formations and economic anxieties. But when you consider first and last words together, you see that neither explanation can be sufficient. Rather, this interest in first and last words as irreducibly individual and unique serves a broader set of expectations about the passage of time and people's right to have a place in it. Not to conquer it but to mark it. When the individuality of that existence matters more, so do things like linguistic milestones marking their arrival and departure. That's how we know they're really here. It's how we know they're really gone.

One unexpected outcome of this is that caregivers have invented ways to pry open the interaction window, at the beginnings and ends of language. I argue that this is a consequence of an increased focus on sincerity, which motivates the deeper probing of the signifying itself: If the actual truth is going to be ascertained by the witness of the authentic self, then where do the limits of that self lie? Recall the example from seventeenth-century Italy, in which Gian Lorenzo Bernini and his spiritual advisor communicated nonverbally. More recently, Linda Acredolo learned symbolic gesture from her daughter. Other parents told Acredolo they played the same way with their kids, too, but her research accelerated the practice, and now millions of people around the world use "baby sign" with their offspring. In the United Kingdom, dementia researchers Maggie Ellis and Arlene Astell developed a way to interact with people with such advanced dementia that they're no longer verbal. In their approach, called "adaptive interaction," any vocalizations, body movements, or facial expressions that the person makes are reflected back to them; this seems to prompt recognition from the person and even spark some back-and-forth. As in symbolic gesture, family caregivers also reported engaging in adaptive interaction, but it took Ellis and Astell to formalize it. They now teach it to professional and family caregivers as a way to engage with those with dementia.

We need a word in English for this ambition. Push back if you will, but I tentatively label this "percocity," which jumps off from the Latin *percox*, for "overcooked." (It mirrors the *precox* roots of "precocity.") Given all the interest in percocity, I foresee a day when brain-computer interfaces being developed for stroke patients or people with ALS will be used by otherwise cognitively normal dying people. Even though they are unresponsive, will messages from them, even channel-checking ones, be possible? If they can hear, can we get some form of answer back? I doubt we'll be ready for the ethical and legal terrain that this will open up when we can contact people beyond the edge of what we've been able to. What will happen when they weigh in about their care? What will we learn about the experience of dying?

There's a technoscientific hubris at work in percocious explorations of the distant limits of consciousness—scientists attempt to translate the brain's faintest electrical signals into something humanly recognizable simply because they can. A host of emotional reasons also plays a role, as if waving goodbye even after the car turns or the boat disappears over the horizon somehow makes the farewell more complete. However, I sense a deeper motive for relentlessly expanding the borderlands of personhood by forcing open the interaction window in this way: the hypercognitive society I live in fears the individual's loss of their expressive powers. It fears the *infans*, the loss of sense. It fears the impossibility of authoring, animating, and receiving social credit for one's communications, especially if someone remains alive. Our identities are so rooted in our cognitive abilities that we are challenged to imagine how we can retain status as persons without them. Perhaps the last word will be found, not as a final utterance before death, but somewhere along a neurological condition's devastating erosions. Otherwise, the disease will leave linguistic rubble; will anyone bother to raise a ruin for someone who remains among the living?

On the other hand, an emphasis on sincerity doesn't serve people very well in their caretaking activities. Young children don't need their language development accelerated as much as parents need better support. Meanwhile, expecting sensical linguistic expressiveness from the dying is unreasonable. To the degree that such expectations are out of step with the way that people die, they're more likely to create bereavement trauma than soothe it. I've grown in my appreciation for the ritualistic last-word traditions, and I can see why they've endured. From an existential perspective, putting your fingerprints on time is an untenable preoccupation of the living—untenable because you and me and all of us will be folded, no matter what we attempt, into the timeless. That's the truth, unnerving or comforting as it may be.

Fortunately, this trend toward the sincere can't be clean or absolute, at least in the sort of society in which I live. The ritualistic "as if" aura around first and last words will endure. That is because whenever someone is coming or going, mysteries will need to be tamed, boundaries clarified, transitions eased. The beauty of "mama" and other cultural first words is that they enfold the child, carrying them over the threshold. (Problems arise when the science is organized to explain the cultural first word, or when people uncritically impose their cultural transformations onto others.) Consider the tension over the meaning of delirious language, or how vastly different attitudes toward early child language coexisted in Trackton and Roadville. The "as if" and "as is" of first and last words remain inextricably interwoven.

Maybe linguistic fuzziness has been the driver for "as if" receptions all along. Did these evolve together? A few from the previous pages come to my mind. My son's "ka," for example. Or the way that clusters of physical and verbal behaviors that usually co-occur in time can still count, as if the person has uttered them, even if only one element occurs. A Japanese child who bows in gratitude (but who can't yet speak the associated words) has still taken their turn in a conversation-like structure. Similarly, a dying Muslim who is only able to raise a finger is considered to have "said" the *Shahadah*. All of this service to the "as if" has an intense, poignant beauty.

So what's next? Babies drive toward the interaction window; the dying retract from it. The early instinct to engage in a back-and-forth finally fades at the end. As to whether or not these bookends of the signifying self mirror each other—that a hand wave or eye gaze persists because a dying person learned it first as a baby, or because it came first in the evolution of language—will have to be worked out elsewhere. It's certainly too extreme to say that last words are evolutionary fossils of the first first ones. But it seems more than plausible, at least to me at this point, that these abilities and their declines have some symmetry. That we don't revert but come full circle, not by accident but through the whole of the design.

§

When people find out what I'm writing about, they ask what I want my last words to be.

I tell them I don't fear dying, and I don't fear the incommunicado. It's not about leaving a specific message—I've planted those seeds already. What terrifies me most is what you might do to me. That you might inflict Trixie's Dilemma on me. To want to connect, not necessarily to express anything in particular but to reach out and get a response, then to misinterpret my attempts. That, for me, is the nightmare. "Does nobody understand?" James Joyce said. *You're pretty good with words, but words won't save your life.*

I hold close the thing my wise friend Louis said: "Your last words shouldn't be the first time you share a truth or tell a secret, they should be the last time you say the thing you've been saying your whole life." His point is that your words have a handhold in people's memories through repetition, not through their lastness.

I would never compose something in advance and count on the intact ability to deliver it. And I would never think I could use my last moments to confess the crime, point to the treasure, reveal the true love. It's no time for plot points. You can't stage a rainbow.

Other than that, embrace the rain. Treat me like a baby. Don't just wash and spoon-feed me—use a conversational praxis that recognizes that my abilities are dwindling, but that also soothes me. I don't want the contact to stop. Let me moan—don't slam drugs into me because I make a little noise. Moan back. Squeeze my hand. Or let me be silent. Don't rouse me, don't probe. If approaches are necessary, let them be subtle. Let's hold hands. I always liked a good snuggle. I know we were fascinated by our babies' words but we connected as much through touch. By then I'll have said and written the things you should know, and which will stay with you. After that I don't need to express any more. Don't bug me. That's the praxis.

You should know that I wish I had a tradition of prayer or song to carry me along, but the time to start that would have been a long time ago. Don't start chanting now.

Interpret my confused speech with judgment. You know who I am, who I was. When I'm delirious, that's not me, that's my brain's collapsing architecture playing at the role of author. My body will dutifully animate. Who gets social credit? Not the "me" you know. Unless, of course, they're wise or sarcastic.

Enjoy our last swaps and offers at the interaction window. At a certain point, halt the praxis. You might in fact be elevating my physiology by creating the conditions by which I feel obliged to continue interacting. If

I seem to be lingering, please leave the room, free me from my organism's own obligation. Don't keep me here by making me fulfill it.

Come to me when I'm well enough to respond, and don't feel guilty if you can't be by my side when I pass. The moment of death isn't as important as we think. Toina died alone in the puckerbrush, maybe muttering to the stars. Billions of humans have died alone in the puckerbrush of one sort or another. Worlds have ended before. Why should I be exempt? Let your care for me in the community of the dead begin once I've joined them. Do all the right things then, do them faithfully. We will join each other in the house of the dead someday.

Of course all of this can go sideways. What I want, the I that wants, is fragile and doesn't much matter in the big picture. Sure, let's indulge it. At the same time, let's acknowledge that human life foils most plans. That's what it's best at.

Epilogue: Back to the Puckerbrush

Every summer I go back to the section of puckerbrush where I encountered Toina's remains, though the precise spot has become obscured as saplings become trees and erosion slowly demolishes the slope. Time, too, does its demolition on my memory. Still, as best as I can, I find a spot that serves, and there I talk to Toina, as if she were really there.

In the years that immediately followed my discovery, I became obsessed with finding out as much about her as I could and writing about it. I learned that she'd been loved, that she was a fierce person who was devoted to her own survival. She hadn't fallen through the social safety net as much as been born underneath it, in an economic class for whom dying in the woods alone was as plausible as any other end.

After all that research, I had a piece of writing but no peace, not until I learned I should go talk to her. The first time I did this, it felt strange—*if you don't believe in spirits, ghosts, or souls, who are you actually talking to? You didn't even know her among the living.* Yet the result was an enormous relief. The best way I have to describe it is that as soon as I went to the puckerbrush and made her social as a dead person, I completed her death. Not in the sense that I killed her. But in the sense that I moved her to the place she belonged, and that was somehow beneficial to me too.

I tell this story to complete the book for two reasons. First, our conversations with people don't end with their deaths. We might revise the stories we tell about their deaths, to arrive at understandings that benefit us, and we might revisit the final moments and reinterpret them, over and over, for the rest of our lives. Last, as long as there are people who know the right ways to care for the dead, then none of us need to fear it, and if you don't know the right ways, you can always learn some.

Acknowledgments

This book came together through the generous guidance, observations, and input from a significant number of people, to whom I am forever grateful. A life-changing year at the Max Planck Institute for Psycholinguistics set me on this course, and I thank Simon Fisher for making it possible. Along the way I was aided by a 2022–2023 Public Scholars Fellowship from the US National Endowment for the Humanities, the Books program of the Sloan Foundation, and a travel grant from the Osler Library of the History of Medicine at McGill University.

For early journalistic assignments on these topics, I'm thankful to Julie Beck at the *Atlantic*, Nadja Spiegelman at the *Paris Review*, and Michael Regnier at *Mosaic Science*. For opportunities to test out ideas, I'm thankful to editors and reviewers with *Omega: The Journal of Death and Dying*, *Language and Communication*, and *Anthropologie et Sociétés*. I also appreciate the feedback I received when I presented parts of the argument at the Montreal Bilingual Initiative at McGill University; University of Chicago; Tilburg University; the Language Sciences Initiative at the University of British Columbia; Maastricht University; the Freiburg Institute for Advanced Studies; the Deathcare Conference; the Conference for Corpora on Language and Aging; the Ego Document group at the University of Amsterdam; and the Max Planck Institute for Psycholinguistics.

I thank the many people who offered stories about first and last words—those stories, whether or not they appear in the book, have changed me immeasurably. Dozens of experts in the language sciences, history, medicine, psychology, and other fields enabled the interdisciplinary scope of this book by answering questions and helping me tie the threads together. Any inaccuracies and mis-tied threads are my responsibility alone. I wish to thank Linda Acredolo, Jeannie Anderson, David Armstrong, Maurizio Bettini, Shivam Bhatt, Elizabeth Blundon, Kees de Bot, Alisa Brownlee, Greg Bryant, Andy Byford, George Carnevale, Marisa Casillas, Laura Chahda, Andrea Chiba, Sylvia Chou, Nina Christensen, Eve Clark, Pieter Coppens, Leonie Cornips, Cynthia Cress, Philip Dale, Douglas Davies, Matt Davis, Rudolf Dekker, Peter Desain, Mark Dingemanse, Holger Dissel, Maggie Ellis, Jason Farquhar, Larry Fenson, Megan Figueroa, Joel Frader, Michael Frank, Romayne Gallagher, Gerard Van Gelder, Annette Gerstenberg, Janet Golden, Candy Goodwin, David Gramling, Robert Gramling, Jackie Guendouzi, Darla Hagge, Adriana Hanulikova, Heidi Hamilton, Mary Beth Happ, Carmen Harris, Jon Henner, Christian Herff, Ingo Hertrich, Cat Hobaiter, Christopher Joby, Peter Jeffrey, Mary Lee Jensvold, Sarit Kattan, Maureen Keeley, Leelo Keevallik, Allan Kellehear, Scott Kendall, Wendy Kinton, Daniel Kondziella, Pim Levelt, Steve Levinson, Yifan Lou, William Lunsford, Kathryn Mannix, Virginia Marchman, Mel McEvoy, Mira Menzfeld, Paul Mueller, Beth Moulam, Kim Oller, Marc van Oostendorp, Marwan Othman, Adrian Owen, Wendy Pearce, Simone Pika, Kevin Pitt, Robin Pollens, Linda Pollock, Anantanand Rambachan, Kate Riley, Caroline Rowland, Asif Saddiqi, Adam Seligman, Amalia Skilton, Bettina Sorger, Lameen Souag, Michael Stolberg, Enzo Tagliazucchi, Donna Thal, Michael Tomasello, Bambi Schieffelin, Eric Venbrux, Marilyn Vihman, Lawrence Ward, Alison Wray, and Jessica Zitter. Apologies to anyone whose name I've inadvertently admitted—know that I'm grateful for your contribution.

I'm grateful to Richard Adams, Tashi Bradford, Monica Elaine Campbell, Beth Hutchinson, Sacha Jackson, and Charlene LeBlanc for relating their experiences with signing. I thank Lisa Smartt for sharing her experiences as well. I'm also grateful for those who served as sounding boards, especially Robin Pollens and Susan Barnett, but also those whose early encouragement and interest was so valuable: Edwin Battistella, Nancy Berlinger, Scott Blackwood, John Butman, Marisa Casillas, Walter Glannon, David Lancy, Sharon Kaufman, Thomas Laqueur, and Cullen Murphy. I'm sad that Sharon, Scott, and John are no longer alive to read the finished book. I'm also grateful for readers of early drafts, among them Vigjilenca Abazi, Geoff Amsel, Stefano Bertolo, Lynn Davey, Mark Dingemanse, Marcel Giezen, Robert Lawrence, Andy Rosen, and my parents, Michael and Jeanette Erard. Anthony Shore, namer extraordinaire, generously provided advice on titles, and Phil Kirkman gave me image help. I'm immensely grateful for the attention of my editor, Phil Laughlin, and to the careful input from anonymous peer reviewers at the MIT Press, whose encouraging compliments and incisive criticism kept me motivated over the long haul. I thank Rachel Fudge for meticulous copyediting and Judith Feldmann for her expert contributions to the production process.

Roger Gathman provided his usual word magic, and Audra Wolfe gifted me with structural advice. Tim Hipp gave me excellent transcription help. I'm grateful to Julie Hochsegang for connecting me with Deaf hospice providers and giving the text a sensitivity read on issues of sign language and Deaf culture. I'm also thankful to Antonio Benítez-Burraco and David Leavens for fact-checking chapter 3. Thanks to Mel McEvoy for his wonderful poems and a sensitivity read on medical issues. I appreciate that Gary Bradshaw spent time looking for photos of Viki. Thanks to Nataly Kelly and Cindy Roat, who connected me to medical interpreters in the United States; thanks to Tatiana Cestari, Liliana Crane, Niuvis Ferro-Gonzalez, Filsan Abdullahi Ismail, Patricia Leadley, and Yvonne Simpson. Thanks to Michael Skaggs of the Chaplaincy Innovation Lab for connecting me to US chaplains, and I appreciate Linda Golding, Josiah Hoaglund, Wendy Manuel, Rebecca Mokos, Taqwa Surapati, and Zac Willette for their insights. I'm also appreciative that Emma Clare of End-of-Life Doula UK connected me with Julie Andrassy, Diane Roberts, and Naomi Wood. Mary Hague-Yearl of the Osler Library of the History of Medicine has provided superb, generous guidance to Osleriana over many years. I am also grateful to Monica Soeting of the Dutch Diary Archive; Russell Johnson at the University of California, Los Angeles Library Special Collections; and Nikola Illeová at the Moravian Culture Museum.

As always, the life I share with Misty McLaughlin and our two sons has been and continues to be the most remarkable gift that a writer could ask for.

Notes

Prelude

Page 2 *it's knowing how to be with the dead.* "There is no social space entirely outside the shared space with the dead. To learn to live is to learn to inhabit this space in a responsible way." Hans Ruin, *Being with the Dead: Burial, Ancestral Politics, and the Roots of Historical Consciousness* (Stanford, CA: Stanford University Press, 2018), 201.

Introduction

Page 6 *greet that dark night in silence* Poet Dylan Thomas's last words were "I've had 18 straight whiskies . . . I think that's the record." Conventional literary history holds that Thomas drank himself to death, but modern medical forensics says he died of untreated pneumonia. Moreover, eighteen whiskies might have been a Thomasian exaggeration, as the evidence says he had only eight. John Ezard, "History Has Dylan Thomas Dying from Drink. But Now, a New Theory," *Guardian*, November 27, 2004, https://www.theguardian.com/uk/2004/nov/27/books.booksnews.

Page 7 *a closing window of interaction.* Or is interpreted to be such.

Page 7 *a rubble of interactive abilities.* In a previous book, *Um . . . : Slips, Stumbles, and Verbal Blunders, and What They Mean* (New York: Pantheon, 2007), I explored verbal rubble and its function around "uhs," "ums," and the like. There I tried to show that "um" has specific functions in our communication. In this book, I am similarly investigating the place of elements that frame linguistic structure.

The relationship of "rubble" to "ruin" distinction comes from anthropologist Gaston Gordillo's *Rubble: The Afterlife of Destruction* (Durham, NC: Duke University Press, 2014), an ethnography of the relationship between ruins and rubble on the Argentinian landscape. Gordillo argues that the ruin is reconstituted rubble, a distinction that Rose Macaulay, in *Pleasure of Ruins* (London: William Clowes and Sons, 1953), misses.

Much of what we see when we visit Greece, Rome, Mexico, Egypt, and other places used to be rubble, but someone reconstituted it to make ruins. Similarly, language has an architecture; at the end of life, that architecture weakens and collapses, leaving something with varying degrees of intactness. The tradition of "famous last words" creates a legible ruin, a monument to the past, out of the rubble. We're very familiar with these linguistic ruins; I want to modestly suggest a science of linguistic rubble as well as an anthropology of linguistic ruin-making.

Page 8 *like tears in rain.* One of the most famous last-words scenes in contemporary cinema is from the 1982 sci-fi movie *Blade Runner.* As Batty, a bioengineered humanoid, is dying, he says: "I've [pause] *seen* things you people wouldn't believe [pause]. Attack ships on fire off the shoulder of Orion [pause]. I watched C-beams [pause] glitter in the dark near the Tannhauser Gate. [Long pause] All those [pause] moments will be lost [pause] in time [pause] like [pause, small choke] tears [pause] in rain [pause.] Time [brief pause] to die."

Then his head drops, and he closes his eyes. How lucky we would be to testify about life so defiantly, with such poetic compression. Buddhist monks in Japan were often supposed to be able to prepare poems as their last words. A close inspection of the practice reveals that these were not composed on the spot but rather ahead of time.

Page 8 *was delighted.* I've chosen to use "deaf" as the term that includes people who don't hear, are hard of hearing, and late-deafened. Where I can confirm that an individual prefers "Deaf" as a marker of identity, I use that.

Page 10 *the authoritative work on the genre.* Karl Guthke, *Last Words* (Princeton, NJ: Princeton University Press, 1992).

Page 10 *Harriet Tubman's last words.* "I go to prepare a place for you."

Page 10 *Marie Antoinette's.* "*Pardonnez-moi, monsieur,*" to her executioner, for stepping on his foot.

Page 10 *"Thanks, Ollie"?* Jenny Cavilleri, in the novel *Love Story.* Erich Segal, *Love Story* (London: Harper & Row, 1970).

Page 10 *"I commend my spirit."* Originally attributed to Jesus but also to Saint Augustine, Charlemagne, Thomas Becket, Cardinal Newman, among many other Christians.

Page 10 *"Oh wow."* Steve Jobs.

Page 10 *"I love you."* "'Alex & Me': The Parrot Who Said 'I Love You,'" NPR, August 31, 2009, https://www.npr.org/2009/08/31/112405883/alex-me-the-parrot-who-said-i -love-you.

Page 10 *attributed to the Mars rover* Opportunity. This was a "poetic translation" by science reporter Jacob Margolis of a final data transmission by the vehicle. To NASA's dismay, these last words became wildly popular. Aristos Georgiou, "No, the Last Words of NASA's Opportunity Rover Weren't 'My Battery Is Low and It's

Getting Dark,'" *Newsweek*, February 28, 2019, https://www.newsweek.com/nasa-mars
-opportunity-rover-new-york-daily-news-jet-propulsion-laboratory-1334615.

Page 12 *inversely proportionate to their charm.* Guthke, *Last Words*, 202, note 1.

Page 13 *"Oh, that is what she was talking about."* Bargainsmarts, "Expiratory vocalizations at the end of life," AllNurses.com, October 3, 2012, https://allnurses.com
/expiratory-vocalizations-end-life-t451382.

Page 14 *occur during illness dying.* One comment made me bolt upright when I read
it, in American linguist Leonard Bloomfield's magnum opus, *Language* (New York:
Holt, Rinehart, and Winston, 1933): "There is no hour of the day when we can say
that a person has finished learning to speak, but, rather, to the end of his life, the
speaker keeps on doing the very things which make up infantile language learning." Did Bloomfield really mean the literal end? Probably not—nearly all studies of
language "across the life span" do not fully span the life.

Page 14 *wrote historian Thomas Laqueur.* Thomas Laqueur, *The Work of the Dead: A
Cultural History of Mortal Remains* (Princeton, NJ: Princeton University Press, 2015),
556.

Page 16 *eyes, hands, and faces as with our brains and mouths.* "Embodied" has several
academic definitions, but I use it here in the vernacular sense: something you do
with your body. In other words, language is instantiated by brains, mouths and
vocal tracts, faces, hands, body postures, and eye gaze.

Chapter 1

Page 21 *"mowuh" meant "more."* This anecdote, along with a discussion of Catherine
Snow's essay, is drawn from my article "The Mystery of Babies' First Words," *Atlantic*, April 30, 2019, https://www.theatlantic.com/family/archive/2019/04/babies-first
-words-babbling-or-actual-language/588289.

Page 21 *as likely as one describing a thing.* Katherine Nelson, "Structure and Strategy
in Learning to Talk," *Monographs of the Society for Research in Child Development* 38,
no. 1–2 (1973): 1–135.

Page 21 *didn't pick up any replacements for several months.* Catherine Snow, "The Last
Word: Questions about the Emerging Lexicon," in *The Emergent Lexicon: The Child's
Development of a Linguistic Vocabulary*, ed. Michael D. Smith and John L. Locke (New
York: Academic, 1988), 352.

Page 22 *as presupposed by the linguists.* Catherine Snow, "Doubling Down on Ser-
endipity," *Education Review* 24 (October 11, 2017): 2, http://dx.doi.org/10.14507/er
.v24.2291. Snow's dissertation was published as "Mothers' Speech to Children
Learning Language," *Child Development* 43, no. 2 (1972): 549–565.

Page 23 *(but mainly with their hands)*. Linguists agree that children babble cross-modally but disagree on how long they do it for and whether they need to be in an environment with signing. See Richard Meier and Raquel Willerman, "Prelinguistic Gesture in Deaf and Hearing Infants," in *Language, Gesture, and Space*, ed. Karen Emmorey and Judy Reilly (New York: Psychology Press, 2013), 401–420. Also Laura-Ann Petitto and P. F. Marentette, "Babbling in the Manual Mode: Evidence for the Ontogeny of Language," *Science* 251, no. 5000 (1991): 1493–1496.

Page 23 *"learns how to mean."* M. A. K. Halliday, *Learning How to Mean: Explorations in the Development of Language (Explorations in Language Study)* (London: Edward Arnold, 1975).

Page 24 *rules about how words are formed—does it count?* This happens less than we think; children as young as fifteen months who speak agglutinative languages like Turkish still use proper case inflections on single nouns. Dan Slobin, "From Ontogenesis to Phylogenesis: What Can Child Language Tell Us About Language Evolution?," in *Biology and Knowledge Revisited: From Neurogenesis to Psychogenesis*, ed. J. Langer, S. T. Parker, and C. Milbrath (Mahwah, NJ: Lawrence Erlbaum Associates, 2004). Slobin notes the same pattern for Inuktitut, whose complex word morphology is shared by many American Indigenous languages.

Page 25 *fills the infinitesimal gap.* W. G. Bateman, "Papers on Language Development," *The Pedagogical Seminary* 24, no. 3 (1917): 396, https://doi.org/10.1080/0891 9402.1917.10534749.

Page 25 *rather than an empirical problem.* Snow, "The Last Word," 347.

Page 25 *theories of language and of meaning.* Snow, "The Last Word," 350.

Page 27 *which they carried.* Fray Bernardino de Sahagún, *Primeros Memoriales: Paleography of Nahuatl Text and English Translation* by Thelma D. Sullivan; completed and revised, with additions, by H. B. Nicholson, Arthur J. O. Anderson, Charles E. Dibble, Eloise Quiñones Keber, and Wayne Ruwet (Norman, OK: University of Oklahoma Press, 1997), 88.

Page 28 *ocatl, xochtic, octototl, conechichilli.* Alejandro Díaz Barriga Cuevas, "La representación social de la infancia mexica a principios del siglo XVI," in *Nuevas miradas a la historia de la infancia en América Latina: Entre prácticas y representaciones*, ed. Susana Sosenski and Elena Jackson Albarrán (D.F., México: IIH UNAM, 2012).

Page 28 *something like "first prayers."* I'm indebted to Frances Karttunen, a Nahuatl scholar, and John Schwaller, a historian, for providing these facts via email.

Page 28 *an ability they gain when they taste corn.* "Es necesario aquí mencionar que en ocasiones el primer ritual de paso incorpora al infante al grupo, y le otorga cierta humanidad. Sin embargo, tal como se verá más adelante, para los antiguos nahuas aún era necesario que el niño comenzara a consumir los alimentos de la tierra; en concreto, el maíz, para poder ser considerado como un "hombre verdadero." Alejandro Díaz Barriga Cuevas, "Algunas notas sobre las concepciones del cuerpo," *Cuicuilco Revista de Ciencias Antropológicas* 70 (September–December 2017): 113–137.

Page 29 *"until they could talk clearly."* Leslie Spier and Edward Sapir, *Wishram Ethnography* (Seattle: University of Washington Press, 1930), 218.

Page 29 *"understand the tongue of [their] parents."* Spier and Sapir, *Wishram Ethnography*, 255.

Page 30 *mingling souls can speak each other's languages with ease.* This is described by an unnamed, fictional Beng diviner in an imagined Beng childcare manual, written by Alma Gottlieb for *A World of Babies*, ed. Alma Gottlieb and Judy DeLoache (Cambridge: Cambridge University Press, 2017). Gottlieb expanded on this in *The Afterlife Is Where We Come From: The Culture of Infancy in West Africa* (Chicago: University of Chicago Press, 2004).

Page 31 *or someone without speech,* infans—*without fari.* Rather than complicate matters with the full noun paradigm of *infans* in Latin, I'm going to distinguish only the singular (*infans*) and plural (*infantes*).

Page 31 *the idea of the "speaker" of an utterance.* Erving Goffman, "Footing," in *Forms of Talk*, ed. Erving Goffman (Philadelphia: University of Pennsylvania Press, 1981), 124–159. For objections to Goffman's framework, see Stephen Levinson, "Putting Linguistics on a Proper Footing: Explorations in Goffman's Concepts of Participation," in *Erving Goffman: Exploring the Interaction Order*, ed. P. Drew and A. Wootton (Boston: Northeastern University Press, 1988), 161–227. For my purposes here, Goffman is sufficient.

Page 31 *"sounding box."* Goffman, "Footing," 226.

Page 31 *"scripts the lines."* Goffman, "Footing," 226.

Page 32 *"the party to whose position the words attest" (its principal).* Goffman, "Footing," 226.

Page 32 *as in "eat shit!" (or* ai tae). Elinor Ochs, "Talking to Children in Western Samoa," *Language in Society* 11, no. 1 (1982): 77–104.

Page 34 *"one of the most exciting milestones in development."* Kyra Karmiloff and Annette Karmiloff-Smith, *Pathways to Language: From Fetus to Adolescent* (Cambridge, MA: Harvard University Press, 2001), 56.

Page 34 *rank high in a trait called "babiness."* The term appears in Mika Braginsky et al., "Consistency and Variability in Children's Word Learning Across Languages," *Open Mind* 3 (June 2019): 52–67, https://doi.org/10.1162/opmi_a_00026. But the norms of babiness in words were established in Lynn K. Perry, Marcus Perlman, and Gary Lupyan, "Iconicity in English and Spanish and Its Relation to Lexical Category and Age of Acquisition," *PLOS One* 10, no. 9 (2015): e0137147, https://doi.org/10.1371/journal.pone.0137147.

Page 34 *known to say "socks" and "shoes."* Nelson, "Structure and Strategy," 31.

Page 34 *called an "action scheme."* Elizabeth Bates, Laura Benigni, Inge Bretherton, Luigia Camaioni, and Virginia Volterra, *The Emergence of Symbols: Cognition and Communication in Infancy* (New York: Academic Press, 1979), 156. Also Elizabeth Bates, Luigia Camaioni, and Virginia Volterra, "The Acquisition of Performatives Prior to Speech," *Merrill-Palmer Quarterly of Behavior and Development* 21, no. 3 (July 1975): 205–226. "Within the same pointing, giving, reaching vocalizing sequences for [two children in the study], we found a gradual passage from vocalization, to vocalization as a signal, to word as a signal, to word as a proposition with a referential value" (220).

Page 34 *in the first ten that English-speaking children said.* Nelson, "Structure and Strategy," 25.

Page 35 *along with gestures and other bodily actions.* As I'll discuss later, we more or less know which words will be spoken early by babies.

Page 35 *have them among their earliest words.* Early work was done by Eve Clark, "From Gesture to Word: On the Natural History of Deixis in Language Acquisition," *Human Growth and Development* (1978): 85–120. Later work was done by Holger Diessel, "Where Does Language Come From? Some Reflections on the Role of Deictic Gesture and Demonstratives in the Evolution of Language," *Language and Cognition* 5, no. 2–3 (2013): 239–49; Holger Diessel and Kenny Coventry, "Demonstratives in Spatial Language and Social Interaction: An Interdisciplinary Review," *Frontiers in Psychology* 11 (2020): 555265, https://doi.org/10.3389/fpsyg.2020.555265; Amalia Skilton, "Learning Speaker-and Addressee-Centered Demonstratives in Ticuna," *Journal of Child Language* (2022), https://doi.org/10.1017/S0305000922000101. I'm indebted to conversations with Clark, Diessel, and Skilton about the importance of demonstratives in child language.

Page 35 *and even predict when they will occur.* See Brandon C. Roy et al., "Predicting the Birth of a Spoken Word," *Proceedings of the National Academy of Sciences of the United States of America* 112, no. 41 (2015): 12663–12668, https://doi.org/10.1073/pnas.1419773112.

Page 36 *controlling one's anger, sharing, and understanding kinship structures.* Annemieke Milks et al., "Hunter-Gatherer Children in the Past: An Archaeological Review," *Journal of Anthropological Archaeology* 64 (2021): 101369, https://doi.org/10.1016/j.jaa.2021.101369.

Page 36 *"healing aspect of the human spirit."* Rose Ann Tahe and Nancy Bo Flood, *First Laugh: Welcome, Baby!* (Watertown, MA: Charlesbridge, 2018).

Page 36 *opportunities to see what's going on around them.* Marisa Casillas, Penelope Brown, and Stephen C. Levinson, "Early Language Experience in a Papuan Community," *Journal of Child Language* 48 (2021): 792–814, https://doi.org/10.1017/S0305 000920000549.

Page 36 *have very little speech directed at them.* Marisa Casillas, Penelope Brown, and Stephen C. Levinson, "Early Language Experience in a Tseltal Mayan Village," *Child Development* 91, no. 5 (2020): 1819–1835, https://doi.org/10.1111/cdev.13349.

Page 36 *"Why are these women wasting their time?"* "Halima" was the fictional author of an imagined childcare manual, written by Sirad Shirdon, a Somali-born speech language pathologist in the US, for Gottlieb and DeLoache, *A World of Babies.*

Page 36 *Many groups are like this.* The Yucatec Mayan, for example. See Laura A. Shneidman and Susan Goldin-Meadow, "Language Input and Acquisition in a Mayan Village: How Important Is Directed Speech?," *Developmental Science* 15 (2012): 659–673, https://doi.org/10.1111/j.1467-7687.2012.01168.x. For a systematic review of twenty-nine studies around the world, see Alejandrina Cristia, "A Systematic Review Suggests Marked Differences in the Prevalence of Infant-Directed Vocalization Across Groups of Populations," *Developmental Science* 26 (2022): e13265, https://doi .org/10.1111/desc.13265.

Page 37 *probably due to the demands of daily life.* Casillas, Brown, and Levinson, in "Early Language Experience in a Papuan Community," suggest that the daily schedule of an agricultural lifestyle, less so beliefs about babies as speakers, drive the amount of speech directed to children. See also D. Sharma and R. LeVine, "Child Care in India: A Comparative Developmental View of Infant Social Environments," *New Directions for Child and Adolescent Development* 80 (1998): 45–67, https://doi .org/10.1002/cd.23219988005.

Page 37 *"first words are too ambiguous, too subjective,"* she mused. "Why aren't first words more celebrated?" I asked Michael Tomasello, who replied: "I think the more odd thing is why they'd celebrate last words." Tomasello proceeded to relate how the family dog had been hit by a car and killed the week earlier. "There's just something about this life force, this personality—how can it be gone?"

Chapter 2

Page 41 *between their sound or shape and what they represent.* D. W. Massaro and Marcus Perlman, "Quantifying Iconicity's Contribution during Language Acquisition: Implications for Vocabulary Learning," *Frontiers in Communication* 2 (2017): 4, https://doi.org/10.3389/fcomm.2017.00004; A. K. Nielsen and M. Dingemanse, "Iconicity in Word Learning and Beyond: A Critical Review," *Language and Speech* 64, no. 1 (2021): 52–72; and L. K. Perry et al., "Iconicity in the Speech of Children and Adults," *Developmental Science* 21 (2018): e12572, https://doi.org/10.1111/desc.12572.

Page 43 *From there, they spread.* This is discussed in David Lancy, *The Anthropology of Childhood* (Cambridge: Cambridge University Press, 2008), 59.

Page 43 *"references to children's jargon are unusual before the seventeenth century."* Philippe Ariès, *Centuries of Childhood: A Social History of Family Life,* trans. Robert Baldick (New York: Knopf, 1962), 47.

Page 44 *"titota, tetita, y totata."* Ariès, *Centuries,* 47.

Page 44 *only three survived him.* Details about Sewall came from an entry at https://www.findagrave.com/memorial/1494/samuel-e_-sewall. Accessed January 22, 2022.

Page 45 *but to not rush it.* Jean-Jacques Rousseau, *Emile,* trans. Barbara Foxley (New York: Open Road Media, 2020), Kindle edition.

Page 45 *all philosophical speculations are utterly useless.* Rousseau, *Emile.*

Page 45 *"do not understand begins earlier than we think."* Rousseau, *Emile.*

Page 45 *had occurred in the first years of life.* P. Lozzi and D. Fariñas, "Infant and Child Mortality in the Past," *Annales de démographie historique* 1, no. 129 (2015): 55–75, https://doi.org/10.3917/adh.129.0055.

Page 45 *one in five of all children died before their first birthday.* Hugh Cunningham, *Children and Childhood in Western Society Since 1500* (New York: Routledge, 1995), 90.

Page 45 *as far back as the Akkadian civilization in 2500 BCE.* See David Bosworth, *Infant Weeping in Akkadian, Greek, and Hebrew Literatures* (University Park, PA: Eisenbrauns, 2016).

Page 46 *"Apple" isn't, in fact, the earliest.* Readers of Herodotus will know an even earlier instance, which makes for interesting conjecture but is an unreliable account. According to the historian, the Egyptian king Psammetichus ordered that two newborn babies be raised by shepherds in a secluded building and not spoken to. Whatever language they spoke first would indicate the oldest language, hence humans' oldest form. Because the two-year-old children begged the shepherd for "*bekos,*" a Phrygian word for "bread," Psammetichus conceded the Phrygians were older than the Egyptians. For an extensive discussion of this myth, see Deborah Levine Gera, *Ancient Greek Ideas on Speech, Language, and Civilization* (Oxford: Oxford University Press, 2003).

Page 46 *to which his father subjected him.* Michel de Montaigne, "Of the Education of Children," *Essays,* trans. Charles Cotton (Project Gutenberg, released October 25, 2004, updated March 16, 2023), https://www.gutenberg.org/cache/epub/3600/pg3600-images.html.

Page 47 *as literary historian Elizabeth Wirth Marvick wrote.* Elizabeth Wirth Marvick, "Louis XIII and His Doctor: On the Shifting Fortunes of Jean Héroard's Journal," *French Historical Studies* 18, no. 1 (1993): 279–300.

Page 47 *Héroard faithfully noted on January 12, 1604.* Or possibly November 29. Marvick, "Louis XIII," 298.

Page 47 *their pronunciations and what words they understood.* See Rudolf Dekker, *Childhood, Memory and Autobiography in Holland: From the Golden Age to Romanticism* (New York: St. Martin's Press, 1999), 24.

Page 47 *ability at six months to answer in gestures.* Dekker, *Childhood*, 24.

Page 47 *didn't write down any of their first words in any language.* This was clarified for me via email by Christopher Joby, who wrote about Huygens in *The Multilingualism of Constantijn Huygens (1596–1687)* (Amsterdam: Amsterdam University Press, 2014).

Page 48 *"papa," "mama," and "pretty."* Albertine-Adrienne Necker de Saussure, *Progressive Education, Commencing with the Infant,* trans. Emma Willard and Mrs. Lincoln Phelps (Boston: W. D. Ticknor, 1835), 186–189.

Page 48 *"among the first accents he is heard to utter."* Mrs. Lincoln Phelps, "Appendix: Observations Upon an Infant, During Its First Year, by a Mother," in *Progressive Education*, 344.

Page 48 *anthropologists have rightly critiqued the ethnocentrism of this view.* For instance, in a multiauthor invited forum, "Bridging the 'Language Gap,'" *Journal of Linguistic Anthropology* 25, no. 1 (2015): 66–86, https://doi.org/10.1111/jola.12071.

Page 49 *Switzerland, the United Kingdom, and the United States.* Cunningham, *Children*, 155.

Page 49 *whether their efforts were working.* A. W. Siegel and S. White, "The Child Study Movement: Early Growth and Development of the Symbolized Child," *Advances in Child Development and Behavior* 17 (1982): 233–285.

Page 49 *observe their babies in a manner akin to scientists.* Rima Apple, "Constructing Mothers: Scientific Motherhood in the Nineteenth and Twentieth Centuries," *Social History of Medicine* 8, no. 2 (1995): 161–178; Rima Apple, *Perfect Motherhood: Science and Childrearing in America* (New Brunswick, NJ: Rutgers University Press, 2006).

Page 49 *to make detailed observations of their babies. Babyhood: A monthly magazine for mothers, devoted to the care of infants and young children and the general interests of the nursery* (1891), accessed September 1, 2021, https://books.google.nl/books?id=Jbct AQAAIAAJ&printsec=frontcover&source=gbs_ge_summary_r&cad=0#v=onepage&q &f=false.

Page 49 *as scientists would and written down what they saw.* E. A. Kirkpatrick, "Records of Early Childhood," *Worcester Gazette*, 1891, reprinted in *Babyhood* (1891), 136.

Page 49 *"that science calls for and that lies at her threshold,"* wrote the author. Kirkpatrick, "Records," 136.

Page 50 *"syllables, moods, parts of speech."* Elizabeth Stowe Brown, "The Record of the Baby's Mind, and How It May Be Kept," *Babyhood* (1891), 157–1159.

Page 50 *locks of hair, and hand and palm tracings.* Janet Golden and Lori Weiner, "Reading Baby Books: Medicine, Marketing, Money and the Lives of American Infants," *Journal of Social History* 44, no. 3 (2011): 667–687, https://doi.org/10.1353/jsh.2011.0030, 669.

Page 50 *until she was five years old.* Charlotte Appel and Nina Christensen, "Ida's Sparebösse—Den fineste julegave gives igen," *Magasin fra det Kongelige Bibliotek* 30, no. 4 (2017): 19–28, https://doi.org/10.7146/mag.v30i4.103301.

Page 50 *she could see in front of their apartment.* Just Mathias Thiele, "Idas Sparebösse," Manuscript collection, Royal Danish Library, Acc 2020/15 (1831), 19. I thank Nina Christensen and Charlotte Appel for their translation help.

Page 50 *in the 1870s, then became increasingly popular.* Golden and Weiner, "Reading Baby Books," 670.

Page 50 *reflected the perception that babies were increasingly likely to survive.* Golden and Weiner, "Reading Baby Books."

Page 50 *such books in its special collection.* I was first alerted to this collection by Golden and Weiner, "Reading Baby Books."

Page 51 *a founder of Radcliffe College.* John Leonard, ed., *Woman's Who's Who of America: A Biographical Dictionary of Contemporary Women of the United States and Canada, 1914–1915* (New York: American Commonwealth Co., 1914), 328.

Page 51 *about how to raise her children.* Roblyn Rawlins, "The Mother's Club of Cambridge, 1878–1904: Reappropriating, Reconfiguring and (Re)presenting Expert Knowledge of Mothering," *Journal of the Motherhood Initiative for Research and Community Involvement* 5 (2014).

Page 51 *"physical, emotional, and spiritual well-being."* Julia Grant, *Raising Baby by the Book: The Education of American Mothers* (New Haven, CT: Yale University Press, 1998), 31.

Page 53 *and how that affects their experiences in schools.* Shirley Brice Heath, *Ways with Words: Language, Life, and Work in Communities and Classrooms* (Cambridge: Cambridge University Press, 1983).

Page 53 *"afraid that they will not learn to talk by themselves."* Rousseau, *Emile.*

Page 53 *"considered an affront and a strange behavior as well."* Heath, *Ways with Words,* 86.

Page 53 *the adults made fun of them.* Heath, *Ways with Words*, 95.

Page 54 *a "potential conversationalist" from the get-go.* Heath, *Ways with Words*, 245.

Page 54 *"the preferred means of communication is talk."* Heath, *Ways with Words*, 246.

Page 54 *the baby's turn in the interaction.* Heath, *Ways with Words*, 248.

Page 54 *and as a vehicle for asserting their identities.* Heath, *Ways with Words*, 10.

Page 56 *Ross in a dance of joy as he "byes" his son out the door.* Previously, in a blooper that became famous, Ross was holding the baby actor trying to get him to say "dada." In the script, this failed—thus the joke. But the baby actor did say "dada," which ruined the joke.

Page 56 *fostered by middle-class parents.* Elinor Ochs and Tamar Kremer-Sadlik, "How Postindustrial Families Talk," *Annual Review of Anthropology* 44 (2015): 87–103.

Chapter 3

Page 59 *banal.* Writer F. Scott Fitzgerald's first word was "up."

Page 59 *or quirky.* Musician Neil Young's first word was "dombeen." Linguist and writer Arika Okrent scoured eleven biographies of famous people for their first words. Arika Okrent, "The First Words of 11 Famous People," *Mental Floss*, October 11, 2023, https://www.mentalfloss.com/article/53129/first-words-11-famous-people.

Page 62 *"to make possible the miracle of human communication."* Stephen Levinson, "Interactional Foundations of Language: The Interaction Engine Hypothesis," in *Human Language: From Genes and Brain to Behavior*, ed. Peter Hagoort (Cambridge, MA: MIT Press, 2019), 189–200.

Page 62 *(So do lips.)* See Joel Sherzer, "Verbal and Nonverbal Deixis: The Pointed Lip Gesture among the San Blas Cuna," *Language in Society* 2, no. 1 (April 1973): 117–131.

Page 62 *"to direct her attention to some referent in the environment," wrote Michael Tomasello.* Michael Tomasello, *Becoming Human: A Theory of Ontogeny* (Cambridge, MA: Harvard University Press, 2018), 113.

Page 62 *and gorillas 102.* R. W. Byrne et al., "Great Ape Gestures: Intentional Communication with a Rich Set of Innate Signals," *Animal Cognition* 22, no. 4 (2019): 471, https://doi.org/10.1007/s10071-017-1127-1.

Page 63 *as early as two months old.* Maya Gratier et al., "Early Development of Turn-Taking in Vocal Interaction Between Mothers and Infants," *Frontiers in Psychology* 6 (2015): 1167, https://doi.org/10.3389/fpsyg.2015.01167.

Page 63 *or those who could manage their emotions.* For an overview, see Antonio Benítez-Burraco, Zanna Clay, and Vera Kempe, "Editorial: Self-Domestication and

Human Evolution," *Frontiers in Psychology* 11 (2020), https://doi.org/10.3389/fpsyg
.2020.02007.

Page 64 *(such as stimulating synapses to retain memories).* Constantina Theofanopou-
lou, Cedric Boeckx, and Erich D. Jarvis, "A Hypothesis on a Role of Oxytocin in the
Social Mechanisms of Speech and Vocal Learning," *Proceedings of the Royal Society B*
284 (2017): 20170988, http://dx.doi.org/10.1098/rspb.2017.0988.

Page 65 *then said "al-hamdulillah."* "The Truth About Adam," Sunna.info, accessed
September 22, 2022, http://www.sunna.info/Lessons/islam_425.html.

Page 65 *"who is an infant in the cradle?" they asked.* Surah 19; verse 29, Quran.com,
accessed September 22, 2022, https://quran.com/19?startingVerse=29.

Page 65 *"to be given the Scripture and to be a prophet."* Surah 19; verse 30, Quran.com,
September 22, 2022, https://quran.com/19?startingVerse=30.

Page 65 *he answered, "I am he."* "Section IV—The Creation and Its Cause," Wisdom
Library, accessed September 22, 2022, https://www.wisdomlib.org/hinduism/book
/the-brihadaranyaka-upanishad/d/doc117939.html.

Page 66 *"no brute will dare to cross it."* Max Müller, *Lectures on the Science of Language* (Perlego, 2010), 354, https://www.perlego.com/book/1728270/lectures-on-the
-science-of-language-pdf.354.

Page 67 *as William Dwight Whitney put it.* William Dwight Whitney, *Language and
the Study of Language* (London: N. Trübner and Co., 1870), 251.

Page 68 *"apart from probably using the vocal/auditory modality."* Maggie Tallerman,
"Protolanguage," in *The Handbook of Language Evolution*, ed. Maggie Tallerman and
Kathleen R. Gibson (Oxford: Oxford University Press, 2012), 484–487.

Page 69 *"to inform potential recruits of what they had found."* Derek Bickerton and
Eörs Szathmáry, "Confrontational Scavenging as a Possible Source for Language and
Cooperation," *BMC Evolutionary Biology* 11 (2011): 261, https://doi.org/10.1186/1471
-2148-11-261.

Page 69 *"a typical animal communication system."* Bickerton and Szathmáry,
"Confrontational."

Page 69 *"anything in the world, past or future, real or imagined."* Bickerton and Szathmáry, "Confrontational."

Page 70 *more protophones, more spoken words.* Annika Werwach et al., "Infants'
Vocalizations at 6 Months Predict Their Productive Vocabulary at One Year," *Infant
Behavior and Development* 64 (2021): 101588, https://doi.org/10.1016/j.infbeh.2021
.101588.

Page 70 *Chimpanzee mothers and infants also look at each other's faces.* K. A. Bard
et al., "Group Differences in the Mutual Gaze of Chimpanzees (*Pan troglodytes*),"

Developmental Psychology 41, no. 4 (2005): 616–624, https://doi.org/10.1037/0012 -1649.41.4.616.

Page 70 *even ape mothers who look face-to-face with infants don't vocalize back.* Thanks to Kim Oller for this observation.

Page 72 *would certainly have provided an advantage.* Sverker Johansson, *The Dawn of Language* (London: Maclehose Press, 2021), 392.

Page 73 *but don't have any syntax.* Tallerman, "Protolanguage," 481. Also Ray Jack-endoff, "Possible Stages in the Evolution of the Language Capacity," *Trends in Cognitive Sciences* 3, no. 7 (1999): 272–279, https://doi.org/10.1016/s1364-6613(99)01333-9.

Page 74 *the visual and the vocal alongside each other, but in different ways.* Derek Bick-erton agreed. "My own preference, for what it's worth," he wrote in 2007, "is that language (or I should say protolanguage) began as a free-for-all, catch-as-catch-can mode that utilized sounds, signs, pantomime and any other available mechanism that would carry intention and meaning." Derek Bickerton, "Language Evolution: A Brief Guide for Linguists," *Lingua* 117 (2007): 512.

Page 74 *vocal cord control was essential to the origin of language.* Oller's theory is also one of these. See also Greg Urban, "Metasignaling and Language Origins," *American Anthropologist* 104, no. 1 (2002): 233–246.

Page 74 *a paper in Science about the structure of babbling.* Peter MacNeilage and Barbara Davis, "On the Origin of Internal Structure of Word Forms," *Science* 288, no. 5465 (2000): 527–531, https://doi.org/10.1126/science.288.5465.527.

Page 75 *the motor patterns most frequent in the manual babbling.* Adrianne Cheek, Kearsy Cormier, Ann Repp, and Richard P. Meier, "Prelinguistic Gesture Predicts Mastery and Error in the Production of Early Signs," *Language* 77, no. 2 (2001): 292–323, https://doi.org/10.1353/lan.2001.0072.

Page 76 *she said "papa" and "tem."* Hippolyte Taine, "De l'acquisition du langage chez les enfants et les peuples primitifs," *Revue Philosophique* 1 (1876). Reprinted in *Mind,* translator unknown (1877), 255.

Page 76 *"one of the most remarkable and one of the first she uttered."* Taine, "De l'acquisition," 254.

Page 76 *"It is a natural vocal gesture, not learned."* Taine, "De l'acquisition," 255.

Page 76 *"for it did not correspond to any one of our ideas."* Taine, "De l'acquisition," 257.

Page 76 *"a fixed state in the classes of inferior animals."* Taine, "De l'acquisition," 259.

Page 77 *relative to the "childish" cultures they conquered.* Stephen Jay Gould, *Ontogeny and Phylogeny* (Cambridge, MA: Harvard University Press, 1977).

Page 77 *not creating it entirely de novo*. Dan Slobin, "From Ontogenesis to Phylogenesis: What Can Child Language Tell Us About Language Evolution?," in *Biology and Knowledge Revisited: From Neurogenesis to Psychogenesis*, ed. J. Langer, S. T. Parker, and C. Milbrath (Mahwah, NJ: Lawrence Erlbaum Associates, 2004).

Page 77 *"entrusted two new-born infants to a shepherd," he argued*. Müller, *Lectures*, 346.

Page 78 *first conventional words developed by early hominins*. Dean Falk, *Finding Our Tongues* (New York: Basic Books, 2004), Kindle edition, 501.

Page 78 *"their earliest experiences of warmth, safety, and love?"* Falk, *Finding*, 501.

Chapter 4

Page 79 *but not produce the sounds*. R. L. Garner, *Gorillas & Chimpanzees* (London: Osgood, McIlvaine & Co., 1896).

Page 79 *"may almost be considered a universal word of human speech."* Garner, *Gorillas & Chimpanzees*, accessed June 15, 2023, https://www.gutenberg.org/files/44191 /44191-h/44191-h.htm.

Page 80 *the first human word ever spoken by an ape*. This was noted by Greg Lambin, *The Simian Mind: The Long Debate about Animal Language* (Chicago: University of Chicago Press, 2007), 143. My portrait of Garner is indebted to Lambin's book.

Page 80 *"unaded-softly, and hoarsely, but quite acceptably."* Catherine Hayes and Keith J. Hayes, "The Intellectual Development of a Home-Raised Chimpanzee," *Proceedings of the American Philosophical Society* 95, no. 2 (1951): 107.

Page 80 *"papa," "cup," "up."* By and large, first words or first symbol uses by the great apes involved in language experiments have deliberately been left unproclaimed. This is one place that the person-making power of first words is most evident. Because apes can't be persons, goes the thinking, they can't have first words, so there's been no celebratory romanticizing of (for instance) Washoe's first sign, "come-gimme," or productions by other animals.

Page 80 *"I never knew that word could be so amazing."* Heather Armstrong, *Dear Daughter* (New York: Simon & Schuster, 2007), Kindle edition. Armstrong also noted the other words her daughter could say: "hi, mama, bo, no, dank ooh, owwee, dada."

Page 81 *the protophones of their babies as young as two weeks old*. Herbert Goldman, "Parental Reports of 'MAMA' Sounds in Infants: An Exploratory Study," *Journal of Child Language* 28 (2001): 497–506.

Page 82 *because they were accurately recalling what they heard*. Rose Schneider, Daniel Yurovsky, and Michael C. Frank, "Large-Scale Investigations of Variability in Children's First Words," preprint ahead of publication, https://langcog.stanford.edu /papers/SYF_underreview.pdf.

Page 82 *yet it still gets social credit for wanting and loving its mother.* Also, if the baby is imitating a parent's production, then the adult is the animator, the child a sort of reanimator.

Page 83 *which is more normative than historically accurate.* Wet nurses have been a crucial part of the baby care team since forever, as demonstrated in Valerie Fildes, *Wet Nursing: A History from Antiquity to the Present* (Oxford: Blackwell, 1988).

Page 83 *who argued for "mama" along these lines in a 1922 essay.* Sabina Spielrein, "The Origin of the Child's Words Papa and Mama: Some Observations on the Different Stages in Language Development," in *Sabina Spielrein, Forgotten Pioneer of Psychoanalysis,* ed. Coline Covington and Barbara Wharton (New York: Routledge, 2003).

Page 83 *in the early 1920s was Jean Piaget.* Isabelle Noth, "'Beyond Freud and Jung': Sabina Spielrein's Contribution to Child Psychoanalysis and Developmental Psychology," *Pastoral Psychology* 64 (2015): 284.

Page 83 *"common belief that 'Papa' and 'Mama' are the child's first words."* Spielrein, "Origin," 235.

Page 83 *"which are seen as the child's first words."* Spielrein, "Origin," 236; John Kerr, *A Most Dangerous Method: The Story of Jung, Freud, and Sabina Spielrein* (New York: Vintage Books, 1993), 493.

Page 83 *"the ancestor sleeps within the child, and the child within the ancestor."* Spielrein, "Origin," 235.

Page 83 *another said lululu after hearing running water.* Spielrein, "Origin," 236.

Page 83 *didn't mention the first word she said and understood herself.* Spielrein, "Origin," 236.

Page 84 *"between the word and meaningless babble."* Spielrein, "Origin," 236.

Page 84 *to study how young Kaluli children become Kaluli speakers.* Bambi Schieffelin describes this work in *The Give and Take of Everyday Life: Language Socialization of Kaluli Children,* 2nd ed. (Tucson: Fenestra Books, 2005).

Page 84 *they don't consider the children to be speaking.* Schieffelin, *Give and Take,* p. 74.

Page 84 *because the children hadn't said "nɔ" and "bo" yet.* Schieffelin, *Give and Take,* 74.

Page 85 *the goal of which was to "make language harden" in the child.* Schieffelin, *Give and Take,* 74.

Page 86 *"and go where they want to go regardless of the wishes of others."* Don Kulick, "Anger, Gender, Language Shift, and the Politics of Revelation in a Papua New Guinean Village," *Pragmatics* 2, no. 3 (1992): 286.

Page 86 *express a baby's way of engaging with the world.* Don Kulick, *Death in the Rainforest* (Chapel Hill, NC: Algonquin Books, 2019), 108, Kindle edition.

Page 86 *"hold up its end of the conversation."* Kulick, *Death*, 37.

Page 86 *"that toddlers learn by being taught,"* Kulick wrote. Kulick, *Death*, 37.

Page 86 *("that's a lie").* Kulick, *Death*, 38.

Page 87 *nor adequately perform aga.* Elinor Ochs, "Talking to Children in Western Samoa," *Language in Society* 11, no. 2 (1982): 77–104.

Page 87 *meaning "eat shit."* Ochs, "Talking," 91.

Page 87 *didn't actually know the meaning of* tae. "When we asked why young children produced *tae* as their very first Samoan word, we were told that very young children *palauvale* ('use bad or indecent language') or *ulavale* ('make a nuisance of oneself, make trouble') . . . In other words, this is the nature of children." Ochs, "Talking," 91.

Page 89 *"or to the feeding bottle and the mouth is full."* Roman Jakobson, "Why Mama and Papa," in *Studies on Child Language and Aphasia* (De Gruyter, 1941), 26.

Page 90 *seven wanted attention.* Goldman, "Parental Reports," 502.

Page 90 *as well as photos of other men and women.* J. Brooks-Gunn and M. Lewis, "Why Mama and Papa? The Development of Social Labels," *Child Development* 50 (1979): 1203–1206.

Page 90 *by more subjects than "mommy."* Brooks-Gunn and Lewis, "Why Mama and Papa," 1204.

Page 90 *said that "mommy" were first.* Brooks-Gunn and Lewis, "Why Mama and Papa," 1205–1206.

Page 92 *authority, efficacy, and credibility.* Maurizio Bettini, "Weighty Words, Suspect Speech: 'Fari' in Roman Culture," *Arethusa* 41, no. 2 (Spring 2008): 313–375.

Page 92 *"its first vagitus."* Bettini, "Weighty," 341.

Page 92 *either as Fabulinus or Farinus.* Bettini, "Weighty," 344.

Page 93 *"merged his voice with that of the child."* Bettini, "Weighty," 344.

Page 93 *well after the ancient religion Varro mentioned had gone away.* See Michel Manson, "The Emergence of the Small Child in Rome (Third Century BC–First Century AD)," *History of Education: Journal of the History of Education Society* 12, no. 3 (1983): 149–159. See also Jacob Mackey, "Developmental Psychologies in the Roman World: Change and Continuity," *History of Psychology*, 22, no. 2 (2019): 113–129.

Page 93 (pupa, pupus). These Latin words come from Manson, "Emergence."

Page 94 *connecting parent and child emotionally.* Linda P. Acredolo and Susan W. Goodwyn, "Symbolic Gesturing in Language Development: A Case Study," *Human Development* 28, no. 1 (1985): 40–49, https://doi.org/10.1159/000272934; Linda Acredolo and Susan Goodwyn, "Symbolic Gesturing in Normal Infants," *Child Development* 59, no. 2 (April 1988): 450–466; Susan W. Goodwyn, Linda P. Acredolo, and C. A. Brown, "Impact of Symbolic Gesturing on Early Language Development," *Journal of Nonverbal Behavior* 24 (2000): 81–103.

Page 95 *as young as nine months old.* V. J. Rideout, E. A. Vandewater, and E. A. Wartella, *Zero to Six: Electronic Media in the Lives of Infants, Toddlers, and Preschoolers* (Menlo Park, CA: The Henry J. Kaiser Family Foundation, 2003).

Page 95 *relationships between babies and adults.* Patrick Hughes, "Baby, It's You: International Capital Discovers the Under Threes," *Contemporary Issues in Early Childhood* 6, no. 1 (2005): 31.

Page 95 *negligible impact on verbal development.* Elizabeth Fitzpatrick, Jonelle Thibert, Viviane Grandpierre, and J. Cyne Johnston, "How HANDy Are Baby Signs? A Systematic Review of the Impact of Gestural Communication on Typically Developing, Hearing Infants Under the Age of 36 Months," *First Language* 34, no. 6 (2014): 486–509.

Page 96 *even the term "baby sign language" is an appropriation.* See Jolanta Lapiak, "Babysign Language; Myths Debunked," Handspeak, last updated 2021, accessed May 15, 2023, https://www.handspeak.com/learn/415/.

Page 97 *"making their behavior socially influential beyond their numbers."* Ginger Pizer, Keith Walters, and Richard Meier, "Bringing Up Baby with Baby Signs: Language Ideologies and Socialization in Hearing Families," *Sign Language Studies* 7, no. 4 (Summer 2007): 391.

Page 97 *rankings of parental leave support.* "PF2.1. Parental Leave Systems," OECD Family Database, updated December 2022, https://www.oecd.org/els/soc/PF2_1_Parental_leave_systems.pdf.

Page 97 *reduce that stress.* N. Howlett, E. Kirk, and K. J. Pine, "Does 'Wanting the Best' Create More Stress? The Link Between Baby Sign Classes and Maternal Anxiety," *Infant and Child Development*, 20 (2011): 437–445.

Page 97 *Henner's criticism is borne out.* A more overarching critique of ASL studies from a disability perspective that touches on related issues is Octavian Robinson and Jonathan Henner, "Authentic Voices, Authentic Encounters: Cripping the University through American Sign Language," *Disability Studies Quarterly* 38, no. 4 (2018), https://dsq-sds.org/article/view/6111/5128.

Chapter 5

Page 100 *to track the emergence of their soul.* I mentioned this book in chapter 2.

Page 100 *and on learning to speak.* In 1835, the book was first translated into English; one of the translators, Almira Phelps, included her own child's diary as an appendix, as I mentioned in chapter 2.

Page 100 *"the physiological processes of development."* Sally Shuttleworth, *The Mind of the Child: Child Development in Literature, Science, and Medicine, 1840–1900* (Oxford: Oxford University Press, 2010), 222.

Page 100 *who kept a diary from 1791 to 1799.* Wedgewood was a famous abolitionist, as were members of Darwin's extended family. The evangelicals and Quakers had an interest in the human development of all humans—hence the abolitionism, interest in women's equality, and interest in children. Recording children's development might have had something to do with disproving the notion popular among racists that humans had multiple geneses—tracing child development could prove a single origin.

Page 100 *explosion of so-called ego-documents.* A concept introduced by Dutch historian Jacques Presser in 1958, eventually defined as "those documents in which an ego intentionally or unintentionally discloses, or hides itself." See Rudolf Dekker and Arianne Baggerman, "Jacques Presser, Egodocuments and the Personal Turn in Historiography," *European Journal of Life Writing* 7 (August 2018): CP90–CP110, https://doi.org/10.5463/ejlw.7.263.

Page 101 *from 1770 to 1830.* German historian Reinhart Koselleck labeled the period from 1770 to 1830 as a "Sattelzeit," or a transition point, "in which a broad series of political concepts acquired their current meanings, and that both defined and reflected the fundamental experienes of moderntiy." From George Williamson, "Retracing the Sattelzeit: Thoughts on the Historiography of the French Revolutionary and Napoleonic Eras," *Central European History* 51 (2018): 68.

Page 101 *"as a token of her mother's love."* Noted in Shuttleworth, *Mind of the Child,* 222.

Page 101 *"their personal lives and the society they were part of,"* Baggerman and Dekker wrote. Rudolf Dekker and Arianne Baggerman, *Controlling Time and Shaping the Self: The Rise of Autobiographical Writing since 1750* (Leiden: Brill, 2006), 6.

Page 102 *who study the behavior of ants and bees.* Kenji Hakuta, "An Interview with Werner F. Leopold," *Bilingual Research Group Working Papers* (1989): 1–17.

Page 103 *noting Hildegard's preferences.* Werner Leopold, "The Study of Child Language and Infant Bilingualism, *Word* 4, no. 1 (1947): 1, https://doi.org/10.1080/00437956.1948.11659322.

Page 103 *a phonetic variant of "mama."* Leopold, "Study of Child Language," 1.

Page 104 *emerging over time, not discrete events.* The best demonstration of this is in linguist Deb Roy's research on the emergence of early words by his son. In a well-known TED talk, he describes wiring his entire house to capture the slow transformation of babblings into words. In his talk he plays an uncanny time-lapse recording in which the phonetic string "gaga" merges into a clearly articulated word, "water." He also shows remarkable transformations of acoustic and visual data in order to aid the search for spots for "the birth of a word." His talk is frequently mentioned by people I meet who hear that I'm writing about first words. Deb Roy, "The Birth of a Word," TED Talk, March 2011, https://www.ted.com/talks/deb_roy_the_birth_of_a_word?.

Page 104 *"the occurrence of the first word."* Alan Cruttenden, "A Phonetic Study of Babbling." *British Journal of Disorders of Communication* 5, no. 2 (1970): 114.

Page 104 *"the myths about language development."* Alan G. Kahmi, "Three Popular Myths About Language Development," *Child Language Teaching and Therapy* 4, no. 1 (1988): 2.

Page 104 *"are generally not accurate."* Kahmi, "Three Popular Myths," 3. Kamhi's surliness was principled—he pointed out that the costs of first-word myths are paid by language-disordered children, whose parents can't accurately tell what they said when or which baby utterances grow up into words.

Page 105 *"in what was overlooked as well."* Lois Bloom, "Language Development Review," in *Review of Child Development Research*, vol. 4, ed. F. Horowitz (Chicago: University of Chicago Press, 1975), 246.

Page 105 *enrolling thirty children at a time.* For a good overview of methodological developments, see David Ingram, *First Language Acquisition* (Cambridge: Cambridge University Press, 1989), particularly the chapter "The History of Child Language Studies." The most comprehensive account of the entire field of psycholinguistics, with numerous details from various traditions, is Pim Levelt, *A History of Psycholinguistics* (Oxford: Oxford University Press, 2013).

Page 105 *each one every month for a year.* Nelson, *Structure and Strategy.*

Page 106 *captured in recordings.* In one study, children were deliberately selected for clear articulation. Elizabeth Bates, Inge Bretherton, and Lynn Snyder, *From First Words to Grammar: Individual Differences and Dissociable Mechanisms* (Cambridge: Cambridge University Press, 1988), 53.

Page 106 *with only 1.5 percent of them.* Evan Kidd and Randi Garcia, "How Diverse Is Child Language Research?" *First Language* 42, no. 1 (2022): 1–38.

Page 106 *into charts and graphs.* Bruno Latour and Steven Woolgar, *Laboratory Life* (Beverly Hills, CA: Sage, 1979).

Page 106 *"But that's because mama was."* Katherine Nelson, "A Matter of Meaning: Reflections on Forty Years of JCL," *Journal of Child Language* 41 (2014): 100, https://doi.org/10.1017/S0305000913000496.

Page 107 *"decayed in some way?"* Elizabeth Bates and George Carnevale, "Julia Notes: Nine to Twenty-Four Months," entry for 3/3/84. These notes are posted on the website for the CHILDES database, https://childes.talkbank.org/diaries/Julia.txt.

Page 108 *to be born later.* Nelson, *Structure and Strategy*, 60.

Page 109 *"a casual albeit intimate observer."* Bates, Bretherton, and Snyder, *From First Words*, 69.

Page 110 *came out in 2021.* Michael C. Frank, Mika Braginsky, Daniel Yurovsky, and Virginia A. Marchman, *Variability and Consistency in Early Language Learning: The Wordbank Project* (Cambridge, MA: MIT Press, 2021).

Page 113 *with "extreme bias."* Meaning that they were more than 2.25 standard deviations from the mean difficulty on that dimension.

Page 114 *"question about child language development."* Frank et al., *Variability*, chapter 18.2.

Page 115 *how many words young children can produce.* Beate St. Pourcain et al., "Common Variation Near *ROBO2* Is Associated with Expressive Vocabulary in Infancy," *Nature Commununications.* 5, no. 4831 (2014), https://doi.org/10.1038/ncomms5831.

Chapter 6

Page 117 *a very old phenomenon: ritual.* Adam B. Seligman, Robert P. Weller, Michael J. Puett, and Bennett Simon, *Ritual and Its Consequences: An Essay on the Limits of Sincerity* (Oxford: Oxford University Press, 2008).

Page 117 *perform in a particular way.* Adapted from a definition of ritual from Roy Rappaport, who is quoted in Seligman et al., *Ritual*. For Rappaport, ritual is "the performance of more or less invariant sequences of formal acts and utterances not entirely encoded by the performers." *Ritual and Religion in the Making of Humanity* (Cambridge: Cambridge University Press, 1999), 24.

Page 118 *"as it really is."* Seligman et al., *Ritual*, 8.

Page 119 *"a record of his life from babyhood."* Kirkpatrick, "Records," 136.

Interlude

Page 121 *"syntactic ergativity."* Too complicated to get into here.

Page 127 *"which covered his legs."* Joseph Kaines, *Last Words of Eminent Persons* (London: George Routledge, 1866), 149–150.

Page 127 *about what, if anything, was he gesturing?* Eventually George Henry Lewes would shift his energies to scientific pursuits, away from literary ones. But he'd studied medicine—perhaps this is why he wrote about these gestures. Appropriately, Lewes has also been credited with writing one of the earliest explorations in English of infant development, in 1863.

Page 127 *"to be permitted to the dying man."* William Munk, *Euthanasia: Or, Medical Treatment in Aid of an Easy Death* (London: Longmans, Green, 1887), 47–48.

Page 128 *and a new set of terms.* Menzfeld's book is *The Anthropology of Dying: A Participant Observation with Dying Persons in Germany* (Springer: Wiesbaden, 2017). Her work introduced me to the useful term "exitus," or "the irreversible loss of a body's physical capacities of respiration and blood circulation" (27), which makes it possible to point out that the Western conception of dying begins before and ends with exitus. However, the anthropological breadth acknowledges that some cultures place death pre-exitally and others post-exitally. Exitus contrasts with "dying," which refers to the disconnection of a person with *"Leib,"* a term that "describes the spatial extension of an animated sensual body (26).

Page 128 *analyzing them with a linguist's eye.* Lisa Smartt's book is *Words at the Threshold: What We Say as We're Nearing Death* (Novato, CA: Near World Library, 2017).

Page 129 *being present in the final moments.* For example, see Otani Hiroyuki et al. "Meaningful Communication Before Death, But Not Present at the Time of Death Itself, Is Associated with Better Outcomes on Measures of Depression and Complicated Grief Among Bereaved Family Members of Cancer Patients," *Journal of Pain and Symptom Management* 54, no. 3 (2017): 273–279.

Chapter 7

Page 132 *mentioned a name.* Joseph W. Lewis, *Last and Near-Last Words of the Famous, Infamous, and Those In-Between* (Bloomington, IN: AuthorHouse, 2016).

Page 132 *"a systematic and scientific study of the dying hour."* Arthur MacDonald. "The Study of Death in Man," *The Lancet* (Sept. 18, 1926): 24.

Page 132 *artists and scientists used the fewest.* Arthur MacDonald, "Death-Psychology of Historical Personages," *American Journal of Psychology* 32, no. 4 (1921): 552–556.

Page 132 *asked John Abernathy [1764–1831]).* Lewis, *Last and Near-Last Words.*

Page 133 *"the specific words they spoke."* Paul Christiansen, "The Meaning of Speech Melody for Leoš Janáček," *Journal of Musicological Research* 23, no. 3–4 (2004): 242, https://doi.org/10.1080/01411890490884454.

Page 133 *as she lay dying in 1903.* I'm indebted to linguist Marten van der Meulen for alerting me to these records.

Page 134 *"But he couldn't do otherwise."* Christiansen, "The Meaning of Speech Melody," 255.

Page 135 *"God be with you, my darling."* These translations are from Christiansen's article.

Page 135 *notes for her reminiscence.* Zdenka Janáčková, *My Life with Janáček: The Memoirs of Zdenka Janáčková,* trans. John Tyrrell (Boston: Faber and Faber, 1998).

Page 135 *obsession with a cuckoo clock.* Janáčková, *My Life,* 89.

Page 135 *any public piece of music.* Christiansen, "The Meaning of Speech Melody," 260.

Page 136 *"they should be expressed" as talk.* Lyn Lofland, *The Craft of Dying* (Cambridge, MA: MIT Press), 99.

Page 137 *"expresses those states."* Lofland, *Craft of Dying,* 100. Emphasis in the original.

Page 137 *a nursing journal in 1986.* Maggie Pflaum and Patricia Kelley, "Understanding the Final Messages of the Dying," *Nursing* 16, no. 6 (1986): 26–29.

Page 137 *"patterns of speech or gesture."* Maggie Callanan and Patricia Kelley, *Final Gifts: Understanding the Special Awareness, Needs, and Communications of the Dying* (New York: Simon & Schuster), 1992), 35.

Page 138 *"seem to make no sense."* Callanan and Kelley, *Final Gifts,* 21.

Page 138 *"however vague or garbled."* Callanan and Kelley, *Final Gifts,* 213.

Page 138 *"said by the dying person."* Callanan and Kelley, *Final Gifts,* 213.

Page 138 *"resentful and angry."* Callanan and Kelley, *Final Gifts,* 60.

Page 139 *"expressive death talking."* John Troyer, "Introduction," to Lyn Lofland, *Craft of Dying,* xvii.

Page 141 *for* The Atlantic. This portrait of Smartt as well as other details, such as Arthur MacDonald's study, are drawn from a piece I wrote: "What People Actually Say Before They Die," *Atlantic,* January 16, 2019, https://www.theatlantic.com/family/archive/2019/01/how-do-people-communicate-before-death/580303/.

Page 142 *"neurochemical commotion."* Lichter and Hunt, "The Last 48 Hours," 14.

Page 143 *a quarter of hospice patients.* P. Jackson et al., "Communication Impediments in a Group of Hospice Patients," *Palliative Medicine* 10 (1996): 79–80.

Page 144 *in the evolution of speech.* A helpful deep dive on this neurobiology is Andreas Nieder and Richard Mooney, "The Neurobiology of Innate, Volitional and Learned Vocalizations in Mammals and Birds," *Philosophical Transactions Royal Society B* (2009), http://dx.doi.org/10.1098/rstb.2019.0054.

Page 145 *"the digital tape recorder . . ."* Philip Lieberman, *Eve Spoke: Human Language and Human Evolution* (Cambridge: W. W. Norton & Company, 1998), excerpted in the *New York Times*, accessed May 20, 2022, https://archive.nytimes.com/www .nytimes.com/books/first/l/lieberman-eve.html.

Page 145 *their language abilities.* Philip Lieberman, Athanassios Propapas, and B. G. Kani, "Speech Production and Cognitive Deficits on Mt. Everest," *Aviation Space and Environmental Medicine* 66, no. 9 (1995): 857–864.

Page 146 *unpredictably hyperassociative.* Camila Sanz et al., "The Entropic Tongue: Disorganization of Natural Language under LSD," *Consciousness and Cognition* 87 (2021): 103070, https://doi.org/10.1016/j.concog.2020.103070.

Page 146 *"radical abundance."* See, for instance, this X (formerly Twitter) thread: Aella (@Aella_Girl), "Comment below, IN ALL CAPS, a 'psychedelic mantra' - a word or phrase that came up repeatedly during a psychedelic experience - that you've had before. One mantra at a time, ALL CAPS, no explanation," March 2, 2023, 4:16 p.m., https://twitter.com/Aella_Girl/status/1631448540991066112.

Page 147 *diagnosed with dementia or have a stroke.* Susan Kemper and Cheryl Anagnopoulos, "Language and Aging," *Annual Review of Applied Linguistics* 10 (1989): 37–50.

Page 147 *an unripe child."* Susan R. Hemer, "Preparing for Death: Care, Anticipatory Grief and Social Death in Lihir, Papua New Guinea," *Mortality* 23, no. 2 (2018): 126, https://doi.org/10.1080/13576275.2017.1346596.

Page 147 *"quotations and proverbs."* Maurice Bloch, "The Uses of Schooling and Literacy in a Zafimaniry Village," in *How We Think They Think* (New York: Routledge, 1998), 183.

Page 149 *last three days of life.* Kristin Turner et al., "Dignity in Dying, a Preliminary Study of Patients in the Last Three Days of Life," *Journal of Palliative Care* 12, no. 2 (1996): 10.

Page 149 *terminal agitation, and others.* Turner et al., "Dignity in Dying," 9.

Page 150 *"even when the theme is complex."* Tatsuya Morita et al., "Impaired Communication Capacity and Agitated Delirium in the Final Week of Terminally Ill Cancer Patients: Prevalence and Identification of Research Focus," *Journal of Pain and Symptom Management* 26, no. 3 (2003): 827–834, https://doi.org/10.1016/S0885 -3924(03)00287-2.

Chapter 8

Page 153 *the last thing he said.* This is a reconstruction.

Page 153 *the devil?* "He" might be Satan, as 2 Corinthians 2:11 of the King James Bible warns, "Lest Satan should get an advantage of us."

Page 154 *"to the wards."* Harvey Cushing, *The Life of Sir William Osler* (London: Oxford University Press, 1940), vol. 1, 596.

Page 154 *"literally worshiped him."* Michael Bliss, *William Osler: A Life in Medicine* (Oxford: Oxford University Press, 1999), x.

Page 156 *gaunt male patient.* Pictured above. https://collections.nlm.nih.gov/catalog /nlm:nlmuid-101448227-img.

Page 156 *his medical knowledge.* He still attended dissections, however, and perhaps even assisted. B. P. Lucey and G. M. Hutchins, "Did Sir William Osler Perform an Autopsy at the Johns Hopkins Hospital?" *Archives of Pathology and Laboratory Medicine* 132, no. 2 (2008): 261–264.

Page 156 *the human experience of dying.* This is Michael Bliss's interpretation. Another speculation is that the autopsy room at Johns Hopkins was run by William Welch, who made it clear that Osler was welcome to attend but not do autopsies on his own. James Wright, "Why Did Osler Not Perform Autopsies at Johns Hopkins?" Letters to the Editor, *Archives of Pathology and Laboratory Medicine* 132, no. 11 (2008): 1710.

Page 156 *and similar subjects.* Cushing, *Life of Sir William Osler*, vol. 2, 298.

Page 156 *a thing it is to die.* Munk, *Euthanasia*, 10.

Page 157 *the next thirty years.* Pat Jalland, *Death in the Victorian Family* (Oxford: Oxford University Press, 1996), 85.

Page 157 *a calm and easy death.* Munk, *Euthanasia*, 5.

Page 157 *inseparable from it.* Munk, *Euthanasia*, 7–8.

Page 157 *last twenty-four hours.* Ivan Lichter and Esther Hunt, "The Last 48 Hours of Life," *Journal of Palliative Care* 6, no. 4 (1990): 7–15.

Page 157 *"to be painful."* William Osler, "Review of Munk's Euthanasia," *Canada Medical and Surgical Journal* (March 1888), 511.

Page 157 *stronger evidence for the assertion.* Bliss, "William Osler," 290. Also, Paul Mueller wrote that "Osler's interest in death and dying, coupled with the popular opinion that the dying process is uncomfortable, an opinion he did not hold, and the lack of systematic empirical observations on the dying process, likely accounted for his desire to conduct his 'Study of the Act of Dying.'" Paul Mueller, "William Osler's Study of the Act of Dying: An Analysis of the Original Data," *Journal of Medical Biography* 15, Suppl. 1 (2007): 60.

Page 158 *ensure healthy families.* Collective investigation was uncomfortably close to the eugenics movement—its founder Frederick Akbar Mahomed collaborated with Francis Galton on creating *The Life History Album*, the eugenicist tool promulgated in the parenting periodical *Babyhood*. However, there's no evidence that Osler knew collective investigation or Mahomed. Like most prominent intellectuals of his era, Osler believed in eugenicist ideas. See Nav Persaud, Heather Butts, and Philip Berger, "William Osler: Saint in a 'White Man's Dominion,'" *Canadian Medical Association Journal*, 192, no. 45 (2020): E1414–E1416, https://doi.org/10.1503/cmaj.201567, and Charles S. Bryan, "Sir William Osler, Eugenics, Racism, and the *Komagata Maru* Incident," *Baylor University Medical Center Proceedings* 34, no. 1 (2021): 194–198, https://doi.org/10.1080/08998280.2020.1843380.

Page 158 *as Milton terms it.* Cushing, *Life of William Osler*, vol. 1, 598.

Page 158 *as a pioneering move.* See Emily Abel, *The Inevitable Hour: A History of Caring for Dying Patients in America* (Baltimore: Johns Hopkins University Press, 2013). Sharon R. Kaufman, in *And a Time to Die . . . How American Hospitals Shape the End of Life* (Chicago: Chicago University Press, 2004), writes on page 64, "His project was a pathbreaking attempt to understand the physiology of the dying transition and its expression in individual difference."

Page 158 *about the study either.* Osler's first major biographer, his Oxford colleague Harvey Cushing, describes the study as focused on "the last sensations of the dying." "For the head nurses in the wards had taken down at his request, for some time, the exact words of dying patients." Cushing, *Life of William Osler*, vol. 1, 639. Michael Bliss, writing in the early twenty-first century, described the study only in passing.

Page 158 *"premonitions and fears."* Dorothy Reed Mendenhall, "Autobiography," 17, Box 1, Folder 11-12. Dorothy Reed Mendenhall Papers, Sophia Smith Collection, SSC-MS-00101, Smith College Special Collections, Northampton, Massachusetts. I note with interest her recollection about the study's interest in "last remarks."

Page 158 *set him apart.* Abel, *Inevitable Hour*, 4.

Page 161 *"did not speak English."* Baltimore, like many large Atlantic Coast cities, was a major stop for the North German Lloyd line of steamships bringing immigrants from Germany and Eastern Europe. The city boasted a half-dozen German language newspapers in the 1890s. See, for example, Ron Cassie, "City of Immigrants," *Baltimore,* accessed January 20, 2023, https://www.baltimoremagazine.com/section/historypolitics/city-of-immigrants-the-people-who-built-baltimore/.

Page 162 *50.7 for women.* M. Heron, "Deaths: Leading Causes for 2016," *National Vital Statistics Reports* (Hyattsville, MD: National Center for Health Statistics, 2018).

Page 162 *deaths of women.* Mueller, "William Osler's Study," 59.

Page 162 *articulations of consciousness.* My analysis of all the data cards appeared in a peer-reviewed article. Michael Erard, "Beyond Last Words: Patterns of Linguistic and Interactional Behavior in a Historical Sample of Dying Hospital Patients," *Omega* 86, no. 3 (2023): 1089–1107, https://doi.org/10.1177/00302228211000938.

Page 163 *hold his hand.* This was detailed at length in an unpublished manuscript by Dorothy Reed Mendenhall, one of two women doctors on staff at the time. Her account is the only independent discussion of the study and how it was conducted that I could find. "In only one case do I remember fear or apprehension before the end. One of our heart cases was evidently dying and I had him put in a private room for the sake of the ward. To my astonishment when I went to see him some hours before the end, he was shaking with fear though perfectly lucid. He cried out in agony over his sins and his apprehension of hell, begging me to do something to keep him alive. I stayed with him most of the time, many hours, only leaving him for some necessary ward duty. During the last half hour of his life, he held both my hands and nearly wrung them to pieces. When he finally breathed his last, helped by the hypo I had ordered, my hands were numb and my spirit shaken. My report to Dr. Osler was full and complete, and he showed much interest in it and the old man's ravings. For my part, I was glad it was the only such case I was compelled to witness." Dorothy Reed Mendenhall, Autobiography, 18.

Page 165 *after the words.* Mel McEvoy, "The Lightness of Self," *Emptied Space* (Middlesbrough, UK: Mudfog Press, 2012).

Page 166 *late stages of the illness.* Nages Nagaratnam et al., "Screaming, Shrieking and Muttering: The Noise-Makers Amongst Dementia Patients," *Archives of Gerontology and Geriatrics* 36, no. 3 (2003): 247–258, https://doi.org/10.1016/s0167-4943(02)00 169-3. You can expect to find little of this at the end of life—in one study, only 4 percent of palliative care patients were diagnosed with advanced dementia. See A. T. Lo, J. Karuza, A. Berall, and G.-A. Perri, "Prevalence of Dementia in a Geriatric Palliative Care Unit," *American Journal of Hospice and Palliative Medicine* 35, no. 5 (2018): 799–803, https://doi.org/10.1177/1049909117737300.

Page 166 *laughter-like vocalizations.* Nieder and Mooney, "Neurobiology," 3; also J. D. Rohrer et al., "Abnormal Laughter-Like Vocalisations Replacing Speech in Primary Progressive Aphasia," *Journal of the Neurological Sciences* 284, no. 1–2 (2009): 120–123, https://doi.org/10.1016/j.jns.2009.04.021.

Page 166 *Sharon Kaufman.* Kaufman, *And a Time to Die*, 107.

Page 167 *"a low muttering."* Munk, *Euthanasia*, 32.

Page 167 *afraid, panicked, and insecure.* Gill Sörensen Duppils and Karin Wikblad, "Patients' Experiences of Being Delirious," *Journal of Clinical Nursing* 16 (2007): 810–818.

Page 167 *"Osler has come."* Letter, E. M. Brockbank to William Osler [date?], pasted into John Ferriar, *Illustrations of Sterne: With Other Essays and Verses*, 2nd ed. (London: Printed for Cadell and Davies, By J. and J. Haddock, Warrington, 1812), Bibliotheca Osleriana 4806.

Page 167 *"comfort it has been!"* Cushing, *Life of Sir William Osler*, vol. 2, 671.

Page 168 *"sensations of dying."* William Osler, *Science and Immortality* (Boston: Houghton Mifflin, 1904), 37.

Page 168 *Osler famously wrote.* Osler, *Science and Immortality*, 37.

Page 168 *"careful records."* Cushing, *Life of Sir William Osler*, vol. 2, 639.

Page 169 *for the study.* Bliss, *William Osler*, 291.

Page 169 *"in the mind."* William Osler, "Maeterlinck on Death," *The Spectator*, November 4, 1911, 740.

Page 169 *"experienced discomforts."* Mueller, "William Osler's Study," 60.

Page 169 *and restlessness.* Lichter and Hunt, "Last 48 Hours," 8.

Chapter 9

Page 171 *as the model for everyone else's.* Alison Berlinger traces this model in "The Death of Christ as a Focus of the Fifteenth-Century Artes Moriendi," *Journal of English and Germanic Philology* 113, no. 4 (2014): 497–412.

Page 171 *all over Europe.* My account of the history draws from the analysis by Sister Mary Catharine O'Connor in *The Art of Dying Well: The Development of the Ars Moriendi* (New York: AMS Press, 1966). O'Connor traces possible source texts for the manuscript that emerged from the Council of Constance and evaluates potential authors. Her claim that the *Tractatus* was composed at Constance appears on page 54.

Page 172 *including English.* O'Connor, *Art of Dying Well*, 1.

Page 172 *a year earlier.* O'Connor, *Art of Dying Well*, 1n2.

Page 172 *thanks to missionaries.* See Erik R. Seeman, "Reading Indians' Deathbed Scenes: Ethnohistorical and Representational Approaches," *Journal of American History* 88, no. 1 (June 2001): 17–47.

Page 172 *the next 250 years.* The suggestion of its diffusion is from O'Connor, *Art of Dying Well*, 58. The suggestion that the *Tractatus* is the original text is also O'Connor's; see *Art of Dying Well*, 7.

Page 172 *"inescapable hour."* O'Connor, *Art of Dying Well*, 5.

Page 172 *in his library.* One was an 1881 reproduction of the British Museum's copy of the earliest existing edition of the *Ars Moriendi*, which dates to 1465. The other was a 1917 collection, *The Book of the Craft of Dying and other early English tracts concerning Death*. This info is from William Osler, *Bibliotheca Osleriana: A Catalogue of Books Illustrating the History of Medicine and Science* (Kingston: McGill-Queen's University Press, 1969), 177.

Page 172 *and the fourth.* As for the other parts, the first part of the *Tractatus* coaches people how to give up their soul; the second lays out the five temptations they'll face; the fifth tells friends what to do; and the sixth lists prayers for bystanders. All of the devotional Christian literature about dying keeps this general shape well into the nineteenth century.

Page 172 *saying certain prayers.* Caxton's *The Arte and Crafte to Know well to Dye* lays this out: "Now it is soo that our Lord dyd fyue thynges pryncipally hangyng on the crosse: he adoured & prayd, he wepte, he cryed, he commaunded his soule to God, and he yelded to hym his sperite. Thus semblably euery seke man constytuted in thartycle of deth oughte to [do]." In David William Atkinson, *The English Ars Moriendi* (New York: Peter Lang, 1992), 27.

Page 172 *in the name of Christ.* Laqueur, *Work of the Dead*, 187. Before saying *ja*, Luther had repeated three times *"Her, in deien Hände befehle ich meinen Geist,"* or "into thine hands I commend my spirit." He said *ja* in response to the question, "Reverend father, do you die in constant reliance on the faith you have taught?"

Page 174 *"he may not with his mouth."* Translator unknown. "The Book of the Craft of Dying," in *The Book of the Craft of Dying and Other Early English Tracts Concerning Death,* ed. Francis M. M. Comper (New York: Longmans, Green, and Co., 1917), 27.

Page 174 *"by some outward sign."* Caxton, in Atkinson, *English Ars Moriendi,* 30.

Page 174 *Gian Lorenzo Bernini (1598–1680).* More about Marchese can be found here. https://www.treccani.it/enciclopedia/francesco-marchese_(Dizionario-Biografico)/. Accessed 4 April, 2024.

Page 174 *feared being incommunicado.* It's possible that Marchese picked this up from, or was inspired by, monastic communities in Europe that developed sign systems for communicating because they had taken vows of silence. But given that these are described first in 909 CE, I would have expected a greater influence on deathbed behavior. See Robert Barakat, "On Ambiguity in the Cistercian Sign Language," *Sign Language Studies* 8 (1975): 275–289. None of the multiple chapters in Thomas Sebeok and Jean Umiker-Sebeok, *Monastic Sign Languages* (Berlin: De Gruyter Mouton, 1987) describe signing at the deathbed.

Page 175 *"without speaking."* I was first alerted to this story by Robert Westin's "Ars Moriendi Tradition and Visualization of Death in Roman Baroque Sculpture: Death Education in the Seventeenth Century," *Death Education* 4, no. 2 (1980): 111–123. The quotes come from Irving Lavin, *The Art of Gianlorenzo Bernini, Vol. 1* (London: Pindar Press, 2007), 297. Lavin provides full descriptions from the biographies by Filippo Baldinucci and Bernini's son, Domenico.

Page 175 *the ability entirely.* Lavin, *Art of Gianlorenzo Bernini,* 293.

Page 175 *clear his throat.* Lavin, *Art of Gianlorenzo Bernini*, 293 and 298. The two accounts differ. In one, Bernini is pointing to the equipment; in the other, he is mimicking the shape or movement of the equipment.

Page 175 *"to his end."* Lavin, *Art of Gianlorenzo Bernini*, 293.

Page 175 *in the face of medical challenges.* I'm grateful for the insight about implications of late signing from Monica Elaine Campbell, the former director of the Ottawa Deaf Health Care Team, which ensures language access for deaf people in palliative and hospice care.

Page 175 *again with corpses.* James Harrod, "The Case for Chimpanzee Religion," *Journal for the Study of Religion, Nature and Culture* 8, no. 1 (2014): 21, https://doi-org.mu .idm.oclc.org/10.1558/jsrnc.v8i1.8.

Page 175 *with the living.* Lucy Baehren, "Saying 'Goodbye' to the Conundrum of Leave-Taking: A Cross-Disciplinary Review," *Humanities and Social Sciences Communications* 9, no. 46 (2022), https://doi-org.mu.idm.oclc.org/10.1057/s41599-022 -01061-3.

Page 176 *"for the priest."* Edward Muir, *Ritual in Early Modern Europe* (Cambridge: Cambridge University Press, 2005), 54.

Page 176 *proof that one already enjoyed God's favor.* David W. Atkinson, "The English Ars Morendi: Its Protestant Transformation," *Renaissance and Reformation / Renaissance et Réforme* n.s. 6, no. 1 (February 1982): 2.

Page 176 *"various deaths of men."* Michel de Montaigne, *Essays*, trans. Charles Cotton, ed. William Carew Hazlitt (1877), accessed January 23, 2023, https://www .gutenberg.org/files/3600/3600-h/3600-h.htm#link2HCH0001. The quote appears in Chapter XIX, "That to study philosophy is to learn to die."

Page 176 *what he wanted.* Montaigne, *Essays,* accessed January 23, 2023, https:// www.gutenberg.org/files/3600/3600-h/3600-h.htm#link2HCH0001.

Page 176 *or infidels.* Karl Guthke, "Anthologies of Last Words: A Tour d'Horizon of a Literary Cyrpto-Genre," *Harvard Library Bulletin* 35, no. 3 (Summer 1987): 312.

Page 176 *moment of character development.* Mary Ann Lund, "Being Dead in Shakespearen Tragedy," in *Interdisciplinary Perspectives on Mortality and Its Timings*, ed. Shane McCorristine (London: Palgrave MacMillan, 2017), 17–31. Also Michael Cameron Andrews, *This Action of Our Death: The Performance of Death in English Renaissance Drama* (Newark: University of Delaware Press, 1989).

Page 177 *anti-vaccine status.* For an example, see Sharon Pruitt-Young, "Before Dying, An Unvaccinated TikTok User Begged Others Not to Repeat Her Mistake," NPR, September 9, 2021, https://www.npr.org/sections/coronavirus-live-updates/2021/09/09 /1035489298/tiktok-covid-vaccination-megan-blankenbiller-hospital.

Page 177 *twenty-first century.* The opposite reaction, in which patients dying from COVID apparently doubled down on denialism, were apparently overstated, if not fabricated outright. David Zweig, "Are Covid Patients Gasping 'It Isn't Real' As They Die?," *Wired*, November 19, 2020, https://www.wired.com/story/are-covid-patients-gasping-it-isnt-real-as-they-die/.

Page 177 *"is obscene."* "Dying COVID Patients Begging Southwest Virginia Doctors for the Vaccine with Their 'Final Breaths,'" WFXR, August 4, 2021, https://www.wfxrtv.com/news/health/coronavirus/dying-covid-patients-begging-area-doctors-for-the-vaccine-with-their-final-breaths/.

Page 177 *"it's too late."* Antonio Planas, "'It's Too Late': Alabama Doctor Shares Final Moments 'of Covid Patients, Urges Vaccination," NBCNews, July 21, 2021, https://www.nbcnews.com/news/us-news/it-s-too-late-alabama-doctor-shares-final-moments-covid-n1274659.

Page 177 *"alphabetical eminences."* Author unknown, "Last Words of Eminent Persons," *Littell's Living Age* (March 30, 1867): 820–822.

Page 178 *Denis Diderot (1713–1784).* The translation is Kaines's; a better one might be "But what devil harm do you expect that could do to me?" His wife had just warned him against eating an apricot, which he did anyway. She was right; he died immediately after. Guthke's *Last Words* mentions another last word attributed to Diderot: "The first step toward philosophy is incredulity."

Page 178 *"well informed Swedish sources."* Guthke, *Last Words*, 5.

Page 179 *bicentenary of his death.* Guthke, *Last Words*, vii.

Page 180 *"humanistic tradition," he wrote.* Guthke, *Last Words*, 152.

Page 180 *has always been, ruin-minded.* Rose Macaulay, *Pleasure of Ruins* (London: Walker and Co., 1953), 20.

Page 180 *cannot be taken back.* Guthke, *Last Words*, 11.

Page 181 *"personal preference."* Anantanand Rambachan, "Like a Ripe Fruit Separating Effortlessly from Its Vine: Religious Understandings of a Good Death: Hinduism," in *Religious Understandings of a Good Death in Hospice Palliative Care*, ed. Harold Coward and Kelli I. Stajduhar (Albany: SUNY Press, 2012), 29–50.

Page 182 *Vishnu's realm.* Rambachan, "Like a Ripe Fruit," 37–38.

Page 182 *"the name of God."* Rambachan, "Like a Ripe Fruit," 38.

Page 182 *"released from mortality."* In a lovely way this resonates with Helen Nearing's account of her husband Scott's death, when "he was gone out of his body as easily as a leaf drops from the tree in autumn, slowly twisting and falling to the ground." Nearing is quoted in Sallie Tisdale, *Advice for Future Corpses* (New York: Simon & Schuster, 2018), 118.

Page 183 *Islamic chaplains in hospitals.* Pieter Coppens, "Islamic Ars Moriendi and Ambiguous Deathbed Emotions: Narratives of Islamic Saints and Scholars on the End-of-Life," in *End-of-Life Care, Dying and Death in the Islamic Moral Tradition*, ed. Mohammed Ghaly (Leiden: Brill, 2023), 152–172.

Page 184 *to say the Shahadah.* The Islamic Bulletin, *What to Do When a Muslim Dies*, accessed September 30, 2022, https://islamicbulletin.org/en/ebooks/Muslim _Funeral_Guide/index.html; see also Anonymous poster, "Ordering dying person to say Shahaadah," Islam Web, February 14, 2017, https://www.islamweb.net/en /fatwa/339616/ordering-dying-person-to-say-shahaadah.

Page 184 *"the Highest Companion."* Coppens, "Islamic Ars Moriendi," 164. This essay and the volume it is from contains a rich, informed source on death, end of life, and grieving in Islamic traditions. Also, Salih Al-Humsi, who died in 1943, repeated the Koranic verse, "Peace be upon you for the patience that you have shown; How excellent is the final abode!" until some minutes before he expired. Then he began saying "Allah, Allah," over and over, until he died.

Page 185 *("nama Amida Butsu").* Jacqueline I. Stone, "Just Open Your Mouth and Say 'A': A-Syllable Practice for the Time of Death in Early Medieval Japan," *Pacific World Journal* 3rd series, no. 8 (2006): 167–189. Stone has written numerous fascinating articles on esoteric Buddhist death practices, such as "The Secret Art of Dying: Esoteric Deathbed Practices in Heian Japan," in *The Buddhist Dead*, ed. Bryan J. Cuevas and Jacqueline I. Stone (Honolulu: University of Hawai'i Press, 2011).

Page 185 *"all-pervasive."* Stone, "Just Open Your Mouth," 168.

Page 185 *do not say 'A'!").* Ajikan gi 阿字觀儀, in *Kōgyō Daishi zenshū*, 2 vols., ed. Tomita Kōjun (1935; repr., Tokyo: Hōsenji, 1977), 2:999–1001; quoted in Stone, "Just Open Your Mouth," 170.

Page 185 *"that he did."* "My Grandfather's Deathbed Experience," *Purelanders*, December 15, 2011, https://purelanders.com/2011/12/15/my-grandfathers-deathbed -experience/.

Page 187 *indignant to the racist.* I owe this idea to Susan Barnett.

Page 187 *named Darnella Frazier.* Associated Press, "Darnella Frazier, Who Recorded George Floyd's Death, Loses Uncle in Police Crash," *PBS News Hour*, July 7, 2021, https://www.pbs.org/newshour/nation/darnella-frazier-who-recorded-george-floyds -death-loses-uncle-in-police-crash.

Page 187 *from PEN America.* Rachel Treisman, "Darnella Frazier, Teen Who Filmed Floyd's Murder, Praised for Making Verdict Possible," NPR, April 21, 2021, https://

www.npr.org/sections/trial-over-killing-of-george-floyd/2021/04/21/989480867
/darnella-frazier-teen-who-filmed-floyds-murder-praised-for-making-verdict-possib.

Page 187 *Black form of witnessing.* Alicia Richardson, *Bearing Witness While Black: African Americans, Smartphones, and the New Protest #Journalism* (Oxford: Oxford University Press, 2020). Also Zoe Corbyn, "Allissa Richardson: 'It's Telling That We're OK with Showing Black People Dying,'" *Guardian*, August 16, 2020, https://www
.theguardian.com/world/2020/aug/16/allissa-richardson-its-telling-that-were-ok
-with-showing-black-people-dying.

Page 188 *"her last wish."* Wasia Hamid and Mohmad Saleem Jahangir, "Dying, Death and Mourning amid COVID-19 Pandemic in Kashmir: A Qualitative Study," *Omega* 85, no. 3 (2022): 700, https://doi.org/10.1177/0030222820953708.

Page 188 *wrote two Spanish scholars.* Oscar Fernandez and Miguel González-González, "The Dead with No Wake, Grieving with No Closure: Illness and Death in the Days of Coronavirus in Spain," *Journal of Religion and Health* (2020): 703–721.

Page 189 *not just the hours before death.* Karlotta Schloesser, Steffen T. Simon, Berenike Pauli, Raymond Voltz, Norma Jung, Charlotte Leisse, et al., "'Saying Goodbye All Alone with No Close Support Was Difficult'—Dying During the COVID-19 Pandemic: An Online Survey Among Bereaved Relatives About End-of-Life Care for Patients with or without SARS-CoV2 Infection," *BMC Health Services Research* 21, no. 1 (September 22, 2021): 998, https://doi.org/10.1186/s12913-021-06987-z, 6.

Chapter 10

Page 192 *"fitness for salvation."* Pat Jalland, *Death in the Victorian Family* (Oxford: Oxford University Press, 1996), 33.

Page 192 *"the sublime to the mundane."* Jalland, *Death in the Victorian Family*, 33.

Page 193 *"readiness for heaven."* Jalland, *Death in the Victorian Family*, 34.

Page 193 *"none at all."* Jalland, *Death in the Victorian Family*, 35.

Page 193 *"Get me some porridge."* Quoted in Jalland, *Death in the Victorian Family*, 172.

Page 193 *"pointing up to heaven."* Quoted in Jalland, *Death in the Victorian Family*, 172. Jalland adds: "William seemed to be clutching at a straw in his search for a sign of salvation in the absence of Holy Communion or edifying last words."

Page 193 *"Hold up my head."* Bliss, *William Osler*, 476. However, Harvey Cushing places his death in his sleep; the last words he spoke were to wish his nephew, W. W. Francis, goodnight: "Nighty-night, a-darling." Cushing, *The Life of Sir William Osler*, vol. 2, 685.

Page 193 *"natural expression of a patient."* *Littell's Living Age*, 822.

Page 193 *power of speech was gone.* The diary of Susanna Vickers is quoted in Françoise Noël, *Family Life and Sociability in Upper and Lower Canada, 1780–1870: A View from Diaries and Family Correspondence.* (Montreal: McGill-Queen's Press, 2003), 251–252.

Page 194 *"tet d'armée."* Halford, quoted in Kaines, *Last Words of Pre-Eminent Persons*, x.

Page 194 *"dying there."* Kaines, *Last Words of Pre-Eminent Persons*, x.

Page 194 *lecture about death.* Jalland, *Death in the Victorian Family*, 36.

Page 195 *Beckett wrote.* Jalland, *Death in the Victorian Family*, 36.

Page 195 *meaningful last word.* To resurrect Goffman's framework: Even if the dying person remained an animator and were able to author their utterances, they weren't credible any longer as the principal, the social actor who would be be recognized through their utterance. Doctors like Savory and Beckett, and others like Kaine, were saying that dying people couldn't play that role.

But the author role was also unstable. Guthke noted how pastors, usually Protestants, offered theological adjustments—or "theological contortions" and "benevolent interpretations," as he put it—meant to mitigate the effects of an inability to perform. He found in printed German funeral sermons "some very curious examples of the preachers' recklessly well meant efforts to interpret a last word, dutifully represented even in cases of sudden death, as a valid equivalent of 'I commend my spirit into your hands'" (*Last Words*, 175). Here is an example of pragmatic generosity in service to theological necessity.

Page 195 *from a dying person.* A very good, accessible discussion is by Brendan Koerner. "Last Words: Why Are We So Sure That Death and Honesty Go Together?" *Legal Affairs*, November–December 2002, https://www.legalaffairs.org/issues/November -December-2002/review_koerner_novdec2002.msp.

Page 195 *"breathe their words in pain."* Shakespeare, *King Richard II*, act 2, scene 1. Harriet Frazier also wrote about dying declarations in Shakespeare's plays. "'Like a Liar Gone to Burning Hell': Shakespeare and Dying Declarations," *Comparative Drama* 19, no. 2 (Summer 1985): 166–180.

Page 196 *legal historians have traced.* See, for instance, Michael J. Polelle, "Death of Dying Declarations in a Post-Crawford World," *Missouri Law Review* 71, no. 2 (2006); Tim Donaldson and J. Preston Frederickson, "Dying to Testify? Confrontation vs. Declarations in Extremis," *Regent University Law Review* (2009): 35–79; "The Admissibility of Dying Declaration," *Fordham Law Review* 38, no. 509 (1970), http://ir.lawnet.fordham.edu/flr/vol38/iss3/5.

Page 196 *bleeding in the back yard.* For an account of the resulting legal fracas, see Roderick Munday, "The Judge Who Answered His Critics," *Cambridge Law Journal* 46, no. 2 (July 1987): 303–314.

Alexander Cockburn also played an important role in legal precedents about whether a dying person can change their will on the deathbed. For a long time, the law said that someone who was mentally ill, dying or not, lacked "capacity." All that changed in 1870, when the English high court, headed by Cockburn, ruled that John Banks, a wealthy British man who suffered delusions and spent time in an asylum, indeed possessed capacity when he willed his estate to his niece. Banks only needed to understand what making a will meant, Cockburn ruled. Banks also had to grasp the extent of his estate, to appreciate what his beneficiaries would get and that conflicts might exist, to communicate why he made certain decisions, and not to have any "insane delusion" that influenced those decisions. Even though Banks said that demons and evil spirits visited him, Cockburn couldn't see how this influenced Banks's decisions. Since then, courts have repeatedly held that this test, called the "Banks versus Goodfellow test," is valid. This is quoted in Megan Brenkel et al., "A Case for the Standardized Assessment of Testamentary Capacity," *Canadian Geriatrics Journal* 21, no. 2 (2018): 26–31. See also Chris Rattigan-Smith, "Case Review: Banks v Goodfellow," Willpack, October 16, 2020, https://www.willpack .co.uk/case-review-banks-v-goodfellow/.

Of course, one's last words might also be to change a will. But more likely, their language ability will be used by medical professionals as evidence of their capacity (or its absence) if a court asks for an opinion. Which is exactly what happens when a will is contested in court: one side or both will bring in doctors, nurses, psychiatrists, or other experts to testify about a person's capacity. Not surprisingly, deciding whether or not someone has "testamentary capacity" is a hot area of cooperation between lawyers and doctors, especially now. As Brenkel and coauthors pointed out in 2018, families have become more diverse and nontraditional at the same time that a huge amount of wealth—US$6 trillion in the United States, US$830 billion in the United Kingdom—is being transferred from dying baby boomers to their heirs (Brenkel et al., "A Case for the Standardized Assessment," 26). That means more people to argue they have a claim in an estate—and a bigger financial reward if they win. In such an environment, observations of a person's language are critical, especially because there's no standardized clinical tool for assessing capacity (though some have tried).

Page 196 *to the moment of death.* Interestingly, there is less of a requirement that dying declarations be spoken words—courts have admitted written words and non-verbals like head nods as valid utterances.

Page 197 *people live in anymore.* See anonymous, "Religious Belief as Affecting the Credibility of Dying Declarations," *Harvard Law Review* 24, no. 6 (April 1911): 484–486; also Bryan A. Liang, "Shortcuts to Truth: The Legal Mythology of Dying Declarations," *American Criminal Law Review* 35, no. 2 (Winter 1998): 229–278.

Page 197 *wryly observed.* Aviva A. Orenstein, "Her Last Words: Dying Declarations and Modern Confrontation Jurisprudence," *University of Illinois Law Review* (2010): 1426, https://www.repository.law.indiana.edu/facpub/6.

Page 197 *hours before death.* Christine L. Watt et al., "The Incidence and Prevalence of Delirium Across Palliative Care Settings: A Systematic Review," *Palliative Medicine* 33, no. 8 (2019): 865–877; P. G. Lawlor et al., "Occurrences, Causes, and Outcome of Delirium in Patients with Advanced Cancer: A Prospective Study," *Archives of Internal Medicine* 160 (2000): 786–794.

Page 197 *two thousand years ago.* Zbigniew J. Lipowski, *Delirium: Acute Confusional States* (Oxford: Oxford University Press, 1990), 4.

Page 197 *Latin for "furrow."* Lipowski, *Delirium*, 3.

Page 198 *shows up most often.* Watt et al., "Incidence and Prevalence of Delirium," 874.

Page 198 *or psychosis.* Cecily Pollard et al., "Delirium: The Lived Experience of Older People Who Are Delirious Post-Orthopaedic Surgery," *International Journal of Mental Health Nursing* 24, no. 3 (2015): 214, https://doi.org/10.1111/inm.12132.

Page 198 *on cognitive test scores.* Michael Leonard et al., "Phenomenological and Neuropsychological Profile across Motor Variants of Delirium in a Palliative-Care Unit," *Journal of Neuropsychiatry and Clinical Neurosciences* 23, no. 2 (2011): 180–188. https://doi.org/10.1176/jnp.23.2.jnp180.

Page 198 *or at least not to fight it.* Miki Namba et al., "Terminal Delirium: Families' Experience," *Palliative Medicine* 21, no. 7 (2007): 587–594, https://doi.org/10.1177/0269216307081129.

Page 200 *"shortly before death."* Michael Nahm and Bruce Greyson, "Terminal Lucidity in Patients with Chronic Schizophrenia and Dementia: A Survey of the Literature," *Journal of Nervous and Mental Disease* 197, no. 12 (2009): 942–944.

Page 200 *the precipice of life.* The connection between delirium and terminal lucidity is stronger in descriptions like this one: it involves "an emergence of unusually clear mental state, offering wisdom and coherent speech, experiencing deathbed visions of deceased relatives and friends or religious figures, often communicating with them, hearing music, seeing shapes, and they may have the ability to perform bodily movements or skills that seemed impossible before." Raya Elfadel Kheirbek, "Terminal Lucidity," *Journal of Palliative Medicine* 22, no. 9 (2019): 1023.

Page 200 *"Cheerio!"* Lamerton, *Care of the Dying*, 59.

Page 200 *forty-eight hours of life.* Sandy MacLeod, "Lightening Up Before Death," *Palliative and Supportive Care* 7 (2009): 513–516.

Page 201 *happened around them.* Edith Andersson et al., "Acute Confusional Episodes in Elderly Orthopaedic Patients: The Patients' Actions and Speech," *International Journal of Nursing Studies* 39 (2002): 307.

Page 201 *"they were so nice before."* Gill S. Duppils and Karin Wikblad, "Patients' Experiences of Being Delirious," *Journal of Clinical Nursing* 16, no. 5 (2007): 812, https://doi.org/10.1111/j.1365-2702.2006.01806.x.

Page 201 *mixed up with the present.* Duppils and Wikblad, "Patients' Experiences," 814.

Page 201 *without adequate assessment.* Callanan and Kelley, *Final Gifts*, 24–25.

Page 202 *did not have have biomedical origins.* S. Grover and R. Shah, "Perceptions Among Primary Caregivers About the Etiology of Delirium: A Study from a Tertiary Care Centre In India," *African Journal of Psychiatry* 15, no. 3 (2012): 193–195, https://doi.org/10.4314/ajpsy.v15i3.26.

Page 202 *"listen specifically to the words."* Gilles Bédard, *"Final Gifts:* An Interview with Maggie Callanan on Nearing-Death Awareness," January 19, 1998, https://maggiecallanan.com/pdf/interview_bedard.pdf.

Page 202 *"The patient knows what's going on."* Barbara Brotman, "Striking Similarity of Dying Words," *Chicago Tribune*, June 19, 2013, https://www.chicagotribune.com/news/ct-xpm-2013-06-19-ct-x-dying-words-0619-20130619-story.html.

Page 203 *necessarily co-occur.* D. A. Counts and D. R. Counts, "Introduction: Linking Concepts Aging and Gender, Aging and Death," in *Aging and Its Transformations: Moving toward Death in Pacific Societies*, ed. D. A. Counts and D. R. Counts (Pittsburgh: University of Pittsburgh Press, 1985), 1–24.

Page 203 *in patient outcomes.* Abel, *Inevitable Hour*, 38–39.

Page 204 *in hospitals.* J. B. Broad, M. Gott, H. Kim, M. Boyd, H. Chen, and M. J. Connolly, "Where Do People Die? An International Comparison of the Percentage of Deaths Occurring in Hospital and Residential Aged Care Settings in 45 Populations, Using Published and Available Statistics," *International Journal of Public Health* 58, no. 2 (2013): 257–267, https://doi.org/10.1007/s00038-012-0394-5.

Page 204 *dying in America.* David Sudnow, *Passing On: The Social Organization of Dying* (Englewood Cliffs, NJ: Prentice-Hall, 1967).

Page 204 *"impersonal environment."* Sudnow, *Passing On*, 170.

Page 205 *"more constant vigilance."* Sudnow, *Passing On*, 85.

Page 205 *"infrequent scrutiny."* Sudnow, *Passing On*, 49.

Page 205 *"empathetic dismay,"* Sudnow wrote. Sudnow, *Passing On*, 170.

Page 205 *"dying' patients,"* Sudnow, *Passing On*, 74.

Page 205 *"essentially dead."* Sudnow, *Passing On*, 88.

Page 205 *"the 'dying' stage."* Sudnow, *Passing On*. 87.

Page 205 *"the nonpaying patient."* Sudnow, *Passing On*, 170.

Page 206 *"an intelligent nurse."* William Osler and Thomas McRae, *The Principles and Practice of Medicine* (New York: D. Appleton and Co., 1920), 38.

Page 206 *"lonely and dehumanizing experience."* Abel, *Inevitable Hour*, 53–54.

Page 206 *which shook her.* In one anecdote, Osler comes in with medical students, hailing Reed. "Here's Dr. Reed, she can report on what she's done on the negro wards," he said. "When I faltered out, 'Six deaths from pneumonia on the men's wards, sir," the clinic racked with laughter. I was completely unnerved—seeing six young adults die within a few hours was no laughing matter for me." Fortunately, Osler hushed the laughter and praised Reed's work. Dorothy Reed Mendenhall, *Autobiography*, 13.

Chapter 11

Page 207 *online nursing forum.* Bargainsmarts, "Expiratory Vocalizations at the End of Life," AllNurses.com, October 3, 2012, https://allnurses.com/expiratory-vocalizations -end-life-t451382/.

Page 208 *include verbal utterances.* One study identified "(i) persistent screaming, (ii) perseverative vocalization, (iii) continuous chattering, muttering, singing or humming, and (iv) swearing, grunting and bizarre noise-making." Nagaratnam et al., "Screaming, Shrieking and Muttering," 247.

Page 208 *"let me die."* Peter D. Sloane et al., "Management of the Patient with Disruptive Vocalization," *The Gerontologist* 37, no. 5 (1997): 678, https://doi.org/10.1093 /geront/37.5.675.

Page 208 *as a part of "disorganized" vocalizations can be interrupted.* Luciana Frade, Rui Carvalho Santos, and Isabel Galrica Neto, "The Importance of Appropriate Management and Differential Diagnosis of Patient's Vocalizations (Groaning or Moaning) in the Last Days and Hours of Life," *Applied Medical Research* 8, no. 1 (2001): 1–6. Also Christina Samuelson and Lars C. Hydén, "Intonational Patterns of Nonverbal Vocalizations in People with Dementia," *American Journal of Alzheimer's Disease & Other Dementias* 26, no. 7 (2011): 563–572.

Page 208 *makes them feel helpless.* Sloane et al., "Management of the Patient," 675.

Page 209 *vocalized this way.* Ingalill R. Hallberg et al., "A Comparison Between the Care of Vocally Disruptive Patients and That of Other Residents in Psycho Geriatric Wards," *Journal of Advanced Nursing* 15, no. 4 (1990): 410–416.

Page 209 *of their brain.* See, for instance, Andreas Nieder and Richard Moone, "The Neurobiology of Innate, Volitional, and Learned Vocalizations in Mammals and Birds," *Philosophical Transactions of the Royal Society B* 375 (2019): 20190054, http:// dx.doi.org/10.1098/rstb.2019.0054.

Page 209 *indicating pain.* A fascinating discussion can be found in Andrey Anikin, Rasmus Bååth, and Tomas Persson, "Human Non-Linguistic Vocal Repertoire: Call Types and Their Meaning," *Journal of Nonverbal Behavior* 42 (2018): 53–80.

Page 209 *yet they're not words.* Leelo Keevallik and Richard Ogden, "Sounds on the Margins of Language at the Heart of Interaction," *Research on Language and Social Interaction* 53, no. 1 (2020): 1–18.

Page 209 *vocalizations and pain.* Lise Bouchard, "A Linguistic Approach for Understanding Pain in the Medical Encounter," in *Culture, Brain, and Analgesia: Understanding and Managing Pain in Diverse Populations,* ed. Mario Incayawar and Knox Todd (Oxford: Oxford University Press, 2013), 10.

Page 209 *speak the same language.* See, for example, how Mohawk English speakers use evidentials as they do in Mohawk, which seems like indecision to white English speakers. Peter Woolfson et al., "Mohawk English in the Medical Interview," *Medical Anthropology Quarterly* 9, no. 4 (1995): 503–509.

Page 209 *biography of his father.* Sean Day-Lewis, *Cecil Day-Lewis: An English Literary Life* (London: Weidenfeld & Nicolson, 1980), 305.

Page 210 *one day before death.* Tatsuya Morita et al., "Impaired Communication Capacity and Agitated Delirium in the Final Week of Terminally Ill Cancer Patients: Prevalence and Identification of Research Focus," *Journal of Pain and Symptom Management* 26, no. 3 (2003): 827–834. Interestingly, this same research team developed a "Good Death Inventory," which included seventy potential dimensions of what Japanese family members would consider a good death. See Mitsunori Miyashita, "Good Death Inventory: A Measure for Evaluating Good Death from the Bereaved Family Member's Perspective," *Journal of Pain and Symptom Management* 35, no. 5 (2008): 486–498, https://doi.org/10.1016/j.jpainsymman.2007.07.009.

Such inventories index cultural priorities and reflect cultural values. Thus, it's interesting to note that only one dimension involved speaking: "Patient was able to say what he or she wanted to dear people." It was not highly ranked. Only two other dimensions implied language production by the patient: "Patient had people who listened" and "Patient had family to whom he or she could express feelings." In this cultural frame, a good death doesn't require the preservation of the dying person as a communicative subject.

Page 210 *last three days of life.* Turner et al., "Dignity in Dying," 7–14.

Page 210 *last forty-eight hours of life.* C. Mazzocato et al., "The Last Days of Dying Stroke Patients Referred to a Palliative Care Consult Team in an Acute Hospital," *European Journal of Neurology* 17 (2010): 73–77.

Page 210 *meaning of words.* R. M. Adapa et al., "Neural Correlates of Successful Semantic Processing During Propofol Sedation," *Human Brain Mapping* 35, no. 7 (2014): 2935–2949, https://doi.org/10.1002/hbm.22375.

Page 210 *pain level, comfort, or thirst.* H. C. Muller-Busch et al., "Sedation in Palliative Care—A Critical Analysis of 7 Years Experience," *BMC Palliative Care* 2, no. 2 (2003): 2, https://doi.org/10.1186/1472-684X-2-2.

Page 211 *psychological distress.* Muller-Busch, "Sedation," 2.

Page 211 *palliative care tool kit.* M. T. Heijltjes et al., "Changing Practices in the Use of Continuous Sedation at the End of Life: A Systematic Review of the Literature," *Journal of Pain and Symptom Management* 60, no. 4 (2020): 828–846, https://doi.org/10.1016/j.jpainsymman.2020.06.019.

Page 211 *"I feel ready."* Mel McEvoy, "He Swims in the Silence," *Wading into the Light* (South Lanarkshire, UK: Red Squirrel Press, 2022), 29.

Page 213 *wrote a hospice doctor in 1973.* Richard Lamerton, *Care of the Dying* (Westport, CT: Technomic Publishing, 1973), 50.

Page 214 *his pack, who protected him.* In some parts of the world, children make difficult experimental subjects because of how they're raised. Where children are raised in groups, separating one out so that you could ask them questions is so artificial, the kids freeze or aren't willing to participate. I appreciate hearing this detail from Marisa Casillas, now at the University of Chicago.

Page 216 *conscious level of processing going on.* Elizabeth G. Blundon et al., "Electrophysiological Evidence of Preserved Hearing at the End of Life," *Scientific Reports* 10, no. 1 (2020): 10336, https://doi.org/10.1038/s41598-020-67234-9; Elizabeth G. Blundon et al., "Resting State Network Activation and Functional Connectivity in the Dying Brain," *Clinical Neurophysiology* 135 (2022): 166–178, https://doi.org/10.1016/j.clinph.2021.10.018; Elizabeth G. Blundon et al., "Electrophysiological Evidence of Sustained Attention to Music among Conscious Participants and Unresponsive Hospice Patients at the End of Life," *Clinical Neurophysiology* 139 (2022): 9–22, https://doi.org/10.1016/j.clinph.2022.03.018.

Page 217 *"no rascal to succeed me!"* Kaines, *Last Words of Eminent Persons*, 116.

Page 218 *it was remembered.* Kaines, *Last Words of Eminent Persons*, 116.

Page 220 *for ten years.* Her first scholarly paper on the topic was published in 2004. Robin Pollens, "Role of the Speech-Language Pathologist in Palliative Hospice Care," *Journal of Palliative Medicine* 7, no. 5 (2004): 694–702, https://doi.org/10.1089/jpm.2004.7.694.

Page 221 *beginning to embrace.* Robin Pollens, "Facilitating Client Ability to Communicate in Palliative End-of-Life Care," *Topics in Language Disorders* 40, no. 3 (2020): 264–277. https://doi.org/10.1097/TLD.0000000000000220.

Page 221 *It's time to be comfortable.* This anecdote appears in Kaufman, *And a Time to Die*, 264.

Chapter 12

Page 224 *said linguist David Gramling*. I wrote about this project in 2019. Erard, "How Can Doctors Find Better Ways to Talk—and Listen—to Patients Close to Death?," *Mosaic Science*, August 27, 2019, https://web.archive.org/web/20220922044255 /https:/mosaicscience.com/story/end-of-life-care-conversations-dying-palliative -doctors-linguistics-ai/.

Page 224 *palliative care patients and their doctors*. David Gramling and Robert Gramling, *Palliative Care Conversations: Clinical and Applied Linguistic Perspectives* (Berlin: De Gruyter, 2019).

Page 224 *what's said to them*. Samatha Green et al., "Investigating Speech and Language Impairments in Delirium: A Preliminary Case-Control Study," *PLOS One* 13, no. 11(2018): e0207527, https://doi.org/10.1371/journal.pone.0207527.

Page 225 *so long ago*. "Like other motor skills, [grammar] has to be mastered with great effort and considerable experience; however, once mastered it is just like riding a bicycle—that is, very hard to lose." Bates, Bretherton, and Snyder, *From First Words*, 285.

Page 226 *"Mommy" or "Mama" with the last breath*. Hajo Schumacher, "The Milf Complex," *Der Spiegel*, September 20, 2018, https://www.spiegel.de/panorama/maenner -und-ihre-muetter-der-milf-komplex-a-40b6d23f-0677-4c9c-9e3a-3a43cab12d0d.

Page 226 *it happens infrequently*. Of 338 deaths reported in a South Korean hospital, six cases of terminal lucidity were reported. Chi-Yeon Lim et al., "Terminal Lucidity in the Teaching Hospital Setting," *Death Studies* 44, no. 5 (2020): 285–291, https://doi .org/10.1080/07481187.2018.1541943.

Page 227 *over and over*. Portsmouth Herald, "Dying Soldiers' Last Words Both Called 'Out for 'Mom,'" Seacoastonline, May 15, 2012, https://eu.seacoastonline.com/story /news/local/hampton-union/2012/05/15/dying-soldiers-last-words-both/496350 58007/.

Page 227 *experiences in other domains*. George Lakoff and Mark Johnson, *Metaphors We Live By* (Chicago: University of Chicago Press, 1980).

Page 227 *or a coma*. Edith Andersson et al., "The Meaning of Acute Confusional State from the Perspective of Elderly Patients," *International Journal of Geriatric Psychiatry* 17 (2002): 652–663.

Page 228 *milk he called lolo*. Taine, "De l'acquisition," 256.

Page 228 *even our own, are strangers*. Necker de Saussure, *Progressive Education*, 52.

Page 228 *going the opposite way*. See Gina Kolata, "More Americans Are Dying at Home Than in Hospitals," *New York Times*, December 11, 2019, https://www.nytimes .com/2019/12/11/health/death-hospitals-home.html.

Page 230 *decades of experience.* On the advice of a sensitivity reader, I should acknowledge that many deaf people have upsetting experiences with interpreters, even in routine medical and dental visits, let alone more severe emergencies and quite possibly the end of life.

Page 231 *language plays at the end of life.* Milagros Silva et al., "Interpreting at the End of Life: A Systematic Review of the Impact of Interpreters on the Delivery of Palliative Care Services to Cancer Patients with Limited English Proficiency," *Journal of Pain and Symptom Management* 51, no. 3 (2016): 569–580, https://doi.org/10.1016/j .jpainsymman.2015.10.011.

Page 232 *into their languages in a way they understand.* Zara Latif et al., "Experiences of Medical Interpreters During Palliative Care Encounters with Limited English Proficiency Patients: A Qualitative Study," *Journal of Palliative Medicine* 26, no. 6 (June 2023): 784–789, http://doi.org/10.1089/jpm.2022.0320.

Page 233 *a person would typically use.* On the other hand, typical utterances are already short—an average of three words in a half-second duration. See Andrew Liesenfeld and Mark Dingemanse, "Building and Curating Conversational Corpora for Diversity-Aware Language Science and Technology," *Proceedings of the 13th Conference on Language Resources and Evaluation (LREC 2022)*: 1178–1192, https:// aclanthology.org/2022.lrec-1.126.pdf.

Page 233 *Because I can't.* Stephen Nachmanovitch, "Old Men Should Be Explorers," 118.

Page 234 *"known to the native speaker."* Kelly Ann Bridges and Diana Van Lancker Sidtis, "Formulaic Language in Alzheimer's Disease," *Aphasiology* 27, no. 7 (2013): 2. Elsewhere Sidtis uses "familiar phrases" as the family term, composed of formulaic expressions, lexical bundles, and collocations. Diana Sidtis, *Foundations of Familiar Language: Formulaic Expressions, Lexical Bundles, and Collocations at Work and Play* (New York: Wiley, 2021).

Page 234 *everyday spontaneous language production, it's been estimated.* Diana Van Lancker Sidtis and Gail Rallon, "Tracking the Incidence of Formulaic Expressions in Everyday Speech: Methods for Classification and Verification," *Language and Communication* 24 (2004): 155.

Page 234 *polite phrases.* Bates, Bretherton, and Snyder, *From First Words*, 7. Maybe as much as 8 percent of their vocabulary. Nelson, *Structure and Strategy*, 19.

Page 234 *status in the brain.* Diana Van Lancker Sidtis and Whitney A. Postman, "Formulaic Expressions in Spontaneous Speech of Left- and Right-Hemisphere-Damaged Subjects," *Aphasiology* 20, no. 5: 411–426, https://doi.org/10.1080/026870 30500538148.

Page 235 *as one of these types.* The chart in figure 11.1 originally appeared in Sidtis, *Foundations of Familiar Language.*

Page 236 *he was dead.* Munk, *Euthanasia*, 33.

Page 237 *the conversational focus.* Jackie Guendozi et al., "Avoiding Interactional Conflict in Dementia: The Influence of Gender Styles in Interactions," *Journal of Language Aggression and Conflict* 4, no. 1 (2016): 8–34.

Page 237 *This pioneering study.* Alisa Brownlee and Lisa Bruening, "Methods of Communication at End of Life for the Person with Amyotrophic Lateral Sclerosis," *Topics in Language Disorders* 32, no. 2 (2012): 168–185.

Page 238 *to use speech before death.* Miechelle McKelvey et al., "Communication Styles of Persons with ALS as Recounted by Surviving Partners," *Augmentative and Alternative Communication* 28, no. 4 (2012): 232–242, https://doi.org/10.3109/0743 4618.2012.737023.

Page 238 *for generating speech.* There's also a range of eye-tracking devices now available, but not when Brownlee and Bruening did their study.

Page 238 *actually increased.* Brownlee and Bruening, "Methods," 178.

Page 239 *"whether you were sick or well."* Carol Levine, "Family Caregivers: Burdens and Opportunities," in *Geriatric Palliative Care*, ed. R. Sean Morrison and Diane E. Meier (Oxford: Oxford University Press, 2013), 376.

Page 239 *"How you will die."* Nathan Yau, "How You Will Die," FlowingData, accessed September 30, 2022, https://flowingdata.com/2016/01/19/how-you-will-die/.

Page 240 *in the United States are sudden.* Leslie A. Saxon, "Sudden Cardiac Death: Epidemiology and Temporal Trends," *Reviews in Cardiovascular Medicine* 6, Suppl. 2 (2005): S12–S20; Omair Yousuf et al., "Clinical Management and Prevention of Sudden Cardiac Death," *Circulation Research* 116, no. 12 (2015): 2020–2040, https://doi.org/10.1161/CIRCRESAHA.116.304555.

Page 241 *organ failure.* The shape of, and rationale for, the trajectories of functional decline and end of life are laid out in June Lunney et al., "Patterns of Functional Decline at the End of Life," *Journal of the American Medical Association* 289, no. 18 (2003): 2387–2392.

Page 241 *among cancer patients.* Takahiro Hosoi, Sachiko Ozone, Jun Hamano, Kazushi Maruo, and Tetsuhiro Maeno, "Prediction Models for Impending Death Using Physical Signs and Vital Signs in Noncancer Patients: A Prospective Longitudinal Observational Study," *Palliative Medicine Reports* 2, no. 1 (October 21, 2021): 287–295, http://doi.org/10.1089/pmr.2021.0029.

Page 241 *registering as a cause of death.* D. S. Jones et al., "The Burden of Disease and the Changing Task of Medicine," *New England Journal of Medicine* 366 (2012): 2333–2338, https://doi.org/10.1056/NEJMp1113569.

Conclusion

Page 243 *through the night.* Many of the details for this reconstruction come from Mary Catherine Bateson, "Six Days of Dying," *CoEvolution Quarterly* 28 (Winter 1980): 4–11.

Page 243 *transmigration of souls.* Stephen Nachmanovich added this detail in his account of Bateson's death. "Old Men Ought to Be Explorers," *Leonardo* 12, no. 2 (1984): 117.

Page 245 *learn, recall, and use.* See Bates, Bretherton, and Snyder, *From First Words*, 355–361.

Page 246 *interacting with newborns.* Mary Catherine Bateson, "Mother-Infant Exchanges: The Epigenesis of Conversational Interaction," *Annals of the New York Academy of Sciences* 263 (1975): 101–113, https://doi.org/10.1111/j.1749-6632.1975 .tb41575.x.

Page 246 *at the baby's level.* Bateson, "Mother-Infant Exchanges," 110.

Page 246 *"coos and murmurs."* Mary Catherine Bateson, "The Epigenesis of Conversational Interaction: A Personal Account of Research Development," in *Before Speech: The Beginning of Interpersonal Communication*, ed. Margaret Bullowa (Cambridge: Cambridge University Press, 1979), 65.

Page 246 *oxytocin-induced back-and-forth.* Subsequent research into neonatal acquisition of turn-taking corroborates this. For a good review, see M. Gratier et al., "Early Development of Turn-Taking in Vocal Interaction Between Mothers and Infants," *Frontiers in Psychology* 6 (2015): 1167, https://doi.org/10.3389/fpsyg.2015.01167. Also S. Dominguez et al., "The Roots of Turn-Taking in the Neonatal Period," *Infant and Child Development* 25 (2016): 240–255, https://doi.org/10.1002/icd.1976.

Page 247 *back to the rhythm.* Since 1975, the field of child language studies has learned this isn't a behavior that all mothers universally engage in. For instance, urban infants receive three times the speech directed at them than urban infants. See Cristia, "A Systematic Review."

Page 247 *"several linguistic codes."* Bateson, "Mother-Infant Exchanges," 110.

Page 247 *also been present at his death.* Nachmanovitch, "Old Men," 117.

Page 247 *"smiling, seeing, pointing."* Nachmanovich, "Old Men," 118.

Page 251 *"they're no longer verbal."* Maggie Ellis and Arlene Astell, "Communicating with People Living with Dementia Who Are Nonverbal: The Creation of Adaptive Interaction," *PLOS One* 12, no. 8 (2017): e0180395, https://doi.org/10.1371/journal .pone.0180395; Arlene Astell et al., "Using Adaptive Interaction to Simplify Caregiver's

Communication with People with Dementia Who Cannot Speak," *Frontiers in Communication* 6 (2022): 689439, https://doi.org/10.3389/fcomm.2021.689439.

Page 251 *"percocity."* From the Latin, *percox*, for "overcooked." This mirrors the *precox* roots of "precocity," for "undercooked."

Page 254 *save your life.* "Stuck Between Stations," track 1 on The Hold Steady, *Boys and Girls in America*, Vagrant Records, 2006.

Further Reading and Selected Sources

Many directions in this book were inspired and informed by a range of works about death and dying.

Ariès, Philippe. *The Hour of Our Death: The Classic History of Western Attitudes Toward Death Over the Last One Thousand Years*. Translated by Helen Weaver. New York: Vintage, 1982.

Jenkinson, Stephen. *Die Wise: A Manifesto for Sanity and Soul*. Berkeley, CA: North Atlantic Books, 2015.

Kaufman, Sharon, and Lynn Morgan. "The Anthropology of the Beginnings and Ends of Life." *Annual Review of Anthropology* 34 (2005): 317–341. https://doi.org/10.1146/annurev.anthro.34.081804.120452.

Macaulay, Rose. *Pleasure of Ruins*. London: Weidenfeld & Nicolson, 1958.

Moody, Raymond. *Life After Life*. Mockingbird Books, 1975.

Moody, Raymond. *Making Sense of Nonsense: The Logical Bridge Between Science and Spirituality*. Woodbury, MN: Llewellyn Publications, 2020.

Osis, Karlis, and Haraldsson, Erlendur. *At the Hour of Death*. New York: Avon Publishers, 1977.

Owen, Adrian. *Into the Gray Zone: A Neuroscientist Explores the Border Between Life and Death*. New York: Scribner, 2017.

Smith, Barbara Hernnstein. *Poetic Closure: A Study of How Poems End*. Chicago: University of Chicago Press, 1968.

Swinton, John. *Dementia: Living in the Memories of God*. Grand Rapids, MI: William B. Eerdmans, 2012.

Tisdale, Sallie. *Advice for Future Corpses and Those Who Love Them: A Practical Perspective on Death and Dying*. New York: Gallery Books, 2018.

In addition to cited works, here is a selection of other works on language, development, and aging that were consulted:

Bates, Elizabeth. *Language and Context: The Acquisition of Pragmatics*. New York: Academic Press, 1976.

Bates, Elizabeth, Laura Benigni, Igne Bretherton, Luigia Camaioni, and Virginia Volterra. *The Emergence of Symbols: Cognition and Communication in Infancy*. New York: Academic Press, 1979.

Bergelson, Elika, and Daniel Swingley. "At 6–9 Months, Human Infants Know the Meanings of Many Common Nouns." *Proceedings of the National Academy of Sciences* 109, no. 9 (2012). https://doi.org/10.1073/pnas.1113380109.

Bergenholtz, Heidi, Malene Missel, and Helle Timm. "Talking About Death and Dying in a Hospital Setting: A Qualitative Study of the Wishes for End-of-Life Conversations from the Perspective of Patients and Spouses." *BMC Palliative Care* 19, no. 1 (2020): 168. https://doi.org/10.1186/s12904-020-00675-1.

Berko-Gleason, Jason. "Insights from Child Language Acquisition for Second Language Loss." In *The Loss of Language Skills*, edited by R. D. Lambert and B. F. Freed. London: Newbury House, 1982.

Bloom, Lois. "Language Development Review." In *Review of Child Development Research*, edited by Francis Horowitz, 245–303. Chicago: University of Chicago Press, 1975.

Bloom, Paul. "Précis of *How Children Learn the Meanings of Words*." *Behavioral and Brain Sciences* 24 (2001): 1095–1103.

Bornstein, Marc, Diane Putnick, Linda Cote, O. Maurine Haynes, and Joan Suwalsky. 2015. "Mother-Infant Contingent Vocalizations in Eleven Countries." *Psychological Sciences* 26, no. 8 (August 2015): 1272–1284. https://doi.org/10.1177/0956797615586796.

Boysson-Bardies, Bénédicte de, and Marilyn May Vihman. "Adaptation to Language: Evidence from Babbling and First Words in Four Languages." *Language* 67, no. 2 (June 1991): 297–319.

Bullowa, Margaret, Lawrence Jones, and Thomas Bever. 1964. "The Development from Vocal to Verbal Behavior in Children." *Monographs of the Society for Research in Child Development* 29, no. 1 (1964): 101–107.

Burke, Deborah M., and Meredith A. Shafto. "Aging and Language Production." *Current Directions in Psychological Science* 13, no. 1 (2004): 21–24. https://doi.org/10.1111/j.0963-7214.2004.01301006.x.

Caraceni, Augusto, and Grassi, Luigi. *Delirium: Acute Confusional States in Palliative Medicine*. Oxford: Oxford University Press, 2003.

Coward, Harold, and Kelli Stajduhar. *Religious Understandings of a Good Death in Hospice Palliative Care*. Binghamton: SUNY Press, 2012.

DeLeon, Jessica, Boon L. Tee, and Adolfo M. Garcia. "Neurodegenerative Disorders of Speech and Language: Language-Dominant Diseases." In *Reference Module in Neuroscience and Biobehavioral Psychology* (2020). https://doi.org/10.1016/B978-0-12-819641-0.00030-X.

DeZeeuw, Katrina, and Emilie Myers. "The Role of Speech-Language Pathologists in Medical Assistance in Dying: Canadian Experience to Inform Clinical Practice." *Canadian Journal of Speech-Language Pathology and Audiology* 44, no. 2 (2020): 49–56.

Dingemanse, Mark. "Beyond Sound and Speech: Liminal Signs in Interaction." *Research in Language, Society, and Interaction* 53, no. 1 (2020): 188–196. https://doi.org/10.1080/08351813.2020.1712967.

Donnellan, Elizabeth, Christopher Bannard, Mark L. McGillion, Kirsten E. Slocombe, and Danielle Matthews. "Infants' Intentionally Communicative Vocalizations Elicit Responses from Caregivers and Are the Best Predictors of the Transition to Language: A Longitudinal Investigation of Infants' Vocalizations, Gestures, and Word Production." *Developmental Science* (2019): e12843. https://doi.org/10.1111/desc.12843.

Eliott, Jaklin, and Ian Olver. "Hope and Hoping in the Talk of Dying Cancer Patients." *Social Science & Medicine* 64 (2007): 138–149. https://doi.org/10.1016/j.socscimed.2006.08.029.

Engelman, Michelle. "Propositional Density and Cognitive Function in Later Life." *Journals of Gerontology: Series B, Psychological Sciences and Social Sciences* 65, no. 6 (2010): 706–711. https://doi.org/10.1093/geronb/gbq064.

Ferguson, Charles. "Baby Talk in Six Languages." *American Anthropologist* 66, no. 6 (December 1964): 103–114.

Gera, Deborah Levine. *Ancient Greek Ideas on Speech, Language, and Civilization*. Oxford: Oxford University Press, 2003.

Golden, Janet. *Babies Made Us Modern: How Infants Brought America into the Twentieth Century*. Cambridge: Cambridge University Press, 2018.

Goodman, Judith, and Philip Dale. 2008. "Does Frequency Count? Parental Input and the Acquisition of Vocabulary." *Journal of Child Language* 35 (2008): 515–531.

Gratier, Mallo, Emilie Devouche, Baptiste Guellai, Renata Infanti, Emine Yilmaz, and Elisabeth Parlato-Oliveira. "Early Development of Turn-Taking in Vocal Interaction Between Mothers and Infants." *Frontiers in Psychology* 6 (2015): 1167. https://doi.org/10.3389/fpsyg.2015.01167.

Gross, William L., Korrina K. Lauer, Xufeng Liu, Charles J. Roberts, Shan Liu, Sravya Gollapudy, Jonathan R. Binder, Sheng Li, and Andrew G. Hudetz. "Propofol Sedation

Alters Perceptual and Cognitive Functions in Healthy Volunteers as Revealed by Functional Magnetic Resonance Imaging." *Anesthesiology* 131, no. 2 (2019): 254–265. https://doi.org/10.1097/ALN.0000000000002669.

Hadjistavropoulos, Thomas, Keela Herr, Kenneth M. Prkachin, Kenneth D. Craig, Stephen J. Gibson, Ann Lukas, and John H. Smith. "Pain Assessment in Elderly Adults with Dementia." *The Lancet Neurology* 13, no. 12 (2014): 1216–1227. https://doi.org/10.1016/S1474-4422(14)70103-6.

Hertrich, Ingo, Susanne Dietrich, and Hermann Ackermann. "The Margins of the Language Network in the Brain." *Frontiers in Communication* 5 (2020). https://doi.org/10.3389/fcomm.2020.519955.

Hobaiter, Catherine, Kirsty E. Graham, and Richard W. Byrne. "Are Ape Gestures Like Words? Outstanding Issues in Detecting Similarities and Differences Between Human Language and Ape Gesture." *Philosophical Transactions of the Royal Society B: Biological Sciences* 377, no. 1860 (2022): 20210301. https://doi.org/10.1098/rstb.2021.0301.

Holler, Judith, Kobin Kendrick, Marisa Casillas, and Stephen Levinson. "Editorial: Turn-Taking in Human Communicative Interaction." *Frontiers in Psychology* 6 (2015): 1919. https://doi.org/10.3389/fpsyg.2015.01919.

Howard, Lorraine, and Gwyneth Doherty-Sneddon. "How HANDy Are Baby Signs? A Commentary on a Systematic Review of the Impact of Gestural Communication on Typically Developing, Hearing Infants Under the Age of 36 Months." *First Language* 34, no. 6 (2014): 510–515.

Hutz, Margarete. "Is There a Natural Process of Decay? A Longitudinal Study of Language Attrition." In *First Language Attrition: Interdisciplinary Perspectives on Methodological Issues*, edited by Monika S. Schmid, Barbara Köpke, Merel Keijzer, and Lina Weilemar, 189–206. Amsterdam: John Benjamins, 2004.

Kemper, Susan, Jennifer Marquis, and Martie Thompson. "Longitudinal Change in Language Production: Effects of Aging and Dementia on Grammatical Complexity and Propositional Content." *Psychology and Aging* 16, no. 4 (2001): 600–614. https://doi.org/10.1037/0882-7974.16.4.600.

Kemper, Susan, Robert Schmalzried, Ruth Herman, and Deirdre Mohankumar. "The Effects of Varying Task Priorities on Language Production by Young and Older Adults." *Experimental Aging Research* 37, no. 2 (2011): 198–219. https://doi.org/10.1080/0361073X.2011.554513.

Leonard, Michael, Shane Donnelly, Maria Conroy, Peter Trzepacz, and David Meagher. "Phenomenological and Neuropsychological Profile across Motor Variants of Delirium in a Palliative-Care Unit." *Journal of Neuropsychiatry and Clinical Neurosciences* 23, no. 2 (2011): 180–188. https://doi.org/10.1176/jnp.23.2.jnp180.

Levinson, Stephen C., and Francisco Torreira. "Timing in Turn-Taking and Its Implications for Processing Models of Language." *Frontiers in Psychology* 6, no. 731 (2015). https://doi.org/10.3389/fpsyg.2015.00731.

Lim, Chang Yong, Jae Young Park, Dong Yul Kim, Ki Dong Yoo, Hyun Ju Kim, Yun Kim, Sang Ju Shin, Yeonjung Kim, and Jin Suk Sung. "Terminal Lucidity in the Teaching Hospital Setting." *Death Studies* 44, no. 5 (2020): 285–291. https://doi.org/10.1080/07481187.2018.1541943.

Lohaus, Arnold, Heidi Keller, Bettina Lamm, Manuel Teubert, Ina Fassbender, Claudia Freitag, Claudia Goertz, Frauke Graf, Thorsten Kolling, Sibylle Spangler, Marc Vierhaus, Monika Knopf, and Gudrun Schwarzer. "Infant Development in Two Cultural Contexts: Cameroonian Nso Farmer and German Middle-Class Infants." *Journal of Reproductive and Infant Psychology* 29, no. 2 (2011): 148–161. https://doi.org/10.1080/02646838.2011.558074.

Maldonado, José R. "Delirium Pathophysiology: An Updated Hypothesis of the Etiology of Acute Brain Failure." International Journal *of Geriatric Psychiatry* 33, no. 11 (2018): 1428–1457. https://doi.org/10.1002/gps.4823.

Maynard, Douglas W., Dagoberto Cortez, and Toby C. Campbell. "'End of Life' Conversations, Appreciation Sequences, and the Interaction Order in Cancer Clinics." *Patient Education and Counseling* 99, no. 1 (2016): 92–100. https://doi.org/10.1016/j.pec.2015.07.015.

Morgan, Dierdre D., Jennifer J. Tieman, Samuel F. Allingham, Magnus P. Ekström, Alanna Connolly, and David C. Currow. "The Trajectory of Functional Decline over the Last 4 Months of Life in a Palliative Care Population: A Prospective, Consecutive Cohort Study." *Palliative Medicine* 33, no. 6 (2019): 693–703. https://doi.org/10.1177/0269216319839024.

Morgan, Laura, and Yvette Wren. "A Systematic Review of the Literature on Early Vocalizations and Babbling Patterns in Young Children." *Communication Disorders Quarterly* 40, no. 1 (2018): 3–14. https://doi.org/10.1177/1525740117748071.

Morrison, Catriona and Martin Conway. "First Words and First Memories." *Cognition* 116, no. 1 (2010): 23–32.

Roberts, Sean. Causal Hypotheses in Evolutionary Linguistics database. Accessed March 1, 2023. https://correlation-machine.com/CHIELD/.

Index

Page locators in italics indicate figures.